Sh
CH

WHISTLEBLOWING:
THE NEW LAW

AUSTRALIA
LBC Information Services—Sydney

CANADA AND USA
Carswell—Toronto

NEW ZEALAND
Brooker's—Auckland

SINGAPORE AND MALAYSIA
Sweet & Maxwell Asia
Singapore and Kuala Lumpur

WHISTLEBLOWING: THE NEW LAW

By

John Bowers Q.C.
Jeremy Lewis
&
Jack Mitchell

LONDON
SWEET & MAXWELL
1999

Published in 1999 by
Sweet & Maxwell Limited of
100 Avenue Road
Swiss Cottage
London NW3 3PF
http://www.smlawpub.co.uk

Typeset by Servis Filmsetting Limited, Manchester
Printed and bound in Great Britain
by MPG Ltd, Bodmin, Cornwall

No natural forests were destroyed
to make this product, only farmed
timber was used and replanted.

ISBN 0 421 656 905

A CIP catalogue record for this book
is available from the British Library

Preface

Whistleblowing is an issue which spans law and morality. It is also important as a matter of corporate and public governance, since only if people are prepared to come forward about concerns in the public interest can the public interest be properly safeguarded. From the practitioner's viewpoint, the Public Interest Disclosure Act 1998 is highly significant, in part because of the lack of any ceiling to awards for detriment or dismissal and the likelihood that cases will be protracted and bitterly fought. On a practical level, employers who wish to avoid the publicity attracted by damaging disclosures on a public stage would be well advised to develop appropriate whistle-blowing policies.

Ultimately a consensus developed in support of the new Act. This was in part due to the obvious need for legislation demonstrated in a number of disasters which might have been averted if only whistleblowers had been prepared to come forward or had been heeded (as we outline in Chapter 1). However the consensus was also the result of sterling work by politicians and academics alike. We refer in Chapter 1 to those who have made the key political contributions. Amongst the academic community, we note the pioneering work on the subject by Yvonne Cripps, *The Legal Implications of Disclosure in the Public Interest* (2nd ed., Sweet & Maxwell, 1994). The charity Public Concern at Work have also played a central role in promoting the new Act, and we are grateful that they have allowed us to reprint (in Appendix 1) their annotations of the Act which first appeared in *Current Law Statutes*. Guy Dehn, the director of Public Concern at Work, has also contributed ideas to the book itself and we thank him for that. We are also grateful for the assistance on particular chapters of Julia Palca of Olswangs, Richard Price O.B.E., Q.C. and Rebecca Ellis. We would also like to thank our families for all their support and tolerance.

We have written the book at the very outset of the new Act without any caselaw specifically relating to the new Act to guide us on its interpretation. We have however endeavoured to incorporate developments up to proof stage in September 1999.

JOHN BOWERS Q.C.   JACK MITCHELL
JEREMY LEWIS   Enfield Chambers
Littleton Chamber, Temple

Preface

Contents

APPENDICES

Table of Cases

Table of Statutes

Table of Statutory Instruments

CHAPTER 1

Introduction

"I hope that the Bill will signal a shift in culture so that it is safe and accepted for employees . . . to sound the alarm when they come across malpractice that threatens the safety of the public the health of a patient public funds or the savings of investors. I hope that it will mean that good and decent people in business and public bodies throughout the country can more easily ensure that where malpractice is reported in an organisation the response deals with the message not the messenger" (Standing Committee, Richard Shepherd M.P., March 11, 1998, p. 4).

1–01 This aspiration was expressed by Mr Richard Shepherd M.P., who introduced the Private Members Bill which led to the enactment of the Public Interest Disclosure Act 1998. It encapsulated the pressing need for a radical change in organisational culture in so far as it affects the whistleblower. We use the term "whistleblowing" in this book to denote the act of an individual worker or a group of workers raising a concern so as to prevent possible malpractice or dangers to the public. We refer to the person raising the concern as a "whistleblower". These matters raised by the whistleblower typically involve a risk to health and safety, fraud, criminal activity, environmental dangers or miscarriages of justice.

In an organisation (whether public or private) the people who are "on the ground" may be the first to spot trouble or potential trouble, whether threats to health and safety or financial corruption. In the whistleblower, companies and public bodies alike possess a valuable resource to discover or uncover risk. However all too often the culture at work causes staff, through fear of victimisation or dismissal, to react by doing and saying nothing. Further, in cases where an employee has spoken up, the reaction has often been to regard the employee as a troublemaker, to be at best ignored and ostracised, "sent to Coventry" and sometimes disciplined or dismissed for speaking up. The IRLB report "Whistleblowers at Work" (Bulletin 563 in February 1997) summarised this ethos as "the 'old' culture of fear, inertia and secrecy" in a situation where such legal protection as existed was, outside the area of health and safety, "piecemeal and in many respects ineffective".

1–02 The need to engender a change in the pervasive culture, and to strengthen the protection available to the whistleblower, has been illustrated and acknowledged in the reports upon many recent tragedies and scandals which could have been prevented, or the impact reduced, had people spoken out or had the warnings of those who did speak out been heeded. These cases have also demonstrated the pressing need for a change in the workplace culture relating to whistleblowers and the need to bolster the legal protection afforded to them. At the risk of over generalisation, we categorise these recent events under the rubrics "turning a blind eye", "turning a deaf ear", "blaming the messenger" and "the triumph of the whistleblower".

A TURNING A BLIND EYE

1–03   In a number of recent cases, workers have been afraid to speak up and this has had the most serious consequences.

A1 The Piper Alpha disaster

1–04   The Cullen Inquiry[1] was set up following the Piper Alpha Disaster, in which 167 people died in 1988 on a North Sea oil rig some 110 miles off the Scottish coast. The Inquiry uncovered a culture in which staff felt unable to raise health and safety concerns with management. The staff were placed on short term contracts. This factor, together with the lack of other employment in the region, created job insecurity that manifested itself in the reluctance of staff to raise concerns over safety. The Cullen Report found that when staff were faced with clear health and safety dangers:

> "workers did not want to put their continued employment in jeopardy through raising a safety issue which might embarrass management".

Even though Piper Alpha employees had wanted to raise concerns over the health and safety dangers, the endemic culture was enough to prevent staff from doing so. It is doubtful that any of the staff envisaged the disastrous effects of their silence. Nevertheless, such a disaster highlights that, especially where workers are concerned about their job security, staff can be placed in a position where a culture leads them to turn a blind eye to danger, even where the danger is to themselves or their colleagues.

The Cullen Inquiry led directly to legislation specifically designed to protect against victimisation of employees carrying out health and safety functions or raising grievances in relation to health and safety. This is now contained in sections 44 and 100 of the Employment Rights Act (ERA) 1996.

A2 The Clapham Rail disaster

1–05   The Hidden Inquiry into the Clapham rail[2] crash, in which 35 people died and some 500 were injured, heard from one employee who revealed that whilst carrying out an inspection of the rail tracks and the wiring he came across some faulty loose wiring. At 8.10 a.m. on December 12, 1988 a signalling failure resulted in a crowded commuter train running head-on into a stationary train near Clapham Junction. Whilst the signal failure was not necessarily caused solely by the loose wiring, it was a contributory factor. When asked why the employee had not raised his concerns as to the loose wiring, he openly replied that he did not want to "*rock the boat*". This response reflected poorly not only on the individual employee whose responsibility was to check the wiring, but also on the organisational culture. This contributed to a reluctance to report concerns even where to do so fell squarely within the employee's duties.

A3 BCCI

1–06   The Bank of Credit and Commerce International SA was compulsorily wound up in 1991 following frauds estimated to run to £2 billion. The Bingham

---

[1] *Public Inquiry into the Piper Alpha disaster* Cm. 1310 (1990).
[2] *Investigation into the Clapham Junction railway accident* Cm. 820 (1989).

Inquiry[3] investigated BCCI's collapse. It identified an *"autocratic environment"*, where nobody dared to speak up, as a *decisive* factor in the failure to bring an end to the fraud in time to prevent BCCI's collapse. When, in 1990, one brave internal auditor did speak up about fraud he was dismissed purportedly on grounds of redundancy. Such a reaction fuelled fear which was present in the organisation.

The Bingham Inquiry led to a raft of new regulations imposing specific duties of disclosure on auditors in the banking, building society, insurance, and financial services sector (see Chapter 9).

A4 1993—Insurance Fraud

1–07 Roger Levitt's Group was one of the top life insurance companies of the 1980s. It collapsed in 1990, leaving unpaid debts of £34 million. The Investors Compensation Scheme has had to pay out £657,000 to 27 individuals. Levitt pleaded guilty to a lesser charge and was sentenced to 180 hours' community service. *The Mail on Sunday* reported that former employees were aware of odd goings-on for years:

"We knew that people were coming in at weekends to print out forged computer records and we knew where the files for the mugs were locked away".[4]

A5 Barings Bank

1–08 In relation to the collapse of Barings Bank the regulator found that a senior manager had failed to blow the whistle loudly or clearly.

B TURNING A DEAF EAR

1–09 Even where a worker has, courageously, been willing to come forward with concerns, in all too many cases these have simply been either ignored or not brought to the attention of the relevant decision makers in the employing organisation.

B1 Zeebrugge Ferry Disaster

1–10 The *Herald of Free Enterprise* ferry sunk at Zeebrugge in 1987 resulting in the death of 193 people because the ferry bow doors were left open at the port. The Sheen Inquiry[5] found that on five separate occasions staff had raised concerns that the ferries were sailing with the bow doors open. The employees' concerns were either ignored or were not passed on by middle management. The inquiry went to great lengths to examine the many variables that occurred in conjunction to cause the ferry to sink. Nevertheless the failure of the organisation to investigate or have proper regard to the concerns raised by staff was a serious and fundamental error. One member of staff had even put forward a constructive suggestion highlighting the possibility that a light in the bridge could alert a captain if the bow doors were still open. The Sheen Inquiry noted that if this sensible suggestion had received the serious consideration it deserved the disaster may well have been prevented.

---

[3] *Inquiry into the supervision of the Bank of Credit and Commerce International* Cm. 198c (1992).
[4] *The Mail on Sunday* November 28, 1993.
[5] Court inquiry, Department of Transport, Ct no.8074, 1987, HMSO.

B2 Child Abuse

1–11 Between 1973 and 1986 countless children in care were assaulted and sexually abused in Leicestershire County Council's childrens' homes. Three men were convicted of assault in 1991, including Frank Beck, director of the homes involved. Mr Beck received five life sentences for crimes of rape and buggery. The Official Inquiry, chaired by Andrew Kirkwood Q.C., revealed that over the 13-year period there had been no less than thirty occasions on which concerns had been raised about Beck and his colleagues by children, staff and others. However no effective action was taken. The Inquiry noted that:

> "The pressures on middle and junior care staff not to be seen to 'rock the boat' with adverse consequences for themselves made it all the more important to take very seriously (their) concern or complaints".

As a result of the Kirkwood Inquiry, steps have been taken by Leicestershire County Council to ensure that staff concerns about serious malpractice are properly considered.

B3 Lyme Bay Canoe disaster

1–12 The Lyme Bay canoe tragedy is an example of a whistleblower being unable to prevent the tragedy from occurring but enabling action to be taken against the person who was accountable for the tragedy.

Joy Cawthorne worked in an activity centre at Lyme Bay. Her responsibilities included teaching children how to canoe. She became concerned that there were insufficient safety precautions for canoeing. She raised these concerns with the managing director responsible for running the centre but he refused to acquire the necessary equipment. Mrs Cawthorne felt she was unable to continue working and she resigned. However she wrote a letter to the managing director setting out clearly her concerns over the safety standards. In March 1993 four schoolchildren were killed during a canoeing expedition at Lyme Bay. The managing director of the centre was jailed and became the first person in the United Kingdom to be jailed for "corporate manslaughter". The prosecution relied heavily on the fact that despite the clear and graphic warning he had been given by Mrs Cawthorne about the grave risk to life if safety standards were not improved, the required improvements were not made and he could not give a good reason for ignoring the warning.

B4 1993—Cancer Misdiagnosed

1–13 Two thousand bone tumour cases had to be re-examined after an inquiry discovered that a senior pathologist at Birmingham's Royal Orthopaedic Hospital had misdiagnosed 42 cancer cases. While some patients unnecessarily underwent treatment, others who had needed attention were given the all clear. The inquiry, headed by Dr Archbald Malcolm, discovered that two consultants had expressed doubts about the diagnoses over several years, and criticised them for failing to speak up through official channels.

B5 1986—Space-Shuttle explodes

1–14 On January 26, 1986 the space shuttle *Challenger* exploded 73 seconds into its flight, killing seven astronauts on board. The explosion was a result of a seal failure in one of the shuttle's solid rocket booster joints. Specific expert warnings of this risk were repeated right up to the launch day. The first, a year earlier, was when a senior rocket engineer with the aerospace company Morton Thiokol (manufacturers of the rocket booster for the *Challenger*) alerted his superiors to problems with the joint seals and warned of the potential catastrophe if the problems were not corrected. This information was not passed on to those in charge at NASA and the seals were not changed. Despite persistent protests by the engineer up to and on the eve of the launch, his superiors took the decision to launch the *Challenger*. In the subsequent investigation the Rogers Commission concluded that underlying the disaster was a:

> "serious flaw in the decision-making process which insulated top management from the substantial concerns of line engineers".

C BLAMING THE MESSENGER

1–15   In a number of high profile cases, rather than follow up the concerns raised by the worker, the employer has instead victimised the worker. The inadequacy of protection for the whistleblower has therefore been highlighted.

C1 *R. v. Ponting* [1985] Crim. L.R. 318

1–16   A Minister of the Crown provided evidence to a House of Commons Select Committee on Foreign Affairs with regard to the Falklands Conflict and the sinking of the *Belgrano* ship. Subsequently Clive Ponting, a senior Foreign Office civil servant, revealed to Tam Dalyell M.P. information he had received as a civil servant, which indicated that the then Minister had been less than "fulsome with the truth" when providing evidence to the Select Committee. Clive Ponting was arrested over this disclosure and charged with a breach of the Official Secrets Act.

On January 28, 1985, the case was heard at the Central Criminal Court. The jury were in effect presented with a defence case that required them to consider whether or not it was Clive Ponting's duty to communicate the information to Tam Dalyell M.P. The jury acquitted him and the case resulted in a new Official Secrets Act.

C2 Dr Stephen Bolsin—Bristol Royal Infirmary

1–17   Dr Stephen Bolsin was an anaesthetist who questioned operating techniques at Bristol Royal Infirmary. These techniques were alleged to have been instrumental in the high death rates of infants during heart surgery. Over a period of five years Dr Bolsin sought to raise his concerns through the proper channels. Although he was vindicated by the General Medical Council, he was shunned by the medical profession and was forced to relocate. He now works in Australia.[6] The whole issue is now the subject of a public inquiry under the chairmanship of Professor Ian Kennedy. Notwithstanding the treatment of Dr Bolsin, the high profile nature of this inquiry may also have encouraged other potential whistleblowers to come forward. Brian Langstaff Q.C. who leads the Bristol inquiry's team, received a letter from an anonymous whistleblower making allegations relating to child heart surgery at the

---

[6] *The Guardian*, February 11 and June 29, 1999.

Royal Brompton hospital. As a result, in June 1999 the Royal Brompton and Harefield NHS trust set up an inquiry to investigate the allegations.[7]

C3 Andrew Millar—British Biotech

1-18   British Biotech, an Oxford based company established in 1986 with 10 scientists and shares trading at 40 pence, was applauded as one of the success stories of the 1990s. In 1996 it had the prospect of joining the FTSE 100 with shares valued at 350p, providing it with a market value of approximately £1.6 billion. Although it employed more than 450 people, in the last 11 years the company had, surprisingly, failed to bring one product to the market. Despite other parties pushing for the company to expand, in 1996 the company faced losses in the region of £30 million against a turnover of less than £10 million.

Dr Andrew Millar joined British Biotech in 1992 as the Director of Clinical Research. His concerns appear to have arisen on May 12, 1997 when British Biotech issued two press releases announcing the result of trials, together with a request for authorisation to the European drug safety agency—EMEA. At the same time many high level appointments to the commercial team were made which gave the appearance that there was to be a launch of a drug in Europe. However by virtue of his position with the company Dr Millar was aware of disappointing results on drug trials both in Europe and in America. Ironically at the very same time as these press releases were made Dr Millar was in America providing a deposition to the Securities and Exchange Commission with regard to alleged misleading company press releases in America.

In February 1998 EMEA reported that the results of the American trial of the drugs had resulted in no marketing authorisation being permitted for the drugs. This came as a great shock to the shareholders. An analyst with Goldman Sachs contacted Dr Millar with regard to him not attending some company presentations. Apparently he proffered an explanation that he had problems with the company's business plan. The analyst was concerned and contacted two fund managers who represented one of British Biotech's largest shareholders. Dr Millar spoke candidly to the fund managers. The pattern was easy to establish. Press releases promising new drugs were released followed by further impartial tests failing to support the claims of the earlier press release. Perpetual approached Mercury Asset Management, the biggest shareholder of British Biotech. Dr Millar attended a meeting suggested by Mercury Asset Management with Kleinwort Benson, Biotech's bankers.

Dr Millar was suspended and then summarily dismissed. In a circular to shareholders British Biotech accused Dr Millar of acting "improperly and unprofessionally". Biotech then sued Dr Millar for breach of his contractual duty of confidence. In this case, however, the apparent attempt to blacken the name of the whistleblower ultimately failed. In June 1999 Biotech issued a statement exonerating Dr Millar and agreed to pay him substantial compensation (reported to be in the region of £250,000 plus costs).[8] As a result of Dr Millar's disclosures Biotech was censured by the Stock Exchange for making misleading statements about the prospects of one of its drugs.[9]

---

[7] *The Guardian*, August 9, 1999.
[8] *The Guardian*, June 9, 1999.
[9] *The Guardian*, June 25, 1999.

C4 1992—Patient abuse

1–19 In July 1992, the report of a Committee of Inquiry revealed that patients at Ashworth Special Hospital, Merseyside, had been subjected to a brutalising regime of physical and mental abuse by members of hospital staff for more than three years. The Inquiry, chaired by Sir Louis Blom-Cooper Q.C., uncovered a "developed pattern of intimidatory behaviour against staff and professionals who were brave enough to speak out", including death threats, vandalism and physical assault. The Report concluded that the culture at Ashworth had allowed the abuse to continue unexposed. It recognised that the problem of non-reporting would be "endemic" wherever such a culture persists. The Committee recommended that the hospital management make provision for nurses and staff to speak out about malpractice and "blow the whistle" on abuse.

C5 The University of Portsmouth

1–20 Bonnie Tall's case illustrates that even where the whistleblower is not victimised by the employer, if the concerns are not addressed, the whistleblower may feel that she has little alternative but to resign rather than be associated with her employer's conduct. Even if the employee then has a claim for wrongful dismissal or unfair dismissal, this may not provide an adequate remedy for prejudice to which the whistleblower may be subjected.

Bonnie Tall blew the whistle on the Vice Chancellor of Portsmouth University, Neil Merritt. Ms Tall had been asked by Mr Merritt to process what she regarded as dubious expenses claims. She properly raised the matter with the finance officer who informed her that this would be "sorted out". No action appeared to have been taken and, when Ms Tall was faced with more suspicious claims, she felt she was in an impossible situation and resigned.

The Employment Tribunal held that Bonnie Tall had been placed in an invidious position and was entitled to compensation for unfair dismissal. In the circumstances Ms Tall received £10,000 compensation from the University. Mr Merritt received a "golden handshake".

After blowing the whistle Bonnie Tall could only obtain work "temping". Companies with whom she was "temping" would consider offering full-time employment but lost interest as soon as they discovered her connection with the university.

C6 Genetically modified potatoes

1–21 In other cases the whistleblower has successfully focused attention on matters of public concern but, notwithstanding this has, it appears, been victimised for blowing the whistle.

Dr Arpad Pusztai conducted research which showed that rats which ate genetically modified potatoes suffered damage to their immune systems. This led him to be concerned as to the effect on humans. In August 1998 he revealed his concerns in an interview for a *World in Action* television programme, stating that in his view the general public were being used as guinea pigs. Initially Dr Pusztai's employers, the Rowatt Institute, were supportive. However the remarks caused a furore and the institute then issued a press release which referred to Dr Pusztai having carried out an incomplete set of experiments and having "muddled data". Dr Pusztai claims that he was "sent to Coventry", that his data was confiscated and he was denied any right to clarify scientific points at issue.[10] He was also suspended and then ordered to retire.

In February 1999, however, twenty two eminent scientists from thirteen different countries announced that they had reviewed Dr Pusztai's data and that they indeed supported his conclusions that there was reason for concern.[11] In March 1999, Dr Pusztai gave evidence as to his concerns to the Parliamentary Select Committee on Science and Technology. Subsequently, in May 1999, a group of scientists, specially convened by the Royal Society, criticised Dr Puszlais' research.[12] The issue however, remains highly controversial. Although Dr Pusztai has not been reinstated, partly as a result of his efforts, media attention has focused on the safety of genetically modified foods and the issue has itself become a political "hot potato".

C7 Fraud in the European Commission

1–22 Paul Van Buitenen, a Dutch assistant auditor in the European Commission's audit unit compiled a dossier detailing widescale corruption, fraud and cronyism within the European Commission. It appears that Mr Van Buitenen had first raised the matter internally and was threatened with disciplinary action if he passed the matter to the European Parliament.[13] Despite this Mr Van Buitenen passed the dossier to the Green Party in the European Parliament. As a result in early December 1998 he was suspended on half pay whilst dismissal proceedings were considered. He was accused of "imparting information to unauthorised and non-competent persons", notwithstanding that the European Parliament is responsible for assessing whether E.U. money has been properly spent. He also claims that his family has suffered death threats and that there has been a campaign to blacken his name such as by insinuating that he was politically motivated.

Following receipt of Mr Van Buitenen's dossier, on January 14, 1999 the European Parliament resolved that a committee of indendependent experts should be formed to investigate the way in which the Commission detects and deals with fraud, mismanagement and nepotism. The Committee delivered its first report on March 15, 1999. The report was so damning that all 20 commissioners felt compelled to resign en masse and Mr Van Buitenen was able to claim that he had been vindicated by the report. Notwithstanding this, Mr Van Buitenen's suspension on half pay was only lifted when the maximum four month disciplinary period expired. He was reassigned to a department auditing the furniture in the commission's office.[14] It has also been reported that he has been threatened with fresh disciplinary action if he makes further disclosures about fraud and mismanagement in Brussels.[15]

D TRIUMPH OF THE WHISTLEBLOWER

1–23 Notwithstanding the litany of cases in which the potential whistleblower has declined to come forward, or in which the whistleblower has been either ignored

---

[10] *The Guardian*, March 9, 1999.
[11] *The Guardian*, February 12 and February 16, 1999.
[12] *The Guardian*, May 28, 29, 1999.
[13] *The Guardian*, January 5, 1999.
[14] *The Guardian*, July 24, 1999.
[15] *Accountancy Age*, June 17, 1999.

or victimised, there are other cases in which whistleblowing has prompted a positive response.

D1 Scott Report

1–24   Sir Richard Scott V.-C.'s *Report of the Inquiry into the Export of Defence Equipment and Dual-Use goods to Iraq and Related Prosecutions*, relating to the *Arms to Iraq affair*, resulted in large part from the actions of a whistleblower. A Matrix Churchill employee warned the Foreign Office that the company was supplying munitions making equipment to Iraq. This letter, which Sir Richard Scott V.-C. described as "highly significant", was kept a secret from ministers for over three years. However the letter played a crucial part in Michael Heseltine M.P.'s decision not to sign a public interest immunity (PII) certificate for the purposes of the *Matrix Churchill* trial—which led to the trial being aborted. With the existence of this letter it was clear to the officials advising Mr Heseltine that there was a "whistleblower" who might well go to the press alleging a cover up. A Department of Trade and Industry official, recognising the significance of the letter, wrote in a minute that:

> "The difficulty of course is not simply that the letter exists but that the writer of the letter no doubt exists and even if he has not so far been involved in the proceedings by either the prosecution or the defence he may well make the existence of his letter public. The chances of his doing so will no doubt be all the greater if he is the one of those who is already made redundant or will be made redundant next month. It is tempting to suggest that we might claim PII for (the) letter, but I fear that doing so in the face of the possibility that the informant in it may well appear across the front of the tabloid press during the course of court proceedings, makes me diffident about suggesting it."[16]

The position taken by Mr Heseltine, as demonstrated by his own markings on the memo and by his evidence to the Inquiry, was that the letter showed that "everyone knew"[17] the contract was for military equipment. This became the catalyst to his refusal to sign the PII certificates and, accordingly, the withdrawal of the charges taken out against the directors of the Matrix Churchill company for supplying arms to Iraq.

Whilst the opinion of the DTI official suggested that the whistleblower was still regarded as a troublemaker, there is also some evidence that others within Government acknowledged, or wished to be seen to acknowledge, the value of the whistleblower. A PII was successfully claimed by the then Foreign Office Minister, Tristan Garel Jones, to keep the identity of the whistleblower secret. This was because:

> "it is undoubtedly in the public interest that the identity of a person carrying out his duty to inform the authorities of suspected wrong doing and thereby jeopardise himself and his livelihood should as far as possible be kept confidential."

---

[16] at p. 1271, para. G10.29.
[17] pp. 1344–5.

D2 Abbey National

1–25   Gary Brown, a manager with Abbey National, received £25,000 from his employers as a reward for blowing the whistle on a superior who he believed was involved in corrupt dealings. Mr Brown was a sales promotion manager in 1993 when his suspicions were aroused over malpractice. He left Abbey National in 1994 but continued to assist the investigators. He appeared in the Old Bailey as a witness in the case against his superior. The superior, who once had been considered a possible chief executive, received an eight year prison sentence for his malpractice. Shortly after the sentence Mr Brown received a letter from the chairman of Abbey National stating that he had appreciated Mr Brown's behaviour. To express his gratitude in an explicit manner a cheque for £25,000 was sent the following week.

Whilst Mr Brown never embarked upon the whistleblowing for any pecuniary reason, the chairman's gesture demonstrated to staff that Abbey National supported those who came forward to report serious wrongdoing.

THE NEED FOR CHANGE

1–26   As the above cases illustrate, there are many people who could have averted a safety or financial disaster had they been encouraged or enabled to speak out. There are a brave few who have managed to succeed in raising their concerns despite facing cultural prejudice and practical barriers in doing so. It may be that there are many more cases in which whistleblowers have been effective in allowing matters to be addressed internally and as such the matter has not needed to come to public knowledge. Nevertheless the above cases illustrate that, prior to the Public Interest Disclosure Act 1998, there was an urgent need for action. In many cases employees may witness serious malpractice but be reluctant to report this for fear of blighting their career by appearing difficult or disloyal. As illustrated by the above cases of "blaming the messenger", there have been good grounds for fears of physical violence, intimidation or dismissal for blowing the whistle. Indeed a recent survey of more than 230 whistleblowers in the United Kingdom and the U.S.A. (cited in *The Independent* for January 28, 1999) found that 84 per cent lost their jobs after informing their employer of fraud, even though they were not party to the fraud but were merely reporting the fact that it was going on.

The reluctance of potential whistleblowers to come forward has however been attributable not only to justified fears of reprisals. As illustrated by the cases of workers turning a blind eye, an additional factor has often been the prevailing "culture" within many organisations where the whistleblower is contemptuously regarded as a "*grass*" or a "*sneak*". This culture has sometimes been supported (notably in the NHS) by the use of gagging clauses. Indeed the Nolan Committee, in its first report on Standards in Public Life[18] (from which we include extracts in the Appendix) noted that:

> "There is a public concern about 'gagging clauses' in public employees' contracts of employment, which prevent them speaking out to raise concerns about standards of public propriety."

---

[18] Cm. 2850–1 (1995).

Even in the absence of an express gagging clause, the culture of secrecy was supported by the employee's knowledge that the duty of confidence was owed to the employer and by the example sometimes set by the employing organisation in failing to respond to concerns when raised. This culture was further sustained by deficiencies within the law which ensured that staff became trapped in an environment breeding inaction and apathy within the workplace despite the presence of dangers and malpractice.

Obviously as a bare minimum, therefore, it is necessary to provide protection against reprisal for workers courageous enough to blow the whistle. Beyond that, as illustrated by some of the above cases of "turning a deaf ear", staff must be provided with clear support and guidance to ensure that they are able to raise concerns and that they are aware that there are appropriate channels through which to do so. In addition, guidance is needed as to what concerns justify the potential whistleblower coming forward. Many staff have a misplaced fear that to raise a concern they must *prove* that the malpractice or crime is or was being committed. Such proof is actually not required, at least not where the information is to be passed on within the employing organisation. If there are genuine grounds for suspicion or concern, this can be investigated by the employer (or by a relevant regulatory body) so as to identify whether there is malpractice or crime or a danger to safety.

Disclosure to more senior personnel within the employing organisation may in practice be the most likely way in which to resolve the problem, since there is actually less incentive for the employer then to take a defensive approach. Such a disclosure does not involve public opprobrium, humiliation, or bad publicity for the organisation, and the employee will not be considered disloyal, as he might be if he went straight to the press to expose wrongdoing. One aspiration of those who promoted the Public Interest Disclosure Act 1998 was thus that it would reduce the need for disclosure *outside* the employing organisation by encouraging the employer to provide adequate mechanisms to receive the warnings of the whistleblower and then to take appropriate action in the light of such warnings. In the absence of such mechanisms, there is a risk that the employer might turn a deaf ear to complaints not only because of active hostility to the whistleblower but due to inadequate reporting structures. Indeed the ideal of encouraging the employer or the public body to put its own house in order was identified by the Nolan Report which noted that:

> "it is striking that in the few cases where things have gone badly wrong in local public spending bodies, it has frequently been the tip-off to the press or the local Member of Parliament—sometimes anonymous, sometimes not—which has prompted the regulators into action. Placing staff in a position where they feel driven to approach the media to ventilate concerns is unsatisfactory both for the staff member and the organisation."[19]

There is likely to be an immediate impact, at least to the extent of encouraging the development of formal channels for whistleblowing. A survey commissioned by Public Concern at Work and Industrial Relations Services reported, in August 1999, that two thirds of private companies and nine out of ten public sector organisations have a whistleblowing policy or plan to introduce one soon.[20]

---

[19] Committee on Standards in Public Life, Second Report, Cm. 3270–1 (1996) p. 21.
[20] *The Guardian*, August 2, 1999.

Nevertheless there will no doubt still be occasions in which the employee justifiably fears that internal disclosure would merely result in reprisals against him or her. In other cases, as illustrated by the examples of "turning a deaf ear", inadequate notice is taken when the matter is raised internally. One challenge for those legislating to protect the whistleblower was, therefore, to encourage disclosure within the employing organisation, whilst providing adequate protection where wide disclosure is appropriate.

MOMENTUM FOR REFORM

1-27   To a considerable extent even prior to the enactment of the Public Interest Disclosure Act there was already a sea change in the cultural perception as to the value of whistleblowers. This was prompted by the Nolan Report and by the observations of a number of public inquiries such as those relating to the Clapham rail crash, the Piper Alpha disaster and the collapse of BCCI. As a result there has been a growing recognition that:

> "It takes special courage and a special person to blow the whistle on malpractice in the workplace. They often suffer loss of a job, and income and career prospects — not to mention isolation, pressure and sometimes intimidation especially in the early stages of making such a move. The cases of Maxwell, Barlow Clowes, BCCI and a host of lower profile and smaller examples of whistleblowing underline the need for people to be able to report malpractices with confidence."[21]

The very term "whistleblowing" has subtly changed in its usage over the last 10 years from a generally pejorative word used as a label denoting a stance against the establishment, to a word synonymous with openness and informed decision making. This itself reflects changing public attitudes to someone who is prepared to breach confidence to bring matters to a wider public attention. It may also say something more generally about the perceived need to bring matters to public attention because of a lesser confidence in the integrity of both public and private administration.

The changing connotations of the term "whistleblower" were epitomised in the observations of the Court of Appeal in *Camelot plc v. Centaur Communications Limited* [1998] I.R.L.R. 80. The Court of Appeal allowed an application by Camelot for the disclosure of documents which would reveal the identity of an employee who had leaked a copy of Camelot's draft accounts to a journalist. There was no question of the leak being in the public interest. The information which was leaked would in any event have become publicly available five days after the document was leaked. It is however perhaps significant that Schiemann L.J. in *Camelot* specifically pointed out that:

> "This is not a case of disclosing iniquity, it is not a whistleblowing case."

The positive connotations of whistleblowing have also been recognised in the use of the heading "Blowing the Whistle" in relation to statutory obligations of disclosure relating to pensions.[22]

---

[21] John Healey M.P., *Hansard* 30 March 1999, col. 877.
[22] Pension Schemes Act 1993, and Pensions Act 1995, s. 48 and see Chapter 9, below.

Despite the change in the connotations attaching to the term "whistleblower", the 1998 Act itself seeks to avoid baggage carried by a word too often misunderstood. Nevertheless, by the time the Public Interest Disclosure Bill was introduced to Parliament a wide consensus had developed as to the need for such legislation. There had been previous attempts to legislate for public interest whistleblowing. Dr Tony Wright M.P. introduced a ten minute rule bill in 1995 for which there was not enough parliamentary time available and this was followed in the next parliamentary session by a Bill introduced by Don Touhig M.P. However the Bill which became the 1998 Act was able to sail through Parliament due to an unusual case of cross party co-operation on a matter impinging on employment law. It also had support in the two sides of industry.

The Act is largely a product of the tireless work of Public Concern at Work, an independent consultancy and legal advice centre launched in 1993, which has campaigned for many years for such legislation. It was introduced as a Private Member's Bill into the House of Commons by the Conservative M.P. Mr Richard Shepherd and taken into the Lords by the Labour peer Lord Borrie Q.C. It received strong support from the Labour Government in its first year in office, especially the Minister of State at the Department of Trade and Industry, Mr Ian McCartney M.P. There was, unusually, no debate at the Second Reading in the House of Commons or at the Third Reading in the House of Lords because of the consensus that had developed in support of the measure.

The new protection forms part of the reform of employment legislation and was put forward in the *Fairness at Work* White Paper Cm. 3968 (1998) as one of the key new rights for individuals. It is also linked with measures to encourage freedom of information. It is referred to in the White Papers on Freedom of Information *Your Right to Know* Cm. 3818 (1997) and on *Modern Local Government* Cm. 4014 (1998) and also in ministerial guidance to the NHS (*Freedom of Speech in the NHS*, letter from Health Minister to NHS Trust chairs, September 25, 1997).

THE PUBLIC INTEREST DISCLOSURE ACT 1998

1–28   The Public Concern at Work Consultation Paper, issued before the Public Interest Disclosure Bill was enacted, defined the aim of changing the law as being:

> "to make it more likely that where there is malpractice which threatens the public interest, a worker will—rather than turn a blind eye—raise the concern and do so in a responsible way".

The Act offers protection to the whistleblower, in broad terms, provided that the disclosure is proportionate and in relation to one of the specified subjects of public concern. The Act is a major step towards recognising the vital importance of those who selflessly, and often at great risk, draw attention to malpractice in the public interest. It seeks to do so whilst not giving protection to those making wild allegations or simply "gold digging". The difficulty faced by the framers of the legislation in seeking to confine protection to appropriate cases of proportionate disclosure may explain the complex structure of the Act. However, for the first time, essential protection for the whistleblower has been put on a statutory footing. Even aside from those who rely upon its provisions in litigation, it should have a powerful educative effect throughout industry and should encourage employers to develop enlightened policies to encourage proper internal disclosures. Indeed Lord Borrie Q.C. stated in the House of Lords debates that:

"This is the most far reaching piece of whistleblowing legislation in the world".

The Act operates by incorporating sections into the Employment Rights Act 1996, and throughout the book we refer to the section as thus incorporated rather than the section of the 1998 Act itself. By section 17, the Act applies only to England, Scotland and Wales. This section enables its provisions to be extended to Northern Ireland by Order in Council, subject to the negative resolution procedure and this has been the effect of the Public Interest Disclosure (Northern Ireland) Order 1998 (S.I. 1998 No. 1763 (N.I. 17)).

BEYOND THE 1998 ACT

1-29   In addition to offering our analysis of the 1998 Act and how it is likely to be interpreted by tribunals, accompanied in the appendices by some worked examples, this book also considers the common law. In many respects the statute builds on experience gained in common law cases and adopts some concepts derived from the common law. The question of a public interest defence affects actions for breach of confidence, defamation, breach of copyright and unfair dismissal.[23] Indeed the Act goes along with other developments in the common law, such as the development of a public interest defence to claims of breach of confidence, which have facilitated a more sympathetic approach to those acting in the public interest. Further development of the common law will need to take into account the provisions of the European Convention of Human Rights in the light of the recent passage of the Human Rights Act 1998. We discuss the way in which whistleblowing has been and is likely to be treated by the European Court of Human Rights. We also consider how protection for the whistleblower has been approached in other jurisdictions.

One general theme running throughout the 1998 Act, and the thinking of those who have promoted it, is the need to provide support and protection for whistleblowers in order to encourage them to come forward. However since disclosure by a whistleblower might prevent a disaster or perpetuation of fraud, the question arises as to whether there should also be a duty to blow the whistle. This has been reflected over the last decade in a number of statutory provisions imposing specific duties of disclosure, such as duties upon an auditor. We therefore consider the development of the common law and statutory duties of disclosure and the interrelation of these obligations with the new provisions of the Act. Since the Act seeks to foster a new workplace culture which leaves behind the petty schoolyard perception of the whistleblower as a "sneak", it might be suggested that there should be a fresh emphasis on the responsibilities of workers and therefore of the obligation, rather than merely the right, to disclose matters of genuine concern.

---

[23] For a detailed exposition of the various guises in which a public interest may arise see Cripps, *The Legal Implications of Disclosure in the Public Interest* (2nd ed., Sweet and Maxwell, 1994).

CHAPTER 2

Structure of the Public Interest Disclosure Act 1998

2–01 During the passage of the Public Interest Disclosure Bill in the House of Lords, Lord Nolan stated that his Committee on Standards in Public Life had been persuaded of the urgent need for protection for public interest whistleblowers. He commended those behind the Bill:

> "for so skilfully achieving the essential but delicate balance in this measure between the public interest and the interests of employers."[1]

PROTECTED DISCLOSURES

2–02 In seeking to attain this balance, the 1998 Act introduces a new species of protection into employment law with its own structure and terminology. A worker has a right not to suffer a detriment for making a "protected disclosure" (section 47B of the ERA). A disclosure is a "protected disclosure" if:

(a) it is a "qualifying disclosure" as defined in section 43B of the ERA (which relates to the subject matter of the disclosure); and

(b) it is made by a worker in accordance with any of sections 43C to 43H of the ERA (section 43A of the ERA) (which sets out conditions which depend on to whom the disclosure is made).

The definition of a "protected disclosure" therefore encompasses two key elements —the subject matter of the disclosure and the identity of the recipient of the disclosure—which are at the heart of the delicate balance which the Act seeks to achieve.

SUBJECT MATTER OF THE DISCLOSURE

2–03 Only a disclosure which relates to one of six specified categories may qualify for protection under the Act. These protected disclosures include (by section 43B) concerns about actual or apprehended breaches of civil, criminal, regulatory or administrative law; miscarriages of justice; dangers to health, safety and the environment; and the cover-up of any such malpractice.

---

[1] *Hansard*, H.L., June 5, 1998, col. 614.

TO WHOM IS DISCLOSURE MADE?

2–04   The other axis around which protection in each case revolves, and which is central to the delicate balance referred to by Lord Nolan, is the person(s) or bodies to whom or to which the disclosure is made. A different regime covers disclosure which takes place (broadly speaking) within the organisation of the employer (or to selected "outsiders"), and outside. We describe the former as first level disclosures and the latter as second level disclosures. More hurdles must be overcome in respect of second rather than first level disclosures, especially where a disclosure is made to the media than otherwise. The chart on page 00 sets this out in a graphical form.

First level protection under the Act is where a worker, who is concerned about matters falling within one or more of the six categories, raises the matter with those closest at hand. This will be those within the organisation or those responsible for policing the malpractice, who may be able most readily to address the problem identified. The employer cannot retaliate by dismissing that whistleblower or subjecting him to a detriment. It is hoped that a culture will develop in which workers feel that they are secure if they raise such concerns internally, safe in the knowledge that they will be protected by the Act and, ideally, an internal whistleblower policy. The employer may also benefit. The potential whistleblower may be encouraged to bring to the attention of senior management problems which the employer may not have known about and which may otherwise have remained hidden at the instance of middle management.

The more complete protection in this respect mirrors the common law where the courts have said that where disclosure is made to "one with a proper interest to receive the information" no breach of confidence occurs (Lord Denning M.R. in *Initial Services Ltd v. Putterill* [1968] 1 Q.B. 396 at 405). Indeed, in most cases, disclosure within the organisation would not itself amount to a breach of confidence.

In providing for protection in relation to second level disclosure the Act recognises that there are some circumstances where disclosure of the malpractice outside of the organisation is in the public interest and should therefore be protected. A subtle line is drawn by the statute between what may be seen as "good" or acceptable disclosures which are considered to be deserving of protection, and disclosures which are too wide and therefore do not merit specific statutory protection. We consider this in Chapter 5.

INITIAL OBSERVATIONS

2–05   The following features of the Act are noteworthy at the outset:

(a) The Act does not amend the common law, save to the extent that section 43J, inserted by the 1998 Act into the Employment Rights Act 1996, renders void a provision in an agreement precluding a worker from making a protected disclosure.

(b) The Act provides, in effect, for restricted disclosures in respect of which the normal remedies of unfair dismissal and victimisation are available, and in respect of which no agreement to exclude disclosure may be enforced.

(c) The Act specifically refers to confidentiality only in relation to determining whether a second level disclosure is protected. In determining whether it is reasonable for the worker to make the second level disclosure, one of the relevant criteria is "whether the disclosure is made in breach of a duty of confidentiality owed by the *employer* to any other person" (section 43G(3)(d)). The issue of confidentiality between *employer and employee*, which is the subject matter of most common law claims (and is covered in Chapter 7 of this book), is not referred to as being relevant under the Act.

(d) The Act renders various disclosures protected but only if the employee passes certain hurdles. These hurdles vary primarily depending on the extent of the disclosure in question.

(e) There is no residual class of protection in addition to the six specific defined categories of subject matter. It is therefore not open for the courts to determine on a case by case basis that there are other disclosures which should be protected under the Act in the public interest. In this the Act differs from some other jurisdictions which have legislated to protect whistleblowers. There are indeed several different models which have been adopted in foreign jurisdictions which are summarised in Appendix 8. Other potential models include protection in all cases where the worker thinks disclosure would be in the public interest (*e.g.* UKCC Code of Professional Conduct for Nurses 1992). Alternatively the Act might have been more closely integrated with the common law so that any disclosure of "iniquity" would suffice. The result achieved by the Act is, we think, in overall terms very successful although some have criticised it as too complex.

(f) The Act effectively sets out the circumstances in which a whistleblower will be protected. It does not follow that a whistleblower who falls outside the ambit of the Act will have no protection. The worker may still be able to rely upon the general unfair dismissal protection under the Employment Rights Act 1996 and may have a contractual claim for wrongful dismissal.

COMMENCEMENT

2–06   The substantive provisions of the Act came into force on July 2, 1999, a full year after it was enacted.

CHAPTER 3

Protectable information under the Public Interest Disclosure Act 1998

3–01 The first building block in the wall of protection created by the 1998 Act is based on the concept of a "qualifying disclosure". This focuses on the nature of the information which may attract protection if other conditions set out in the Act are satisfied in the particular case. Section 43B(1) of the ERA provides that:

> "a 'qualifying disclosure' means any disclosure of information which in the reasonable belief of the worker making the disclosure tends to show one or more of the following:
>
> (a) that a criminal offence has been committed, is being committed or is likely to be committed;
>
> (b) that a person has failed, is failing or is likely to fail to comply with any legal obligation to which he is subject;
>
> (c) that a miscarriage of justice has occurred, is occurring or is likely to occur;
>
> (d) that the health or safety of any individual has been, is being or is likely to be endangered;
>
> (e) that the environment has been, is being or is likely to be damaged
>
> (f) that information tending to show any matter falling within any of the preceding paragraphs has been, is being or is likely to be deliberately concealed."

A qualifying disclosure therefore extends to a wide range of information, applying to most malpractice about which a whistleblower might feel the need to complain. Protection is not tied to whether the information is confidential or to whether a common law defence to breach of confidence can be established. Indeed a disclosure within the employing organisation would only in very exceptional circumstances constitute a breach of the duty of confidentiality at all, whether express or implied in the contract of employment. Nor need the action of the employee in a general sense be reasonable, although the reasonableness of the belief in the truth of the information, or the more general reasonableness of the conduct of the worker, is relevant at various subsequent stages in ascertaining whether the disclosure is protected, especially in respect of an external, second level disclosure. Equally there is no requirement that the person to whom the disclosure is made is not already aware of the information from other sources (section 43L(3)). The whistleblower need not be telling him something which he did not already know.

REASONABLE BELIEF IN TRUTH

3–02 To achieve protection under any of the several parts of the Act, the worker must have a "reasonable belief" in the truth of the information as tending to show one or more of the six matters listed which he has disclosed, although that belief need not be correct (section 43B(1)). This has led some to criticise the statute as giving too much licence to employees to cause trouble, since it pays no regard to issues of confidentiality in this respect. Nor need the employee actually prove, even on the balance of probabilities, the truth of what he is disclosing. This is probably inevitable because the whistleblower may have a good "hunch" that something is wrong without having the means to prove it beyond doubt or even on the balance of probabilities. An example is the *Herald of Free Enterprise* disaster where no one had the resources to check on the hunch which several employees had about the safety of the bow doors. The notion behind the legislation is that the employee should be encouraged to make known to a suitable person the basis of that hunch so that those with the ability and resources to investigate it can do so.

The control on abuse is that it must have been reasonable for the worker to believe that the information disclosed was true. This means, we think, that the following principles would apply under the Act:

(a) It would be a qualifying disclosure if the worker reasonably but mistakenly believed that a specified malpractice is or was occurring or may occur.

(b) Equally if some malpractice was occurring which did not fall within one of the listed categories, the disclosure would still qualify if the worker reasonably believed that it did amount to malpractice falling within one of those categories.

(c) There must be more than unsubstantiated rumours in order for there to be a qualifying disclosure. The whistleblower must exercise some judgment on his own part consistent with the evidence and the resources available to him. There must additionally be a reasonable belief and therefore some information which tends to show the specified malpractice occurred. In the Guidance Note of March 1997 published by the Occupational Pensions Regulatory Authority in relation to the obligation on auditors and pension trustees to report to the regulator where they have "reasonable cause to believe" there has been (amongst other things) a relevant breach of the law, it is suggested (at paragraph 6.1) that:

> "Having reasonable cause to believe that a breach has occurred means more than acting on someone's unsubstantiated suspicion. It makes sense . . . to make checks before sending a report to OPRA."

Notwithstanding the different context, we think that this common sense suggestion, made in the *Guidance Note* after wide consultation, applies equally in relation to whether a worker could reasonably believe that information is true.

(d) The reasonableness of the belief will depend in each case upon the volume and quality of information available to the worker at the time the decision to disclose is made. Employment tribunals will have to guard against the use of hindsight to assess the reasonableness of the belief in this respect in the same way as they are bound, in considering liability in unfair dismissal cases, to consider only what was known to the employer at the time of dismissal or appeal (*e.g. Devis v. Atkins* [1977] A.C. 931). As in unfair dismissal cases, what happens subsequent to the dismissal (or, in a whistleblowing case where there is no dismissal, victimisation) may have an impact on the level of compensation to be awarded but not directly on liability itself.

(e) It does not matter at this stage whether the malpractice about which the disclosure is made was in the past, in the present or is prospective when the disclosure is made, nor whether it relates to particular conduct or to a state of affairs. These considerations may however be relevant to the issue of the reasonableness of a second level disclosure (see Chapter 5).

THE SIX CATEGORIES

3–03   There are six defined categories of protectable disclosures which are described by the Act as "qualifying disclosures" in section 43B(1). There is scope for considerable overlap between the six categories set out in the Act in particular cases. Damage to the environment may for example fall within subsections (a) (b) and (e) of section 43B(1) of the ERA.

It is also noteworthy that there is no necessity for a link between the matters disclosed and the actual employment of the worker. The discloser may simply be acting as a concerned employed citizen, although gratuitous interference in a matter of no concern to the employee may reflect on the good faith requirement, which we consider in Chapter 4.

We now consider in turn the scope of the categories of information referred to in the statute:

(a) That a *criminal offence* has been committed, is being committed or is likely to be committed: this involves a criminal offence of whatever degree of seriousness or otherwise, and may include breach of a minor regulation. There is no specific geographical scope placed on where the crime may be committed.

(b) Failure to comply with a *legal obligation* includes a breach of any statutory requirement, contractual obligation, common law obligation (*e.g.* negligence, nuisance, defamation) or an administrative law requirement. This might include a legal obligation imposed by a different jurisdiction.

The category of administrative law requirement may be especially wide in that an anticipation that a decision or procedure was susceptible to judicial review would fall within its scope. It may for example be sufficient that a public body has taken into account irrelevant considerations, or failed to take account of relevant considerations or has acted for an improper purpose in reaching a decision. It may also extend to breach of codes of practice such as the concern of a civil servant that he had been asked to act in a way which breached a provision of the Civil Service Code or the code for staff of non-departmental public bodies (NDPBs) (*e.g.* the requirement to act with "integrity, impartiality and honesty"). The Government confirmed by letter to Mr Shepherd M.P. (the sponsor of the Bill) that compliance with such codes is in its view a contractual requirement binding on public servants, so that a disclosure of a breach of it can be protected.

The Act does not, however, cover a failure to fulfil what might be considered to be a moral (but not legal) obligation of the employer to an outsider. Further, whether disclosure of a breach of a self-regulatory code qualifies for protection will turn upon whether there is a legal obligation to comply with the rule. In some cases this may give rise to difficult issues of construction. Whilst a breach of a code of conduct might enable the self-regulatory organisation to take disciplinary action it may in some contexts be difficult to identify a *legal* obligation which has been flouted. In such circumstances the extent of the common law defence of disclosure in the public interest will continue to be of crucial importance (see Chapter 7).

(c) *Miscarriage of justice* would include all interference with the proper judicial process, such as perjury or failure to disclose evidence, although the direct impact is diminished at present since police officers are specifically excluded from the scope of the Act (section 13 of the Act). It should be noted that the Government has given a firm commitment that police officers will be provided with equivalent protection in due course[1] although the form that protection will take remains to be seen. It may be done, for example, through amending the Police Regulations.

"Miscarriage of justice" is not a widely used term of art, although it is mentioned in section 2 of the Criminal Appeals Act 1968. As such there is little caselaw to guide tribunals and they can be expected to adopt a common sense broad brush approach to this term. An instructive case in this context, which shows the potential ambit of the term, is *Lion Laboratories v. Evans* [1985] Q.B. 526 (CA). Two employees of Lion Laboratories disclosed to the press information casting doubt on the reliability of breathalyser equipment produced by the employer company. These machines were used by the police to measure levels of intoxication in drink driving cases. The Court of Appeal decided that because of the public interest in the matter wide disclosure was justified since it related to potential miscarriages of justice. An injunction was therefore refused.

(d) *Health and safety risks.* The ERA 1996 (in sections 44 and 100) already provides some protection on victimisation for health and safety matters, being protection against detriment and dismissal if the employee is (in summary) disadvantaged or dismissed for carrying out health and safety activities or because he is a member of a works safety committee or refuses to work in circumstances of danger which the employee "reasonably believed to be serious and imminent and which he could not reasonably have been expected to avert". This test is naturally a difficult one to prove.

The protection relating to disclosure of health and safety risks applies whether the risk threatens a worker or any individual. As such, this could

---

[1] *Hansard*, H.C., Vol. 310, cols 1143–4; H.C. Standing Committee D March 11, 1998, cols 16–17.

apply to employees, visitors to public places, or customers in a restaurant or the general public. In *Masiak v. City Restaurants (U.K.) Limited* EAT 683/97 it was held that section 100(1)(e), relating to vicitimisation for health and safety matters, is not confined to concerns as to the health and safety of other employees but covers concerns as to the health and safety of the general public.

(e) That the *environment* has been, is being or is likely to be damaged. This would cover potential oil spills, toxic waste emissions, and threats to the rain forest.

(f) *"Cover ups"*. This category provides that qualifying disclosures include information not only about the substantive malpractice, but information which "in the reasonable belief of the worker" tends to show that "any matter falling within any of the preceding paragraphs has been, is being or is likely to be deliberately concealed". It is one of the first reactions (and perhaps a natural reaction) in those about whom the whistle is blown to seek to restrict information about the malpractice. If that is done deliberately, disclosures about the cover up are as well protected as would be the original information about the malpractice itself. This would not, however, cover accidental or unintended concealment.

These six categories constitute a complete statutory regime. There is no concluding catch-all provision to give flexibility to the concept of protected disclosure. Tribunals therefore have no licence to go outside the parameters of these six protected areas. There is also no specific reference to financial irregularities, although these will usually fall within the rubric of criminal offences of one sort or another, such as fraud, theft or false accounting. In the USA, by contrast, the Whistleblower Protection Act 1989 covers disclosures of "gross mismanagement", "gross waste of funds" and "abuse of authority". These are more elastic concepts in the hands of the courts, although it is not immediately obvious what set of facts would be covered in the USA but not in the United Kingdom (see Appendix 8).

CRIMINAL DISCLOSURES

3–04   There is special provision (section 43B(3)) that where the disclosure of the information is itself a crime (*e.g.* it breaches the Official Secrets Act) it does not qualify as being a "qualifying disclosure" under the Act. This is especially controversial since it might be said that one area where the whistle could most usefully be blown in the public interest is in the civil service or the security services where to do so would often in fact amount to a crime that is a breach of the Official Secrets Act (although compare the Ponting case described in Chapter 1). David Shayler, who seeks to make disclosures about wrongdoing in MI5, would not be protected, even if the Act had been in force at the time he made his disclosures (and indeed MI5 has some form of internal whistleblowing procedure although the details have not been made public).

Because of this provision there may be an overlap of jurisdictions dealing with a particular disclosure. Where the disclosure is alleged to constitute a criminal offence and proceedings are in progress or anticipated, it is likely that an employment tribunal will postpone any hearing under the 1998 Act because of the risk that proceedings in the tribunal might prejudice those in the criminal court, and because it would be better for a criminal court to make the determination as to whether the disclosure concerned a criminal act. This is the approach normally taken when an employee has been dismissed for misconduct and that misconduct may be the subject of criminal proceedings.[2] If the worker is acquitted at trial, he will be able to invoke the protection of the Act in the normal way. The tribunal is not however bound in every case to allow an adjournment. In considering whether to allow an adjournment the tribunal will ordinarily consider the degree of similarity between the issues before the tribunal, the extent of the delay likely to be caused, how late the application is made and the reasons for the delay in making an application for an adjournment.[3]

Lord Nolan[4] and Lord Borrie Q.C.,[5] speaking on the Bill in the House of Lords, opined that where no such proceedings were in prospect but the employer alleges that the disclosure constituted a crime, the standard of proof which the tribunal should apply should be effectively a criminal one. Both based their comments on the decision in *Re A Solicitor* [1992] 2 All E.R. 335. The Government spokesman, Lord Haskell,[6] while pointing out that the effects of such a finding would not be the same as in a criminal court, stated that a "high standard of proof" would be required. This is consistent with the ordinary approach where matters which would constitute a criminal offence are raised in civil proceedings. Ordinarily the civil standard of proof of the balance of probabilities will continue to apply but the evidence required to satisfy this standard will be at the high end of the scale because the Court will take into account the improbability of guilt as part of the range of circumstances to be weighed in determining the balance of probability.[7]

LEGAL PROFESSIONAL PRIVILEGE

3–05   The 1998 Act makes special provision to prevent a legal advisor claiming protection under the Act if he discloses information which was supplied by a worker if the worker could have claimed legal professional privilege in relation to such information. The legal advisor will not be able to assert that he has made a qualifying disclosure if he discloses the information without authority from the worker client (section 43B(4) of the ERA). This does not, however, affect the lawyer's ability to make disclosures to others on the express instructions of a worker who is his client, in which case there would be a disclosure as agent for the worker client and that would be judged in the normal way.

GEOGRAPHICAL SCOPE

3–06   To fall within the Act, the relevant failure or malpractice may occur or be anticipated to occur either inside or outside the United Kingdom (section 43B(2) of

---

[2] *e.g. Evans v. Wyre Forest District Council*, COIT 1590/129; see generally Bowers, Brown and Mead, *Employment Tribunal Practice and Procedure* (Sweet & Maxwell, 1999), p. 126–130.
[3] *Bastick v. James Lane (Turf Accountants) Limited* [1979] I.C.R. 778 (EAT).
[4] *Hansard*, H.L., June 5, 1998, col. 614.
[5] *Ibid.*, cols. 616–7.
[6] *Ibid.*, col. 616.
[7] *Hornal v. Neuberger Products Ltd* [1957] 1 Q.B. 247 (CA).

the ERA). Thus, an employee in the United Kingdom may raise concerns about the felling of rainforests in South America, or human rights violations in East Timor (provided that this amounted to a crime). Nor does not it matter what law applies to the disclosure as a matter of private international law (section 43B(2) of the ERA).

THE LEVELS OF PROTECTION

3–07   The Act provides various levels of protection for which different hurdles must be surpassed. In outline these relate to disclosure:

(a) to the employer (section 43C).

(b) to any one other than the employer legally responsible for the situation in respect of which the disclosure is made (section 43C).

(c) to a legal adviser (section 43D).

(d) to a Minister if the individual is appointed under any enactment by the Minister (section 43E).

(e) to a regulator as prescribed in regulations (section 43F).

(f) to any other person when it is reasonable to do so according to set criteria (section 43G).

(g) where the disclosure is of exceptionally serious matters (section 43H).

We now turn to consider these in detail.

CHAPTER 4

First level disclosure under the Public Interest Disclosure Act 1998

4–01   We use the phrase first level disclosure (which does not appear in the Act) as a shorthand to describe disclosure to the employer, to any one legally responsible for the situation in respect of which the disclosure is made, to a legal adviser, to a Minister if the individual is appointed under any enactment by the Minister, or to a regulator as prescribed in Regulations (section 43F). These are in general those individuals who are most obviously in a position to influence and redress the malpractice about which the disclosure is made. In these circumstances the whistleblower deserves the highest level of protection. There is nothing in the Act to require an employer to act on the basis of a disclosure. However a failure to do so may lead him to be found criminally or civilly liable for failing to exercise due care. In this chapter, we consider in turn the new section 43C, 43D, 43E and 43F of the Employment Rights Act 1996.

DISCLOSURE TO EMPLOYER OR OTHER RESPONSIBLE PERSON: SECTION 43C

4–02   An employee who makes a disclosure to his employer has the greatest level of protection under the 1998 Act. The new section 43C of the ERA provides:

"(1) A qualifying disclosure is made in accordance with this section if the worker makes the disclosure in good faith—

(a) to his employer, or
(b) where the worker reasonably believes that the relevant failure relates solely or mainly to—

(i) the conduct of a person other than his employer, or
(ii) any other matter for which a person other than his employer has legal responsibility,

to that other person.

(2) A worker who, in accordance with a procedure whose use by him is authorised by his employer, makes a qualifying disclosure to a person other than his employer, is to be treated for the purposes of this Part as making the qualifying disclosure to his employer."

This was described by Lord Borrie Q.C. as being "absolutely at the heart" of the Act.[1] No additional evidential test applies in this section beyond the requirement to act in good faith and that the worker "reasonably believes the information tends to show" the malpractice or misconduct (section 43B). This is one of the lowest standards of proof in the legal system and is lower than the need for a prima facie case for arrest. The term "employer" has a rather wider definition than is normal because of the special cases which are fitted within the employer–employee straitjacket which we consider below.

a. Good faith

4–03   The worker must act in "good faith" even in respect of an internal disclosure. This requirement naturally also appears in relation to sections 43E to 43H where further hurdles must also be surpassed. In other contexts a requirement of good faith has been equated with an honest belief in a state of affairs, albeit that a person might not act in good faith if he had a suspicion that the belief might be unfounded and deliberately refrained from questioning further.[2] As such, a person who was "honestly blundering and careless" would still be acting in good faith.[3]

We suggest therefore that a disclosure is made in good faith if it is made honestly, even though made negligently or without due care being taken by the person making it. Where the disclosure is demonstrably made for an ulterior and undesirable purpose, in particular something approaching blackmail, it would not be found to have been made in good faith. Other such purposes which are likely to be held as made in bad faith (depending on the precise circumstances) may be those made in the pursuance of a grudge, retaliation against a colleague who has in some way harmed the person making the disclosure, general resentment against the employer's policy or a desire for publicity. In *Shillito v. Van Leer (U.K.) Limited* [1997] I.R.L.R. 495 a case on victimisation on health and safety grounds, the EAT held that a health and safety representative might be said to have acted in bad faith since he had been pursuing a personal agenda of embarrassing the company but that there was no requirement that he generally behave reasonably.[4] However motivations may often be mixed in making a disclosure and difficult questions will be posed for the tribunals in many cases.

Employment tribunals are already required to consider whether an employee has acted in good faith in relation to victimisation provisions of the sex,[5] race[6] and disability discrimination[7] legislation and in relation to victimisation for assertion of a statutory right.[8] There is little case law in relation to the concept of good faith. However in *Bham v. CFM Group Limited* EAT 1254/95 the EAT upheld a finding that a complaint of race discrimination had been made in bad faith in circumstances where Mr Bham complained that his dismissal constituted victimisation for having made a discrimination complaint. The employment tribunal found that Mr Bham had deliber-

---

[1] *Hansard*, H.L., June 19, 1998, cols. 1801/2.
[2] See *Jones v. Gordon* [1877] A.C. 616, HL (in the context of bills of exchange), *Dodds v. Yorkshire Finance Bank* (1992) C.C.L.R. 92 and *Chartered Trust Plc v. Commissioner of the Police for the Metropolis* (unreported, May 26, 1999, CA) (each in the context of hire purchase transactions).
[3] *Jones v. Gordon* [1877] A.C. 616, HL, *per* Lord Blackburn at p. 628.
[4] See also *Goodwin v. Cabletel U.K. Ltd* [1997] I.R.L.R. 665; [1998] I.C.R. 112 (EAT).
[5] Sex Discrimination Act 1975, s. 4(2).
[6] Race Relations Act 1976, s. 2(2).
[7] Disability Discrimination Act 1995, s. 55(4).
[8] ERA, s. 104(2).

ately declined to raise any complaint of discrimination as part of a grievance which he had brought but had indicated to an employee of the respondent that he would do so if the grievance hearing did not appear to be going well. Mr Bham subsequently wrote to councillors of the local authority indicating a concern that he was the victim of race discrimination. He was later dismissed after he failed to attend a meeting to investigate his absences from work on the grounds of ill health. The tribunal found that Mr Bham was unfairly dismissed but that there was no discrimination on grounds of race and no vicitimisation. It also held that the complaint of victimisation had not been made in good faith because it had been raised as a "tactical tool" in the hope of extending Mr Bham's employment by any means at his disposal. The tribunal appear to have concluded that if there was a genuine belief in the complaint it would have been raised earlier rather than being held back for tactical purposes. Further the EAT upheld the decision of the tribunal to take account of the finding that the complaint had been made in bad faith in reducing compensation for unfair dismissal.

b. To whom should the employee take his concern internally?

4–04 There is a real question about the scope of disclosure by a worker "to his employer" when the employer is (as will usually be the case) a large organisation with many layers of management. We think that this concept would include a disclosure to any person senior to the worker, who has been expressly or implicitly authorised by the employer as having management responsibility over the worker. It would probably not, however, cover a disclosure to a colleague on precisely the same level, unless that person had a particular role in receiving such complaints whether pursuant to a special whistleblowing policy or just the normal chain of command. In some cases, there may be no "disclosure" at all.

The scope of the persons to whom the whistle may be blown in this way might be covered expressly in a whistleblowing procedure, and it is best practice for the employer to do so, although there is no statutory duty to do so. If there is a whistleblowing procedure covering these matters, this may influence the determination by the tribunal whether the employee is acting in good faith. An employee who wholly fails to abide by the terms and conditions of that policy may be more likely to be held not to be acting in good faith.

c. Other responsible persons

4–05 Section 43C(1)(b) of the ERA provides that, if the worker reasonably believes that the relevant failure relates solely or mainly to the conduct of a person other than the employer or to matters for which that other person has legal responsibility, there is a qualifying disclosure if the disclosure is made to that person. This would we think protect, for instance:

(1) a nurse employed by an agency who raises in the care home where he/she works (*i.e.* where he/she is placed by the agency) a concern about malpractice in that home. The care home might have vicarious liability for the malpractice and therefore this might be regarded as conduct of the care home or a matter for which it has legal responsibility.

(2) a worker in an auditing firm who raises a concern with the client (in relation to a matter for which the client would be legally responsible), and

(3) someone who works for a local authority highway contractor raising a concern with the local authority that the performance of the contract exposes the authority to negligence claims from injured pedestrians.

While such action may be protected, the following special aspects about such disclosure should be noted:

(a) Subject to section 43C(2) (see below), it does not amount to raising the matter with the employer for the purposes of a subsequent wider disclosure (under section 43G) when it is in some cases possible to build on the failure to act on one disclosure to make another (see p. 30 below).

(b) The Act does not place any obligation on the person responsible to respond to the concern or to investigate it in any way; and

(c) If the worker is victimised for making a disclosure under this subsection, any claim which he may have is only to be made against his employer, and not against the person to whom he made this disclosure.

Section 43C(2) expressly provides that where the organisation has a whistleblowing procedure which involves raising the concern with someone other than the employer, a disclosure to that person will be treated as if it were a disclosure to the employer. This would typically apply to a procedure authorising a disclosure to a health and safety representative, a union official, its parent company, a retired non-executive director, its lawyers or external auditors, or to a commercial reporting hotline. The procedure need not be agreed between employer and employee or employer and the union or works council. It is sufficient if it is "authorised" by the employer.

As such, the reasonableness of the response made by the employer to the concern is relevant in determining whether a subsequent wider disclosure may be protected: section 43G(3)(e). While the Act does not require employers to set up whistleblowing procedures, a worker who makes a wide, public disclosure is more likely to be protected if there was no such procedure or it was not reasonable to expect him to use it (section 43G(3)(f)), so that it makes sense for the employer to set up such a procedure.

DISCLOSURE TO AND BY A LEGAL ADVISER: SECTION 43D

4–06   The new section 43D of the ERA is a short section which covers a disclosure made in the course of seeking legal advice about a concern. It provides that:

"A qualifying disclosure is made in accordance with this section if it is made in the course of obtaining legal advice".

This is the only sort of disclosure within the Act which does not have to be made in good faith in order to be protected. The legal adviser, in turn, cannot, however, of his own volition make a protected disclosure of the information if it would be covered by legal professional privilege (section 43B(4)). He can make only such disclosure as the client instructs him to make on his behalf. If the legal adviser discloses the privileged information without authority, he will be unable to assert that he has made a qualifying disclosure. If he is authorised to make the disclosure, this will be judged as having been a disclosure made by the client, and it will only be protected if it is made in accordance with the other provisions of the Act. Disclosure to the lawyer therefore does not give the client any rights beyond those which he would normally have.

DISCLOSURE TO A TRADE UNION

4–07   Disclosure to a trade union is not an express statutory right but where a trade union is recognised in a workplace, we would expect that in most cases disclosures to trade union officials will be protected under the whistleblowing procedures to which reference is made in section 43C(2). This provides:

> "A worker who, in accordance with a procedure whose use by him is authorised by his employer, makes a qualifying disclosure to a person other than his employer, is to be treated . . . as making the qualifying disclosure to his employer."

The implications of this provision (and others) for general disclosures to union officials were considered at some length in the House of Lords at the Committee and subsequent stages of the progress of the Bill. Lord Borrie Q.C. made the point that a disclosure by a union member for the purpose of obtaining legal advice from the union solicitor will, in any event, be protected under this section.[9] Nevertheless a concerted effort was made in the House of Lords to mention trade union officials specifically in the Act itself on the basis that such officials (who will often not be employed by the same company as the whistleblower) were in reality in a similar position to legal representatives, and would often be the first port of call especially in a health and safety issue. Reference was made in the Lords debates to Mr Templeton, a trustee of the Maxwell pension fund at the *Scottish Daily Record*, who felt that something was wrong with the administration of the fund, raised it with his union and at a trustees' meeting and was then dismissed. This amendment was opposed by the Government and was not pursued.

MINISTERS OF THE CROWN AND GOVERNMENT APPOINTED BODIES: SECTION 43E

4–08   Section 43E of the ERA provides that workers are protected if, in good faith, they disclose their concerns to a Minister of the Crown provided that their employer is:

> "(i) an individual appointed under any enactment by a Minister of the Crown, or
>
> (ii) a body any of whose members are so appointed".

This therefore applies to Government employees. It would also apply to, amongst others, employees of utility regulators such as OFWAT, OFTEL and OFGAS and to NHS Trusts, tribunals and all kinds of non-departmental public bodies whose

---

[9] *Hansard*, H.L., June 5, 1998, col. 624.

members are appointed by a Minister of the Crown. The section refers to disclosure to a Minister as, legally, this is taken to be the effect of a disclosure to a department.

This provision is based on the recommendations that the Committee on Standards in Public Life made in its First[10] and Second Reports.[11] We include relevant extracts in Appendix 6. An employee may be more comfortable making the disclosure to the department since it is at one remove from the work relationship, and thus disclosure may not be seen so directly as diminishing trust and confidence in the relationship with the employer. The department may also have far greater ability to put matters right in response to the concerns expressed.

The following matters should be noted about this subsection:

(a) As under section 43C(1)(b), a disclosure under this section is not treated as one to the employer for the purposes of any subsequent, wider disclosure (section 43G) (see below pp. 36–37).

(b) If the worker is victimised for making a disclosure under this subsection, any claim he may have is made against his employer and not against the Minister to whom he made this disclosure.

(c) Subsection 1(b) requires the worker to act in "good faith" (which we have considered above).

Disclosure to a person prescribed by the Secretary of State: section 43F

4–09   Section 43F protects a worker who makes a qualifying disclosure to a person prescribed by the Secretary of State for Trade and Industry by Order, provided that the disclosure relates to matter for which that person is prescribed. The Public Interest Disclosure (Prescribed Persons) Order (S.I. 1999 No. 1549) sets out a list of the persons who are prescribed, and the purposes for which they are prescribed, for the purposes of this section (see Appendix 3).

An amendment was made to the Bill in Committee[12] for the purposes of enabling classes of person to be prescribed so as to ensure that health and safety representatives might be prescribed, should it transpire that employers were not including them within internal reporting procedures. Other classes of persons capable of being prescribed under this section could include certain trade union officials.[13]

There are lesser restrictions on the nature of disclosures to such persons than to others outside the employing organisation and which we treat as second level disclosures within section 43G. By section 43F(1)(a) the worker must act in good faith in order to qualify for these purposes. The worker must reasonably believe that the malpractice falls within the matters prescribed for that regulator and reasonably believe "that the information disclosed, and any allegation in it, are substantially true" (section 43F(1)(b)). It is thus appropriate to check which is the prescribed regulator and whether the concern is within its remit. By way of example, disclosure in good faith to the Health and Safety Executive would be a protected disclosure under

---

[10] Cm. 2850–I pp. 60 and 91–92.
[11] May 1996 p. 22.
[12] Parliamentary Debates, H.C. Standing Committee D, March 11, 1998, col. 8.
[13] *Hansard*, H.L., June 5, 1998, col. 623.

section 43F provided that two further conditions were satisfied. First, the worker must have reasonably believed that the information disclosed, and any allegation contained in it, was substantially true. Secondly, the worker must have reasonably believed that the disclosure concerned fell within the relevant description set out in S.I. 1999 No. 1549 as matters to be disclosed to that body. The worker making the disclosure to the Health and Safety Executive must therefore reasonably have believed that the disclosure concerned matters which might affect the health or safety of an individual at work or might affect the health or safety of any member of the public arising out of or in connection with the activities of persons at work.

While this provision contains a higher evidential burden than that required for raising the concern under section 43C, the worker will not lose protection if his belief was mistaken, provided it was reasonable for him to hold it. To be protected under this section, where a worker discloses the fact that another person has told him that a fraud has taken place, he would have to show that he himself had a reasonable belief—and some factual basis for it—that the fraud has in fact taken place. The concept of a disclosure being "substantially true" will be addressed in detail below in relation to second level disclosures. It should be noted that the test remains one of a subjective nature so that it remains an issue of fact for the tribunal on all the information whether the concern raised was substantially true.

Thus, although the worker must meet a higher evidential burden than in section 43C relating to internal whistleblowing, where a regulator has been prescribed, there is no requirement:

(a) that the particular disclosure was reasonable (although it must be made in good faith);

(b) that the malpractice was serious; nor

(c) that the worker should have first raised the matter internally.

The favoured position of the whistleblower who makes disclosure to a regulator is explicable on the basis that:

(a) the regulators have a statutory duty to investigate such matters and they can only perform their role if members of the public are prepared to come to them with information. Employees will only do so if there is no danger of retaliation in the workplace for disloyalty;

(b) the regulator can usually be relied upon to maintain confidentiality of the material once it is in their domain, whether the allegation is right or wrong;

(c) the motivation of anyone revealing material to a regulator is likely to be one of concerned public interest because the regulator will not pay money for the material (although someone who makes such a disclosure may qualify for a Community Action Trust award).

These considerations have also been persuasive in forging a preferential position under the common law of confidence for disclosures made to prescribed regulators over other external disclosures. In *Re A Company* [1989] 1 Ch. 477, where an employee reported an internal matter to the Financial Investment and Broker's

Regulatory Authority which was then the relevant regulator under the Financial Services Act 1986 (and whose functions are now performed by the Financial Services Authority), Scott J. said:

> "It may be the case that the information proposed to be given, the allegations to be made by the defendant to FIMBRA and for that matter by the defendant to the Inland Revenue, are allegations made out of malice and based upon fiction or invention. But if that is so, then I ask myself what harm will be done. FIMBRA may decide that the allegations are not worth investigating. In that case no harm will have been done. Or FIMBRA may decide that an investigation is necessary. In that case, if the allegations turn out to be baseless, nothing will follow from the investigation. And if harm is caused by the investigation itself, it is harm implicit in the regulatory role of FIMBRA."

If it is not clear whether the matter should be raised internally or with a pre-scribed person, the worker or his adviser might first contact the particular regulator informally to check if it is prescribed and, without initially identifying the employer, to discuss the nature of the concern in order to establish whether it is within the regulator's remit and to explore what action the regulator considers appropriate. It is assumed that the regulator will maintain the confidentiality of that enquiry.

CHAPTER 5

Second level external disclosures under the Public Interest Disclosure Act 1998

5–01 Sections 43G and 43H set out the circumstances in which other disclosures, including those to the media, may be protected. These provisions give the tribunal much more scope for determining the reasonableness of aspects of the employee's behaviour than the earlier provisions.

SECTION 43G DISCLOSURES

5–02 Section 43G provides:

"(1) A qualifying dislcosure is made in accordance with this section if—

    (a) the worker makes the disclosure in good faith,

    (b) he reasonably believes that the information disclosed, and any allegation contained in it, are substantially true,

    (c) he does not make the disclosure for purposes of personal gain,

    (d) any of the conditions in subsection (2) is met, and

    (e) in all the circumstances of the case, it is reasonable for him to make the disclosure.

(2) The conditions referred to in subsection (1)(d) are—

    (a) that, at the time he makes the disclosure, the worker reasonably believes that he will be subjected to a detriment by his employer if he makes a disclosure to his employer in accordance with section 43F,

    (b) that, in a case where no person is prescribed for the purposes of section 43F in relation to the relevant failure, the worker reasonably believes that it is likely that evidence relating to the relevant failure will be concealed or destroyed if he makes a disclosure to his employer, or

    (c) that the worker has previously made a disclosure of substanitally the same information—

        (i) to his employer, or

        (ii) in accordance with section 43F.

(3) In determining for the purposes of subsection (1)(e) whether it is reasonable for the worker to make the disclosure, regard shall be had, in particular, to —

    (a) the identity of the person to whom the disclosure is made,

    (b) the seriousness of the relevant failure,

(c) whether the relevant failure is continuing or is likely to occur in the future,

(d) whether the disclosure is made in breach of a duty of confidentiality owed by the employer to any other person,

(e) in a case falling within subsection (2)(c)(i) or (ii), any action which the employer or the person to whom the previous disclosure in accordance with section 43F was made has taken or might reasonably be expected to have taken as a result of the previous disclosure, and

(f) in a case falling within subsection (2)(c)(i), whether in making the disclosure to the employer the worker complied with any procedure whose use by him was authorised by the employer.

(4) For the purposes of this section a subsequent disclosure may be regarded as a disclosure of substantially the same information as that disclosed by a previous disclosure as mentioned in subsection (2)(c) even though the subsequent disclosure extends to information about action taken or not taken by any person as a result of the previous disclosure."

Under section 43G, therefore, disclosures must meet three quite stringent tests in order to be protected. The first of these (section 43G(1)(a)–(c)) deals in general terms with the good faith or other motive of the whistleblower. The second (section 43G(2)) sets out three preconditions, one of which must be met if the disclosure is to be capable of protection. Finally, to be protected the disclosure must be reasonable in all the circumstances (section 43G(1)(e) and (3)). If the concern had been raised internally beforehand or with a prescribed regulator, the reasonableness of the worker's belief in the substantial truth of the information disclosed will be assessed having regard to what happened in a first level disclosure and any response which he may have received from management or the prescribed regulator to the original complaint. Thus, if the response was a stony silence or an ineffectual remedy, the employee may be justified in continuing with his campaign and taking the matter further to a wider audience.

"SUBSTANTIALLY TRUE"

5–03   A second level disclosure only qualifies for protection if the worker reasonably believes that the information disclosed, and any allegation contained in it, is "substantially true".[1] This raises the possibility of a divergence between the law of defamation at common law and public interest disclosure under the new Act. An employee may have protection from dismissal on this basis but, despite a reasonable belief in the substantial truth of the allegation, not be able to justify the matter in defence to a defamation action or qualify for qualified privilege in answer to a defamation claim (see Chapter 12).

It is not clear precisely how the courts and tribunals will approach the phrase "substantially true". There are some dicta which might be applied by analogy to this situation. In the criminal case of *R v. Lloyd* [1966] 1 All E.R. 107 the court said that the word "substantial" should be approached in a broad common sense way. It meant

---

[1] s. 43G(1)(b); s. 43H(1)(b).

more than some trivial degree but less than total. In the Australian authority, *Tillmanns Butcheries Pty Ltd v. Australasian Meat Industry Employees Union* (1979) 42 F.L.R. 331 at 348, the court declared that when used in a quantitative sense it does not necessarily mean "most" but may mean only "much" or "some". What must be recognised in this context is that it must be the concern raised which is substantially true. An employee may have a concern that money is being withdrawn from his employer's bank account. He may have independent evidence to that effect in the form of a bank statement showing that withdrawal. Whilst he is protected in respect of an allegation of withdrawal he may not be able to demonstrate that an allegation of fraud is substantially true.

PERSONAL GAIN

5–04   A second level disclosure does not qualify for protection if the purpose of the disclosure is for personal gain.[2] This is aimed primarily at the grosser excesses of "cheque book journalism". It covers not only payments of money, but benefits in kind. It would also catch a situation where the benefit did not go directly to the worker but to a member of his family, provided that its purpose was personal gain. The concept of personal gain does not, however, catch any reward payable by or under any enactment (section 43L(2)), such as a payment made by Customs and Excise for information received.[3] The exception does not cover private rewards of any sort such as an award by the Community Action Trust. The effect of section 43L is that where a reward is made by a regulator who is not prescribed under section 43F, it shall not be a bar to protection. Such rewards are occasionally made by statutory agencies in return for information supplied. Banks also often provide rewards for information received.

THE THREE PRECONDITIONS: SUBSECTION (2)

5–05   Even where an allegation is made in good faith, without a personal profit motive, and it is reasonably believed to be substantially true, a second level disclosure will still only qualify for protection under section 43G if one or more of the three further preconditions are met. These conditions are that the worker reasonably believes that he will be victimised by the employer if he makes the disclosure (section 43G(2)(a)); that he reasonably believes that there is likely to be a cover-up such that "evidence relating to the relevant failure will be concealed or destroyed if he makes a disclosure to his employer" (section 43G(2)(b)); or that the matter or substantially the same matter had previously been raised internally or with a prescribed regulator (section 43G(2)(c)). It is only necessary to meet one of these three preconditions. Albeit not raised as a specific condition, there is clearly underlying these preconditions the presumption that, before any wider disclosure is protected, there should be a first level disclosure and that only if the first level has not addressed the problem should it be taken outside the organisation. Even if the precondition is met the tribunal must still consider whether the worker acted reasonably in all the circumstances of the particular case (which we consider later).

---

[2] s. 4G(1)(c); s. 43H(1)(c).
[3] Standing Committee D, Hansard, March 11, 1998.

a. Precondition 1: reasonable belief in victimisation: Subsection 2(a)

5–06   The first of the alternative preconditions which may be met is that the worker reasonably believes that he will be victimised were he to raise the matter internally or with a prescribed regulator. The relevant belief that he will be victimised must exist at the time when he makes the external disclosure. This belief must be objectively reasonable and it must be to the effect that he will be "subjected to a detriment by his employer if he makes a disclosure to his employer or to a prescribed person".

The employee seeking to rely on this precondition may face problems of proof that his employer is the sort who would react by victimisation. Reporting to a prescribed regulator in such circumstances more readily secures protection for the employee. There may however be some unusual situations in which the worker fears a close relationship between his employer and the regulator in question, such that the worker may reasonably fear that the concern will not be properly addressed.

It is important to note the use of the words "will be" before the word "victimised". This places a positive burden on the whistleblower to demonstrate that he will suffer a detriment and it is not enough if the fear is groundless.

b. Precondition 2: reasonable belief in a cover-up: Subsection 2(b)

5–07   This second precondition deals with circumstances where the worker reasonably believes a cover-up of the malpractice is likely to occur if he makes the disclosure at the first level. It can only be satisfied where there is no regulator prescribed under section 43F to whom the reporting of that malpractice should be made. If there is, his door is the correct door towards which he should whistle. Accordingly where there is a prescribed regulator, the Act states that a concern about a cover-up should be raised with that regulator before any wider disclosure might be capable of protection unless the matter is exceptionally serious (section 43H).

c. Precondition 3: previous internal disclosure: Subsection 2(c)

5–08   The third alternative is that wider second level disclosures may be protected where the matter has previously been raised internally or with a prescribed regulator. However if the employer is doing his best to remedy the wrong, even if that best is misguided, imperfect and slow, the employee will probably not be protected due to the test of reasonableness (section 43(G)(3)(e)), although this will depend on all the circumstances of the particular case.

It should be noted that the disclosure at this second level does not have to be of *exactly* the same information as was disclosed at the first, provided it is *substantially* the same. Typically the employee will build in further information with the second or subsequent disclosure of his concern as compared with the first, and specially cover the failure of the employer to respond to his initial concerns. Indeed the brush off or contemptuous response to the first disclosure will often light the touch paper for more explosive and wider disclosure. Section 43G(4) specifically deems a disclosure to be "substantially the same" where the subsequent disclosure "extends to information about action taken or not taken by any person as a result of a previous disclosure".

In assessing reasonableness in relation to whether the particular disclosure should be protected under this precondition, where the concern was previously raised with the employer, the tribunal must have particular regard (section 43G(3)(f)) to whether the worker had complied with the terms of any whistleblowing procedure the organisation has. This need not be an expressly agreed procedure since the statute refers to "any procedure whose use by [the worker] was authorised by the employer". An agreed procedure is, however, clearly to be recommended and leaves less room for any argument before a tribunal about reasonableness.

REASONABLENESS: SUBSECTION (3)

5–09   The test of reasonableness thus applies only when an employee has crossed the threshold of one of the three preconditions. The Act draws on several threads in the common law fabric in determining what is reasonable in the circumstances. Subsection (3) expounds some of the factors in determining reasonableness but it is important to stress that the tribunal, in weighing the balance, has a wide discretion. It is likely that it will be difficult successfully to appeal from the exercise of that discretion by the tribunal.

In deciding whether the disclosure was reasonable in all the circumstances, the tribunal should have particular regard to; the identity of the recipient, the seriousness of the relevant failure and whether the relevant failure is continuing or is likely to occur in the future, any duty of confidentiality to a third party and the nature of previous disclosure(s).

a. Identity of the person to whom the disclosure is made: Subsection 3(a)

5–10   The tribunal must have regard to "the identity of the person to whom the disclosure is made". The range of people to whom such a disclosure might be made is potentially vast. It could include the police, a professional body, a non-prescribed regulator, a union official, an M.P., the relatives of a patient at risk, a contracting party whose rights were being flouted, an internet gossip service, a web site, shareholders (who have a role as stakeholders in the business), friends and neighbours, membes of voluntary groups or the media.

It is likely that tribunals will have regard, at least in the first few decisions, to the decisions at common law where similar issues have been considered in the courts under the common law of confidence (see Chapter 7 below). Disclosures of confidential information to the media were held to be justified in *Initial Services v. Putterill* [1968] 1 Q.B. 396, where a disclosure to the *Daily Mail* about price fixing was held to be lawful by the Court of Appeal because the public were being misled. Similarly in *Lion Laboratories v. Evans* [1985] 1 Q.B. 526 the Court of Appeal held the press was an appropriate recipient of the information in relation to suspect roadside breathalysers as it was important that people had the information needed to challenge criminal charges and it seemed that the Home Office—which had approved the breathalyser—was an interested party. In *Cork v. McVicar, The Times,* October 31, 1985 the High Court allowed the *Daily Express* to publish allegations of corruption in the Metropolitan Police.

However the Court of Appeal in *Francome v. Daily Mirror* [1984] 1 W.L.R. 892, held that the *Daily Mirror* could not publish confidential information which suggested that a jockey had been engaged in misconduct as the public interest would be just as well served by a disclosure to the police or the Jockey Club. This position was explained in *A–G v. Guardian Newspapers Ltd (No. 2)* [1990] 1 A.C. 109 (HL) (*per* Lord Griffiths at p. 268):

"In certain circumstances the public interest may be better served by a limited form of publication perhaps to the police or some other authority who can follow up a suspicion that wrongdoing may lurk beneath the cloak of confidence. Those authorities will be under a duty not to abuse the confidential information and to use it only for the purpose of their inquiry."

A hierarchy in terms of the desired route for raising concerns might be as follows; internal within the organisation—to a regulator with power to redress the concern —to a trade union—to the responsible Minister—to a Secretary of State appointed body— to an M.P.— to shareholders—to interested third parties e.g. to a concerned citizens group—to the local or trade media— to the national media.

b. The seriousness of the failure: Subsection 3(b)

5–11   A further consideration in assessing reasonableness is "the seriousness of the relevant failure". A higher level of seriousness would be expected where a second level disclosure of confidential information is made to the police or a non-prescribed regulator, than if the same information was disclosed to the media.

c. Whether the relevant failure continues: Subsection 3(c)

5–12   The third matter which must be weighed in the balance of reasonableness is "whether the relevant failure is continuing or is likely to occur in the future". The sense of this provision is that it will be reasonable if the disclosure is about a continuing or future threat as opposed to something which has blown over in the sense that it has already happened and it is not considered likely that it will happen again. The importance of wider disclosure was illustrated by a concern which was raised in 1994/95 with Public Concern at Work about a dangerous ride found in an amusement park. The concern was raised with the Health and Safety Executive which stated that they could not attend at the park for several weeks if not months. The worker would receive protection in such a case if the media were told. He would have no other outlet to which to take the concern.

Conversely disclosure to the media is likely to be more difficult to justify where the concern has already been satisfactorily addressed, whether within the employment organisation or otherwise, or where the person making the disclosure does so for the purposes of personal gain rather than to right a wrong. This picks up on a theme in the jurisprudence on the law of confidence (see Chapter 7). This has been touched on in for example *Weld-Blundell v. Stephens* [1919] 1 K.B. 520; *Initial Services v. Putterill* [1968] 1 Q.B. 396 at 405; *Schering Chemicals v. Falkman* [1982] Q.B. 1 at 27. Where the threat has passed, there must be a particularly clear public interest in any confidential information being disclosed.

d. Subsection 3(d): duty of confidentiality owed to a third party

5–13   This provision was inserted in the House of Commons at committee stage in order to ensure that tribunals took account of the interests of a third party about whom confidential information had been disclosed. It should be stressed that it does not make confidentiality as between *employer and employee* an issue in determining reasonableness here (or indeed for anything else in the Act). If the duty of confidentiality to the employer was a strong factor against granting protection this would empty the Act of much of its content.

In introducing the amendment the sponsoring Minister explained that it was necessary in order to deal with information which was subject to particular confidence, such as arising out of a banker-client or doctor-patient relationship. In such cases, tribunals should—it is submitted—have close regard to the decision that would be reached if the third party sued the employer for breach of confidence. At report stage in the Commons, the Minister[4] stated that:

> "It is certainly not the intention that, where a bank has acted diligently, it should be liable for a breach of confidence by a client when a bank employee has made a public interest disclosure."

Banks also have duties of disclosure already pursuant to the European Union Money Laundering Directive 1991, implemented by the Money Laundering Regulations 1993 (S.I. 1993 No.1933).

The effect of the reference to the duty of confidentiality to third parties is merely that it is one matter which is expressly declared to be material in determining the reasonableness of the particular disclosure. A helpful example of this at common law is to be found in *W v. Egdell* [1990] 1 Ch. 359, where the Court of Appeal held that it was lawful for a consultant psychiatrist to disclose information about an in-patient to the medical director at the patient's hospital, where the consultant genuinely believed that a decision to release the patient was based on inadequate information and posed a real risk of danger to the public. However the court held that the sale of his story to the media would not have been justified. Nor would an article in an academic journal have been justified unless it had concealed the patient's identity.

A further example would be the position of a doctor who carries out a blood test on an individual and becomes aware that he is HIV positive. The doctor might find it difficult to argue that it is in the public interest to inform the public about this through the media. In the event that the patient had a partner, the disclosure might be reasonable.

Where the disclosure does breach a duty of confidence owed by an employer to a third party, in determining the reasonableness of the disclosure it will be important to assess the effect of the breach on the rights of the third party and, in particular, any unjustifiable damage it caused him.[5] It is not, however, a precondition of protection that such a duty of confidentiality is not breached. It may be that the provision will have only a narrow impact since the common law has recognised that the disclosure of iniquity cannot be a breach of confidence.

e. Subsection 3(e): previous disclosures

5–14   The tribunal is also required to have regard to whether the employee has previously made a disclosure of substantially the same information to his employer or to a person nominated by the Secretary of State by Regulations. If the employer has investigated the concern and taken all reasonable action in respect of it, the further disclosure is unlikely to be reasonable unless, perhaps, the whistleblower does not know the action has been taken and could reasonably believe that it had not been taken. This section also applies where the concern has been raised with a prescribed regulator.

---

[4] *Hansard*, H.C. April 24, 1998, col. 1137.
[5] Mr Shepherd, Parliamentary Debates, H.C. Standing Committee D, March 11, 1998, col. 9.

The clear policy behind this provision is to ensure that the whistleblower remains informed as to the outcome of any investigation which has taken place into the concern he has expressed; what action has been taken if the allegation is found to be substantiated, and if the allegation is found not to be substantiated why not and what the employer may do in the circumstances. Thus if the worker raises a concern internally or to the regulator and they inform the worker about the outcome of the investigation, it is necessary for the employer to have acted in clear terms and appropriately in response to the concern raised. If for example the employer investigates and does not report back any outcome or reasons for the outcome to the worker, it may be reasonable for the worker to take the matter further, perhaps to the media. Conversely, should the employer openly investigate and report back to the worker with a thorough examination as to why the allegation is not substantiated it may not be reasonable for the worker to proceed further down the line of disclosure.

Where the concern has been addressed to a regulator the same principle may apply save that the employer remains potentially vulnerable if the regulator does not report back any findings and the worker decides to report the matter externally. It thus makes sense for employers to press the regulators to report back as promptly and fully as possible so as to avoid such further disclosure being held to be reasonable. The employer might also ask the prescribed regulator to communicate its findings to any whistleblower and to seek confirmation that this has been done.

f. Subsection 3(f): Whistleblowing procedures

5–15   Where a second level disclosure is to be made on the basis that the worker has previously made a disclosure of substantially the same information to the employer, in considering reasonableness the tribunal must consider whether the worker complied with any whistleblowing procedure authorised by the employer. However it is suggested it will not be enough to introduce such a procedure in a workplace. Reasonable steps should also be taken to promote the whistleblowing procedure amongst the workforce. Ideally once such a procedure is introduced, its use should be monitored and its role should be mentioned to the workforce (routinely, depending on the size of the organisation), for example through team briefings, newsletters or posters. We discuss elsewhere what would be appropriate to put in these procedures (Appendix 7).

It should be noted that a grievance procedure is different from a whistleblowing procedure—a point made by Lord Borrie[6]—in that under a grievance procedure it is for the worker to prove his case, whereas under a whistleblowing procedure he raises the matter so that it may be investigated. This may be significant in relation to the extent of any evidence which the worker must adduce.

Disclosures of exceptionally serious matters: Section 43H of the ERA

5–16   Section 43H provides an alternative basis for protecting second level disclosures relating to matters of an exceptionally serious nature. It provides:

---

[6] *Hansard*, H.L., June 5, 1998, col. 627.

"(1) A qualifying disclosure is made in accordance with this section if—

(a) the worker makes the disclosure in good faith,

(b) he reasonably believes that the information disclosed, and any allegation contained in it, are substantially true,

(c) he does not make the disclosure for purposes of personal gain,

(d) the relevant failure is of an exceptionally serious nature, and

(e) in all the circumstances of the case, it is reasonable for him to make the disclosure.

(2) In determining for the purposes of subsection (1)(e) whether it is reasonable for the worker to make the disclosure, regard shall be had, in particular, to the identity of the person to whom the disclosure is made."

The essential difference between section 43H of the ERA and section 43G, therefore, is that in place of the three alternative pre-conditions in section 43G(2), under section 43H it is sufficient to establish that the relevant failure is exceptionally serious in nature. As in section 43G, there is still a requirement that the worker must act in good faith, must possess a reasonable belief that the information disclosed is substantially true, must not be acting for personal gain and it must be reasonable for him in all the circumstances to make that disclosure. However in relation to reasonableness the only factor which must be taken into consideration is the identity of the person to whom the disclosure is made. The other factors listed in section 43G(3) in relation to reasonableness may still be taken into account but there is no express statutory requirement to do so.

The requirements as to the identity of the recipient of the disclosure and the requirement for reasonableness in all the circumstances (section 43H(1)(e),(2)) were inserted by a Government Amendment in Committee in the Commons.[7] The Minister said:

"The Government firmly believe that where exceptionally serious matters are at stake, workers should not be deterred from raising them. It is important that they should do so, and that they should not be put off by concerns that a tribunal might hold that they should have delayed their disclosure or made it in some other way. That does not mean that people should be protected when they act wholly unreasonably: for example, by going straight to the press when there could clearly have been some other less damaging way to resolve matters".[8]

The scope of what is "exceptionally serious" as opposed to a matter of ordinary concern is likely to be seen as a matter of fact and degree for the tribunal. It is a matter on which there may be legitimate room for disagreement, and not much room for appeal to the Employment Appeal Tribunal since this is pre-eminently a matter of appreciation by the tribunal hearing all the evidence. By way of example, if a worker was genuinely concerned that a child was being sexually abused, he would be protected under this section if he went direct to the police. Other examples would include Piper Alpha, the *Herald of Free Enterprise*, the defects leading to the Clapham rail

---

[7] Parliamentary Debates, H.C. Standing Committee D, March 11, 1998.
[8] *ibid.*, col. 10.

disaster and the Maxwell pensions scandal. The features which may regulate an assessment of whether something is "exceptionally serious" include:

(a) the nature of the concern;

(b) the number of potential victims;

(c) the degree of suffering, financial or otherwise of those victims;

(d) the quality and extent of the evidence available.

CHAPTER 6

The scope and mechanics of protection under the Public Interest Disclosure Act 1998

6–01   Here we consider the mechanisms and mode of delivering protection under the Act. The statute is fitted firmly within the mainstream of employment law in terms of its coverage and remedies, but the specific mechanics raise several interesting points, in particular in rendering certain agreements void insofar as they seek to restrain the making of protected disclosures.

THE SCOPE OF THE WORKERS WHO HAVE PROTECTION: SECTION 43K OF THE ERA

6–02   Section 43K of the ERA provides an extended meaning to the definition of "worker" and, as such, the scope of this Act goes beyond much of existing employment law. This is necessary to deal with the various circumstances in which a person may come upon malpractice. It may reflect a widened appreciation of the proper scope of employment protection as may be seen in recent provisions such as the Working Time Regulations 1998 and the National Minimum Wage Act 1998. In addition to employees (whether or not the employee has started work), the Act expressly protects independent contractors who provide services other than in a professional-client or business-client relationship. It also expressly covers certain agency workers, homeworkers, NHS doctors, dentists, ophthalmologists and pharmacists, and trainees on vocational or work experience schemes. We consider below some of these categories and the special arrangements made for identifying the employer.

a. Agency workers

6–03   Section 43K(1)(a) provides that a worker includes a person who:

"works or worked for a person in circumstances in which—

    (i) he is or was introduced or supplied to do that work by a third person, and

    (ii) the terms on which he is or was engaged to do the work are or were in practice substantially determined not by him but by the person for whom he works or worked by the third person or by both of them."

Section 43K (1)(a) therefore makes special provision to cover agency workers, where the agency introduces workers or finds them the post and the terms of employment are substantially determined by the agency or the organisation where he performs the work. In this case the "employer" will be deemed to be the person who substantially determined the *terms of engagement* (see 43K(2)(a)). This will normally be the organisation where the person performs the work. This widening of scope represents a somewhat different provision to that introduced (controversially) into the Working Time Regulations 1998 which renders as the employer the body which actually pays the worker. The person or body determining the terms of engagement seems to denote the person or body who or which provides the details of the work to be performed, and the level and terms of remuneration.

b. Independent contractor

6–04   Under section 230(3) of the ERA 1996, the definition of a worker includes a person who has entered into or works under a contract of employment or under:

> "any other contract, whether express or implied and (if it is express) whether oral or in writing, whereby the individual undertakes to do or perform personally any work or services for another party to the contract whose status is not by virtue of the contract that of a client or customer of any profession or business undertaking carried on by the individual"

This covers an independent contractor who himself provides services other than in a professional–client or business–client relationship. The definition is a wide and flexible one which includes the self-employed.[1] Further under section 43K (1)(b) protection extends to independent contractors who provide services under contract "whether personally or otherwise". This therefore widens the provision in section 230(3)(b) of the ERA so as to include workers who engage others to provide the work or services. It is not however sufficient that as part of the contract work or labour is carried out. This must be the "dominant purpose". In *Uttley v. St John Ambulance* September 18, 1998 EAT/635/98 a member of St John Ambulance, Mrs Uttley, alleged that she had suffered sexual harassment. She attended weekly meetings, took training courses and had supervisory responsibilities for other members when attending public events at which first aid services were provided. She was also a leader, trainer and supervisor of the children's arm of St John's Ambulance ("the Badgers"). She worked over 50 hours a year but received no salary and was not required to attend events. She was reimbursed her actual out of pocket expenses, given meals and refreshments by the organisers of the events she was attending and given free entry to those events. When she was on duty Mrs Uttley was subject to the discipline and requirements of St. John Ambulance and she was also the subject of its grievance and disciplinary procedure. However the EAT held that she was not engaged under a contract personally to execute work or labour since there were many incidents of membership that could not be described as labour, such as training and attendance at meetings and she could also remain a member but cease to be active. As such, the dominant purpose of the agreement was not personally to execute work or labour.

---

[1] *Quinnen v. Hovells* [1984] I.C.R. 525 (EAT); *Loughran and Kelly v. Northern Ireland Executives* [1998] I.R.L.R. 593.

c. NHS

6–05 The Act applies across virtually the whole of the NHS, where much whistleblowing takes place. Doctors, dentists, ophthalmologists and pharmacists in the NHS are usually independently contracting professionals and are otherwise covered under the Act although they would not necessarily otherwise come under the definition of employee or worker in the ERA. For these people, the Health Authority (or in Scotland, the Health Board) with which they contract is deemed to be their employer for the purposes of this Act (see section 43K(2)(b)).

d. Trainees

6–06 A trainee on work experience or on a vocational scheme receives protection, if he is a person who is:

> "provided with work experience pursuant to a training course or programme or with training for employment otherwise than (i) under a contract for employment or by an educational establishment on a course run by that establishment" (section 43K(1)(d)).

For these people, the person providing the training is deemed to be the employer for the purposes of this Act (see section 43K(2)(c)). This does not, however, cover trainees or students in education. It would probably cover a student on a sandwich year since the training is not run by the educational establishment. Whilst it is supported by and often set up by, or with the help, of an educational establishment, the year out does not possess the necessary integration with the educational establishment to fall within the relevant words "run by".

LIMITS OF THE DEFINITION OF "WORKER"

6–07 The broad definition of a "worker" allows the protection of the Act to extend to a very wide range of circumstances in which a person may come across malpractice. All of the following circumstances would be covered:

(a) trainees aware of abuse of public money on government funded programmes;

(b) employed accountants working in private practice who become aware of financial malpractice in a company or charity;

(c) actuaries who blow the whistle on a pension fund fraud;

(d) an employed book-keeper who becomes aware of a VAT or Revenue fraud.

Two important limits of the definition should however be noted.

a. Non-executive directors

6–08 Non-executive directors who blow the whistle on malpractice would not be protected. They are self-employed and would not be a person performing work or services even allowing for the extended definition in section 43K(1)(b) of the ERA.

b. Volunteers

6–09   Although there is an extended definition of the term "worker", there must still be a contractual relationship. In order for there to be a contractual relationship there must be an agreement supported by consideration, an intention to create legal relations and reasonable certainty of terms. Where a person works as a volunteer it may be that the requirements for consideration and for an intention to create legal relations are not satisfied but the tribunal will have regard to the reality of the situation.

As to the requirement for consideration, one common feature of a volunteering relationship is the absence of any obligation to provide the volunteer with work and of any minimum commitment of time from the volunteer. If so there will not be an umbrella or global contract of employment linking each occasion on which the volunteer has worked for the "employer".[2] However on the facts it may be that there is an obligation to offer and accept work even if the work is only of a sporadic or casual nature.[3] Even where there is no minimum commitment of time the volunteer may still be a "worker" as a result of entering into a contractual relationship on the occasions when work has in fact been done by the volunteer.[4]

A further common feature of a volunteering relationship is the absence of any payment for the work except for expenses. Payments made to workers will not constitute consideration if they are genuinely *ex gratia* (though tribunals may be sceptical of this if payments are made as a matter of course). Nor will payments made genuinely by way of reimbursement of expenses constitute consideration. In these cases, even where there may be a right to terminate the volunteer relationship which is akin to a dismissal, and even though the volunteer may gain status and skill from acting as a volunteer, the volunteer is unlikely to be a "worker", at least where there is no mutual minimum time commitment and no other mutual obligations such as an obligation to provide training.[5] However whilst it may be that expenses have merely been estimated in broad brush terms to save administrative costs, in a series of cases flat rate payments made to volunteers have been a crucial factor leading to a finding that the volunteer was in employment (either under a contract for services or personally providing work or labour). The fact that the payment is low is irrelevant since the tribunal is not concerned with assessing the value of the consideration.[6] Further where there is no or no immediate payment, it may be that other mutual obligations are accepted such as an obligation to train, supervise and provide a safe system of work.[7]

Even where there is an agreement supported by consideration this will not be binding unless there is an intention to create legal relations. As explained by Stuart-

---

[2] *Clark v. Oxfordshire Health Authority* [1998] I.R.L.R. 125 (CA).

[3] See *Carmichael v. National Power Plc* [1998] I.R.L.R. 301 (CA) (currently under appeal to the House of Lords).

[4] *Clark v. Oxfordshire Health Authority* [1998] I.R.L.R. 125 (CA); *McMeehan v. Secretary of State for Employment* [1997] I.R.L.R. 353 (CA); *Asila Elshami v. Welfare Community Projects and Leema* (London North I.T., Case No. 6001977/1998).

[5] *Gradwell v. Council for Voluntary Service, Blackpool, Wyre & Fylde* (Manchester E.T., Case No. 2404313/97); *Alexander v. Romania at Heart Trading Co. Limited* (Brighton E.T., Case No. 310206/97).

[6] *Migrant Advisory Service v. Chaudri* (EAT Case No. 1400/97); *Asila Elshami v. Welfare Community Projects and Leema* (London North I.T., Case No. 6001977/1998); *Rodney v. Harrambee Organisations Limited* (Birmingham E.T. Case No. 36684/86).

[7] *e.g. Armitage v. Relate* (Middlesbrough E.T., Case No. 43238/94) where there was a minimum time commitment and a provision for recoupment of training expenses if obligations were not met.

Smith L.J. in *R v. Lord Chancellor's Department ex p. Nangle* [1991] I.R.L.R. 343 (DC):

> "the concept of an intention to create legal relations in this context means an intention to enter into a contract legally enforceable in the courts. But the converse of the situation is that the relationship is *purely voluntary* or is binding in honour only."

The test of intention is to be ascertained objectively.[8] However where the parties have reduced their agreement to writing the question is one of construction of the documents in the context of the surrounding circumstances.[9] Where there is an express agreement, the onus of proving that there is no intention to create legal relations is on the party who asserts that there is no such intention. Where the agreement contains obligations, rights and entitlements going both ways, the burden of showing that there is no such intention is a heavy one.[10]

The label placed on the agreement by the parties, such as whether the worker is referred to as a "volunteer" may be relevant but is not determinative as to whether there was an intention to create legal relations. The tribunal can also have regard to the context in which an agreement was made in order to ascertain whether there was the requisite intention. On this basis, in *Rogers v. Booth* [1937] 2 All E.R. 751 the Court of Appeal held that an officer of the Salvation Army had no contract because the relationship was a purely spiritual one. This was so even though she was paid a maintenance payment. The payment was expressly stated to be purely hardship money since the officer had no other means of earning a living.[11] Further, where the agreement lacks precision and is informal this may be more consistent with an absence of intention to create legal relations than a formal agreement.[12] The mere fact that there is a recognised practice of using volunteers and an informal relationship may not however be sufficient to persuade a tribunal of an absence of an intention to create contractual relations.[13]

EXCLUSIONS

6–10 Consistently with the familiar employment law pattern, there are a series of exclusions from the scope of the Act:

a. Members of the armed forces and those involved in national security

6–11 There are various exclusions from the scope of protection offered under the statute which broadly mirror those found in other parts of the employment legislation. The Act applies to people who are employees of, work for, or are in the service of the Crown (section 191 ERA) but does not extend to those in the armed forces (section 192 ERA) or to those involved in national security (section 11, below). The

---

[8] *Diocese of Southwark v. Coker* [1998] I.C.R. 140, CA.
[9] *Nangle* at 346, para. 21.
[10] *Nangle*; *Edwards v. Skyways Limited* [1964] 1 W.L.R. 349 at 355.
[11] See also *Diocese of Southwark v. Coker* [1998] I.C.R. 140, CA (assistant curate in Church of England not an employee as no contractual intention).
[12] *Chitty Contracts*, 27th ed., para. 2–118.
[13] See, *e.g. Asila Elshami v. Welfare Community Projects and Leema.*

general rule in section 193 ERA applies, to the effect that a Crown servant is protected under this Act, unless the worker is the subject of a ministerial certificate that his work safeguards national security. This is a conclusive answer to a claim, and would not be open to review by the employment tribunal.

A worker in the security service or at GCHQ will therefore not be protected from victimisation even where he raises a concern internally. There was indeed some concern expressed in the House of Commons Committee debate whether the scope of the definition of security service was clear beyond doubt. An amendment was sought to apply the Act to non operational employees, for example office cleaners and messengers who might come across waste or maladministration which did not impinge on sensitive and secret matters. However the amendment was withdrawn. It may be that with experience with the Act, such bodies will be brought under the umbrella of some form of whistleblower protection.

b. Those who ordinarily work outside of Great Britain

6–12   Section 12 of the Act applies section 196 of the ERA with the effect that the Act does not protect people who *ordinarily work outside of Great Britain*. Under section 196(5), someone who ordinarily works on a ship will, however, be protected under the Act unless (a) the ship is registered outside Great Britain; (b) the employment is wholly outside Great Britain; or (c) the worker is not ordinarily resident in Great Britain. The tribunals normally apply to this the "base test", that is to identify where the employee ordinarily starts and finishes his work, even if he does not work in that place throughout his work.[14] This is not, however, a rule of law and tribunals should apply a broad brush approach to the words of the statute. In *Janata Bank Ltd v. Ahmed* [1981] I.R.L.R. 457, indeed, the Court of Appeal was anxious to prevent this hardening into a rule of law and said that:

> "The use of the words 'ordinarily' and by implied contract 'extraordinarily' points the way inexorably and rightly in a labour law context, to a broad brush approach which, on a given set of marginal acts, one tribunal may decide one way and one another".

This means that if someone comes across malpractice abroad whilst engaged on a business trip, he may make a protected disclosure.

c. Police officers

6–13   Section 13 of the Act extends section 200 of the ERA to this Act and thereby excludes police officers from this new legislative protection. This does not affect the rights of civilian staff in the police service to claim protection.

The proposed exclusion of police officers was criticised by both the Police Complaints Authority and the Association of Chief Police Officers and other consultees, particularly when miscarriages of justice are one of the specified malpractices expressly covered by the Act (see section 43B(1)(c)). As a result of this criticism, the Government gave "an absolute commitment" that police officers will be given equivalent protection by regulation.[15] The Minister told the Standing Committee that the

---

[14] *Wilson v. Maynard Shipbuilding Consultants AB* [1978] Q.B. 665.
[15] *Hansard*, H.C. April 24, 1998, cols. 1143–44.

Home Office would immediately commence a review of the police regulations once the Bill was enacted and that if the police regulations could not provide "equivalent" protection then other measures would be taken.[16]

VICTIMISATION: SECTION 2 OF THE PIDA, SECTION 47B OF THE ERA

6–14   The remedial mechanisms adopted by the Act are to render a dismissal for making a protected disclosure an automatically unfair dismissal and to provide redress for victimisation for making such a disclosure and rendering agreements not to make protected disclosure void.

a. General

6–15   The protection against victimisation (including dismissal) is the back bone of the Act. A new section has been inserted into Part V of the ERA, which protects *inter alia* categories of workers who are performing statutory functions, such as health and safety representatives, from victimisation. The same method of protection is thus provided to all employees (as widely defined) as is currently available to those who have been designated to carry out health and safety duties or are members of a health and safety committee (section 44). Similar protection under ERA 1996 applies to one who refuses to work on Sunday (section 45), is a trustee of an occupational pension scheme (section 46) and is an employee representative (section 48). The original model was what is now section 146 Trade Union and Labour Relations (Consolidation) Act 1992, that an employee has the right not to have action short of dismissal taken against him for the purpose of preventing or deterring him from being or seeking to become a member of an independent trade union or penalising him for doing so.

This new section thus protects employees from action short of dismissal and protects other workers (who cannot be dismissed as they are not technically employees) from any form of victimisation, including the termination of their contract. By section 47B(2) an employee who is dismissed cannot claim under this section but must claim under sections 5 and 6 of the 1998 Act (sections 103A and 105(6) of the ERA), which is considered below.

As originally enacted, the 1998 Act (inserting in s. 47B ERA) provided that where an employee on a fixed term contract had agreed to waive the right to claim unfair dismissal if the contract was not renewed in accordance with section 197 of the ERA, the employee could bring a claim that the contract was not renewed due to making the protected disclosure. However this will no longer apply once the Employment Relations Act 1999 comes into force. Section 18 of that Act repeals the provisions permitting exclusion of the right to claim unfair dismissal and makes consequential amendments to section 47B ERA. At the time of writing no commencement date for the Employment Relations Act 1999 has been announced.

No qualifying period or upper age limit applies to this protection.

b. Subjecting a worker to a detriment

6–16   An employer subjects a worker to a detriment not only if he acts to the worker's detriment but if he causes him detriment by deliberately failing to act.

---

[16] Parliamentary Debates, H.C., Standing Committee D, March 11, 1998, cols. 16–17.

Examples would include refusing promotion; not giving a pay rise; being disciplined; being singled out for relocation; or being denied facilities or training which would otherwise have been provided. Where the worker is not an employee, detriment includes termination of his contract (for services).

The concept of detriment has received most consideration in the fields of race and sex discrimination where it has featured in the legislative framework since 1976 and 1975 respectively as a criterion of when the employee may sue for differential treatment. In that context detriment has been construed as including any disadvantage to the worker which is *de minimis*.[17]

The Act does not however provide protection against the refusal to offer employment. As such an employer who regards a known whistleblower as a troublemaker for having blown the whistle can refuse to offer employment on that ground. A whistleblower may therefore still run the risk that if he/she speaks out future job prospects will be damaged. The failure to offer protection against this contrasts with the position in relation to sex and race discrimination[18] and protection for refusal to employ on grounds of trade union activities.[19]

c. Causation

6–17   In order to establish victimisation, it must be shown that the detriment was incurred "on the ground that" the worker made a protected disclosure. It is for the employer to show the ground on which he subjected the worker to a detriment and in effect to disprove the proposition that the basis for that detriment was the act of whistleblowing: section 48(2) of the ERA. Causation is thus crucial. This may be seen as an inversion of the normal burden of proof being on the applicant, but in practice it has the effect of doing no more than placing an evidential burden on the employer in respect of a matter with which he will best be able to deal. Only the employer knows what prompted him to act as he did. The formal onus of proof as to the grounds for his action or failure to act therefore rests on him. It does however mean that prima facie there is a presumption that any detriment applied is for the blowing of the whistle.

In the context of victimisation relating to race discrimination, the requirements in relation to causation have recently been clarified by the House of Lords in *Nagarajan v. London Regional Transport* [1999] I.C.R. 877. Conscious motivation is not needed in order to establish a claim for victimisation. The test to be applied is the same test of causation as that applied for direct discrimination on grounds of race or sex. The alleged victimiser must have had knowledge of the protected act (for example that the victim had complained of race discrimination) and that knowledge must have caused or influenced the victimiser to treat the victimised person less favourably than he treated or would treat others. As such there must still be a subjective element for there to be victimisation but it is sufficient if the discrimination is subconscious.

Further, the approach taken in relation to victimisation for carrying out health and safety or trade union duties suggests that it will be difficult for an employer to argue that the detriment was the result of the *manner* in which a disclosure is made (for example the intemperate language used) rather than the *fact* of the disclosure. In

---

[17] *De Souza v. A.A.* [1986] I.C.R. 514 (CA).
[18] Sex Discrimination Act 1975, s. 6; Race Relations Act 1976, s. 4.
[19] Trade Union and Labour Relations (Consolidation) Act 1992, s. 137.

Shillito v. Van Leer (U.K.) Ltd [1997] I.R.L.R. 495 the EAT held that it was irrelevant that the health and safety representative acted in an unreasonable manner. The EAT proceeded to find, relying partly on a finding that Mr Shillito had acted in bad faith with a personal agenda of embarrassing the employer, that his health and safety representative activities were not the reason he was disciplined. However in other cases, while recognising that there might be some cases where the conduct was so extraneous, malicious or unreasonable as to fall outside the scope of the protection, tribunals and courts have refused to uphold submissions by employers that victimisation was due to the manner in which the safety representative or trade union official carried out their activities rather than the activities themselves.[20]

d. Action against a third party

6–18   The section does not confer a right of action against any third party who victimised the worker other than the employer (as widely defined by the statute). As such there could not be a claim under the Act against clients of the employer (unless that third party comes within the extended definition of employer in section 43K(2)). However, the failure of the employer to protect the worker against such action by others might itself be a detriment where the employer has sufficient control over that third party to prevent the worker being exposed to such action.[21] It may also be possible to sue that third party for the economic torts of interference in the contract or intimidation, although an inducement to carry out an unfair dismissal without more is not itself actionable in tort.[22]

It is interesting to compare this position with that obtaining in Australia. In South Australia, the Whistleblowers Protection Act 1993 created a specific tort of victimisation, which could be enforced against third parties whilst a tort of unlawful reprisal was introduced in the Queensland Whistleblowers Protection Act 1994 and the Australian Capital Territory Public Interest Disclosure Act 1994.[23]

e. The threat of a detriment

6–19   We think that detriment in this context also includes the *threat* of a detriment. As the Government spokesman said in the House of Lords debates.[24]

> "An employee who has made a disclosure to his employer could be threatened with relocation to a remote branch of a company, for instance, where promotion prospects are poorer. That kind of threat is a detriment and even though the worker can be assured that the employer could not lawfully carry out the threat, the fear of the threat may well amount to detrimental action. Any threat which puts a worker at a disadvantage constitutes in itself detrimental action".

In *Mennell v. Newell & Wright* [1997] I.R.L.R. 519, a case of assertion of statutory rights, the Court of Appeal agreed with the EAT (while allowing an appeal on

---

[20] *Goodwin v. Cabletel U.K. Ltd* [1997] I.R.L.R. 665; [1998] I.C.R. 112 (EAT) paras 39–40; *Bass Taverns Limited v. Burgess* [1995] I.R.L.R. 596 (CA).

[21] *Burton and Rhule v. De Vere Hotels* [1996] I.R.L.R. 596 (EAT).

[22] *Wilson v. Housing Corporation* [1998] I.C.R. 150.

[23] See Lewis, Schroder and Homewood, *A Short Guide to the Public Interest Disclosure Act* (1998).

[24] *Hansard*, H.L. June 5, 1998, col. 634.

other grounds) that asserting a *threatened* infringement of a statutory right came within section 104 of the ERA.

A different question arises as to an attempted disclosure rather than an attempted threat to the applicant. On a literal reading of the Act there is no provision for protection of the worker until there has been a protected disclosure. It may be that the courts will feel able to construe this broadly in accordance with the underlying intention of the Act so as to protect a worker attempting to make a protected disclosure. Otherwise the employer could victimise the worker before the disclosure is actually made. It is however by no means clear that the Act is capable of being construed in this way, although it can be said that a threat to cause an employee a detriment is an attempt to cover up.

f. Complaints to the employment tribunal

6–20   By section 3 of the 1998 Act, inserting into section 48 of the ERA, the employee may make a complaint to an employment tribunal that he has been subjected to a detriment in breach of section 2 of the 1998 Act and section 47B of the ERA. Claims of an infringement of this right are not enforceable in any other forum.

Under section 48(3) claims should be brought within three months of the act or the deliberate failure of which complaint is made, or the last act or failure if the worker was subjected to a series of detriments. Where it was not reasonably practicable to claim within three months, the period may be extended to such extra time for presentation as is reasonable to bring the particular claim before the tribunal. This provision is the same as that which applies for unfair dismissal and the same case law is likely to be applied by analogy. The approach taken is not as liberal as the extension on grounds which are just and equitable as is provided in the sex and race discrimination provisions.

Under section 48(4) ERA where the complaint relates to a deliberate failure to act, time runs from the date the employer decided not to act. In the absence of other evidence of this time, it is the date the employer did an act inconsistent with the failed act or, in the absence of such evidence, the date by when the employer might reasonably have been expected to have acted. A properly drawn internal procedure should include provision that the employer should normally bring his concerns forward within one or two months of his becoming aware of them. There will be an exception for concerns of an exceptionally serious nature.

g. Remedies for victimisation

6–21   Where a tribunal has found that a worker was victimised in breach of section 2 of the 1998 Act (section 47B of the ERA), it must make a *declaration* to that effect and may make an award of *compensation* for loss incurred by reason of any such victimisation: section 49(1) of the ERA. Compensation awards are assessed on the basis of what is "just and equitable in all the circumstances", having regard to the infringement complained of and any loss suffered by the worker as a result of the detriment: section 49(2) of the ERA. These losses specifically include expenses reasonably incurred by the complainant and the loss of any benefit which he might otherwise have expected to obtain from the employment, and might include legal expenses: section 49(3) of the ERA.

The worker is under a duty to mitigate his losses (section 49(4)) by taking another job or acting reasonably in seeking another job. The tribunal must reduce the award by such sum as it considers just and equitable where it finds the worker himself had contributed to or caused the detriment: section 49(5). In practice, a well-known whistleblower may find mitigation of loss very difficult because he may be regarded as a potential troublemaker by prospective employers. Thus, where credible evidence to this effect is presented to a tribunal, very large awards may be made.

DISMISSAL: SECTION 103A ERA

a. The reason for dismissal

6–22   This new provision in section 103A of the ERA makes the dismissal of an employee because or principally because he made a protected disclosure automatically unfair. To achieve this it is made a prohibited reason, within sections 99–103 of the ERA, to dismiss. The effect is that the tribunal is not to consider whether or not the employer's actions were reasonable (although this may have an impact on the compensation to be awarded). If there were a number of reasons for the dismissal, it is automatically unfair if the protected disclosure was the *principal* reason for dismissal. It thus does not apply if disclosure is only one of the reasons for dismissal.

In the context of unfair dismissal generally, the question as to what is the principal reason is usually addressed by way of the test as to what was "uppermost in the mind of the employer" when he came to dismiss. This derives from the decision of the Court of Appeal in *Abernethy v. Mott Hay & Anderson* [1974] I.C.R. 323. The Whistleblower Protection Act 1989 in the USA, by way of contrast, requires only that the employee demonstrate that the whistleblowing was a contributory factor to the dismissal.

b. Selection for redundancy

6–23   An employer may seize the opportunity of a redundancy exercise to weed out "trouble makers", including whistleblowers. It was necessary that special provision should be made to cover this eventuality. Thus, if the reason for dismissal was a redundancy affecting more than one employee, it is unfair to select an employee for dismissal on the ground that he made a protected disclosure. Neither the normal qualifying period of one year, nor the upper age limit, apply to detriment or dismissals.

The effect is that the dismissal is unfair (section 105(1) of the ERA) if (a) the principal reason for it was redundancy; (b) other employees in a similar position were not dismissed in the same circumstances; and (c) the reason or the principal reason the employee was selected was because he had made a protected disclosure.

Similar provisions render unlawful selection for redundancy on the grounds of trade union activities, refusal to work Sundays and other matters which may render a dismissal automatically unfair.

COMPENSATION ISSUES COMMON TO VICTIMISATION AND THE TERMINATION OF CONTRACT

6–24   In its White Paper, *Fairness at Work*, the Government proposed a removal on the ceiling of compensation for unfair dismissal. The Employment Relations Act 1999 (section 30(4)) increases the ceiling on compensatory awards for unfair dismissal to £50,000. This sum is to be index linked. However there is no ceiling on compensation for a breach of the 1998 Act (section 37(1) of the Employment Relations Act 1999—previously provided for in S.I. 1999 No. 1548). This provision was introduced at the Report Stage of the Bill on March 30, 1999. When introducing the amendment, the Secretary of State for Trade and Industry, Stephen Byers, explained that:

> "we must send out a clear message underlining how seriously we regard this issue".

He also stated in responding to criticism that the absence of a ceiling on compensation would be difficult for small firms, that:

> "Any tribunal can take into account the size of an organisation or company in deciding whether an approach has been fair and reasonable in particular circumstances. . . . If a small business does not have the amount of back-up that is available to a larger company, the tribunal can take that factor into account in deciding the appropriate level of compensation to apply".[25]

The Government had also proposed that employee whistleblowers would be entitled to a special award. However section 33(1) provides for an end to all special awards. Instead there will be an entitlement to an additional award payable upon a failure to comply with an order for reinstatement or reingagement unless it is not practicable to comply. The additional award will consist of between 26 and 52 weeks' pay (section 117 Employment Rights Act 1996 and section 33(2) Employment Relations Act 1999). However only employees will be able to claim an additional award. As such there is a risk that this provision will create an anomaly in that employees will be afforded significantly better protection than that available to a worker where their job is lost in breach of the 1998 Act.

The level of compensation was one of the most controversial areas as between the Government and the sponsors of the Bill. As the Government and Mr Shepherd were unable to agree on the correct approach to compensation for unfair dismissal at the time the Bill was introduced, a wide regulation making power was introduced and Public Concern at Work was asked to consult key interest groups on the various options which might be adopted. These were (a) applying the normal regime on unfair dismissal; (b) awarding compensation for losses, without any ceiling; or (c) extending the special provisions for health and safety representatives to whistleblowers.

The Government initially favoured the third option. This would provide for the compensatory award (to be increased from £12,000 to £50,000 under the Employment Relations Act 1999), a basic award and a special award (to be replaced by the new Additional Award under the Employment Relations Act).

A surprising consensus emerged among business, unions and professional interests in response to the consultation. Eighty five per cent of consultees opposed the Government's initial approach and favoured full compensation for whistleblowers. The Institute of Directors—which alone favoured normal awards—felt the precedent of health and safety representatives was "wholly inappropriate", while the

---

[25] *Hansard* 30 March 1999 col. 877.

Confederation of British Industry expressed reservations about the high minimum and the low maximum awards in it. Both bodies emphasised that they saw this Act primarily as a corporate governance measure, rather than as a traditional employment matter. During the Public Interest Disclosure Bill's passage,[26] the Government came under pressure from all sides to endorse the view of the interested parties. This it did when, shortly before the Bill completed its passage, the Government published its White Paper *Fairness at Work*.

Along with the proposal to remove the ceiling on unfair dismissal awards generally (which has now been replaced by the £50,000 ceiling), the Government stated in *Fairness at Work* that public interest whistleblowers should additionally receive the protection for health and safety representatives (outlined above) or, alternatively, be able to claim aggravated damages.

Section 49(3) provides that where a (non-employee) worker's contract is terminated (such as that of a G.P. or dentist in the NHS), he cannot be awarded more compensation than he would have received if he had been an employee who was unfairly dismissed.

INTERIM RELIEF: SECTION 9 PUBLIC INTEREST DISCLOSURE ACT 1998

6–25   Section 9 of the 1998 Act provides that employees (but not other workers) who are dismissed because they made a protected disclosure are able to claim interim relief. At present this is only available to those dismissed on the grounds of trade union activities, health and safety activities, as trustees of occupational pension schemes, or because they are employee representatives (sections 100, 102 and 103 of the ERA). This is a potentially significant provision because, if the tribunal finds that the employee is likely to win at the full hearing, it will order that, *pro tem.*, the employee is re-employed or that his employment is deemed to continue so that he will receive his pay and normal benefits. If after the full hearing the tribunal finds for the employee, such an interim order is likely to increase the chances that the tribunal find it is practicable for the employer to comply with any re-employment order made at the full hearing.

For interim relief to be available the claim for it must be made within seven days of the dismissal (section 128(2) of the ERA). The tribunal must determine the application as soon as practicable thereafter (section 128(3) of the ERA) but must give the employer not less than seven days notice of the hearing (section 128(4) of the ERA). The tribunal cannot postpone the hearing of an application for interim relief unless it is satisfied there are exceptional circumstances (section 128(5) of the ERA).

If at the interim relief hearing the tribunal considers it likely that, at a full hearing, it will find that the reason or the principal reason for the dismissal was because the employee made a protected disclosure, then a series of provisions apply (section 129(1) of the ERA). In the case of trade union action, "likely" has been interpreted as demanding more than a reasonable chance of success; rather the prospects must be "pretty good".[27]

---

[26] See *Parliamentary Debates*, H.C. Standing Committee D, March 11, 1998, cols. 12–14; *Hansard*, H.C. April 24, 1998, cols. 1124–1139; *Hansard*, H.L. May 11, 1998, cols. 893, 895, 899, 900, 903.
[27] *Taplin v. Shippam Ltd* [1978] I.R.L.R. 450.

The procedure laid down in the Act is the same as that to be found in other rubrics for interim relief. The tribunal first explains its powers (section 129(2) of the ERA) and asks the employer if he will re-employ the employee, pending the full hearing (section 129(3) of the ERA). If the employer is willing to do so, then an order is made to that effect: section 129(4)–(6) of the ERA. If the employee does not accept re-engagement (that is a different post, though on terms no less favourable: section 129(3)(b) of the ERA) then the tribunal decides whether that refusal is reasonable. If it is reasonable then the employee's contract is deemed to continue until the full hearing. If the refusal is not reasonable then no order is made pending full hearing: section 129(8) of the ERA.

If the employer fails to attend the hearing for interim relief or says he is unwilling to re-employ the employee (section 129(9)), then the tribunal makes an order under section 130 that the employee's contract is deemed to continue until the full hearing. Even if the employee does not actually return to work, such an order will strengthen the employee's bargaining position in negotiations and may have some influence on the tribunal's decision whether to grant a re-employment order at full hearing and on whether it was practicable for the employer to comply with it.

Agreements rendered void: Section 43J of the ERA

6–26   Section 43J of the ERA is an important mechanism for ensuring that those making protected disclosures are free to do so and cannot be silenced. It is a relatively new departure for employment law (although it echoes the restrictions on contracting out from rights found in most statutory employment protection). It provides that:

"(1) Any provision in an agreement to which this section applies is void in so far as it purports to preclude the worker from making a protected disclosure.

(2) This section applies to any agreement between a worker and his employer (whether a worker's contract or not), including any agreement to refrain from instituting or continuing proceedings under this Act or any proceedings for breach of contract."

As such any clause or term in an agreement between a worker and his employer is void insofar as it purports to preclude the worker from making a protected disclosure. The agreement may be in an employment contract, in a contract of a worker who is not an employee or in any other agreement between a worker and employer. The section therefore applies to "gagging clauses", though only insofar as they relate to a protected disclosure.

In particular, it should be noted that section 43J covers settlement agreements of tribunal proceedings. These have regularly contained confidentiality clauses as part consideration for the money to be paid in settlement. The employer may only be prepared to make any payment to the ex-employee if he can feel secure against the risk not only of further legal proceedings but, also, the risk of having his "dirty linen" further washed in front of an interested public. This may be of particular importance where the employer is concerned to prevent the employee contacting a prescribed regulator under section 43F. The provision would apply with equal strength and immediacy where a public body seeks to stop workers contacting the sponsoring department under section 43E. However confidentiality clauses in a compromise agreement are in any event notoriously difficult to enforce. Even prior to the 1998 Act, there would have been significant difficulties in obtaining injunctive relief to prevent disclosure to a prescribed regulator or sponsoring department.[28]

In the event that an employee accepts a specific sum in return for not making a protected disclosure, it is likely that (subject to a defence of change of position), the employer would be entitled to claim for the return of that sum. Ordinarily money paid under a void contract could be reclaimed by means of an action for money had and received.[29] In *Credit Suisse First Boston (Europe) Limited v. Padiachy* [1998] I.R.L.R. 504, in the context of a void term in relation to a transfer of an undertaking, Longmore J. said that he could see no answer to a claim for the return of money paid in consideration for entering into a void restrictive covenant.

UNOFFICIAL INDUSTRIAL ACTION; SECTION 16 PUBLIC INTEREST DISCLOSURE ACT

6–27   While section 237(1A) Trade Union and Labour Relations (Consolidation) Act 1992 provides that generally an employee who is taking part in unofficial industrial action at the time of his dismissal cannot bring a claim for unfair dismissal, this bar will not apply where the employee was dismissed or made redundant because he had made a protected disclosure.

---

[28] See *re A Company* [1989] 1 Ch. 477.
[29] *Guinness Mahon & Co. Limited v. Kensington & Chelsea LBC* [1998] 3 W.L.R. 829 (CA).

CHAPTER 7

Whistleblowing and confidentiality

7–01 Notwithstanding the enactment of the Public Interest Disclosure Act 1998, there will still be circumstances relevant to the whistleblower where it is important to have regard to the scope of equitable and contractual obligations of confidentiality. From the perspective of the potential whistleblower the duty of confidence may remain significant where the whistleblower fails to comply with the requirements for protection under the 1998 Act. It will then be important to consider whether the whistleblower has acted in breach of the duty of confidence or other contractual obligation owed to the employer and to what extent the Courts are likely to be influenced by the fact that an employee has exceeded the protection offered by the 1998 Act.

THE WHISTLEBLOWER'S DUTY OF CONFIDENTIALITY

7–02 Even in the absence of a relevant express term of the contract of employment, during the course of employment the employee will owe an implied duty of confidence to the employer as an aspect of the duty of good faith and fidelity.[1] After employment, unless an employee has obtained a springboard advantage by using, copying or disclosing confidential information whilst still employed,[2] the employee will only be under an implied obligation not to use or disclose information which is sufficiently highly secret as to be akin to a trade secret. On this basis the Court of Appeal held that there had been no breach of confidence by a former managing director in *Brooks v. Olyslager OMS (U.K.) Limited* [1998] I.R.L.R. 590 (CA). After entering into a compromise agreement terminating his employment, the managing director disclosed to an investment banker, who was interested in the company as a professional adviser and option holder, that the company was insolvent and that its budgets were considered too optimistic by its holding company. The Court of Appeal held that the disclosures were not a breach of any implied term of the compromise agreement. Since the employment had ended there was no implied duty to keep merely confidential information secret and that no information akin to a trade secret had been disclosed.

In order to be regarded as confidential, information must have the necessary quality of confidence and must have been imparted in circumstances importing an

---

[1] *Faccenda Chicken Limited v. Fowler* [1984] I.C.R. 589 (CA).
[2] *Roger Bullivant v. Ellis* [1987] I.R.L.R. 491; *Johnson and Bloy (Holdings) Ltd v. Wolstenholme Rink plc and Tallon* (1987) I.R.L.R. 499, CA; Universal Thermosensors Limited v. Hibben [1992] 1 W.L.R. 840; *M3 Consultants v. Tillman* (Unreported, September 31, 1998, Garland J.).

obligation of confidence.[3] Information which is in the public domain generally cannot have the necessary quality of confidence[4] although, as in the case of a customer list, something constructed solely from information in the public domain may be confidential because the information as collected together is not in the public domain.[5] By way of exception to this, confidentiality will probably remain as against a confidant who has been responsible for the disclosure.[6] In any event, even if the confidence has been destroyed, an employee responsible for the leak would clearly have acted in breach of his/her contract of employment unless a defence to the disclosure can be made out. It is the defence of just cause by reason of the disclosure of iniquity in which the whistleblower has traditionally had to seek refuge.

THE DEFENCE OF JUST CAUSE AND EXCUSE

Development of the defence

7–03   It is possible to negative a duty of confidence on the grounds that the disclosure was made for just cause or excuse. This may be on the basis that the disclosure was under compulsion of law, that there was express or implied consent of the person to whom the duty is owed to make disclosure or where disclosure was in the public interest.[7] From the perspective of the whistleblower the scope of the defence of disclosure in the public interest is of central importance, at least if he/she does not fall within the protection of the 1998 Act or is making a disclosure outside of the context of worker and employer. It is necessary to review the authorities in some depth because judges have not spoken with one voice on the matter.

In *Gartside v. Outram* (1857) 26 LJ Ch 113, the *fons et origo* of the doctrine, Wood V.-C. (at 114) adopted the general principle that:

"there is no confidence as to the disclosure of iniquity. You cannot make me the confidant of a crime or a fraud, and be entitled to close up my lips upon any secret which you have the audacity to disclose to me relating to any fraudulent intention on your part: such a confidence cannot exist."

In *Initial Services Limited v. Putterill* [1968] 1 Q.B. 396 (CA), Lord Denning M.R. (at 405G-406B)[8] expressed the opinion that this principle:

---

[3] *Saltman Engineering Co. Limited v. Campbell Engineering Co. Ltd* (1948) 65 R.P.C. 203 (CA); *Coco v. A.N. Clark (Engineers) Ltd* [1969] RPC 41; at 47; *A.-G. v. Guardian Newspapers (No.2)* [1990] 1 A.C. 109 (HL) at 258A–B, 268A–C; *R. v. Department of Health ex parte Source Informatics Limited, The Times*, June 14, 1999, Luthum J.

[4] *A.-G. v. Guardian Newspapers (No.2)* [1990] 1 A.C. 109 (HL).

[5] *Coco v. A.N. Clark (Engineers) Limited* [1969] R.P.C. 41; *Lansing Linde Limited v. Kerr* [1991] 1 W.L.R. 251, CA *per* Staughton L.J. at 260B–D; *SBJ Stephenson Limited v. Mundy* (Unreported, July 30, 1999, Bell J.); *M3 Consultants v. Tillman* (Unreported, July 31, 1998, Garland J.).

[6] *Speed Seal Products Limited v. Paddington* [1986] 1 All E.R. 911; *A.-G. v. Guardian Newspapers* [1990]1 A.C. 109 *per* Lord Griffiths at 268E (but see the doubt expressed as to the reasoning in *Speed Seal* by Lord Goff at 285B–286A.

[7] *Tournier v. National Provincial and Union Bank of England* [1924] 1 K.B. 461 (CA) *per* Bankes L.J. at 473.

[8] Approved in *British Steel Corporation v. Granada Television Limited* [1981] A.C. 1096 (HL) *per* Lord Wilberforce at 1169B–C; *per* Lord Fraser at 1201C–F; *Beloff v. Pressdram Limited* [1973] 1 All E.R. 241 at 260A–D; *Malone v. Commissioner of Police for the Metropolis (No.2)* [1979] 1 Ch. 344 at 362B–C,377B.

"should extend to crimes, frauds and misdeeds, both those actually committed as well as those in contemplation, provided always—and this is essential—that the disclosure is justified in the public interest. . . .

The disclosure must be to one who has a proper interest to receive the information. Thus it would be proper to disclose a crime to the police . . . There may be cases where the misdeed is of such a character that the public interest may demand, or at least excuse, publication on a broader field, even to the press."

The balance of authority now suggests that there can be a public interest defence to disclosure in breach of confidence even if there is no wrongdoing. A narrower approach was suggested in *Beloff v. Pressdram Limited* [1973] 1 All E.R. 241 at 260G where Ungoed-Thomas J. expressed the opinion that:

"Public interest, as a defence in law, operates to override the rights of the individual (including copyright) which would otherwise prevail and which the law is also concerned to protect. Such public interest, as now recognised by the law, does not extend beyond misdeeds of a serious nature and importance to the country and thus, in my view, clearly recognisable as such."

In that case Nora Beloff, a well known lobby correspondent with *The Observer* newspaper, sought damages for breach of copyright after *Private Eye* printed without her permission a memorandum she had written. The claim failed because she had no copyright in the memorandum. However Ungoed-Thomas J. expressed the view that a claim for breach of confidence would have succeeded. It was argued against this claim that publication was in the public interest in that the public should know how lobby correspondents obtained their information and how the lobby system worked. Ungoed-Thomas J. rejected this proposition, without entering into any balancing of competing public interests, on the grounds that the memorandum did not disclose any "iniquity" or "misdeed".

The matter was taken further in *British Steel Corporation v. Granada Television Limited* [1981] A.C. 1096 (HL) which arose when Granada Television broadcast a programme relating to a national steel strike in 1980 relying on confidential documents leaked by an employee informant. British Steel made an application for delivery up of the documents and for disclosure of the identity of the informant. It was conceded that it was not possible to rely on the iniquity exception but this concession received some approval in the House of Lords. Lord Wilberforce noted (at 1169C–D;1175B–C) that:

"given the widest extension of the expression 'iniquity' nothing within it is alleged in the present case. The most it is said the papers reveal is mismanagement and government intervention. . . .

Granada had on its side . . . the public interest that people should be informed about the steel strike, of the attitude of BSC, and perhaps that of the government towards settling the strike. But there is no 'iniquity' here—no misconduct to be revealed.[9]"

---

[9] See to like effect *per* Viscount Dilhorne at 1176C (emphasising that at most the documentation showed mismanagement rather than iniquity or misconduct) and Lord Fraser at 1200H–1201B.

A broader defence of disclosure required in the public interest was recognised by Lord Denning M.R. (with whom Davies L.J. agreed) in *Fraser v. Evans* [1969] 1 Q.B. 349 at 362. He explained that the defence that there is no confidence in iniquity:

"is merely an instance of just cause or excuse for breaking confidence. There are some things which may be required to be disclosed in the public interest, in which event no confidence can be prayed in aid to keep them secret."

This formulation was adopted in *Malone v. Commissioner of Police of the Metropolis (No.2)* [1979] 1 Ch. 344 where Sir Robert Megarry V.-C. asserted (at 363C–D) that:

"There may be cases where there is no misconduct or misdeed but yet there is a just cause or excuse for breaking confidence. The confidential information may relate to some apprehension of an impending chemical or other disaster, arising without misconduct, of which the authorities are not aware, but which ought in the public interest to be disclosed to them."

Similarly in *Lion Laboratories Limited v. Evans* [1985] 1 Q.B. 526 the Court of Appeal rejected the narrow proposition that the public interest defence was confined to iniquity. O'Connor L.J. explained that:

"Everything depends on the facts of the case; thus the court will not restrain the exposure of fraud, criminal conduct, iniquity; but these are only examples of situations where the conflict will be resolved against the plaintiff. I do not think that confidence can be overridden without good reason to support the contention that it is in the public interest to publish.[10]"

In *A-G v. Guardian Newspapers (No.2)* [1990] 1 A.C. 109 (HL) both Lords Griffiths and Goff referred to a balancing of public interests and Lord Goff expressly recognised that the principle that there is no confidence in iniquity is just one aspect of this. Lord Griffiths explained (at 268G-269D) that:

"The courts have . . . always refused to uphold the right to confidence where to do so would be to cover up wrongdoing. In *Gartside v. Outram* (1857) 26 LJ Ch 113 it was said that there could be no confidence in iniquity. This approach has been developed in the modern authorities to include cases in which it is in the public interest that the confidential information should be disclosed: see *Initial Services Limited v. Putterill* [1968] 1 Q.B. 396; *Beloff v. Pressdram Limited* [1973] 1 All E.R. 241 and *Lion Laboratories Limited v. Evans* [1985] Q.B. 526. This involves judges in balancing the public interest in upholding the right to confidence, which is based on the moral principles of loyalty and fair dealing, against some other public interest that will be served by the publication of the confidential material. . . . I have no doubt . . . that in the cases of a private claim to confidence, if the three elements of quality of confidence, obligation of confidence and detriment are established, the burden will lie upon the defendant to establish that some other overriding public interest should displace the plaintiff's right to have his confidential information protected."

---

[10] See to like effect Stephenson L.J. at 537F–538D; Griffiths L.J. at 550B–E.

In the same case Lord Goff also emphasised that the defence rests on consideration of the public interest. He noted (at 282E–H) that:

> "although the basis of the law's protection of confidence is that there is a public interest that confidences should be preserved and protected by the law, nevertheless the public interest may be outweighed by some other countervailing public interest which favours disclosure. . . . It is this limiting principle which may require a court to carry out a balancing operation, weighing the public interest in maintaining confidence against the countervailing public interest favouring disclosure.
>
> Embraced within this limiting principle is, of course, the so called defence of iniquity. . . . it is now clear that the principle extends to matters of which disclosure is required in the public interest"

Although there has been a broadening of the category of considerations which can be relied upon to justify disclosure, it remains necessary to establish a genuine public interest in making the disclosure. It is not sufficient that the subject matter of the disclosure may be of interest to the public.[11] It remains relevant to have regard to the types of disclosure which have been held to give rise to a public interest defence since a court may well be more sympathetic to such a defence if the disclosure falls within or is analogous to one of these recognised categories. We shall then turn to other considerations bearing upon whether the disclosure is likely to be justified.

CATEGORIES OF INFORMATION

(1) Crime and civil frauds

7–04   Clearly disclosure of crimes and frauds, whether past or contemplated, are amongst the clearest examples of "iniquity" and provided that disclosure is within proper bounds will often be justified in the public interest. *Gartside v. Outram* itself concerned disclosure by an ex-employee of accounting and business information which it was alleged showed that the employer had been carrying on business in a fraudulent manner. Wood V.-C. held that this would be a good defence if the factual basis for it was made out at trial.

Similarly in *Malone v. Commissioner of Police of the Metropolis (No.2)* [1979] 1 Ch. 344 Megarry V.-C. observed that:

> "If what is overheard, though confidential, is itself iniquity, it is plain that it is subject to no duty of confidence."

However, although the public interest in disclosing past or proposed crimes will often be a determinative consideration, it may still be necessary to consider whether in the particular circumstances, having regard to the nature of the crime or fraud, the person to whom disclosure is made and any countervailing public interest in preserving confidentiality, the disclosure is justified.[12]

---

[11] *British Steel Corporation v. Granada Television Limited* [1981] A.C. 1096 *per* Lord Wilberforce at 1168G; *Lion Laboratories Limited v. Evans* [1985] 1 Q.B. 526 *per* Stephenson L.J. at 537C.
[12] See also *Initial Services Limited v. Putterill* [1968] 1 Q.B. 396 (at 405) where Lord Denning M.R. emphasised that overall qualification that disclosure must be justified in the public interest.

As to the significance of the nature of the crime or fraud, in *Weld-Blundell v. Stephens* [1919] 1 K.B. 520 (affd [1920] A.C. 956) the Court of Appeal appeared to distinguish between different degrees of wrongdoing. That case concerned disclosure of a document containing libellous material rather than a crime. However Warrington L.J. emphasised that in *Gartside v. Outram* the fraud had been a systematic fraud and the disclosure of the relevant documents would tend to prevent such frauds in the future. By implication Warrington L.J. appeared to suggest that disclosure might not be justified in the case of a minor fraud, or a one off instance, where disclosure would not have an effect in preventing future frauds.

Similarly in *Kitson v. Playfair* (1896) *The Times* March 28, Hawkins J. held that a doctor could inform the Public Prosecutor if he learnt in his professional capacity of circumstances showing that a crime was to be committed. However Hawkins J. acknowledged that there were limits to this principle. He suggested that it would be a "monstrous cruelty", and an unjustified breach of confidence, if a doctor, having been called to provide physical aid to a woman having an abortion, then reported to the police that she had (unlawfully) been seeking to procure an abortion.

Further, even where a disclosure relates to serious criminal conduct there may, exceptionally, be a countervailing public interest which prevents confidentiality being overridden. In *Bunn v. BBC* [1998] 3 All E.R. 552, an application was made to restrain the BBC from making reference in a television programme to an interview with the police under caution by Mr Bunn, the former Deputy Managing Director of Robert Maxwell Group plc. The interview was said to show that Mr Bunn was engaged in conspiracy to defraud. The statement was also said to contain material which would enable the public fairly to assess the workings and efficiency of the Serious Fraud Office since it would be relevant to whether the SFO had had sufficient material to proceed with the second criminal trial relating to the fraud by Robert Maxwell and his companies. Lightman J. held that the statement made under caution was confidential in that it was only to be used for the purposes of criminal proceedings. Although Lightman J. refused the injunction on the grounds that the information was already in the public domain and on the ground of delay, he held that the public interest defence to the claim of breach of confidence would not have succeeded because there was a countervailing public interest in an accused person being able to make full disclosure in a statement to the police without fear of that statement being used for extraneous purposes.[12a]

A broader exception to the public interest defence even in cases of disclosure of criminal conduct was suggested by dicta of the Employment Appeal Tribunal in *Byford v. Film Finances Limited* EAT/804/86. In that case Mrs Byford had disclosed information to minority shareholders in a company which she genuinely believed disclosed illegal and possible criminal activity on the part of the directors and which was or might be in fraud of the minority shareholders. When this was discovered she was dismissed and she then brought a complaint of unfair dismissal. Unfair prejudice proceedings were also brought but these had not been resolved by the time of the unfair dismissal proceedings and it had therefore not been determined whether the allegations were well-founded. The EAT rejected a submission that confidentiality was overriden on the basis that the Applicant had genuinely believed that she was disclosing

---

[12a] Contrast *Woolgar v. Chief Constable of the Sussex Police* [1993] 3 All E.R. 604, CA where the public interest was in favour of disclosure of statements made to the police because the disclosure was to the appropriate regulatory authority in the interests of public health or safety.

wrongdoing. *Gartside v. Outram* was said to be distinguishable on the basis that it related to disclosure by an ex-employee.

Notwithstanding these dicta, *Byford* does not establish that confidentiality cannot be overriden by a public interest defence prior to termination of an employee's employment. This would be inconsistent with the broad terms in which the public interest defence has been expressed in the line of cases leading to *A-G v. Guardian Newspapers (No.2)* (see above). In any event, the decision in *Byford* is explicable on the basis that the EAT was concerned not with whether there was a breach of confidence but with whether, for the purposes of a claim of unfair dismissal, the employer acted fairly in dismissing Mrs Byford. As such it was not necessary in *Byford* to determine the issue as to breach of confidence. Aside from whether there was a breach of obligations of confidence, the EAT was satisfied that Mrs Byford's employers had been entitled to conclude that Mrs Byford had "entirely betrayed the trust reposed in her" and that as such the dismissal was fair. Further, there was a failure in *Byford* to follow a more appropriate route for disclosure, such as disclosure to the Department of Trade and Industry, and the motive for the disclosure was held to be a loyalty to the minority shareholder rather than a desire to bring injustice to light.

(2) Civil wrongs

7–05   Disclosure of confidential information may also in some circumstances be justified where the information relates to civil wrongs. This parallels the provision in the 1998 Act that there is a qualifying disclosure if a worker reasonably believes that a person has failed, is failing or is likely to fail to comply with any legal obligation to which he is subject.[13]

In *Initial Services Limited v. Putterill* [1968] 1 Q.B. 396 upon resigning as sales manager of the claimant launderers, Mr Putterill removed documents belonging to the claimants which he passed to *Daily Mail* reporters. Relying upon these documents, the newspaper alleged that there was an unlawful price fixing agreement and that the laundries had misled the public in claiming to have increased their prices to offset tax when in reality they were increasing their profits. Breach of the Restrictive Trade Practice Act 1956 was not a criminal offence and it was argued that the disclosure could only be justified in cases of information relating to crime and fraud. The Court of Appeal rejected this submission and refused to strike out the defence that the disclosures were made in the public interest.

It may be, however, that *Initial Services Limited v. Putterill* is explicable on the basis that although there was a civil wrong, this concerned breach of a statute regulating competition in the public interest. This might be distinguished from other civil wrongs which essentially raise private concerns. Certainly in other cases civil wrongs have not been held to be sufficient to override the duty of confidence. In *Weld-Blundell v. Stephens* [1919] 1 K.B. 520 (affd [1920] A.C. 956) the Court of Appeal held that disclosure could not be justified on the basis that it revealed libellous material. It was apparent however that there could be no public interest justifying disclosure since it would have no useful purpose other than to enable the person libelled to recover damages for a libel the existence of which might not otherwise have become known (*per* Warrington L.J. at 534).

Even where the civil wrong raises matters of concern for the wider public, it may

---

[13] Employment Rights Act 1996, s. 43B(1)(b).

be that if the allegation is merely of negligence or incompetence rather than deliberate wrongdoing, this would not be sufficient to justify disclosure. In *Distillers Co. (Biochemicals) Limited v. Times Newspapers Limited* [1975] 1 All E.R. 41 Talbot J. (at 50A) expressed the opinion that negligence could not come within the class of misdeeds justifying disclosure. This was notwithstanding that the negligence would have concerned the handling of the thalidomide drug and that it was acknowledged that there was a public interest in the general public learning of what had happened with the thalidomide drug and that any light this might throw on obviating similar problems in future was welcome. Similarly in *British Steel Corporation v. Granada Television Limited* [1981] A.C. 1096 (HL) mismanagement of a public company was not considered to be a sufficient justification for disclosure even though this was of obvious public interest.

(3) Breach of rules of self-regulatory schemes

7–06   It is also clear that disclosure of a breach of the rules of a self-regulatory scheme, particularly in the financial services sector, is capable of justifying disclosure in breach of confidence, at least where the disclosure is to the relevant regulatory body. In *A Company's Application* [1989] 1 Ch. 477 it was alleged that a former employee of a company involved in providing financial advice and management threatened that if he did not pay £10,000 as compensation for dismissal he would report breaches of the Financial Investment Management and Brokers' Regulatory Authority ("FIMBRA") regulations to FIMBRA and would report tax improprieties to the Inland Revenue. The defendant sought an injunction to prevent any disclosures using confidential information. Scott J. refused to grant an interlocutory injunction but also held that the duty of confidentiality did not extend to a duty not to make disclosure to the appropriate regulatory body of a possible breach of that bodies' regulatory rules.

Similarly in *Francome v. Mirror Group Newspapers Limited* [1984] 1 W.L.R. 892 secret tapes were made of telephone conversations involving John Francome, a well-known jockey. The tapes were then sold to the press. An attempt was made to justify the apparent breach of Mr Francome's confidence on the basis that the tapes revealed breaches of the rules of racing. The Court of Appeal restrained publication until trial but held that there was a triable issue as to whether the publication could be justified on this basis. Whilst the Court of Appeal was sceptical as to whether disclosure to the press was justified, it was more sympathetic to the claim that publication might be justified if made to the police or to the Jockey Club which had supervisory powers.[14]

(4) Immoral conduct

7–07   In *Stephens v. Avery* [1988] 1 Ch. 449 *The Mail on Sunday* published an article containing details of a lesbian affair on the basis of information passed on by a third party in whom the claimant had confided. The claimant brought a claim for breach of confidence. In refusing to strike out the claim the court accepted that there might be no confidence in relation to matters which have a "grossly immoral tendency". However this could provide no defence in this case since there was no common view that the sexual conduct involved was grossly immoral.

The 1998 Act includes no category of qualifying disclosure akin to matters having

---

[14] *per* Sir John Donaldson M.R. at 899A–C; *per* Stephen Brown L.J. at 902B.

a "grossly immoral tendency". However in the light of the approach of the court in *Stephens* it may well be that conduct would not be regarded as grossly immoral unless a consensus to that effect was indicated by the conduct being unlawful. As such it would fall within section 43B(1)(a) or (b) of the Employment Rights Act 1996 as capable of being a qualifying disclosure.

(5) Conduct misleading to the public

7–08   In a series of cases it has been suggested that disclosure could be justified in order to prevent the public being misled. This is a category with no specific equivalent in the list of qualifying disclosures provided for by the 1998 Act.

In *Initial Services v. Putterill* [1968] 1 Q.B. 396 it was alleged that the public had been misled into believing that laundry prices had been increased due to tax when in fact there was substantial additional profit. This was held to be an arguable ground justifying disclosure of otherwise confidential material. Similarly in *Church of Scientology of California v. Kaufman* [1973] R.P.C. 635 (at 654) one ground for resisting an injunction was that otherwise the public might be deceived into paying for "nonsensical mumbo-jumbo" (being the judge's description of the teachings of the Church of Scientology). It was therefore in the public interest that there should be disclosure of the type of thing for which payment was being requested.

The possible breadth of this ground was illustrated by *Woodward v. Hutchins* [1977] 1 W.L.R. 760 (CA) at 763–764. A former public relations officer wrote a series of articles about pop stars by whom he had been employed (via a management company). An interlocutory injunction was refused. Although the injunction sought was too wide in any event since it covered information in the public domain, Lord Denning M.R. and Bridge L.J. both emphasised that since the pop stars had invited publicity they could not complain if the truth was then told. It may be however that the decision turned not so much upon whether there was a defence to breach of confidence as a matter of law but on whether the discretion should be exercised in favour of granting an injunction. Bridge L.J. left open the possibility that if the defendants could show that the information was true there would only be nominal damages for breach of confidence. Further Lawton L.J. explained the decision on the basis that the breach of confidence was interwoven with the allegation of libel and that the ordinary principle in the case of libel was to allow publication where justification was alleged.

The decision in *Woodward* was however followed in *Khashoggi v. Smith* (1980) 124 S. J. 149 (CA) where the claimant sought to restrain her former housekeeper from disclosing information about her private affairs including allegations of criminal conduct. Roskill L.J. accepted that the allegations about the claimant's private life could not be disentangled from the allegations of offences and that disclosure was therefore justified since there could not be any confidence where the information was to be exploited (by the press) for investigation into the alleged offences. However he also held that the claimant had allowed herself into the public eye to such an extent that she "ran the risk of the whole story being made public", in the sense of giving a full account of matters where only a partial or misleading account had previously been given.

In each case, however, it is necessary to ascertain whether the public interest justifies disclosure. In *British Steel Corporation v. Granada Television Limited* [1981] A.C. 1096 (HL), for example, Viscount Dilhorne (at 1176C) was of the view that disclosure would not have been justified in order to establish that it was not true that there had been no government intervention in the steel strike. Further the fact that no provision is made for such an exception under the 1998 Act may indicate that a whistleblower would be on very dangerous ground in making a disclosure of otherwise confidential information merely on the basis of correcting a misleading impression that had previously been given to the public unless this also falls within one of the qualifying disclosures.

(6) Public interest defence beyond iniquity

7–09   (a) **Matters dangerous to the public**

Without relying upon any wrongdoing, disclosure of otherwise confidential material may be justified on the basis that it reveals dangers to health and safety or to the environment (as provided for in the 1998 Act[15]). In *Hubbard v. Vosper* [1972] 2 Q.B. 84 Lord Denning M.R. (at 96A–B) considered that, in relation to material on Scientology which had been published in breach of confidence, a public interest defence might be established at trial on the basis that it was dangerous material including "medical quackeries of a sort which might be dangerous if practised behind closed doors". Similarly in *Church of Scientology of California v. Kaufman* [1973] R.P.C. 635, Goff J. also held that disclosure by a former student of Scientology was justified on the basis of possible danger to the public in the light of evidence that Scientology had caused some followers to become ill.

Since the justification is based on weighing rival public interests, however, disclosure on the ground of danger to the public will require consideration of the seriousness of the danger and the scope of disclosure required. In *W v. Edgell* [1990] 1 Ch. 359 (CA) the claimant suffered from paranoid schizophrenia and was detained in a secure hospital after killing five people. He applied to a mental health review tribunal and, to support his application, sought a report from the defendant who was an independent consultant psychiatrist. The defendant's report revealed that the claimant had a continuing interest in home-made bombs and expressed the opinion that the claimant was a continuing danger to the public. The claimant then withdrew his application and refused to consent to the defendant disclosing the report. However the defendant disclosed the report to the medical officer at the secure hospital and a copy was sent to the relevant Secretary of State. When the claimant's case was subsequently referred to a mental health review tribunal it became apparent that the report had been disclosed and the claimant applied for an injunction restraining the defendant from communicating the contents of the report and requiring all copies to be delivered up. In refusing the injunction the Court of Appeal held that the public interest in confidentiality was outweighed by the public interest in protecting others against possible violence. The Court of Appeal emphasised the degree of danger to the public, as demonstrated by the nature of the crimes which the claimant had previously committed, and the fact that the disclosure had been made to the appropriate regulatory bodies who should have all relevant information in relation to the claimant before considering his release from hospital.

A further important consideration in this context may be whether the danger is past or is still present. In *Schering Chemicals Limited v. Falkman Limited* [1982] Q.B. 1 (CA) it was alleged that confidential information had been used to make a film relating to the drug Primodos. The claimant company had withdrawn Primodos from

---

[15] Employment Rights Act 1996, s. 43B(1)(d),(e).

the market after suspicions had arisen that it had caused abnormalities in new-born children. The Court of Appeal refused to grant an injunction restraining the broadcast of the film. It was recognised that publication might be justified to prevent danger to the public but this was not a consideration here since the drug had been withdrawn from the market. As Shaw L.J. explained (at 27C–D):

> "If the subject matter is something which is inimical to the public interest or threatens individual safety, a person in possession of knowledge of that subject matter cannot be obliged to conceal it although he acquired that knowledge in confidence. In some situations it may be his duty to reveal what he knows. No such consideration has existed in this case since the time that Primodos was withdrawn from the market. Neither the public nor any individual stands in need of protection from its use at this stage in the history."

A further and related consideration will be whether the information is likely to be used for the purpose of addressing the potential danger to the public interest or for some other purpose. In *The Distillers Co. (Biochemicals) Limited v. Times Newspapers Limited* [1975] 1 All E.R. 41 documents disclosed on discovery in actions against a company which marketed thalidomide, were handed on to a newspaper. An injunction was sought to restrain the use of the confidential documentation for a collateral or ulterior purpose other than in the action in which discovery was given. The Court of Appeal granted the injunction having regard to the public interest in the proper administration of justice which demanded that documents disclosed on discovery should not be used for a collateral purpose. Talbot J. recognised that there was a competing public interest in the public learning of what had happened with the thalidomide drug and also that this might help prevent similar problems in future. He concluded however that having regard to the purposes to which the information was to be put the public interest in the administration of justice should prevail. For example it was suggested that the documents could be made available to others who had suffered from thalidomide, but this would be achieved if proceedings were brought in due course. It may have been therefore, that there would have been a different conclusion if the material was to be used directly to analyse the lessons from what had happened with thalidomide, perhaps through disclosure to the public health authorities.

7–10   (b) Danger to depositors/investors
In addition to dangers to health and safety, dangers to the financial interests of the public may also, at common law, justify disclosure which would otherwise be in breach of confidence, although there is no precise equivalent under the 1998 Act. In *Price Waterhouse v. BCCI Holdings (Luxembourg) SA* [1992] B.C.L.C. 583 the Court of Appeal expressly recognised that the public interest in effective supervision of banking institutions could justify overriding a duty of confidence. Price Waterhouse had acted as auditors to the BCCI Group. After the collapse of the BCCI Group the Bank of England and the Treasury set up a non-statutory enquiry into the supervision of BCCI. The Bank of England and the Serious Fraud Office served notices on Price Waterhouse to disclose various confidential documents and Price Waterhouse sought a declaration that it was entitled to disclose the documents. Millett J. considered that in this case the public interest in preserving confidentiality was outweighed by the public interest in the effective supervision of authorised banking institutions, having regard to the need to protect depositors, and the public

interest in ensuring that the inquiry into the adequacy of such supervision should have access to all relevant material.

7–11   (c) Risk of miscarriage of justice

Disclosure in the public interest may also, as under the 1998 Act,[16] be justified if relating to a miscarriage of justice that has occurred or is likely to occur. In *Lion Laboratories Limited v. Evans* [1985] Q.B. 526 the Court of Appeal was concerned with the risk that but for full disclosure there may be unsafe convictions for drink driving. The claimants manufactured breathalyser equipment. The defendants had been employed by the claimants as technicians. When their employment ended they removed documents which cast doubt on the reliability of the equipment. These documents were passed on to the press. It was admitted that the documents were confidential but an interlocutory injunction was overturned due to the public interest in informing the public that the equipment might not be reliable.

It is arguable that the disclosure in *Lion Laboratories*, being disclosure to the press, would not have qualified for protection under the 1998 Act. There was no suggestion that the defendants' concerns had previously been raised with their employer or that there was reason to believe that the employer would destroy the evidence. Nor is it apparent that the disclosure would constitute an "exceptionally serious failure", being a precondition for protection under section 43H(1)(d) of the Employment Rights Act 1996.

(7) Other public interests

7–12   Notwithstanding the broad public interest test, a defence to disclosure of confidential information has not been found to be justified except where there is an allegation of wrongdoing (including the extended sense such as misleading the public) or a substantial risk to the public (such as danger to health and safety or of financial interests or of a miscarriage or justice). It is likely that broader public interest considerations as to matters which it would be beneficial for the public to know might now be taken into account, applying the broader public interest test, but it remains unlikely that disclosure could be said to be "required" in the public interest or justified by an overriding public interest.

In *X v. Y* [1988] 2 All E.R. 648, Rose J. accepted that there was a public interest in having a free press and an informed debate which could be taken into account in considering whether disclosure was justified. In that case employees of a health authority leaked to the press information identifying two doctors who were continuing in practice after having contracted AIDS. Rose J. granted an injunction restraining publication of this information. The public interests in having a free press and an informed public debate were outweighed by the public interest in actual or potential AIDS sufferers being able to resort to hospitals without fear of this being revealed and in the interest of those owing duties of confidence in their employment being loyal and not disclosing confidential matters. However in reaching this view he expressly took into account the fact that depriving the public of the information would be of minimal significance in its impact upon public debate about AIDS generally and its effect on doctors.

---

[16] Employment Rights Act 1996, s. 43A(1)(c).

General considerations in relation to whether disclosure is justified

7-13 Whilst there are recognised categories of disclosure where confidentiality has been held to be negatived, there are also a number of recurring themes as to the significant considerations to be taken into account. Some of the important considerations are summarised below.

(1) Nature of the matters alleged

7-14 In assessing whether confidentiality is negatived, an important factor will obviously be the seriousness and importance of the matters raised by the prospective whistleblower. This will in turn bear upon the importance of other factors. For example, an employer guilty of fraud is unlikely to be able to complain that wide disclosure of the fraud constitutes a breach of confidence, whereas in other cases more restricted disclosure might be required.

(2) Is the information also privileged?

7-15 Where information is not only confidential but also subject to legal professional privilege the public policy against disclosure is particularly strong. In this context justification for disclosure has been confined to circumstances involving iniquity. For these purposes iniquity includes all forms of fraud and dishonesty but does not extend beyond dishonesty to include disreputable behaviour or a failure to maintain good ethical standards.[17] It is sufficient that the solicitor's advice is sought in furtherance of or in relation to the fraud or crime[18] or that the discovery relates to evidence gathered by fraudulent or criminal conduct.[19] It is not necessary to show that the solicitor was aware of the iniquity. Even within the category of privileged communications, however, the court is required to weigh the public interest in confidentiality in the particular circumstances against the public interest in disclosing iniquity having regard to the seriousness of the alleged iniquity and the circumstances in which privilege is claimed.[20]

(3) Recipient of the information/ proportionality

7-16 In considering whether disclosure of otherwise confidential material is justified, it is necessary for a court to consider not only the nature of the information but also whether disclosure to the particular recipient is in the public interest. In *Initial Services Limited v. Putterill* [1968] 1 Q.B. 396 (CA) Lord Denning M.R. explained (at 405G-406B) that:

> "The disclosure must . . . be to one who has a proper interest to receive the information. Thus it would be proper to disclose a crime to the police; or a

---

[17] *Gamlen v. Chemical Co (UK) v. Rochem (No.2)* (1980) 124 SJ 276 (CA), *per* Goff L.J.; *Barclays Bank Plc v. Eustice* [1995] 1 W.L.R. 1238 (CA), *per* Schiemann L.J. at 1248D–1250D; *Nationwide Building Society v. Various Solicitors* [1999] P.N.L.R. 52, Blackburne J.
[18] *Barclays Bank Plc v. Eustice* [1995] 1 W.L.R. 1238 (CA), *per* Schiemann L.J. at 1251E–1252C; *Nationwide Building Society v. Various Solicitors* [1999] P.N.L.R. 52, Blackburne J.
[19] *Dubai Aluminium Co. Limited v. Al Alawi* [1999] 1 All E.R. 703; [1999] 1 Lloyd's Rep. 478 (Rix J.).
[20] See *Derby v. Weldon (No.7)* [1990] 1 W.L.R. 1156, *per* Vinelott J. at 1173A–F; *Barclays Bank Plc v. Eustice* [1995] 1 W.K.R. 1258 (CA), *per* Schiemann L.J. at 1249H–1250D where it was suggested that the cloak of privilege was less likely to be lifted where advice is sought as to what has already been done and for the purposes of imminent litigation than where advice is sought as to how to structure a fraudulent transaction.

breach of the Restrictive Trade Practices Act to the registrar. There may be cases where the misdeed is of such a character that the public interest may demand, or at least excuse, publication on a broader field, even to the press."

In *A-G v. Guardian Newspapers (No.2)* [1990] 1 A.C. 109 (HL) Lord Griffiths similarly emphasised the importance of the recipient of the information, stating (at 268A–C) that:

"Even if the balance comes down in favour of publication, it does not follow that publication should be to the world through the media. In certain circumstances the public interest may be better served by a limited form of publication perhaps to the police or some other authority who can follow up a suspicion that wrong-doing may lurk beneath the cloak of confidence. Those authorities will be under a duty not to abuse the confidential information and to use it only for the purpose of their inquiry. If it turns out that the suspicions are without foundation, the confidence can then still be protected: see *Francome v. Mirror Group Newspapers Limited* [1984] 1 W.L.R. 892. On the other hand, the circumstances may be such that the balance will come down in favour of allowing publication by the media, see *Lion Laboratories Limited v. Evans* [1985] Q.B. 526."

Similarly Lord Goff (at 282H–283B) emphasised that more limited disclosure might sometimes be required and, in the Court of Appeal (at 176F–G), Lord Donaldson M.R. explained this on the basis that the nature and degree of communication must be proportionate to the cause of or excuse for the disclosure.

On this basis both Lord Goff and Lord Griffiths in *A-G v. Guardian (No.2)* emphasised that since in that case there were a number of avenues of proper complaint it was difficult to envisage a case in which it would be in the public interest for allegations of iniquity to be published in the media (although no issue arose as to what steps could be taken if other avenues of complaint failed to advance the matter).

Similarly in *Re A Company's Application* [1989] 1 Ch. 477 Scott J. held that the ex-employee's duty of confidentiality did not extend to preventing disclosure to FIMBRA and the Inland Revenue of matters that they were responsible for investigating. However disclosure to the public as a whole could have been restrained but for the fact that a suitable undertaking not to make such disclosure had been given. Further, disclosure to the Inland Revenue of information other than fiscal matters would equally have been a breach of the duty of confidence (at 482D–E).

This approach was also adopted in *W v. Edgell* [1990] 1 Ch. 359. Whilst there would have been an obvious breach of confidence if the medical report had been disclosed to the public, the Court of Appeal held that there was no such breach where the report was made available to the authority concerned with deciding whether the claimant should be released from a secure hospital. The authorities in relation to disclosure to a regulatory body have recently been reviewed by the Court of Appeal in *Woolgar v. Chief Constable of the Sussex Police* [1999] 3 All E.R. 604. Mrs Woolgar was a registered nurse and matron of a nursing home. She was arrested and interviewed by the police after the death of a patient in her care. Although no charges were brought, the matter was referred to the United Kingdom Central Council for Nursing, Midwifery and Health Visiting (the U.K.C.C.), which is the regulatory body for nursing midwifery and health visting. Mrs Woolgar sought unsuccessfully to obtain an order restraining the police from disclosing the contents of her interview with the police to the U.K.C.C. The Court of Appeal emphasised that it was for the police in the first instance to assess whether the public interest in disclosure outweighed the public interest in confidentiality. If in the reasonable view of the police they were in possession of confidential information which, in the interests of public health or safety, should be considered by a professional or regulatory body then they were free to pass on that information to the regulatory or professional body for their consideration. The U.K.C.C. would receive the information on the basis that it could only be used for the purposes of its own inquiry.

It has been suggested that wider disclosure might be justified where the information involves concerns involving the wider community.[21] As such in cases where the public has been misled or put in danger by secret practices, publication in the press has been regarded as justified.[22] However, it is doubtful whether the width of permitted disclosure can be neatly associated with the extent to which the public as a whole are affected. In particular:

(a) It may also be necessary to consider the seriousness of any misconduct. Even if there are only a few people affected by a fraud, it seems unlikely that disclosure to the press of the fraud would be a breach of confidence if there was no question as to whether the fraud was established.

(b) The permissible recipients of the disclosure may also vary according to the extent to which the allegations have been proven or require further investigation. Notwithstanding that information concerns a possible harm to the public as a whole, it may be that disclosure to the appropriate regulatory body is particularly appropriate where there are matters requiring further investigation. In *Re a Company's Application* (1989) Ch. 477, for example, Scott J. considered that disclosure to FIMBRA and the Inland Revenue would be permissible irrespective of whether there was substance in the allegations. It did not follow that wider publication would not be permissible if the allegations could be made out. Indeed Scott J. (at 482H) contrasted his approach with the requirement for at least a prima facie case to be established if there was to be publication to the world at large.

(c) As provided for under the 1998 Act,[23] wider disclosure may be permissible where, notwithstanding disclosure to the regulatory body, there has been a failure to take action when the concern was first raised. In *A-G v. Guardian Newspapers* Lord Griffiths observed (at 269G–H) that:

> "if a member of the service discovered that some iniquitous course of action was being pursued which was clearly detrimental to our national interest, and he was unable to persuade any senior members of his service or any member of the establishment, or the police, to do anything about it, then he should be relieved of his duty of confidence so that he could alert his fellow citizens to the impending danger."

---

[21] See *Gurry, Breach of Confidence* (1984), p. 345.
[22] *Church of Scientology v. Kaufman* [1973] R.P.C. 635; *Woodward v. Hutchins* [1977] 1 W.L.R. 760; *Hyde Park Residence Ltd v. Yelland* [1999] E.M.L.R. 654.
[23] Employment Rights Act 1996, s. 43G.

(d) It may also be relevant to consider what use is likely to be made of the information by the recipient in the particular circumstances of the case.[24]

(4) Evidential basis

7-17 An additional consideration when weighing the public interest for and against disclosure will be the evidential basis for any claim that there is a public interest in disclosure, and this also resonates in the 1998 Act. In *Church of Scientology of California v. Kaufman* [1973] R.P.C. 627 Goff J. proceeded on the basis that at the trial of the action, as opposed to the interlocutory stages, it was necessary for the claimant positively to establish that fraudulent claims had been made by the claimant. Similarly in *Woodward v. Hutchins* [1977] 2 All E.R. 751 (CA) it was noted (at 756A) that in order to have a defence to the claim of breach of confidence it would be necessary to establish in a trial the truth of the allegations made. However the balance of authority suggests that the evidential burden at common law will vary according not only to the stage in the proceedings but also the seriousness of what is alleged, the nature of the public interest in favour of confidentiality and the identity of the recipient.

At one end of the spectrum, where the disclosure is to an appropriate regulatory body, there is likely to be a low threshold. Indeed in *Re A Company Application* Scott J. opined (at 482H–483B) that:

"Where the disclosure which is threatened is no more than a disclosure to investigate matters within its remit, it is not, in my view, for the court to investigate the substance of the proposed disclosure, unless there is ground for supposing that the disclosure goes outside the remit of the intended recipient of the information."

As to the evidential basis required where wider disclosure is intended, in *Lion Laboratories* [1985] QBD 526 Griffiths L.J. emphasised that it was necessary at least that a fair reading of the documents disclosed to the press should cast doubt on the accuracy of the breathalyser equipment. Further it was said to be necessary to evaluate the strength of the defence at the interlocutory stage since otherwise the defence of public interest could be a "mole's charter" (at 550G–551A,G).

Similarly the need to consider the merits of the allegations was emphasised (in the context of disclosure other than to a regulatory body) in *A-G v. Guardian Newspapers Limited (No.2)* [1990] 1 A.C. 109 (HL). Lord Keith considered (at 262B) that a prima facie case that the allegations had substance would need to be shown. To like effect Lord Goff's opinion (at 283A–B) was that:

"a mere allegation of iniquity is not of itself sufficient to justify disclosure in the public interest. Such an allegation will only do so if, following such investigations as are reasonably open to the recipient, and having regard to all the circumstances of the case, the allegation in question can reasonably be regarded as being a credible allegation from an apparently reliable source."

The strength of the evidence required may also vary according to the importance of the public interest in preserving confidentiality in the particular case. In the context

---

[24] See *Distillers Co. (Biochemicals) Limited v. Times Newspapers Limited* [1975] 1 All E.R. 41.

of the burden of proof required to remove the cloak of privilege on grounds of iniquity, for example, the balance of authority is that at least prima facie evidence that the allegation of fraud is well founded will be required before privilege is lifted.[25] The evidential burden will however vary according to the particular circumstances—including the public interest in confidentiality, the recipient of the disclosure and the matters being disclosed. As Vinelott J. explained in *Derby & Co. Limited v. Weldon (No.7)* [1990] 1 W.L.R. 1156 at 1173E–F:

> "There is a continuous spectrum and it is impossible to, as it were, calibrate or express in any simple formula the strength of the case that the plaintiff must show in each of these categories. An order to disclose documents for which legal professional privilege is claimed lies at the extreme end of the spectrum."

There may also be evidential issues not only as to whether there has been wrongdoing but, in addition, as to the degree of threat to the public. In *W v. Edgell* the court accepted[26] that whilst it had to decide where the balance of the public interest lay, it was entitled to give such weight to the considered judgment of the psychiatrist who chose to make the disclosure as seemed appropriate in all the circumstances.

(5) Motive for disclosure

7–18 In *Initial Services Limited v. Putterill* [1968] 1 Q.B. 396 Lord Denning M.R. (at 406G) suggested that differing considerations may apply depending on the motive for the disclosure. He commented that:

> "I say nothing as to what the position would be if he disclosed it out of malice or spite or sold it to a newspaper for money or for reward. That indeed would be a different matter. It is a great evil when people purvey scandalous information for reward."

Notwithstanding these observations, generally where it is in the public interest for there to be disclosure, the motive of the person disclosing the information will not be relevant.[27]

In a number of cases disclosure has been held to be in the public interest notwithstanding that the person making the disclosure was paid for doing so.[28] However in a doubtful case, the motive of the person making the disclosure may tip the balance against disclosure.[29] Indeed in *Francome v. Mirror Group* [1984] 1 W.L.R. 892 (CA)

---

[25] *O'Rourke v. Darbishire* [1920] A.C. 581, *per* Viscount Dilhorne at 606; *Nationwide Building Society v. Various Solicitors* [1998] P.N.L.R. 52.

[26] See *per* Bingham L.J. at 422B–C [1990] 1 Ch. 359.

[27] *British Steel Corporation v. Granada Television Limited* [1981] A.C. 1096 *per* Lord Fraser at 1202D; *Lion Laboratories Limited v. Evans* [1985] 1 Q.B. 526 (CA) at 536G; *Woodward v. Hutchins* [1977] All E.R. 751 (CA) at 753G, 755F; *Khashoggi v. Smith* (1980) 124 S.J. 148 (CA).

[28] *Hubbard v. Vosper*; *Church of Scientology v. Kaufman*; *Woodward v. Hutchins*; *Hyde Park Residence Limited v. Yelland* [1999] E.M.L.R. 654 at 662–663, 673–674.

[29] See *Schering Chemicals Limited v. Falkman Limited* [1982] Q.B. 1 (CA) where Shaw L.J. (at 27E) emphasised that freedom of speech did not encompass "the mercenary betrayal of business confidences" and Templeman L.J. (at 37E) said that the defendant had used the confidential information "for his own gain" and (at 40A) that if an injunction was not granted a trusted adviser would have been able to make money out of his dealing in confidential information.

Lord Donaldson M.R. noted that it is almost unheard of for compliance with the moral imperative to make disclosure to be in the financial interests of the person making the disclosure. Further, the motive of the informant may cast doubt on the evidential basis for the allegation and in those cases (as in *W v. Edgell*) where the professional judgment of the informant would otherwise be relevant in assessing the public interest, this might be negatived by reference to the informant's motives.

Even if there is no breach of confidence as a result of the disclosure being in the public interest, if the disclosure is in bad faith the employee is likely to be in breach of the duty of fidelity and of the duty not without reasonable and proper cause to conduct himself in a manner calculated or likely to destroy or seriously damage the relationship of confidence and trust between the employee and employer.[30] Additionally, an employee who owes fiduciary duties would in general be required to account for secret profits made from his employment through acting other than bona fide in the best interests of the employer. Whilst much may depend on the subject matter of the disclosure, in many cases the court would be likely to be sympathetic to such a claim. Similarly there may be an obligation upon an employee to make restitution of any profits resulting from the disclosure if it is something which the employee had specifically contracted not to do.[31] In *Woodward v. Hutchins*, for example, although the Court of Appeal considered that publication by the press of material putting the record straight as to the private lives of various pop stars, the conduct of the employee who leaked the story for reward was clearly regarded with distaste. As Lawton L.J. put it (at 755F):

> "Persons like the first defendant cannot expect much in the way of admiration when they sell their employers' secrets for money."

In any event if the allegation proves to be false, the employee motivated by malice may also be liable in damages for defamation or malicious falsehood.[32] The motive of the person responsible for the disclosure may also be taken into account when the court exercises its discretion as to costs.[33]

(6) Timing

7–19   There may be a public interest in disclosure not only in relation to ongoing and prospective acts but also in relation to past acts.[34] Nevertheless the timing of the disclosure may be important in assessing the weight to be given to the public interest in disclosure, particularly in relation to disclosure concerning a danger to the public.[35]

COMPARISON WITH THE PUBLIC INTEREST DISCLOSURE ACT 1998

7–20   To a substantial degree the 1998 Act is consistent with the common law in relation to which disclosures are protected. In particular:

---

[30] *Malik v. BCCI SA* [1998] A.C. 20 (HL); *Byford v. Film Finances Limited* EAT/804/86 (see Chapter 11).
[31] *Attorney-Gen. v. Blake* [1998] 1 All E.R. 833 (CA) (currently on appeal to the House of Lords [1999] 1 W.L.R. 1279).
[32] *Re A Company's Application* at 483H; *Woodward v. Hutchins* at 757B.
[33] *Church of Scientology of California v. Kaufman* [1973] R.P.C. 635 at 690.
[34] See *Initial Services Limited v. Putterill* [1968] 1 Q.B. 396, *per* Lord Denning M.R. at 405.
[35] See *Schering Chemicals Limited v. Falkman Limited* [1982] Q.B. 1 (CA) (above).

(a) Protected disclosures include misdeeds consisting of criminal offences or failure to comply with legal obligations[36] but also include other subjects where there may be a public interest in disclosure. Two of these categories, that relating to miscarriages of justice[37] and dangers to health and safety,[38] reflect matters recognised as being capable of founding a public interest defence.

(b) The identity of the recipient of the information is a key factor both under the 1998 Act and at common law.

It is difficult to envisage circumstances in which an employee would be protected under the 1998 Act and yet be in breach of a duty of confidence with no public interest defence. During discussions between Public Concern at Work and banking bodies during the passage of the 1998 Act some concern was expressed as to the effect of the 1998 Act on the duty of confidentiality owed by bankers. In particular there was concern that the duty would become difficult to enforce since an employee who disclosed confidential information could not be disciplined if he/she fell within the protection of the 1998 Act. The same concerns would apply to others owing duties of confidentiality, such as lawyers and doctors. However when placed in the context of common law obligations of confidentiality, it is unlikely that the 1998 Act poses significantly new problems for employers concerned with ensuring that its employees observe duties of confidence owed to their customers. In the first place it will usually be necessary for the worker, in order to enjoy protection under the 1998 Act, to report the matter either to the employer or to the relevant regulatory body. Where wider disclosure is made, if this is protected under the 1998 Act then it is most unlikely that there would be a breach of the duty of confidence having regard to the public interest defence.

There may however be some circumstances in which disclosure which would not be protected under the 1998 Act would not constitute a breach of a duty of confidence. In particular:

(a) The 1998 Act sets out a finite list of qualifying disclosures. The public interest defence is more flexible and matters not listed in the 1998 Act may be sufficient for the public interest defence. One rationale for justifying disclosure in *Initial Services v. Putterill* [1968] 1 Q.B. 396 and in *Church of Scientology of California v. Kaufman* [1973] R.P.C. 635 (at 654) was that the public was being misled and the disclosure rectified this. Such a disclosure would not easily fall within any of the qualifying disclosures under the 1998 Act unless it could be shown that in misleading the public the employer was also acting in breach of a legal obligation. Equally it may be difficult to establish that the breach of the rules of a self-regulatory organisation constitutes a qualifying disclosure under the 1998 Act.

(b) The evidential requirements may be greater under the 1998 Act. A worker making disclosure to a prescribed organisation will only be protected

---

[36] Employment Rights Act 1996, s. 43B(1)(a),(b).
[37] Employment Rights Act 1998, s. 43B(1)(c); *Lion Laboratories.*
[38] Employment Rights Act 1996, s. 43(B)(1)(d); *Hubbard v. Vosper; Church of Scientology v. Kaufman; W v. Edgell.*

if the worker not only acts in good faith but also "reasonably believes" that the relevant failure falls within the description of matters in respect of which the person is prescribed and that the information disclosed and any allegation contained in it are substantially true.[39] The requirement to establish that the employee not only honestly but also "reasonably believes" in the truth of the allegations sets a higher standard than that suggested in *Re A Company's Application* [1989] 1 Ch. 478 where it was held that it was not for the court to investigate the substance of a proposed disclosure to a regulated body of matters which that body had a duty to investigate unless there was ground for supposing that the disclosure went outside the remit of that body.

(c) The 1998 Act also gives greater prominence to whether the allegations are made in good faith and for reward. It may be however that there is little substantive divergence from the common law position since even if there is no breach of confidence, an employee who acts maliciously or is paid for leaking to the press, may well act in breach of the duty of fidelity to the employer or breach the term of mutual trust and confidence. If the allegation is false there may also be liability in malicious falsehood or defamation.

We would expect the courts to develop the law so that the gaps between the common law and statute became less wide over time. Where a prospective whistleblower falls outside the protection of the 1998 Act, therefore, there may still be a defence to a claim for breach of confidence but particular care will be needed in assessing whether the whistleblower can safely make the requisite disclosure.

---

[39] Employment Rights Act 1996, s. 43F.

CHAPTER 8

Whistleblowing and copyright

8–01 A potential whistleblower who is considering speaking out will often be concerned to be able to provide evidence in support of his allegations. The employee may, for example, wish to make copies of research gathered in the course of employment if that research demonstrates a health and safety concern. Alternatively the employee may wish to make and disclose copies of internal memoranda which evidence impropriety. In these circumstances, the potential whistleblower, especially if there is a risk that he will be acting outside the protection of the Public Interest Disclosure Act 1998, may have to consider not only whether there is a risk of a claim of breach of confidence, but also a risk of a breach of copyright.[1]

INFRINGEMENT

8–02 Copyright will be infringed where there is unlicensed use of a substantial part of a work, for example by copying or reproducing all or a substantial part of the work. Most documents (being original literary works) and photographs (being artistic works) will be included as works within the meaning of the Copyright Designs and Patents Act 1988 ("CDPA").[2] Ordinarily the author of a work will be the first owner of the copyright in that work.[3] However where the work is made by an employee in the course of his employment, the employer will be the first owner of the copyright subject to any agreement to the contrary.[4] Similarly the Crown will be the first owner of copyright in works produced by an officer or servant of the Crown in the course of his duties.[5] In ascertaining whether work was carried out in the course of employment or in the course of duties, the court will have regard to whether the skill, effort and judgment expended by the employee or officer in creating the work fell within the scope of the normal express or implied duties of the employee or officer or within any special duties assigned to him. The employer will not have copyright in the work merely because it was created in working hours and might be a useful accessory to the contracted work.[6] In addition, even where an employee

---

[1] In addition to general provisions relating to infringement copyright, specific obligations apply in relation to data within the meaning of the Data Protection Act 1998 ("DPA"). The substantive provisions of this Act are due to come into force on March 1, 2000. Under section 55 DPA it is an offence for a person knowingly or recklessly to obtain or disclose personal data (or the information contained in such data), or to procure the disclosure to another person of that information, without the consent of the data controller. However it is a defence to show that the action was necessary for the purpose of preventing or detecting a crime or that disclosure was justified in the public interest.

[2] CDPA, ss. 1,4.

[3] CDPA, s. 11.

[4] CDPA, s. 11(2).

[5] CDPA, s. 163.

[6] *Stephenson Jordan & Harrison Limited v. MacDonald* [1952] R.P.C. 10; *Noah v. Shuba* [1991] F.S.R. 14.

creates a work other than in the course of his employment, the employer may be the owner of that work in equity if the work is created in breach of the employee's fiduciary duty to the employer.[7]

DEFENCE OF FAIR DEALING

8–03   So far as the whistleblower is concerned, the most relevant defences are the public interest and, to a lesser degree, the fair dealing defences. As to the fair dealing defence, the most relevant provisions are contained in section 30 of the CDPA. This provides:

"(1) Fair dealing with a work for the purpose of criticism or review, of that or another work or performance of a work, does not infringe any copyright in the work provided that it is accompanied by a sufficient acknowledgment.

(2) Fair dealing with a work (other than a photograph) for the purpose of reporting current events does not infringe any copyright in the work provided that (subject to subsection (3)) it is accompanied by a sufficient acknowledgment.

(3) No acknowledgment is required in connection with the reporting of current events by means of a sound recording, film, broadcast or cable programme."

"Purpose"

8–04   In *Pro Sieben Media AG v. Carlton UK Television Limited* [1999] 1 W.L.R. 605 the Court of Appeal explained that it is not sufficient that the person seeking to rely upon the defence of fair dealing subjectively intended the work to be for the purpose of criticism or review or for reporting current events or sincerely believed that this was the effect of the work. Whether that is the purpose of the work is to be determined objectively, although the motive of the infringer of the copyright may be relevant in ascertaining whether there has been fair dealing. The Court of Appeal in *Pro Sieban Media AG* concluded that the judge at first instance had wrongly concluded that the use of copyright material was not for the purpose of criticism and review because he had focused too much on the purposes, intentions and motives of those involved in planning and production of the programme, and focused too little on the likely impact on the audience.

Criticism or review of that or another work

8–05   The fair dealing defence in section 30(1) of the CDPA enables the potential whistleblower to use a copyright work only for the purpose of criticising that work or another work. The criticism can be strongly expressed, and even be unbalanced, without forfeiting the fair dealing defence. Any remedy from malicious or unjustified criticism rests in an action for defamation, although the work must be genuinely concerned with criticism or review rather than an attempt to dress up an infringement in the guise of criticism or review.[8] Criticism of a work need not be

---

[7] *Service Corporation International Plc v. Channel Four Television Corporation* [1999] E.M.L.R. 83 at 91.
[8] *per* Robert Walker L.J. in *Pro Sieben Media AG* [1999] 1 W.L.R. 605 (CA) at 613D; *Time Warner v. Channel Four* [1994] E.M.L.R., 1, *per* Henry L.J. at 14.

limited to criticism of style. It can extend to criticism of the thoughts or ideas to be found in the work and its social or moral implications.[9]

In *Pro Sieban Media AG v. Carlton U.K. Television Limited* [1998] F.S.R. 43 Laddie J., at first instance, emphasised that it was not sufficient to use the copyright work for the purpose of criticising something other than the work or another work. Laddie J. emphasised that criticism of the work or another work need not be the only purpose and could be used as a springboard to attack something else. However criticism of the work or another work must be a significant purpose. In *Pro Sieban* the defendants, as part of a series of programmes on chequebook journalism, made a programme including the case of Mandy Allwood who had become pregnant with eight children after undergoing fertility treatment. As part of the programme, the defendants used footage from a programme made by the claimant about Ms Allwood's case. Laddie J. concluded that the use of the copyright footage by the defendant was for the purpose of criticism of the decision to pay for an interview rather than for the purpose of criticism of the claimant's programme. As such he concluded that it was not a criticism or review of that work or another work as required by section 30(1). The Court of Appeal did not take issue with Laddie J.'s analysis that the criticism must be of the work or another work. However it concluded that, on the facts, the use of the copyright footage was for the purpose of criticism or review of the claimant's report, and of other newspaper material, as the fruit of chequebook journalism. This was in turn used as an illustration of the theme that chequebook journalism is inimical to the truth.

In many cases this approach will be wide enough to provide protection to the whistleblower. In a case where a whistleblower seeks to rely on documentary evidence which has been copied and is to be disclosed in breach of copyright, it will often be possible to show that the whistleblower is criticising the ideas of themes contained in those documents. In other cases, however, the whistleblower will not be criticising either the work or the ideas contained in it. In *Lion Laboratories Limited v. Evans* [1985] 1 Q.B. 526 (CA), for example, on leaving employment with the claimant, two of the defendants removed confidential internal memoranda which cast doubt on the accuracy of breathalyser equipment. This material was offered to a newspaper for publication. Although an allegation was made both of breach of confidence and breach of copyright, in refusing an interlocutory injunction the Court of Appeal considered only the common law defence of public interest and not the statutory defence of fair dealing. The memoranda were to be used as evidence but there does not appear to have been criticism either of those documents or the ideas they contained. If however the documents had additionally suggested that the results should not be made public then the criticism of that sentiment, expressed in the document, would have qualified as criticism of the work.

"Reporting current events"

8–06   A potential whistleblower may seek to show that disclosing documents in breach of copyright constitutes reporting current events within section 30(2) of the CDPA. The CDPA does not contain any definition of what constitutes a current

---

[9] *Hubbard v. Vosper* [1972] 2 Q.B. 84, *per* Lord Denning at 94F; *per* Megaw L.J. at 98D; *Time Warner v. Channel Four TV* [1994] E.M.L.R., *per* Henry L.J. at 15; *Pro Sieban Media AG* [1999] 1 W.L.R. 605 at 614H–615B.

event. Unless this is given a very liberal interpretation it may be difficult for a potential whistleblower to fall within the scope of this section. In many (but not all) cases the potential whistleblower will wish to bring to light matters which have not yet been placed in the public spotlight and as such, on a narrow view, might not be regarded as an "event". The whistleblower might also be concerned not merely about something which happened on a particular occasion but with an ongoing concern, such as failings in health and safety practice at the workplace.

Some commentators have argued that "current events" should be given a liberal meaning since it is prima facie in the public interest that the public should be informed regarding matters of public concern.[10] This view has also recently received judicial support.[11] In *The NLA v. Marks & Spencer Plc* [1999] E.M.L.R. 369, Lightman J. expressed the view that the report need not be made in the media or be to the public or accessible to the public. Lightman J. added that the publication of a report or article in the press may itself constitute a current event, but the reporting of current events, does not extend to publishing which are merely currently of interest but are not current events, or to publishing matters not previously known and of historical interest alone. Publication of matters which are not current events can only be justified if reasonably necessary to understand, explain or give meaning to a report of current events.[12]

The liberal approach to what is "current" was illustrated by the decision of Jacob J. in *Hyde Park Residence v. Yelland* [1999] E.M.L.R. 654. In August 1998 the *Daily Mirror* printed an article in which Mohammed Al-Fayed repeated an allegation that shortly before their accident in August 1997 the Princess of Wales and Dodi Al-Fayed had visited Mohammed Al-Fayed's Villa Windsor in Paris. He claimed that they had been accompanied by an Italian designer and were planning to get married and live in the house. The former chief security officer at Villa Windsor, Mr Murrell, had made two video stills which demonstrated that the couple had only been at the villa for 28 minutes. He took these to *The Sun* to support his claim that there had only been a short tour of the house by Diana and Dodi and that there had been no discussion of any plans to live there. *The Sun* printed the story and published the stills. The security company which had employed Mr Murrell brought proceedings against him and *The Sun* for breach of confidence and breach of copyright. Both claims failed. It was argued that there could be no defence of fair dealing under section 30(2) CDPA since the event in question, being the tour of the villa, had taken place a year prior to the publication. Jacob J. emphasised that this was too narrow an approach. It was sufficient that the report was topical and, even aside from the fact that Mohammed Al-Fayed had recently repeated his allegations, the events at the Villa Windsor, were still very much under discussion.

Similarly, in other cases, the general approach has been to assess whether there has been a report as to something which can legitimately be regarded as an "event" having regard to the newsworthiness of the matter. In *Pro Sieban*, for example, the Court of Appeal, in concluding that media coverage of Ms Allwood's case was itself a current event, referred to the volume and intensity of media interest in the case. A

---

[10] Laddie, Prescott and Vitoria, *The Modern Law of Copyright and Designs* (2nd ed., 1995), para. 2.157 at 134.
[11] *Pro Sieben Media AG v. Carlton U.K. Television Limited* [1999] E.M.L.R. 109, CA; *The NLA v. Marks and Spencer Plc* [1999] E.M.L.R. 369, Lightman J. at 381–382.
[12] *The NLA v. Marks and Spencer Plc* [1999] E.M.L.R. 369 at 382.

similar approach appears to have been taken in *PCR Limited v. Dow Jones Telerate Limited* [1998] F.S.R. 170. The claimant issued cocoa reports concerning the status of cocoa crops around the world. The defendant, a specialist commodity news service, published articles containing substantial quotations from the reports. Lloyd J. accepted that the fact that the reports had come out into the market, and their impact on the market, was "news" and, as such, a current event.[13] However in *Associated Newspapers Group Plc v. News Group Newspapers Limited* [1986] R.P.C. 515 Walton J. took the view that the publication of an exchange of letters between the Duke and Duchess of Windsor were not the sort of current event with which the statute was concerned.

In any event an artificially wide interpretation of what constitutes a current event may be unnecessary if it is instead possible to rely on a public interest defence.[14] The scope of such a defence is considered below.

Sufficient acknowledgment—"identifying the author"

8–07   Subject to the exception in section 30(3) of the CDPA, there can be no fair dealing defence under section 30 of the CDPA unless the infringing copy is accompanied by a "sufficient acknowledgment". As to this, section 178 of the CDPA provides that:

> "'sufficient acknowledgment' means an acknowledgment identifying the work in question by its title or other description, and identifying the author unless:
>
> (a) in the case of a published work, it is published anonymously;
> (b) in the case of an unpublished work, it is not possible for a person to ascertain the identity of the author by reasonable inquiry."

Accordingly it is not sufficient to identify the copyright owner. The author must also be identified.[15]

"Fair"

8–08   Even where a publication has been for one of the purposes set out in section 30 of the CDPA, the dealing must be shown to be fair in all the circumstances. Fair dealing is a matter of degree to be assessed on the basis of fact and impression in each case.[16] The dealing must be fair for the approved purpose and the court will take into account such matters as the amount of the extract taken, its proportion to any crit-

---

[13] Note, however, that the term "current event" is narrower than "news" because reporting of "news" can extend to information relating to past events not previously known: *The NCA v. Marks and Spencer Plc* [1999] E.M.L.R. 369 *per* Lightman J. at p. 382.

[14] In *Laddie et al. op. cit.*, para. 2.153 at 130–131 it is argued that Parliament has not legislated in such detail concerning copyright and the public interest that there is now little room for the common law public interest defence. As such the logic of their argument requires a liberal approach to the fair dealing defence in CDPA, s. 30(2). This theory that there is no separate public internal defence was expressly considered and revealed in *Hyde Park Residence Limited v. Yelland* [1999] E.M.L.R. 654, Jacob J.

[15] *Express Newspapers plc v. News (U.K.) Limited* [1990] F.S.R. 359.

[16] *Pro Sieban Media AG* (CA), *per* Robert Walker L.J. at 613B; *Hubbard v. Vosper* [1972] 2 Q.B. 84, *per* Lord Denning M.R. at 94C, *per* Megaw L.J. at 98F.

icism (where section 30(1) applies), the purpose of the infringement and the motive of the person infringing the copyright.[17]

The purpose for which the copyright has been infringed is likely to be particularly important in the context of whistleblowing. Where the copyright work is being used in conjunction with raising matters of public concern, copying of very substantial extracts may be fair dealing. In *Hubbard v. Vosper* [1972] 2 Q.B. 84 (CA), Mr Vosper authored a book critical of Scientology which contained substantial extracts from books and bulletins about Scientology by its founder, Ron Hubbard. In holding that there was an arguable defence of fair dealing, and refusing an interlocutory injunction, the Court of Appeal took account of the fact that Mr Vosper claimed to be seeking to expose Scientology to the public and to criticise and condemn Scientology. This was contrasted with an infringement of copyright in order to attack or compete with a trade rival. In such circumstances there is far less likelihood of establishing fair dealing,[18] albeit that this is not an absolute bar to there being fair dealing.[19]

The circumstances in which the potential whistleblower obtains or discloses the infringing copyright may also be relevant. In *Beloff v. Pressdram Limited* [1973] 1 All E.R. 241 the claimant, who was the political and lobby correspondent for *The Observer*, wrote an internal memorandum to her editor stating that she had had a conversation with a named member of the government to the effect that if the Prime Minister was to be run over by a bus Mr Maudling would become Prime Minister. She then published an article criticising *Private Eye*'s attitude to Maudling. *Private Eye* then published a reply attacking the claimant in personal terms and incorporating in full her internal memorandum. The editor of *The Observer* purported to assign the copyright in the memorandum to the claimant and she then brought an action for infringement of copyright. Ungoed-Thomas J. held that there was no valid assignment but if there had been, no fair dealing defence would have been established. Publication of information known to have been leaked and which could not have been pursued without the leak, was unjustifiable for the authorised purposes of criticism or review and was not fair dealing.

In *Time Warner Entertainments Company LP v. Channel Four Television Corporation Plc* [1994] E.M.L.R. 1 the Court of Appeal distinguished *Beloff* on the grounds that it related to an unpublished work. In *Time Warner* the Court of Appeal was concerned with whether there had been a breach of copyright in use of extracts from the film *A Clockwork Orange* which had already been released. The Court of Appeal emphasised that criticism and review of a work already in the public domain which would otherwise constitute fair dealing, would seldom if ever be rendered unfair because of the method by which the copyright was obtained. This would be of little comfort for the whistleblower or those seeking to publish the matters disclosed by the whistleblower where, as in the ordinary case, the whistleblower seeks to make public matters which are not already in the public domain. It is however

---

[17] See *Hubbard v. Vosper* [1972] 2 Q.B. 84, *per* Lord Denning M.R. at 94B-C; *Associated Newspaper Group Plc v. News Group Newspapers Limited* [1986] R.P.C. 515 at 518; *BBC v. BSB Limited* [1992] Ch. 140 at 157–158. *PCR Limited v. Dow Jones Telerate Limited* [1998] F.S.R. 170 at 185–186; *Pro Sieban Media AG v. Carlton Television Limited*; *Newspaper Licensing Agency Limited v. Marks and Spencer Plc The Times*, January 26, 1999.

[18] See also *Associated Newspaper Group Plc v. News Group Newspapers Limited* [1986] R.P.C. 515 at 518 *Pro Sieban Media AG*; *Walter v. Steinkopff* [1892] 3 Ch. 489; *Weatherby v. International Horse Agency & Exchange Limited* [1910] 2 Ch. 297.

[19] *BBC v. BSB Limited* [1992] Ch. 141 at 158.

unlikely that the surreptitious circumstances in which copyright may have been infringed would be a bar to a fair dealing defence where a whistleblower raises matters of public concern. This would be inconsistent with the public interest defence and with the recent judicial recognition that a distinction is to be drawn between whistleblowing cases and other disclosures: *Camelot v. Centaur Communications Limited* [1998] I.R.L.R. 80 (CA). As the Court of Appeal noted in *Time Warner*, if confidential material is improperly disclosed the remedy usually lies in an action for breach of confidence.

In any event the circumstances in which the copyright is obtained and disclosed is merely one factor to be taken into account, and it is unlikely, especially where the disclosure relates to a matter of public concern, that this would be sufficient to render the dealing unfair. In *Hubbard v. Vosper* [1972] 2 Q.B. 84 the Court of Appeal specifically rejected the claim that there could be no fair dealing defence in relation to unpublished Scientology memoranda. The Court recognised that there might be such general interest in the unpublished material that it is legitimate to criticise it, or the ideas contained in it, without there being any infringement of copyright.[20] Similarly in *Hyde Park Residence Limited v. Yelland* [1998] E.M.L.R. 654[21] the fair dealing defence succeeded notwithstanding that the employee had secretly retained two pairs of video stills which he disclosed to *The Sun* and had been paid for his story. Jacob J. emphasised that the test in all cases was whether what had been done with the copyright work was "fair" and that this might be so even if it was not "necessary" to use the copyright work. In any event, publication of the stills was close to being necessary in order to substantiate *The Sun*'s story.

PUBLIC INTEREST DEFENCE

8–09   Whilst it may be prudent for a potential whistleblower to seek to meet the requirements for a fair dealing defence, where matters of public concern are raised the more straightforward approach is to rely on a defence of public interest akin to that applied in the context of breach of confidence actions. Section 171(3) of the CDPA specifically provides for the preservation of:

> "any rule of law preventing or restricting the enforcement of copyright, on grounds of public interest or otherwise."

The scope of the public interest defence is considered in Chapter 7 above in relation to claims of breach of confidence. The availability of the common law public interest defence in the context of infringement of copyright was recognised in *Beloff v. Pressdam Limited* [1973] 1 All E.R. 241 at 259H, where Ungoed-Thomas J. explained that:

> "Fair dealing is a statutory defence limited to infringement of copyright only. But public interest is a defence outside and independent of statutes, not limited to copyright cases and is based on a general principle of common law."

---

[20] *per* Lord Denning M.R. at 95A–B.
[21] See para. 8–06.

Further recognition was given to the availability of a public interest defence to infringement of copyright in *A-G v. Guardian Newspapers (No.2)* [1990] 1 A.C. 109 (HL). The House of Lords required *The Sunday Times* to account for the profits made in serialisation of *Spycatcher*. Lord Keith explained that in calculating profits no account was to be taken of any sums paid to Peter Wright or his publishers for the copyright because no claim for these sums would have been enforceable. This was because there was no copyright in a work the publication of which was brought about contrary to the public interest.[22]

Similarly Lord Jauncey noted that there could be no enforceable copyright in *Spycatcher* since it "reeked of turpitude".[23]

In two whistleblowing cases involving allegations of infringement of copyright, reliance has been placed on the public interest defence and the court has not considered it necessary to refer to the fair dealing defence. It was on the basis of a common law public interest defence that an interlocutory injunction was refused by the Court of Appeal in *Lion Laboratories* [1985] QBD 526 (see above). The judgment of Stephenson L.J. (with whom O'Connor L.J. agreed) might be explained on the basis that although Stephenson L.J. recognised that the courts would not restrain a breach of copyright where there was just cause or excuse for infringing the copyright, this was consistent with public interest being relevant as a factor relevant to discretionary injunctive relief rather than as a substantive defence. However Griffiths L.J. stated expressly that he considered that the defence of public interest applied to breach of copyright in addition to breach of confidence.

A substantive defence of public interest was also recognised in a whistleblowing context in *Service Corporation International Plc v. Channel Four Television Corporation* [1999] E.M.L.R. 83. One of the defendants, Mr Anderson, was employed by an operator and owner of funeral homes as a trainee funeral director. In fact during the period of his employment he was working under cover and covertly made a film which purported to show corpses being subjected to disrespectful and abusive treatment and coffins with corpses in them being used as rubbish bins. The claimants sought to restrain the showing of the film on Channel Four, claiming that it had been made in breach of confidence and as a result of trespass and also that the claimants owned the copyright in the film. Injunctive relief was refused. Unsurprisingly, in relation to the claim of infringement of copyright Lightman J. concluded that there were good prospects of establishing a public interest defence at trial, raising questions not only as to the funeral home where the filming took place but also as to whether the state of affairs revealed might be prevalent in the claimants' funeral homes or in the industry generally.

Notwithstanding these cases, a determined, but unsuccessful, attempt was made in *Hyde Park Residence Limited v. Yelland* [1998] E.M.L.R. 654 to establish that there is no defence of public interest to a claim of infringement of copyright. Jacob J. accepted that the cases up to 1988 which had tended towards the recognition of a public interest defence had done so with little basis. However he concluded that section 171(3) CDPA was intended to recognise a defence of public interest either by way of refusing to recognise copyright altogether or by way of a defence in the particular circumstances of the case. Jacob J. also rejected the contention that the

---

[22] *per* Lord Keith at 262G–263A.
[23] at 294D.

recognition of such a defence would involve judges in matters of public controversy and make the law too uncertain. This was no more the case than in relation to the defence of just cause or excuse in relation to claims of breach of confidence. In any event the need to balance freedom of expression and the right to respect for private life under the European Convention of Human Rights would involve judges in a similar sort of exercise.

Whilst there is now clear authority for the existence of a public interest defence, it has also been emphasised that the defence may not be of wide scope. Indeed, in *Hyde Park Residence Limited v. Yelland* [1999] E.M.L.R. 654 Jacob J. suggested (at 673) that it was unlikely that the defence could succeed unless:

> "the court can be reasonably certain that no right-thinking member of the society would quarrel with the result."[24]

A very wide public interest defence might be regarded as undermining the statutory balance of rights reflected in the fair dealing defence. Indeed the dangers of too wide a public interest defence is reflected in the judgment of Younger J. in *Glyn v. Weston Feature Film Company* [1916] 1 Ch. 261, upon which Lord Keith placed reliance in *A-G v. Guardian Newspapers*. Younger J. held that there was no enforceable copyright in the novel in that case because it was "grossly immoral", notably because it "advocates free love and justifies adultery where the marriage tie has become merely irksome".[25]

Specific limits to the public interest defence were suggested in *Hyde Park Residence Limited v. Yelland* [1998] E.M.L.R. 654. Jacob J. considered that the defence was unlikely to extend beyond the context of the communication of what was essentially information, such as the disclosure of video stills in that case essentially by way of communication of evidence. From the perspective of the whistleblower, however, it is precisely the communication of information through the copyright work that is likely to be of concern.

Jacob J. also emphasised that (as in the context of breach of confidence) a distinction is to be drawn between the public interest and what is of interest to the public. Further, the disclosure must be proportionate so that, in many cases, disclosure to the newspapers rather than to a regulatory body would not be justified. These considerations were emphasised in *Express Newspapers Plc v. News (U.K.) Limited* [1990] F.S.R. 359 when the *Daily Star* sought to rely on a public interest defence where it had copied part of an interview reported by *Today* with a member of the Royal Family. It was argued that this interview was the first time that a member of the Royal Family had discussed the Family's attitude towards unmarried pregnancy and that its importance lay in exploring and contrasting the conflicting obligations of Royalty towards State and family and the way in which their attitudes have changed. Sir Nicholas Browne-Wilkinson V.-C., in rejecting this defence on the facts, explained that the basis of the public interest defence is the public interest in disclosing secret information which the public needs to know. As such, the whole basis of the defence evaporated once the information had already been disclosed by another paper. Further, reflecting a distinction drawn in the

---

[24] Followed by Jacob J. in *Mars U.K. Limited v. Teknowledge Limited (No. 2)* (Unreported, June 11, 1999).
[25] at 269.

context of breach of confidence, he noted that the defence did not cover information which, as here, was merely of interest to the public rather than there being a public interest in disclosure.

However, in whistleblowing cases there will invariably be a concern to publicise information which, even if not secret, has not been made known sufficiently widely to address the concerns raised by the whistleblower. As such the observations of Browne-Wilkinson V.-C. (as he then was) that there is limited scope for the public interest in relation to information which has already been publicised, is unlikely to be a serious concern to the potential whistleblower.

In some cases when considering the balance of competing interests necessary when addressing the public interest defence, the Court has considered that it is relevant to have regard to the statutory balance implicit in the fair dealing defence. In *PCR Limited v. Dow Jones Telerate Limited* [1998] F.S.R. 170 Lloyd J. acknowledged that there was a defence of public interest which, although more common to claims of breach of confidence, had been recognised as a defence to infringement of copyright and was not limited to disclosure of iniquity. However he considered that the public interest in promoting transparency in the cocoa market was adequately satisifed by the fair dealing defence in section 30(2) of the CDPA.

As illustrated by the approach in *Service Corporation v. Channel Four*, however, in clear cases, for example where allegations of wrongdoing are made, especially if made to an appropriate authority, there will be little need to refer to the fair dealing defence. In other cases, however, it may be less clear whether a public interest defence is available. Relevant considerations will be the nature of the matters disclosed, the identity of the recipient of the information, the extent of the evidential basis, the motive for disclosure and the timing of disclosure (see Chapter 7). The more unclear the availability of the public interest defence, the more important will be compliance with the requirements for a fair dealing defence, albeit that the considerations casting doubt on whether there is a public interest defence may also impact on whether there is a fair dealing defence.

INTERRELATION OF COPYRIGHT PROTECTION AND PUBLIC INTEREST DISCLOSURE ACT 1998

8–10   Where the requirements of the Public Interest Disclosure Act 1998 are not met, it will be necessary for the potential whistleblower who infringes copyright to seek to rely upon the defences of fair dealing and/or public interest. This is unlikely to be necessary where the disclosure is made in accordance with the 1998 Act. There is no express provision in the 1998 Act addressing the extent to which a whistleblower is entitled to infringe copyright in order to supply evidence to support a protected disclosure. However the evidence collected and disclosed, whether or not in breach of copyright, will form part of a qualifying disclosure provided only that, in the reasonable belief of the worker, it tends to show one or more of the matters listed in section 43B of the 1998 Act. The infringing copy will itself be the means by which the requisite information is disclosed. As such if the requirements of the 1998 Act are met, the worker will have the right not to be subjected to dismissal for disclosing the protected information notwithstanding that in making the disclosure, or in order to be able to do so, he infringed copyright. Having regard to the policy underlying the 1998 Act, the courts are unlikely to accept a submission that the detriment was due not to the disclosure but to the manner in which it took place, being an infringement of copyright.[26] Equally, having regard to the policy of the 1998 Act, it is most unlikely that injunctive relief would be granted to enforce copyright where the infringement is part of or in support of a protected disclosure.

---

[26] See para. 6–13, above; *Shillito v. Van Leer (U.K.) Limited* [1997] I.R.L.R. 495 (EAT); *Goodwin v. Cabletel UK Limited* [1997] I.R.L.R. 665; [1998] I.C.R. 112 (EAT); *Bass Taverns Limited v. Burgess* [1995] I.R.L.R. 596 (CA).

CHAPTER 9

The obligation to blow the whistle

9–01 The Public Interest Disclosure Act 1998 does not impose any sanction upon an employee for failing to blow the whistle. This Chapter considers the extent to which there may be a positive obligation upon employees to blow the whistle in particular circumstances, whether at common law or pursuant to specific statutory obligations.

NO GENERAL DUTY OF DISCLOSURE

9–02 Since an employment contract is not a contract of the utmost good faith there is no general duty upon employees and employers to make full disclosure of material facts to each other: *BCCI SA v. Ali (No.1)* [1999] I.R.L.R. 226; [1992] 2 All E.R. 1005. In some circumstances there will be a duty upon an employee to disclose wrongdoing, at least, of other employees. The leading authorities have left open several issues as to the limits of this obligation.

BLOWING THE WHISTLE ON SUBORDINATES

9–03 The question as to the scope of an employee's obligation to disclose wrong-doing has usually arisen in the context of whether an employee can enforce a sever-ance package agreed after failing to disclose the wrongdoing. In *Sybron Corporation v. Rochem Limited* [1984] 1 Ch. 112 (CA) the employers sought to recover sums paid out to an ex-employee, Mr Roques, under a pension and life assurance scheme. Mr Roques was employed by Gamlen Chemical Co. (U.K.) Limited, a subsidiary of the Sybron Corporation group. He was the most senior employee for Gamlen's European operations and had power of hiring and firing over the whole of the European zone. Various employees of Gamlen and Sybron Corp. secretly set up rival organisations to act in competition with Sybron and Gamlen and traded through these rival com-panies whilst still employed by Sybron or Gamlen.

The Court of Appeal recognised that there is no general rule that in every case an employee must disclose any information which he or she has about breaches of duty by fellow employees. It is necessary to have regard to the express terms of the con-tract of employment and to those terms which can be implied in the particular cir-cumstances. In *Sybron Corp.* there was held to be a duty to report the misconduct of fellow employees in the light of Mr Roques' seniority in the organisation and the fact that others involved in the conspiracy were his subordinates. In addition a relevant consideration was the fact that, as Mr Roques was well aware, the fraud was con-tinuing (Fox L.J. at 129E–F).

Sybron Corp. may be regarded as an extreme case. Mr Roques occupied a very senior position in the employing organisation, there was a recognised reporting structure under which he was required to make reports in relation to matters within his zone and there was serious wrongdoing by subordinates within his zone which was clearly a matter which ought to have been dealt with in the monthly reports. Further the wrongdoing was serious and ongoing. The case therefore begs the question as to the extent to which the duty to report wrongdoing would extend to less extreme circumstances.

BLOWING THE WHISTLE ON SUPERIORS

9-04 Although in *Sybron* the Court of Appeal emphasised that Mr Roques was required to report the misdeeds of his subordinates, it may be that it was his managerial status, with its attendant reporting duties, rather than his very senior position in the hierarchy that was crucial. It is clear, however, from the decision of the Court of Appeal in *Swain v. West (Butchers) Limited* [1936] 3 All E.R. 261 that the duty to disclose misdeeds is not necessarily confined to reporting upon subordinates. Mr Swain was employed as the general manager of the employers' business and as such was responsible for the business as a whole except that he was subordinate to the managing director. However, he followed certain unlawful orders of the managing director involving the selling of incorrectly labelled meat. Mr Swain was asked about this by the chairman of the employers and told that if he provided proof of the managing director's dishonesty he would not be dismissed. Mr Swain provided the requisite information, thereby implicating himself in the fraud. He was then dismissed.

The Court of Appeal held that Mr Swain could not enforce the agreement to the effect that he would not be dismissed because he was already under an obligation to report the managing director's wrongdoing and there was therefore no consideration for the agreement with the chairman. The Court of Appeal emphasised that Mr Swain's contract provided that he was to do all in his power to "promote, extend and develop the interests of the company". Of itself this might appear unremarkable. However this was in a context where Mr Swain had control of the business and was responsible for seeing that it was conducted honestly and efficiently by all who came under his control.

In the case of less senior employees the courts are likely to be much more reluctant to find that there is a duty to report the misdeeds of superiors. Such reluctance is evident in the decision of the majority of the EAT in *Ladbroke Racing Limited v. King, Daily Telegraph*, April 21, 1989. Following the dismissal of a manager for gross misconduct including falsification of records and removing money from the shop, an investigation was carried out into the conduct of his subordinates. This revealed that the subordinate employees had, on their manager's instructions, been involved in serious breaches of the rules including allowing unauthorised betting and failing to reconcile the cash. The employer's rules provided that it would not be an answer to a breach of the employer's rules that it had been condoned by management. The subordinate employees were dismissed for their breaches of the rules and for failing to report the breaches of the rules by their manager. By a majority, the EAT held that the dismissal was unfair. There was no sufficiently clear express terms upon which the employer could rely in order to impose an express duty to report the manager's misconduct. Nor was there a breach of the implied term of trust and confidence because this left a discretion in the employees and, in the EAT's view, the employees had not acted unreasonably in choosing not to report their manager's misconduct.

One difficulty in imposing an implied obligation of disclosure even on junior employees is the difficulty of reconciling this with the emphasis in *Sybron Corp* that there is no general duty of disclosure on all employees. This was emphasised by Pumfrey J. in *Cantor Fitzgerald International v. Tradition (U.K.) Limited* (Unreported, June 12, 1998, Pumfrey J.). A claim was brought against Tradition for infringement of copyright. It was alleged that Tradition's employee programmers had constructed a computer programme for Tradition which reproduced a code written for the Claimant, their former employer. The employees had told Tradition that they were not copying the code. Tradition brought third party proceedings against one of the employees and sought leave to serve out of the jurisdiction. This was refused on the basis that there was no good arguable case. Tradition argued that the employee was under an implied duty to disclose the misconduct of his fellow employees in copying the code. Pumfrey J. concluded that this was unlikely to succeed. There was nothing to distinguish Mr Gresham from the ordinary run of comparatively junior employees, he had no independent managerial responsibility and had worked under the direction of a director of Tradition who was principally responsible for any infringements of copyright.

THE LIMITS OF THE OBLIGATION

9–05 Notwithstanding the specific contractual provision in *Swain* the reasoning would appear to apply generally to cases where an employee has managerial responsibilities. This is however difficult to reconcile with the decision of the House of Lords in *Bell v. Lever Brothers Limited* [1932] A.C. 161 (HL) which has held a baleful influence over this area of law for many decades. Messrs Bell and Snelling entered into contracts of employment with Lever Brothers Limited and were also appointed respectively as chairman and vice chairman of Niger Company. Lever Brothers held over 99 per cent of the shares in Niger Company. Bell and Snelling each made personal profits by speculating in Niger Company's business. Before Lever Brothers became aware of this, the service contracts of Bell and Snelling were brought to an end and substantial severance payments were made by Lever Brothers. Upon becoming aware of the secret profits, however, Lever Brothers sought to recover the severance payments. It was argued that Bell and Snelling were under an obligation to disclose their misdeeds in making the secret profits and that the severance agreements were voidable as a result of the non-disclosure. This was accepted by the Court of Appeal but rejected by a majority of the House of Lords.

Since Bell and Snelling occupied the most senior positions for their employer it might have been expected, on the basis of the reasoning in the subsequent cases of *Sybron* and *Swain*, that even if they should not have disclosed their own wrongdoing, that of their colleague should have been disclosed. However in *Sybron* Stephenson L.J. took the view (approving a dictum of Walton J. at first instance) that:

> "it would be very difficult to have submitted, with any hope of success, that Messrs Bell and Snelling, having been appointed to rescue the affairs of their employers' African subsidiary in effect jointly, ought to have denounced each other."

A number of possible explanations were advanced for this in *Sybron* and are considered below. None of the explanations adequately explain the decision on the facts of *Bell* and it may well be that *Bell* cannot be taken as limiting the scope of the duty to disclose wrongdoing of others because the obligation to disclose the wrongdoing of a fellow servant was neither argued nor expressly addressed in *Bell*. Indeed in so far as the obligation to disclose wrongdoing of others was touched upon at all, it supported a wide obligation to disclose the wrongdoing of others. Lord Atkin noted (at 228) that:

> "It is said that there is a contractual duty of the servant to disclose his past faults. I agree that the duty in the servant to protect his master's property may involve the duty to report a fellow servant whom he knows to be wrongfully dealing with the property."

Although *Bell* may be difficult to explain on its facts, the possible bases of distinguishing *Bell* illustrate some of the potentially relevant factors in relation to the scope of the duty to blow the whistle on fellow employees.

BLOWING THE WHISTLE ON EMPLOYEES OF SIMILAR SENIORITY

9–06   Although Bell and Snelling were working together and Stephenson L.J. accepted that they were in joint management where neither was subordinate to the other, this is difficult to reconcile with the facts in *Bell*. Bell was chairman of Niger Company and Snelling was vice chairman and Bell was entitled to a higher salary. In any event, it would be strange if a person in a managerial position had a responsibility to report on wrongdoing both by those more senior (as in *Swain*) and those less senior (as in *Sybron*) but not in respect of those at the same level. If only Bell or only Snelling had been engaged in the fraud then, in the light of the senior management role of Bell and Snelling, there would surely have been an obligation to report the fraud. The fact that Bell and Snelling were both parties to the fraud could not have improved their position.

CONTINUING WRONGDOING

9–07   A further possible basis for distinguishing *Bell*, suggested by Fox L.J. in *Sybron* (at 128D–E), was that in *Sybron* the misconduct was continuing whereas in *Bell* there was only a question as to past misconduct. It is apparent from the judgment of Fox L.J. that he regarded this as one factor to be weighed in the balance in favour of requiring disclosure rather than as necessarily being determinative. Certainly this may be important. The urgency of disclosure to the employer will be all the more obvious in the case of ongoing misconduct.

There are, however, dangers in placing too much importance on this factor. Irrespective of whether the misdeed has been completed, an employer may have an interest in rooting out the culprit. The misdeed may be such as to cast doubt as to whether the culprit is a sufficiently trustworthy employee and there may be concern not only to prevent the same misconduct in future but also other misconduct. In *Camelot v. Centaur Communications Limited* [1998] I.R.L.R. 80, for example, the Court of Appeal was faced with an application to disclose documents which would reveal the identity of an employee of Camelot who leaked a copy of Camelot's draft accounts to a journalist. There was no danger of a further leak of the same nature due to injunctions or undertakings already given in relation to that information and the passage of time. However, the Court of Appeal accepted that an employee sufficiently disloyal or untrustworthy to make the initial disclosure could not be relied upon to refrain from revealing other confidential information such as, in the case of Camelot's employees, the names and addresses of lottery winners.[1]

Further, it is doubtful whether *Bell* can itself properly be regarded as a case which related solely to past misconduct. At the time when the severance agreements were entered into there were no longer any secret profits being made and the jury found that there was no deliberate concealment of the secret profits. However Bell and Snelling held their senior positions at the time when they were engaged in making secret profits. At that time the misconduct was ongoing but it was not held that at that stage there was any duty to disclose the misconduct. If there had been such a duty, then it would have been strongly arguable that Lever Brothers had suffered loss of the sums paid by way of severance payments by reason of the breach of contract by Bell and Snelling.

Conversely it seems very unlikely that the decision in *Sybron* would have been any different even if there was only past misconduct, for example because the wrongful competition had been brought to an end. Mr Roques not only had managerial responsibility but also had an express obligation to report matters within his zone every month. As such he was certainly under an obligation to report the misconduct by other employees. Even if an employee has been dismissed or disciplined it would be relevant for an employer to be made aware of the grounds for this. If this is not properly communicated the employer might be exposed to the risk of a claim for negligence if it subsequently provides a reference indicating that there is no reason to doubt the loyalty or probity of the ex-employee.

DELIBERATE CONCEALMENT

9–08   In *Bell* there was a specific finding that the non-disclosure of wrongdoing was not fraudulent. Deliberate or fraudulent concealment is not however a prerequisite of liability. Where, as in *Sybron* and *Swain*, there is an express or implicit positive obligation arising from employment to report wrongdoing, for example due to a senior managerial role of the employee, there would then be a duty to exercise reasonable care and skill in relation to that duty. A breach of the duty might therefore arise from careless oversight rather than deliberate concealment. It may be however, that in a case where it is less clear that there was a duty to report the wrongdoing, deliberate concealment of the wrongdoing might be sufficient to establish that the non-disclosure amounted to a breach of the duty of fidelity or, in the case of senior employees or directors, a breach of fiduciary duty (see below in relation to directors). In *BCCI v. Ali* (No. 1) [1999] I.R.L.R. 226; [1999] 2 All E.R. 1005 Lightman J., in the context of considering whether there was an obligation upon BCCI to disclose its fraud to its own employees, observed that he could not see how questions of fraudulent concealment could arise unless BCCI was under a duty to disclose. However whilst a mere failure to disclose is unlikely to be deliberate concealment in the absence

---

[1] See further, Chapter 10.

of a duty to disclose, the position may be different where an employee takes positive steps to hide information which would otherwise come to an employer's attention.

HAS THERE BEEN A SPECIFIC REQUEST?

9–09   Similarly it may be important in a marginal case that an employee fails to supply information as to wrongdoing despite receiving a specific request. This is not an essential factor in all cases. In *Sybron* there was indeed a duty to make monthly reports and in *Swain* the employee was expressly asked to blow the whistle on the managing director. However it was made clear in *Swain* that the duty to report acts of which Mr Swain was aware and which he knew were not in the interests of his employer arose irrespective of any specific request. This was reaffirmed in *Sybron* (*per* Stephenson L.J. at 126G).

EXPRESS TERMS OF THE CONTRACT

9–10   The express terms of the contract may impose a clear obligation to disclose wrongdoing. In *Swain* there was some emphasis on the fact of the express duty to "promote, extend and develop the interests" of the employer. The obligation may, however, arise from the circumstances of the employment irrespective of the express terms. By way of example, in *Sybron* no reliance was placed on any express terms of the service agreement. Further a similar obligation to that in *Swain* is likely to apply to most senior employees and directors (and would certainly have applied to Bell and Snelling).

SERIOUSNESS OF THE WRONGDOING

9–11   The nature of the wrongdoing may be crucial. If the wrongdoing is sufficiently serious this may of itself be sufficient to give rise to a duty of disclosure to the employer.[2] As such it is likely that an employee at any level would be expected to report if he/she was aware of a serious imminent health risk. In *Bell v. Lever Brothers* Lord Atkin suggested (at 228) that there might be a duty on employees to protect the employer's property to the extent of reporting a theft by a fellow employee. Although Lord Atkin explained this on the basis of the duty to protect the employer's property, it might also have been explained on the basis of the implied duty of good fidelity or on the basis that an employee who kept quiet about such a theft would thereby seriously damage the mutual trust and confidence between employer and employee.

ABILITY TO RESOLVE THE MATTER WITHOUT REPORTING THE WRONGDOING

9–12   Even where a person is in a managerial position there may be no duty to report misdeeds of others within his/her area of control if the matters can be dealt with satisfactorily without reporting the matter. This consideration would support a more onerous duty of disclosure on subordinates who report misconduct of more

---

[2] See *The Zinnia* [1984] I.R.L.R. 211 at 218.

senior employees. In *Swain* the misconduct was of the managing director and as such there was no question of Mr Swain himself being able to institute disciplinary action. The only means of dealing with this would have been to report the matter to the board of directors.

REPORTING MATTERS OTHER THAN MISDEEDS

9–13 It is also apparent that where an employee has managerial functions he/she may be required to report on matters other than the misdeeds of employees. In *Swain* Greer L.J. noted that it was Mr Swain's duty to report acts of which he knew which were not in his employer's interests. It appears to have been accepted that this flowed from Mr Swain's overall responsibility for the business. In some cases the obligation may be obvious, such as reporting health and safety problems. However considerable difficulty arises in relation to identifying the precise scope of this obligation. There may also be difficult issues as to whether there is an obligation to disclose wrongdoing outside work which tarnishes the image of the employer. It may be, however, that this difficulty could be partially resolved on the basis that it would be for the manager in the first instance to assess in such marginal cases, acting honestly in the employers' interests, whether the matters were such that he or she could deal with them without troubling superiors, or whether it was necessary to take such matters further in order to protect the employer's interest.

DUTY TO DISCLOSE OWN WRONGDOING?

9–14 Traditionally *Bell v. Lever Brothers* has been taken as authority for the proposition that whilst an employee may be obliged to blow the whistle on others, there is no obligation for an employee to disclose his or her own wrongdoing. On this basis Lightman J. held in *BCCI v. Ali* (No. 1) [1999] I.R.L.R. 226; [1992] All E.R. 1005, that BCCI was not under any duty to disclose to its employees the fraudulent manner in which it had been carrying on its business even though this conduct put at risk the employees' own reputation. Lightman J. rejected the contention that the position in *Bell* was altered by the recognition in *Malik v. BCCI* [1997] 3 All E.R. 1 that employees and employers are under a duty not without reasonable and proper cause to act in a manner likely to destroy or seriously damage the mutual trust and confidence between employer and employee even though this duty extends to refraining from damaging an employee's future employment prospects. It made no difference that the employer had acted dishonestly since in *Bell* itself Lord Atkin had expressly stated that there was no duty on an employee to disclose his own wrongdoing even in a case of theft. Further in *Horcal Limited v. Gatland* [1984] I.R.L.R. 288 at 290 the Court of Appeal observed, without deciding, that there was force in the submission that even a director who does wrong has no additional obligation to confess to the wrong (see below in relation to directors). Lightman J. also noted that in *Sybron* Kerr L.J. doubted whether an employee could fraudulently conceal his or her own misconduct. However he considered that, at least in *BCCI v. Ali*, there could be no question of fraudulent concealment unless there was a duty to disclose.

In support of his decision in *BCCI v. Ali* Lightman J. noted that a duty to confess wrongdoing, whether on the part of the employer or the employee, might require "standards extravagant and unattainable in the workplace". This would clearly be a significant problem if every wrongdoing had to be confessed. As Lightman J. noted, the duty to confess would become impossibly onerous if it applied in every case, by for example imposing a duty on an employee to confess taking a day's sick leave when he was not genuinely ill. However there is already a need for the courts to ascertain in what circumstances and in relation to which wrongs an employee may owe a contractual duty to disclose the wrongdoing of others. The same process of reasoning could equally apply to ascertaining in what circumstances an employee should be required to disclose his own wrongs. There would be nothing extravagant in a requirement that an employee who, as in *Sybron*, by reason of his position in the employer's organisation, is under an express or implied duty to report misconduct, should be under a duty to report his own theft from the employer. Limits on the duty could be identified by reference to such matters as the position of the employee in the organisation and the nature of the wrongdoing.

In practical terms, such an obligation may have little impact on the conduct of the employee. A person who is prepared to carry out a theft, for example, is unlikely to be willing to disclose his own wrongdoing merely because of a contractual obligation to do so. However the issue has usually arisen in the context of seeking to set aside a contract such as a severance package. Where there has been a misrepresentation there is no difficulty since the employer would be entitled to rescind for misrepresentation. Indeed this remedy could have been open in *Sybron* where the employee wrote misleading letters to his employer. In the absence of misrepresentation it may (as in *Bell*) be necessary to establish the duty of disclosure in order to prevent an employee, who was guilty of gross misconduct but concealed this from the employer, receiving a windfall from a severance payment made by the employer in ignorance of the employee's conduct.

DIRECTORS AND SENIOR EMPLOYEES

9–15 It may be that different considerations would apply as to the scope of the duty to disclose wrongdoing where an employee, by reason of also being a director or by reason of his or her seniority, also owes fiduciary duties to the employer. The director would have to exercise any discretion as to whether to disclose the wrongdoing bona fide in the best interests of the employer. A director who chooses not to disclose his or her own wrongdoing in order to further his or her own interests, or a director who fails to disclose misdeeds of other employees for fear of disclosing his own wrongdoing or out of loyalty to those employees, would be acting in his own interest or that of the other employees rather than in the interests of the company.

In general a senior employee or director who fails to disclose the wrongdoing of others or himself by way of oversight, rather than self protection or misplaced loyalty, although possibly in breach of a duty of disclosure under his or her contract of employment, would not be in breach of fiduciary duty.[3] However when dealing with his own principal a fiduciary must make full disclosure of all facts material to the transaction and also show that the transaction was fair. If the fiduciary fails to satisfy these requirements then there may be a liability in damages and the transaction can be set aside.[4] This is however difficult to reconcile with *Bell v. Lever Brothers* where Bell and Snelling

---

[3] See *Bristol and West Building Society v. Mothew* [1998] Ch. 1 (CA) at 18A–20C.
[4] *Swindle v. Harrison* [1997] 4 All E.R. 705; *BCCI v. Aboody* [1990] 1 Q.B. 923 at 962E–964C; *Bowstead and Reynolds on Agency* (1996) 16th ed. Art 47 at 223–224.

were senior employees of one company and directors of an associated company but the non-disclosure was found not to have been deliberate (but see *Horcal Limited* (above)).

In any event, even in the case of deliberate non-disclosure by a director it may still be necessary to have regard to the factors relevant to whether there is a duty upon an employee. The scope of a director's duties will depend upon how the business of the company is organised and what part the director could reasonably be expected to play.[5] The scope of the director's responsibilities are therefore likely to be highly relevant. Equally, much will depend upon the nature and seriousness of the matter which it is alleged should have been disclosed. As such there is no breach of fiduciary duty in a director failing to take steps preparatory to setting up in competition after ceasing to be a director, notwithstanding that disclosure would be in the employer's interest and is withheld out of self-interest.[6] Nor is there any duty upon a director to disclose that he or she has it in mind to act unlawfully and in breach of contract in the future before doing anything wrong.[7]

DUTIES OF DISCLOSURE UPON AN EMPLOYEE WHO HAS BECOME MIXED UP IN WRONGDOING

9–16 It may well be that an employee whose acts or omissions, whether innocent or not, have facilitated the wrongful acts of another employee against the employer, thereby comes under a duty to make full disclosure of the wrongdoing, although this does not appear to have been canvassed in *Sybron*. In *Norwich Pharmacal Co. v. Commissioners of Customs and Excise* [1974] A.C. 133 (HL) the Customs and Excise Commissioners were ordered to disclose the identity of importers who were infringing the claimant's patent on the basis that the Commissioners, being responsible for the infringing goods, had become innocently mixed up in the importers' wrongdoing. Lord Reid explained (at 175B) that:

> "If through no fault of his own a person gets mixed up in the tortious acts of others so as to facilitate their wrong-doing he may incur no personal liability but he comes under a duty to assist the person who has been wronged by giving him full information and disclosing the identity of the wrongdoers. . . . justice requires that he should cooperate in righting the wrong if he unwittingly facilitated its perpetration."

The duty to make disclosure applies not only to disclosing the identity of a wrongdoer, but also to disclosing full information about the wrongdoing.[8] Whilst this has generally arisen in the context of applications for an Order for discovery, the discretion to make the Order is founded upon there being a duty upon the person who has become mixed up in the wrongdoing to assist the person wronged by providing full information.[9] Even if there is no enforceable common law obligation to make disclosure, it is

---

[5] *Framlington Group plc v. Anderson* [1995] B.C.C. 611 at 628H.
[6] *Balston Limited v. Headline Filters Limited* [1990] F.S.R. 385 at 412.
[7] *Horcal Limited v. Gatland* [1984] I.R.L.R. 288 (CA).
[8] *Societe Romanaise de la Chaussure SA v. British Shoe Corporation Ltd* [1991] F.S.R. 1 at 5; *Bankers Trust Co. v. Shapira* [1980] 1 W.L.R. 1274; *Axa Equity and Law Life Assurance Society Plc v. National Westminster Bank Plc* [1998] P.N.L.R. 433.
[9] *Norwich Pharmacal, per* Lord Reid at 175; *Bankers Trust Co. v. Shapira* [1980] 1 W.L.R. 1274, *per* Lord Denning M.R. at 1281.

only a short step to imply a term of the contract of employment to the effect that there is such a duty as a legal incident of the contract or as an obvious term.

Interface with the Public Interest Disclosure Act 1998

9–17   There may also be an issue in some circumstances as to the extent to which it is necessary to modify the scope of the duty of disclosure of wrongdoing, or the remedies for breach, in the light of the Public Interest Disclosure Act 1998. A worker has a right not to be subjected to a detriment on the ground that he has made a protected disclosure and a dismissal will be unfair if the reason or the principal reason is that he has made a protected disclosure. These provisions would not have assisted the employee in *Swain*, notwithstanding that he was dismissed after disclosure of the misdeeds of the managing director, since the reason for the dismissal was Mr Swain's misconduct rather than the disclosure.

The position would have been less straightforward if Mr Swain had not himself been guilty of serious misconduct but had only been willing to make partial disclosure of the managing director's misconduct, perhaps due to concern about reprisals or implicating other colleagues. On the Court of Appeal's analysis Mr Swain was plainly obliged to make full disclosure of the wrongdoing. However if he had been dismissed for failing to make full disclosure, he could now argue that it only became apparent to the employers that he had additional information to disclose by reason of the limited disclosure he made and that the principal reason for the dismissal was therefore the disclosure. This argument might be made with still greater force if, rather than having been asked for the information, Mr Swain had voluntarily come forward to provide the partial disclosure and therefore exposed himself to the wrath of the employer for not telling more.

Certainly the protection provided by the Act might be undermined if an employer could justify victimisation of an employee who comes forward to blow the whistle, but is reluctant to make fuller disclosure, on the grounds that the victimisation was not due to the partial disclosure but due to breach of a duty to make fuller disclosure. By way of example, an employee may be under an express contractual obligation to report any incidences of theft of which he becomes aware. Pursuant to that duty, the employee may report that items have been taken from a shop where the employee is based. The disclosure might be made in the hope of encouraging the employer to improve procedures so as to deter a recurrence but the employee may be reluctant to disclose the identity of the culprits. As a result of the employee's whistleblowing it might therefore be apparent to the employer that the disclosure is only partial, since the culprits have not been identified, and that the employee is therefore in breach of the express duty of disclosure. It is unlikely that the employer would be able to justify disciplinary action against the whistleblowing employee on the grounds of his failure to make fuller disclosure in circumstances where the awareness of the inadequacies of that disclosure have arisen out of the partial disclosure, being a protected disclosure under the 1998 Act.

Conclusion as to the Scope of the Duty of Disclosure

9–18   While there will be many cases where there is obviously a duty to disclose misdeeds or other acts, in many cases, as emphasised in *Sybron* an assessment of all relevant circumstances will be necessary. The following matters, whilst not an exhaustive list, are likely to be of particular significance:

(a) The express terms of the contract.

(b) Any works rules or policies clarifying the scope of the duty.

(c) Whether there has been a request to the employee for disclosure.

(d) The seniority of the employee and his or her place in the employer's hierarchy.

(e) Whether the employee has managerial responsibilities and the scope of those responsibilities.

(f) By whom any such wrongdoing was committed.

(g) The nature and seriousness of the wrongdoing or other matter to be disclosed.

(h) The degree of connection between the wrongdoing and the employment.

(i) Whether the wrongdoing or other matter is of a continuing nature and/or is likely to continue unless reported.

(j) Whether there has been deliberate concealment by the employee.

Statutory obligations to disclose information

9–19   In addition to contractual obligations of disclosure, the need for employees and professionals to blow the whistle on impropriety has been recognised by the implementation of statutory duties of disclosure. Section 33A of the Pensions Schemes Act 1993 and section 48 of the Pensions Act 1995 are each expressly headed "Blowing the Whistle" and impose specific duties upon auditors and trustees of pension schemes to report what they have "reasonable cause to believe" are relevant breaches of the law or other matters likely to be of material significance to, respectively, the relevant Secretary of State (in the case of section 33A) and the Occupational Pensions Regulatory Authority (in the case of section 48). Emphasising the importance which it attached to this, OPRA devoted its first guidance note (dated March 1997) to this provision.

Similar obligations have also been imposed upon auditors of banks, insurance companies, building societies, persons authorised to carry out investment business and friendly societies. In each case there is a statutory duty to report to the regulator various matters relating to authorisation criteria or (in the case of building societies and friendly societies) criteria of prudent management, which are likely to be of material significance to the regulator.[10] Various statutory duties are also imposed upon employees, amongst others, to assist with or provide information in relation to investigations.[11]

---

[10] Auditors (Financial Services Act) 1986 Rules 1994 (S.I. 1994 No.526); Auditors (Insurance Companies Act 1982) Regulations 1994 (S.I. 1994 No. 449); Accountants (Banking Act 1987) Regulations 1994 (S.I. 1994 No. 524); Building Societies (Auditors) Order 1994 (S.I. 1994 No.525); Friendly Societies (Auditors) Order 1994 (S.I. 1994 No.132).

[11] Banking Act 1987, s. 41; Building Society Act 1986, s. 55(3); Companies Act 1985, s. 434; Financial Services Act 1986, s. 94 and 177(3); Insolvency Act 1986, ss. 218, 219 and 235; Re Arrows [1995] 2 A.C. 75 (HL).

Statutory duties to disclose also apply in contexts other than financial matters. Section 52(1) of the Drug Trafficking Act 1994 makes it a criminal offence for those who acquire information in the course of their employment that another person is engaged in laundering the proceeds of drug trafficking, to fail to disclosure this to a constable as soon as reasonably practicable. Section 18A(1) of the Prevention of Terrorism (Temporary Provisions) Act 1989 makes similar provision in relation to failure to disclose financial assistance for terrorism. Employees also have a duty under regulation 12 of the Management of Health and Safety at Work Regulations[12] to inform the employer, and any other employee with specific responsibility for health and safety, of any work situation which the employee ought to have considered to represent a serious and immediate threat to health and safety or a shortcoming in the employer's protection arrangements for health and safety where the problem arises out of that employee's activities at work and has not previously been reported.

Whilst the various statutory duties apply only in certain limited circumstances, they illustrate that where disclosure is particularly important it may be necessary to go beyond a permissive approach.

CLARIFICATION BY A WHISTLEBLOWING POLICY

9–20   In the light of the Public Interest Disclosure Act 1998, it is to be expected that many more employers will choose to adopt a whistleblowing policy. So as to ensure that employees are apprised of relevant statutory duties of disclosure and in the light of the difficulties that may arise in ascertaining whether there is a common law duty of disclosure in particular circumstances, it will often be in the employers' interest to seek to identify, as part of that policy, the following matters:

(a) Which employees are required to disclose misdeeds of others.

(b) In relation to what types of misdeeds and what other matters is there a duty to blow the whistle.

(c) To whom should disclosure be made and what procedures exist for making the disclosure.

(d) The disciplinary sanction for a breach of the duty of disclosure.

(e) The fact that an employee should not be victimised for making the disclosure.

Especially where there are likely to be matters which are of particular concern to the employer the prudent course would be to provide as specifically as possible for those matters which must be disclosed and by whom. As the EAT explained in *The Distillers Company (Bottling Services) Limited v. Gardner* [1982] I.R.L.R. 48 (where an employee was disciplined for failing to report theft of a case of whisky):

---

[12] SI 1992 No. 2051, implementing in part Article 13 of Council Directive 89/391 on the *Introduction of Measures to Encourage Improvements in the Safety and Health of Workers at Work.*

"If . . . this is a matter of great importance to the [employer], it would be reasonable to expect in their rules not merely a specific prohibition against misappropriation but a clear obligation placed upon employees who witness such behaviour to report it immediately. It is asking a lot of an employee to require him to report the misdemeanours of his colleagues, but if this is to be the rules it should . . . be very clearly spelled out."

This dictum was followed by the Employment Appeal Tribunal in *Ladbroke Racing Limited v. King, Daily Telegraph*, April 21, 1989. Delivering the majority judgment of the EAT, Wood J. noted that if it was to be asserted that there was an express duty to report any breach of company rules, such a stipulation would have to be written clearly, if necessary in capital letters in the staff handbook.

In addition to spelling out clearly the obligation to report certain matters, it is also likely to be important to identify the disciplinary consequences of failing to do so. This is particularly important if the employer is seeking to impose an onerous or unusual obligation, such as imposing wide obligations on employees with no managerial responsibility, or where the misconduct is to be regarded as gross misconduct.[13]

There may be significant advantages to the employer in including duties to blow the whistle in addition to setting out whistleblowers' rights and relevant procedures in a policy. In particular:

(a) If carefully drafted it would clarify the scope of the duty of disclosure.

(b) It might encourage a sense of corporate responsibility.

(c) It might encourage employees to bring serious matters to light where otherwise the temptation would be simply to ignore the matter.

(d) It would assist in entitling an employee to set aside a severance package or other agreement entered into with an employee guilty of (non-disclosed) wrongdoing.

(e) It may entitle the employer to fairly impose a disciplinary sanction that would otherwise be regarded as too severe.

However the imposition of duties of disclosure is not without problems. In particular:

(a) As noted in *Distillers* any express duty going beyond that which would be implied in the ordinary course would have to be very clearly spelled out. The wider the obligation sought to be imposed, the greater the difficulty there may be in identifying this and then in consistently applying it.

(b) Too wide an obligation upon employees carries the risk of the duties being too unspecific, damaging industrial relations and causing friction and suspicion between employees.[14] If a defensive attitude is then encouraged this may undermine corporate responsibility rather than encourage it.

---

[13] *Dalton v. Burton's Gold Medal Biscuits Limited* [1974] I.R.L.R. 45 (NIRC).
[14] See *Distillers* at p. 50, para. 17.

(c) Even if there is a whistleblowing policy incorporating duties of disclosure, there may be difficulty where there is only partial disclosure. If a sanction is then imposed for failing to make full disclosure this may be regarded as being imposed as a result of the worker having made a protected disclosure and therefore be unlawful victimisation under the Public Interest Disclosure Act 1998.

Notwithstanding these concerns, since employees will in any event be under implied duties of disclosure, including statutory duties, a whistleblowing policy could usefully clarify the scope of the duties. In addition it may be that a whistleblowing policy could helpfully identify certain obvious areas where a duty of disclosure is to be required. Careful identification of duties of disclosure might be regarded as complementing the 1998 Act, providing a rounded carrot and stick approach to encouraging the whistleblower to come forward.

CHAPTER 10

Informants

10–01 A prospective whistleblower may be deterred from coming forward if he has no confidence that his identity will not be kept confidential. Further the whistleblower may also be concerned as to disclosure of the details of the allegations since it may be that this would have the effect of disclosing the whistleblower's identity. An employer who discloses the identity of the whistleblower or the details of the allegations against the whistleblower's wishes may well act in breach of the Public Interest Disclosure Act 1998 if the whistleblower falls within the protection of that Act. This will be so if the court considers that as a result of the employer's disclosure the worker has suffered a detriment on the ground of the worker having made the disclosure.[1]

In most cases, especially where a whistleblower falls within the protection of the 1998 Act, there is not likely to be any question of an employer or other body being required to disclose the identity of the whistleblower. The court has a discretion to order discovery based upon the equitable bill of discovery. However such an order has generally only been made on the basis that the informant is a wrongdoer (usually on the basis that information has been disclosed in breach of confidence) and that the order is made against a person who has become mixed up (innocently or not) in the wrongdoing.[2] There is an additional safeguard in relation to attempts to discover the source of information of matters set out in a publication, in the sense of any speech, writing, broadcast, cable programme or other communication addressed to the public at large or any section of it. In such circumstances, by virtue of section 10 of the Contempt of Court Act 1981, disclosure of the source of information can only be ordered if it is established to the satisfaction of the court that disclosure is necessary in the interests of justice or national security or for the prevention of disorder or crime.

10–02 The test set out in section 10 of the Contempt of Court Act enables the court to distinguish between those cases where the employee is raising issues of public concern and other cases where there is no wider public interest to be protected beyond the general interest in freedom of expression. In *Camelot v. Centaur Communications Limited* [1998] I.R.L.R. 80, for example, where the Court of Appeal ordered a magazine to return documents which would lead to the identification of an employee of Camelot who had leaked confidential draft year-end accounts, the court was careful to emphasise that there was no element of whistleblowing involved. It was apparent that the employee was a wrongdoer and, as such, the Court of Appeal recognised the strong public interest in being able to unmask a disloyal employee so as to be able to dismiss him.

---

[1] ERA, s. 47B(1).
[2] *British Steel Corporation v. Granada Television* [1981] A.C. 1096 (HL); *Axa Equity and Law Life Assurance Society Plc v. National Westminster Bank Plc* [1998] P.N.L.R. 433.

The decision in *Camelot* was followed by Neuberger J. in *O'Mara Books Limited v. Express Newspapers Plc* [1999] F.S.R. 49.[3] Stolen manuscripts of the book *Fergie —Her Secret Life* were found in the possession of two of the defendants and they were ordered to disclose their source. Neuberger J. noted that whoever had stolen the manuscript had done so solely with a view to making a profit. Further there was a likelihood that the source was an employee of either the publishers or their American printers. The existence of a dishonest employee was damaging to employer-employee relations and relations between employees and there was an obvious risk of the dishonest employee making further unlawful disclosures. As such the only public interest against disclosure was the general public interest underlying section 10 of the Contempt of Court Act of encouraging freedom of expression and the interests of justice were clearly in favour of disclosure.

Neither *Camelot* and *O'Mara* were concerned with the case of a whistleblower. Especially having regard to the policy underlying the Public Interest Disclosure Act 1998, where a whistleblower makes a disclosure covered by the Act, it is most unlikely that this would be regarded as wrongdoing or that the interests of justice require disclosure.

10–03   In some cases, however, the interest in protecting the identity of the whistleblower, and perhaps also the details of any allegations, may run directly counter to other considerations bearing on the interests of justice. Fairness requires that the person against whom the allegations are made is properly apprised of the allegations and has an opportunity to answer them. This is a familiar issue in the unfair dismissal context and it is difficult to envisage a situation in which a dismissal could be fair unless an employee is apprised of the gist of the allegations against him.[4] Even aside from the unfair dismissal context, an employee may well have an interest in being apprised of the allegations made against him in order to protect his reputation and so as to be able to clear his name. This may require disclosure of the identity of the whistleblower and of the allegations made so that there is a full opportunity to rebut the allegations.

The court was faced with such a situation in *P v. T Ltd* [1997] 1 W.L.R. 1309. A senior employee was notified that his employer had received serious allegations about him from a third party. He was not told what the allegations were or by whom they were made other than that they related to gross misconduct in the way that he had conducted himself with external contractors. The employer stated that it would not disclose more as to the nature of the allegations since this would disclose the identity of the informant and the employer considered that the informant's request for anonymity was reasonable. The employee was dismissed for gross misconduct. The employers admitted unfair and wrongful dismissal but the employee also sought an order against the employers to disclose the precise nature of the allegations against him and the identity of the informant. Scott V.-C. made the order notwithstanding that no wrongdoing by the informant had yet been made out. There were potential claims of defamation (which would depend on the information being false) and malicious falsehood (which would depend on the information being given maliciously). The employee could not establish that these claims could be made out unless the order was granted. Justice demanded that the order be made in order to give the employee a chance to clear his name.

---

[3] See also to like effect *John Reid Enterprises Limited v. Pell* [1999] E.M.L.R. 675 (Carnworth J.).
[4] *Linfood Cash and Carry Limited v. Thomson* [1989] I.R.L.R. 235 (EAT).

Whilst the informant in *P v. T Ltd* was an outside source, the same considerations would have been relevant if it had been another employee. On the basis that the employee was, in good faith, reporting gross misconduct to the employer, the informant would be entitled to protection under the 1998 Act for having made the disclosure, even if the allegations proved to be false (subject to the safeguards already considered above). In most situations the proper course would be for the employer not to proceed with disciplinary action unless the employer was at least able to put the substance of the allegations to him. Indeed Scott V.-C. branded as outrageous the conduct of the employer in *P v. T Limited*. However where the employer does proceed with disciplinary action without revealing the substance of the allegations it is unlikely that the 1998 Act would affect the assessment that the interests of justice require, at minimum, that the substance of the allegations be disclosed. This might be reconciled with the 1998 Act on the basis that any detriment which the informant worker then suffers is not on the ground of having made the disclosure but on the ground of the need to comply with the order of the court.

CHAPTER 11

Unfair dismissal before or outside the 1998 Act

11–01   Even before the Public Interest Disclosure Act, an employee who was dismissed for whistleblowing could claim unfair dismissal under what is now the Employment Rights Act 1996. Under the 1998 Act dismissal for making a protected disclosure will be automatically unfair. However where there is not a protected disclosure, for example because the employee makes a second level disclosure without complying with the requirements of sections 43G or 43H of the ERA, the tribunal will still need to consider whether the dismissal is unfair under section 98 of the ERA.

REASON FOR THE DISMISSAL

11–02   In general, for a dismissal to be fair, the employer must first establish that the reason for the dismissal, or the principal reason, falls within one of the five categories set out in section 98(1) and (2) of the Employment Rights Act 1996. It is not necessary at this stage to show that the reason in fact justified the dismissal. In a whistleblowing case, the reason typically advanced by the employer for the dismissal is misconduct or "some other substantial reason". The employer will typically assert that the dismissal was a breach of the duty of confidence and/or of the duty of fidelity, that as a result of the disclosure there has been a total collapse in the trust and confidence required between employer and employee and that the disclosure has rendered working relationships impossible or very strained. Of course in some cases more unscrupulous employers may instead seek to invent other reasons for dismissal in order to justify ridding the employer of a person who, as a result of whistleblowing, is regarded as a troublemaker. It will be for the tribunal to ascertain whether the reason given for the dismissal is the real reason but, at least for dismissals on grounds of misconduct or capability, it will be sufficient for the employer to establish that the reason was genuinely held even if it the employer was mistaken.[1]

FAIRNESS

11–03   The tribunal must then determine whether the reason for dismissal is fair "in accordance with equity and the substantial merits of the case". The standard to be applied is whether dismissal fell within the range of reasonable responses of the employer. The tribunal will generally ask in whistleblower cases outside the 1998 Act whether the employer had a reasonable belief based on reasonable grounds after rea-

---

[1] *Maintenance Co. Limited v. Dormer* [1982] I.R.L.R. 491.

sonable investigation that the employee was responsible for the disclosure and should also consider whether the disclosure constituted wrongdoing[2] and if so whether the wrongdoing was sufficiently serious that an employer could conclude that dismissal was justified. The reasonableness of the employer's action is to be judged only up to the time of the dismissal (or appeal). Any vindication of the action taken by the employee after the dismissal, or indeed if it is positively established that the concerns raised by the employee were not well-founded, will not be relevant to the question of fairness if these were not matters known to the employer at the time of the dismissal or appeal and could not have been discovered following a reasonable investigation. Whether the concerns were well founded or adequately supported by evidence may however be important in relation to compensation, which is awarded on the basis that it is just and equitable (for further details, see Bowers and Honeyball, *Textbook on Labour Law* (5th edn., 1998)).

FIRST LEVEL DISCLOSURES

11–04   Where a whistleblower merely makes disclosure to a person in authority within the employing organisation the matter is likely to be a protected disclosure provided that the subject matter falls within one of the categories in section 43B of the ERA. In any event, even aside from the 1998 Act it is unlikely that the tribunal would find that the dismissal was fair. This is so even though the employee may become unpopular with colleagues as a result of the disclosure. In *Callanan v. Surrey AHA* COIT 994/36 (5.2.80) a student nurse at a psychiatric hospital reported the fact that a colleague had hit a patient and other nurses then refused to work with him. Although the decision preceded the 1998 Act, the dismissal was held to be unfair. However this was not a case where there was any suggestion of breach of confidence. The disclosure was to the employer and the tribunal proceeded on the basis that the employer could not justify its dismissal by reference to the threat of industrial action.

In other cases the whistleblower, although not dismissed, may be victimised by other employees for making the disclosure, for example by being "sent to Coventry". The employer will be vicariously liable for harassment by employees if carried out in the course of their employment and, as such, where the whistleblowing employee has made a protected disclosure, the harassment will constitute unlawful victimisation. Even aside from the 1998 Act the employer will be under an implied duty to provide a suitable and safe working environment and to provide reasonable support to the whistleblowing employee.[3] If the employer is in breach of this obligation the employee may be able to leave the employment and claim to have been unfairly constructively dismissed. In practice, however, the whistleblowing employee may be loathe to give up his employment even if there is a prospect of claiming that he was constructively dismissed. Further, there may be considerable evidential difficulties in establishing that the employer was in repudiatory breach. There may for example be a substantial dispute as to whether the employer has failed to take reasonable steps to support the whistleblowing employee where there

---

[2] See Chapter 7.
[3] *Wigan Borough Council v. Davies* [1979] I.R.L.R. 127 (EAT); *Waltons & Morse v. Dorrington* [1997] I.R.L.R. 488 (EAT).

has been a genuine breakdown in the relationship between the whistleblower and other employees.

SECOND LEVEL DISCLOSURES

11–05   More substantial difficulties in assessing fairness are likely to arise where the disclosure is made outside the employing organisation. Within the framework of the 1998 Act, once the other preconditions of sections 43G and 43E of the ERA have been satisfied, the tribunal must consider whether, having regard in particular to the matters set out in section 43G(3) of the ERA, it was reasonable for the worker to make the disclosure. The tribunal must therefore consider the position from the perspective of the employee. Where however there is no protected disclosure, under the general unfair dismissal provisions, the focus is on the *employer's* position since the tribunal must consider whether the employer acted reasonably (*i.e.* within the range of reasonable responses) in treating the employee's conduct as a sufficient reason to dismiss.

In assessing whether the employer has acted reasonably, considerations which underlie the statutory requirements for a protected disclosure, and the common law public interest defence for breach of confidence, are likely to be highly relevant even where there is no protected disclosure and reliance must be placed on the general unfair dismissal provisions. The employer is entitled to expect loyalty from the employee but, to take one extreme, the duty of fidelity could not extend to requiring an employee to conceal fraud. In considering the substantive fairness of the decision to dismiss, therefore, the important considerations in the absence of a protected disclosure are likely to include; the nature and seriousness of the allegation, whether the person receiving the information had a proper interest in receiving it, whether there are others to whom the information could more appropriately have been communicated, the motive for the disclosure, and the evidential basis for the disclosure.

These considerations have been important in the approach taken in the few whistleblowing cases which preceded the 1998 Act. The criteria each supported a finding of unfair dismissal in *Cornelius v. Hackney LBC* EAT/1061/94. Mr Cornelius, who was employed by Hackney LBC as an internal auditor, discovered that a stores officer also employed by Hackney had acted illegally and in a manner detrimental to his employer's interests. He reported on these matters to his employers but became concerned about what he perceived to be an unwillingness amongst senior management to deal with corrupt practices. He passed on details of his concerns, and of documentary evidence in support, to his trade union and to the chairman of the Performance Review Sub-Committee. The employment tribunal[4] held that the dismissal was procedurally unfair. However even though Mr Cornelius had genuinely been seeking to address a perceived cover up of corrupt practices, the tribunal held that he was substantially to blame for his dismissal by reason of having disclosed his concerns to his trade union and to the chairman of the Performance Review Sub-Committee, especially as his report was annotated with unflattering remarks about his colleagues. Compensation was therefore reduced by 50 per cent.

On appeal, however, the EAT concluded that the decision to reduce compensation was perverse. As the EAT explained:

---

[4] COIT 4376/92/LS.

"There is a high duty upon local government officers in the Appellant's position to report dishonesty in any form, and to persist if need be in ensuring that it is brought to the attention of those in authority and that appropriate action is taken. . . . It is difficult to see how the Appellant could be criticised for passing the documents in his possession, all of which related to his duty to uncover corruption, to the Chairman of the Committee which was concerned in investigating the matter, and who had expressly requested to see them. . . .

Equally we are at a loss to understand why the Appellant should be criticised for sending documents to his Union in order to obtain advice from them, if he was unable to resolve the matter satisfactorily by other means."

Although the tribunal had proceeded only on the basis of procedural unfairness, the EAT plainly regarded the dismissal as substantively unfair. It is likely that an employee in Mr Cornelius' position would now be able to succeed under the 1998 Act. Reliance could now be placed on section 43G of the ERA in the light of the fact that the concerns had previously been raised with management. Having done so it was then reasonable to make the wider disclosure in the light of the genuine concern that there was a cover up, together with the fact that the disclosure was made to those with a genuine and legitimate interest in receiving the information either to provide assistance and advice (in the case of the union) or to investigate the handling of corruption (in the case of the councillor).

By contrast to the position of Mr Cornelius, in *Byford v. Film Finances Limited* EAT/804/86 although the applicant had a genuine belief in serious allegations against her employer, other considerations led to a finding that dismissal was fair. Mrs Byford was a long serving employee who felt that she owed obligations of loyalty not only to the company that employed her, but also to its former chairman who was a minority shareholder in the company who had been ousted from a role in managing the company by the majority shareholders. Out of a sense of loyalty to the former chairman, Mrs Byford was persuaded to spy on the activities of the company for the minority shareholders. She discovered what she genuinely believed was evidence of improper and fraudulent conduct by the directors of the employing company (who were associated with the majority shareholders), including conduct constituting a fraud on the minority. She reported her findings to the minority shareholders and, as a result, unfair prejudice proceedings were commenced. Upon discovering Mrs Byford's role, the respondent company dismissed her.

The EAT upheld the employment tribunal's finding that the dismissal was fair. The dismissal had been for "some other substantial reason" in that there was a breakdown in trust in Mrs Byford as a result of her having gone behind the director's back to report her findings to the minority shareholders. Further, the EAT considered that not only was the decision to dismiss within the range of reasonable responses but there was really no other alternative since Mrs Byford plainly could not be trusted. Neither the employment tribunal nor the EAT resolved the issue as whether the allegations made by Mrs Byford were true. As such the decision proceeded on the basis that the employer was entitled to demand loyalty irrespective of the truth of the serious allegations. It may be, however, that the decision would have been different if the allegations had not been raised for the ulterior motive of assisting the minority and had been raised with a person responsible for investigating the allegations. Further, although the minority shareholders might be said to have had a legitimate interest in the information as to a fraud on the minority, the EAT emphasised that if there was to be a disclosure of the concerns it would have been more appropriate to make disclosure to the auditors or, if as Mrs Byford alleged they could not be trusted, to the Department of Trade and Industry.

The employer's entitlement to expect loyalty was similarly emphasised in *Thornley v. ARA Ltd* EAT 669/76. Mr Thornley raised concerns about the aircraft design of a Tornado aircraft. He was not satisfied with the response. Ultimately he sent a letter to *The Guardian* and was then dismissed. The EAT was unimpressed with the argument that unless Mr Thornley publicised his concerns, the aircraft would be sold with flaws. It was not for him to denigrate his employer's product. On the facts, the matters Mr Thornley disclosed would probably not have fallen within any of the six categories of information which could constitute a qualifying disclosure under section 43B of the ERA. However underlying the reasoning of the EAT was its assertion that whilst an employee might genuinely feel bound to follow his conscience and make a disclosure in the public interest, the price of doing so might be dismissal. This is likely to be continue to be a significant risk in cases where an employee cannot rely on the protection of the 1998 Act.

REMEDY

(i) Reinstatement or re-engagement

11–06   Where an employee has been dismissed as a result of making a protected disclosure, the remedies available will be compensation (with no ceiling) and reinstatement or re-engagement and it will be possible to claim interim relief (see Chapter 6). The remedies available to an employee who has been unfairly dismissed for making a disclosure which is not a protected disclosure will also be compensation or reinstatement/re-engagement (subject to the financial ceiling) but there will be no entitlement to claim interim relief.

In practice, orders for reinstatement or re-engagement are relatively rare. The tribunal must consider whether it is practicable for the employer to comply with the order and whether it would be just to make the order where the employee has caused or contributed to the dismissal to some extent.[5] The tribunal may also take into account other considerations. The availability of interim relief may improve the prospects of reinstatement or re-engagement being practicable. However the tribunal is likely to find that the reinstatement or re-engagement is not practicable if trust and confidence between the employer and employee has been lost or where the relationship between the employee and his colleagues has broken down.[6] Whilst it may be that tribunals will take into account the public policy underlying the enactment of the 1998 Act, these considerations may still be significant in a whistleblowing case where the employer may regard the employee as untrustworthy as a result of the leak and the whistleblower's colleagues may, as in *Callanan v. Surrey AHA* (above), have been angered by the whistleblower's disclosures.

(ii) Compensation

11–07   In a case of unfair dismissal not covered by the 1998 Act, subject to reductions, for example due to contributory fault, the unfairly dismissed employee will be

---

[5] ERA, s. 116.
[6] *East Coast Limited v. McGregor* EAT 473/76.

entitled to a basic award and a compensatory award. In addition employee whistleblowers dismissed for making a protected disclosure will be entitled to receive an additional award where the employee has made a request for re-engagement or reinstatement.[7]

The compensatory award for unfair dismissal, whether under the new provisions of the 1998 Act or under general unfair dismissal provisions, will be limited to compensation for financial loss (including a sum for loss of notice rights). The principal heads of loss will be immediate and future loss of earnings, expenses and lost benefits and loss of statutory employment protection rights. Compensation is limited to financial loss and therefore there can be no claim for injury to feelings or for stress and anxiety suffered as a result of the dismissal. However, as in the cases of damages for breach of contract, the employee can be compensated for financial loss due to difficulty in finding alternative work arising out of damage to his reputation due to the employer's breach of contract.[8] Further, where an employee suffers loss as a result of difficulty in being able to mitigate loss due to the manner of the dismissal, for example because the employee is traumatised by his treatment, this can be taken into account in assessing whether loss has been properly mitigated by finding other work subject to principles of remoteness.[9] In this respect the position is more favourable than relation to damages for breach of contract.[10] As such a whistleblower whose reputation is tarnished by being branded a troublemaker, or who is traumatised by his treatment at the hands of the employer, may be able to recover loss resulting from consequent difficulties in finding alternative work.

When introducing the new clause 11 of the Employment Relations Bill, which provided that there is no ceiling on compensation for dismissal for making a protected disclosure,[11] the Secretary of State for Trade and Industry, Stephen Byers, asserted in answer to criticism that the absence of a ceiling on compensation would be difficult for small firms, that:

> "Any tribunal can take into account the size of an organisation or company in deciding whether an approach has been fair and reasonable in particular circumstances. . . . If a small business does not have the amount of back-up that is available to a larger company, the tribunal can take that factor into account in deciding the appropriate level of compensation to apply".[12]

This would be a radical departure from the approach taken in calculating compensation for unfair dismissal. Employment tribunals are accustomed to taking into account the size and administrative resources of an employer organisation when considering whether a dismissal is fair. However once a dismissal is unfair there is no scope for taking into account size and administrative resources as a basis for reducing compensation and it would be very surprising if this is to be a relevant factor on the basis of which compensation can be reduced under the 1998 Act.

In any event, notwithstanding that there is no ceiling on compensation and the

---

[7] See Chapter 6.
[8] *Malik v. BCCI* [1997] 3 W.L.R. 95 (HL). see Chapter 14 para. 14–07.
[9] *Norton Tool Co. Limited v. Tewson* [1972] I.C.R. 501 (NIRC); *Vaughan v. Weighpack Limited* [1974] I.C.R. 261 (NIRC).
[10] *Johnson v. Unisys Ltd* [1999] I.R.L.R. 90 (CA).
[11] Now section 37(1) of the Employment Relations Act 1999.
[12] *Hansard* 30 March 1999, col. 877.

possibility of receiving an additional award where re-employment has been sought, there is a serious risk that the whistleblower will be under compensated. Where a whistleblower has not found work at the date of the hearing it will be necessary for the tribunal to assess how long the whistleblower is likely to be out of work for. In practice a whistleblower may face lengthy periods of unemployment as a result of gaining a reputation as a troublemaker. However it may be difficult for a tribunal to predict such a long period of unemployment at the date of the remedies hearing, especially when the hearing comes on relatively quickly after the dismissal.

(iii) Contributory fault

11–08   Contributory fault may be relevant both to whether an order for reinstatement or re-engagement should be made and in relation to reducing compensation (including the basic award). This is so whether or not the dismissal is automatically unfair as being a dismissal for making a protected disclosure. The tribunal may make an order for reinstatement or re-engagement even where there is contributory conduct[13] but this is unusual. It may be however that a tribunal will be more willing to make such an order despite contributory fault in a whistleblowing case having regard to the public policy underlying the 1998 Act.

In a whistleblowing case, the alleged contributory fault will typically consist of the intemperate terms in which the disclosure was made, particularly where there has been unjustified criticism of the employer or of the applicant's colleagues. Although the EAT in *Cornelius v. Hackney LBC* (above) held that the reduction of compensation by 50 per cent was perverse, this was on the basis that there was no blameworthy conduct by the whistleblower. Although Mr Cornelius had annotated his report with comments that were critical of his colleagues, the EAT accepted that the omission to delete the annotations before disclosing the report was justified by reference to standard auditing practice. By contrast in *Friend v. CAA* (unreported, cited in [1998] I.R.L.R. 253) an employment tribunal held that a whistleblower had contributed 100 per cent to his dismissal (prior to enactment of the 1998 Act). Captain Friend was employed by the CAA as a flight operations inspector. As a result of expressing strong views as to safety matters, he enjoyed a poor relationship with some of his colleagues. Ultimately, following allegations made by some of his colleagues, he was dismissed. The employment tribunal held that the dismissal was procedurally unfair but that his compensation should be reduced by 100 per cent due to his contributory fault. In upholding this decision the Court of Appeal explained that there was no need for the tribunal to have investigated whether Captain Friend's safety concerns were well-founded since in relation to compensation:

> "The question for the industrial tribunal . . . was not whether he was right or wrong, reasonable or unreasonable, in the views he expressed; but whether his way of expressing them, and the steps he took, or omitted to take, as a means of emphasising them, amounted to action which caused or contributed to his dismissal . . . [F]or the purpose of answering that question it was unnecessary to enlarge the ambit of an already long hearing by going into the rights and wrongs of the controversy engendered by the helicopter safety issue."[14]

---

[13] *Automatic Cooling Engineers Limited v. Scott* EAT 545/81 (re-engagement despite 75 per cent contribution to dismissal).
[14] [1998] I.R.L.R. 253 at 254, para. 9.

Notwithstanding this decision,[15] it is open to the tribunal to have regard to the whistleblowing context when determining the amount of any deduction which should be made for contributory fault. This is because any deduction for contributory fault is to be by such proportion of the award as the tribunal considers to be "just and equitable".[16] Having regard to the public policy underlying the 1998 Act, and in particular the public intersection encouraging whistleblowers to raise matters of public concern, it may be that where there has been a protected disclosure this will be reflected in any deduction for contributory fault being less than would have been made for similar blameworthy conduct in a non-whistleblowing case.

COMPARATIVE WEAKNESS OF GENERAL UNFAIR DISMISSAL PROTECTION

11–09   Even aside from the difficulties that may be encountered in establishing that a dismissal is unfair where the disclosure is not a protected disclosure, there are other weaknesses in the general unfair dismissal scheme when compared to the protection under the 1998 Act:

(1) Unfair dismissal protection only applies to employees under a contract of service rather than to the wider class of "worker" protected under the 1998 Act.

(2) There is currently a one year service qualification (save for example for dismissal by reason of health and safety activities).

(3) The cap on compensation is low (although under the Employment Relations Act 1999 the cap on the compensatory award is to be substantially increased to £50,000) and tribunals are reluctant to reinstate or re-engage employees where there has been contributory fault (which would include failing to use the right channels to blow the whistle) or a break down in trust and confidence. The case of Bonnie Tall (see Introduction C5) illustrates the inadequacy of the remedy of compensation for unfair dismissal.

(4) There is no protection for actions short of dismissal, and no right to claim interim relief, except in the special case of victimisation on health and safety grounds or, in a case of disclosure through or by a union, where the dismissal or victimisation can be said to be on the ground of engaging in trade union activity.

---

[15] Also considered at para. 12–09.
[16] ERA, s. 122(2),123(6).

CHAPTER 12

Defamation

12–01 The whistleblower may find himself at the receiving end of a claim for defamation as well as disciplinary action. The general law of defamation is beyond the scope of this book but here we deal with those features of the law which are most relevant to the whistleblower. Truth is generally an absolute defence to an action for defamation, but the onus of proof is on the whistleblower which may be a difficult burden to discharge. The defence most likely to be relied upon by the whistleblower will instead be that of qualified privilege.

QUALIFIED PRIVILEGE

The three stage test

12–02 If a statement is published in circumstances of qualified privilege this will provide a defence even though the statement is defamatory and untrue, unless the person making the statement was actuated by malice. The leading case is now the Court of Appeal decision in *Reynolds v. Times Newspapers Ltd* [1998] 3 All E.R. 961 (which was affirmed and developed in *Gaddafi v. Telegraph Group* (unreported, October 28, 1998, (CA)). The Court of Appeal set out the following tests, each of which must be satisfied:[1]

(a) whether the publisher was under a legal, moral or social duty to those to whom the material was published (the duty test);

(b) whether those to whom the material was published had an interest to receive the material (the interest test);

(c) whether the nature, status and source of the material, and the circumstances of the publication should, in the public interest, be protected in the absence of proof of express malice (the circumstantial test).

The duty and interest tests

12–03 As under the Public Interest Disclosure Act, the identity of the recipient of the disclosure will be a very important consideration as a result of the duty test and the interest test. In some cases of first level disclosure there may be a legal duty to make the disclosure—either to an appropriate regulatory body or to the employer

---

[1] See also *Loveless v. Earl* [1999] E.M.L.R. 530 where the Court of Appeal, in addition to requiring a common and corresponding interest, applied a test of whether the publication was "warranted by any reasonable occasion or exigency". This test was satisfied because the letters which were alleged to be defamatory were akin to references from an employer to a prospective new employer and as such were "clearly capable" of being so warranted.

(see Chapter 9). Even if there is no legal duty, an employee may be under a moral or social duty to blow the whistle. As to whether there is a social or moral duty, the test enunciated in *Stuart v. Bell* [1891] 2 Q.B. 341 by Lindley L.J. (at 350) was:

"Would the great mass of right minded men in the position of the defendant have considered it their duty under the circumstances to make the communication?"

In many cases the legal, moral or social duty will arise out of the whistleblower's position as an employee. In particular, the whistleblower may be able to rely on the dictum of Blackburn J. in *Davies v. Snead* (1870) L.R. 5 Q.B. 608 at 611 that the requisite duty arises:

"[w]here a person is so situated that it becomes right in the interest of society that he should tell to a third person certain facts".

It is not sufficient that the whistleblower *genuinely believes* that the person to whom the disclosure is made had the requisite interest. In general, the recipient must in fact have the requisite interest.[2] However despite the general requirement for reciprocity between the duty to make the disclosure and the interest in receiving the information, the publication may be privileged if made in the ordinary course of business or if it is otherwise reasonably necessary or if it is the only effective way of discharging a duty or protecting an interest.[3]

In relation to disclosure to the employer or to another employee in a supervisory position, the whistleblower will almost always be able to rely on the principle that there is a common interest as between employees in a business and between employees and the employer in the success of the business and the way it is carried on.[4] Similarly in most cases the common interest or duty is likely to be equally apparent in relation to other first level disclosures such as disclosure to an appropriate regulatory authority or disclosure to a trade union in order to obtain advice.

In relation to second level disclosures, the whistleblower may benefit from a more liberal approach to the duty and interest tests following the decision in *Reynolds*. The Court of Appeal (at 1004E–F) expressed the view, in the context of disclosures by the media, that the duty test and the interest test should be more readily satisfied in modern conditions. This was explained on the basis of the duty on the media to inform the public and engage in discussion on matters of public interest and the corresponding interest of the public which is more than prurience in receiving this information. It may be however that the reasoning would also apply to disclosure by a whistleblower to the media of matters of public concern.

The circumstantial test

12–04   Whilst the duty and interest tests are to be taken to be rather more readily satisfied than previously, the Court of Appeal in *Reynolds* emphasised that it would

---

[2] *Hebditch v. MacIlwaine* [1894] 2 Q.B. 54 (CA); but see the qualifications suggested in *Gatley, Libel and Slander* (9th ed., 1998) para. 14.13 at pp.337–338.
[3] *Edmondson v. Birch* [1907] 1 K.B. 371 at 380; *Pullman v. Hill* [1891] 1 Q.B. 524; *R. v. Lancs C.C. Police Authority, ex p. Hook* [1980] Q.B. 603 at 615; *Gatley, Libel and Slander, op. cit.* paras 14.68–14.78 at pp. 381–390.
[4] *Bryanston Finance v. De Vries* [1975] Q.B. 703 (CA); *Hunt v. G.N.Ry* [1891] Q.B. 189; *Gatley, Libel and Slander, op. cit.* para. 14.45 at pp. 361–362.

still be necessary to satisfy the circumstantial test. The Court of Appeal also questioned whether this test was in practice very different from the requirement in Australia that the publication must be reasonable in all the circumstances of the case. Relevant considerations will include the reliability of the source and the extent to which the information has been verified especially where there is a very wide disclosure.[5] As in other contexts the reliability of the source is likely to be less important where there is a narrower disclosure, such as to a regulatory body with a proper interest in receiving the information. This is likely to change in the House of Lords—in *Gadaffi*, for example, the Court of Appeal recognised that sources cannot always be disclosed.

In *Reynolds*, which concerned a newspaper article on the circumstances of the fall of the former Irish Prime Minister, the duty and interest tests were satisfied but not the circumstantial test. This was because particular allegations against Mr Reynolds of lying had been made without (apparently) sufficient support for them. A retrial was ordered because of defects in the judge's direction of the jury in this respect.

The circumstantial test, at least in so far as it is applied to disclosure by the news media, has however been significantly weakened by the decision of the Court of Appeal in *Gaddafi*. In that case, it was held that the defendant who sought to assert qualified privilege did not have to disclose the source of the defamatory material that was the basis of the allegations. The claimant in *Gaddafi* protested that (i) without knowing the source of the information, it would be extremely difficult for the Court to determine whether the circumstantial test had been satisfied and (ii) it would consequently be impossible for the claimant's legal advisors to advise their client on the defendant's prospects of successfully defending the action. Despite this the Court held that the very limited information which had been provided by the claimant would suffice.

Public Officials

12–05   A particularly liberal approach to the defence of qualified privilege has been adopted where the purportedly defamatory statement consists of a complaint against a person in authority or with responsibilities to the public, provided that the complaint is made bona fide to a person with a proper interest in the subject matter.[6] The liberal approach is illustrated by the following examples:

(a) A member of the public may make a complaint before a local authority for investigation even though the report constitutes a libel (*Couper v. Lord Balfour of Burleigh* 1913 S.C. 492).

(b) A police surgeon was able to rely on the privilege when in consequence of an incorrect diagnosis he made an unfounded allegation to his superior officer to the effect that the constable had contracted venereal disease (*A v. B* 1907 S.C. 1154).

(c) In the old case of *Purcell v. Sowler* [1891] 1 Q.B. 474 charges of misconduct against a poor law official were not to be broadcast through the press although it would have been privileged had they been properly laid before the appropriate local authority.

---

[5] *Reynolds* at 995B–D.
[6] *Blagg v. Sturt* (1846) 10 Q.B.D. 899.

Malice

12–06   The defence of qualified privilege can be defeated by malice. The person making the disclosure will have acted maliciously:

> "(a) If he actually knew that what he was publishing was untrue.
>
> (b) If he was reckless as to the truth of what he was publishing and did not consider or care whether what he was publishing was true or not.
>
> (c) If the publisher used the privileged occasion not in order to perform some relevant duty but to give vent to personal spite or ill will towards the person defamed."[7]

As such if the dominant purpose is not to inform but is to injure the claimant, the defence is not available. The fact that the defendant did not believe that what he said was true is usually conclusive evidence of malice to rebut qualified privilege. The use of excessive language in the circumstances of the case may be itself evidence of malice but there must be something so extreme in the words used to afford evidence that the publication was actuated by malice. Although recklessness will suffice, it is not, however, sufficient for the claimant to show that the defendant was careless, impulsive or irrational in arriving at his belief or that he was improvident, credulous or stupid.[8] If the defendant honestly believed a statement to be true, he does not lose the protection because he had no reasonable grounds for so believing.

Further, it is important to distinguish between the objective test which is applied for ascertaining the meaning of what has been published and the subjective test for malice. It may be that, applying the objective test, the words published have a defamatory meaning and that the defendant had no honest belief in the truth of that meaning. However there will still be no malice if the defendant had an honest belief that the words had a different meaning which was honestly believed to be true.[9]

DEFAMATION AND EMPLOYMENT RIGHTS

12–07   In two recent cases the courts have explored the relationship between principles applicable to defamation and rights under a contract of employment.

Qualified privilege

12–08   In *Halpin v. Oxford Brookes University* (unreported, November 30, 1995) an attempt was made, unsuccessfully, to exclude the qualified privilege defence on the basis that the publication was made in breach of the contract of employment. Mr Halpin was a senior lecturer in law in the University's Business School. He complained that he had been defamed by an internal memorandum circulated by Professor Watkins, the head of the Business School which was said to be critical of his performance. Professor Watkins plainly had an interest or duty in relation to Mr Halpin's performance and the memorandum was circulated to others

---

[7] *per* Neill L.J. in *Halpin v. Oxford Brookes University* (unreported, November 30, 1995) (CA).
[8] *Horrocks v. Lowe* [1975] A.C. 135 (HL) at 1500.
[9] *Loveless v. Earl* [1999] E.M.L.R. 530, CA.

who a corresponding duty or interest to receive the information. It was argued, however, that circulation of the criticisms without allowing Mr Halpin to comment on them was a breach of the disciplinary procedure and constituted a repudiatory breach of Mr Halpin's contract of employment. As such, it was argued that since the communication was in breach of contract there could be no defence of qualified privilege. The Court of Appeal rejected this and, in doing so, emphasised the importance of employees being able to raise internally matters of concern to the employing organisation. As Neill L.J. explained:

> "it remains an important public interest that people should be able to communicate freely and frankly on matters of mutual concern. It seems to me to be beyond argument therefore that managers in large organisations must be free to have free and frank discussions on all matters relating to the organisation in which the parties to the discussion have a proper mutual interest. The protection of the individual who may be defamed is that the privilege to communicate is qualified privilege only. It can be destroyed by malice. But I cannot accept that a manager can be prevented from expressing an honest and relevant opinion merely by reason of the fact that the matter or person discussed might have been dealt with in some other way."

We would suggest that the reasoning in *Halpin* should apply equally to a disclosure made without following a whistleblowing procedure. However the decision in *Halpin* preceded the enunciation of the circumstantial test in *Reynolds* and it might yet be argued, therefore, that a failure to follow a whistleblowing procedure or other recognised procedure for raising complaints should be a relevant consideration when applying the circumstantial test.

Consent

12–09   While a breach of the contract of employment does not exclude the defence of qualified privilege, the terms of the employment contract may be a foundation to a defence of consent. A claimant's claim will be defeated in a libel action if the defendant can prove that the claimant consented to the publication of the words complained of. Although the consent may be express or implied by conduct, proof of consent must be clear and unequivocal. The words complained of must be substantially the same as those to which the claimant consented. Malice will then not be relevant.

Friend v. CAA [1998] I.R.L.R. 253[10] concerned an employee of the Civil Aviation Authority who saw himself in the role of whistleblower. He had very strong views about the constitution of inspection teams set up to investigate whether safety standards on helicopters had been complied with. As a result of expressing those views he incurred the displeasure of his colleagues. A number of senior employees wrote memoranda which were highly critical of Captain Friend's conduct including the suggestion that he was rude and discourteous to those colleagues. This formed the basis of formal disciplinary proceedings against Captain Friend. When these had concluded he issued writs claiming damages for defamation in respect of the republication of the allegations against him in the disciplinary procedure. The CAA defended

---

[10] See also para. 11–08 above.

the claim on the ground that he had consented to the republication since the disciplinary procedure was part of his contractual terms. The Court of Appeal upheld this plea and struck out the writ. The essential purpose of the disciplinary procedure, they decided, was to conduct a fair inquiry into an accusation or complaint against the employee and that inevitably required that the accusation or complaint be republished at the various stages of the disciplinary process. Captain Friend was held to have consented to the allegations being republished by accepting the terms of employment including the disciplinary code. The employers were entitled to rely on the defence of *volenti non fit iniuria*. This would not however apply to the initial allegations made prior to the disciplinary process and the authors of those allegations would have only been able to rely on the defence of qualified privilege.

DEFAMATION AND THE PUBLIC INTEREST DISCLOSURE ACT

12–10   The Public Interest Disclosure Act does not provide specific protection against proceedings for defamation being brought against a whistleblower. If such proceedings were to be brought by the employer this might be regarded as subjecting the worker to a detriment within section 47B of the ERA. However nothing in the 1998 Act would cover proceedings brought by another employee or a third party who claimed to have been defamed. It would however be contrary to the underlying policy of the Act if a worker could be the subject of defamation proceedings despite having made a protected disclosure. We think that a worker who makes a protected disclosure would inevitably also succeed in a defence of qualified privilege in relation to that disclosure, especially as the structure of the 1998 Act fits comfortably with the threefold test for qualified privilege unless the defamatory remark was not central to the primary disclosure.

It might also be argued that when a court comes to apply the circumstantial test enunciated in *Reynolds* in a whistleblowing case, it should have regard to the criteria set out in the 1998 Act and should be inclined to find that the circumstantial test is not satisfied if there would not have been a protected disclosure. Such an approach might be supported on the basis that the 1998 Act encapsulates a balance struck by Parliament between the public interest in encouraging disclosure of matters of public concern and the public interest of the employer and those about whom the allegations are made. However whilst the 1998 Act might provide a useful guide as to some relevant considerations, we would suggest that it does not follow that merely because there would not be a protected disclosure the circumstantial test should not be satisfied. The 1998 Act provides a floor of rights for the whistleblower. Even within the employment context it does not purport to set out comprehensive limits upon when an employer can take action against a whistleblower. As we have seen even if there is no protected disclosure an employee may be able to rely upon the general unfair dismissal protection. Equally it does not follow that merely because a worker would not have been entitled to the higher level of protection under the 1998 Act that a defence of qualified privilege should fail despite the duty and interest tests being satisfied.

CHAPTER 13

The European Convention of Human Rights

13–01   The Human Rights Act 1998 ("the HRA") received Royal Assent on November 9, 1998 but will not come into effect until October 2, 2000. Its purpose is to incorporate the substantive rights provided for by the European Convention on Human Rights ("the Convention") into domestic law. Under the HRA it will be necessary to have regard to the Convention and to Strasbourg caselaw in construing domestic legislation. The right to freedom of expression, contained in Article 10 of the Convention, is of obvious relevance in construing the rights contained in the Public Interest Disclosure Act 1998. It may also be of relevance in considering protection offered to whistleblowers who fall outside the protection of the Public Interest Disclosure Act 1998, such as the person who acts honestly but not on reasonable grounds in making disclosure other than to his employer or the whistleblower who discloses an exceptionally serious failure other than to the employer but is motivated by personal gain. In this Chapter we therefore consider the principal provisions of the HRA and relevant Convention case law bearing upon the protection of whistleblowers.

THE HUMAN RIGHTS ACT 1998[1]

13–02   The HRA contains the following key elements:

Strasbourg caselaw

13–03   When a court or tribunal is determining a question "in connection with" a right under the Convention (such as the scope of protection for a whistleblower) it must, insofar as considered to be relevant, take into account relevant Strasbourg case law.[2] By way of example, Article 10 of the Convention will be relevant wherever an Employment Tribunal considers whether a whistleblower has been unfairly dismissed. The principal sources of authority will be judgments, decisions or declaratory or advisory opinions of the European Court of Human Rights ("ECHR"). A further relevant source of authority will be the decisions reached by the European Commission of Human Rights ("the Commission") as to admissibility and its opinions in which it stated its view, upon consideration of a petition, as

---

[1] This chapter largely draws upon an article by J.Bowers and J. Lewis, "Whistleblowing: Freedom and Expression in the Workplace" [1996] 6 E.H.R.R. 637. For a review of the effect of the Convention on United Kingdom employment law see Mr Justice Lightman and J. Bowers Q.C., *Incorporation of the ECHR and its Impact on Employment Law* [1998] 5 E.H.R.R. 1.
[2] section 2 of the Act.

120

whether there was a breach of the Convention, will continue to be a relevant source of authority. This is so notwithstanding that since November 1, 1998, pursuant to Protocol 11, the three-tier judicial system of Commission, Court and Committee of Ministers has been abolished and replaced by a single court exercising all judicial powers.

It will be for the court or tribunal to determine the weight to be given to any relevant authority. There is no strict doctrine of precedent under the Convention. However regard is generally taken of previous relevant decisions. Obviously a decision of the ECHR will carry greater weight than a decision of the Commission and recent decisions, which therefore reflect developments in the law, generally carry greater weight than an earlier decision of the same body.

Construction of primary legislation

13–04   Insofar as possible, primary and subordinate legislation, whether passed before or after the coming into force of the HRA, must be construed consistently with the rights under the Convention. This gives statutory effect to the approach which has developed at common law. As Lord Bridge explained in *R v. Secretary of State for the Home Department, ex p. Brind* [1991] 1 A.C. 696 at 747H–748A:

> "it is already well settled that, in construing any provision in domestic legislation which is ambiguous in the sense that it is capable of a meaning which either conforms to or conflicts with the Convention, the courts will presume that Parliament intended to legislate in conformity with the Convention, not in conflict with it."

Incompatibility between legislation and the Convention

13–05   Where subordinate legislation cannot be construed in a manner consistent with the Convention, the relevant provisions of the subordinate legislation can be disapplied if the originating primary legislation does not prevent this (section 3 of the HRA). However a court or tribunal cannot disapply primary legislation requiring it to act inconsistently with a Convention right or incompatible subordinate legislation where removal of the incompatibility would be inconsistent with primary legislation (section 6(2) of the HRA). Instead certain courts (including the High Court, County Court and House of Lords) can make a "declaration of incompatibility" (section 4). It will then be possible by an accelerated procedure for a ministerial remedial order to be made provided that all appeals have been determined or abandoned or the time for appealing has expired (section 10). Whilst other courts or tribunals (such as the county court or Employment Appeal Tribunal) can highlight the incompatibility in their judgment, they cannot make a declaration of incompatibility.

A declaration of incompatibility will not automatically affect the rights of the parties in the action in which it is made. However a minister has power to give retrospective to the remedial order. It is likely that effect would be given to this on appeal. It may be however that a court making the declaration of incompatibility would be prepared to grant a stay in order to see whether a retrospective remedial order is made to which effect can then be given in the action.[3]

---

[3] This is the course posited by Mr. Justice Lightman and John Bowers Q.C. [1998] 5 E.H.R.R.

Public authorities

13–06   Where a "public authority" acts in a way incompatible with a Convention right (or fails to act in a way compatible with the right), a "victim" can bring infringement proceedings (section 6(1),7(1) of the HRA). A court which finds that there has been a breach of the Convention can grant such relief or remedy within its jurisdiction as it considers "just and appropriate". However no award of damages can be made unless the court is satisfied that this is necessary to afford just satisfaction to the victim.

The HRA contains a wide ranging definition of a public body as including a court or tribunal and any person whose functions include "functions of a public nature". However section 6(5) of the HRA provides that in relation to any particular act, a person is not a public authority by virtue of having functions of a public nature if the nature of the act is private. It is likely that in construing these provisions the approach to identifying whether a decision of a body is susceptible to judicial review will be adopted in determining whether a public body is acting in a private or a public capacity. In the judicial review context there is a substantial body of case law as to whether a body is to be regarded as a public body acting in its public capacity. Principally regard is had to whether there is a sufficient statutory underpinning and to the substance and effect of the function being discharged.[4]

The effect of this approach may be substantially to reduce the effect of the HRA in the employment field. There may be a public law claim where the act of the employer can be regarded as having a public law element, for example, there has been a failure to follow a disciplinary procedure established by statute.[5] However ordinarily, a personal claim by an employee or officer of a public body against the employer is a matter of private law.[6] An employee who is victimised for exercising a Convention right would therefore not be able to bring a claim under section 6 of the HRA, although there may be other remedies, especially construing these in the light of the Convention. The exclusion of a direct claim under section 6 sits uneasily with the approach of the ECHR. It has been emphasised by the ECHR that the obligation upon the State to secure compliance with the Convention applies whether or not the State is exercising a public power and that the obligations under the Convention apply to the "State as employer" whether the State's relations with its employees are governed by public or private law.[7]

Freedom of expression

13–07   In addition to the general provisions in the HRA in relation to rights under the Convention, the importance placed upon the principle of freedom of expression is emphasised by the fact that section 12 makes specific provision for cases where the court is considering whether to grant any relief which might affect the exercise of the Convention right to freedom of expression. In particular:

---

[4] *R. v. Panel on Takeovers and Mergers, ex p. Datafin Plc* [1987] Q.B. 815; Fordham, *Judicial Review Handbook* (2nd ed., 1997) para. 34 at 389–400.
[5] *McClaren v. Home Office* [1990] I.C.R. 824 (CA), *per* Lord Woolf at 836F–837A.
[6] See *R v. East Berkshire Health Authority, ex p. Walsh* [1984] I.C.R. 743 (CA); *R. v. Derbyshire C.C. ex p. Noble* [1990] I.C.R. 808 (CA); *McClaren v. Home Office* [1990] I.C.R. 824 (CA), *per* Lord Woolf at 836; *R. v. Secretary of State, ex p. Prior* [1994] E.L.R. 231 at 240.
[7] *Swedish Engine Drivers' Union v. Sweden* (1976) 1 E.H.R.R. 617 paras 36, 37; *Schmidt and Dahlstrom v. Sweden* (1976) 1 E.H.R.R. 632, paras 32, 33.

(a) The court must have "particular regard to the importance of" that right (section 12(4)).

(b) Where the person against whom the relief is sought is not present, no relief can be granted unless the applicant has taken all practicable steps to notify that person or there is a compelling reason why that person should not be notified (section 12(2)).

(c) No relief is to be granted to restrain publication before trial unless the court is satisfied that the application is likely to succeed at trial in establishing that publication should not be allowed (section 12(3)). It will therefore not be possible to proceed to consider the balance of convenience in relation to restraining publication merely on the basis of establishing a serious issue to be tried in accordance with the test in *American Cyanamid v. Ethicon Limited* [1975] A.C. 396 (HL).

(d) Where the proceedings relate to material which the respondent claims or which appear to the court to be journalistic, literary or artistic material, or conduct connected with such material, the court must have regard to any privacy code and to the extent to which the material has or is about to become available to the public or the extent to which it is in the public interest for the material to be published (section 12(4)).

ARTICLE 10 OF THE EUROPEAN CONVENTION

13–08   The principal instrument offered by the European Convention for the protection of the whistleblower is the presumption in favour of freedom of expression contained in Article 10 of the Convention. This proclaims that "everyone has the right to freedom of expression". However Article 10(2) expressly recognises that competing interests may arise. It provides that:

"The exercise of [freedom of expression] since it carries with it duties and responsibilities, may be subject to such formalities, conditions, restrictions or penalties as are prescribed by law and are necessary in a democratic society, in the interests of national security, . . . for the protection of the reputation or rights of others, for preventing the disclosure of information received in confidence. . . ."

The scheme of Article 10 therefore is to give primary emphasis to the right to freedom of expression but also to recognise that the scope of free expression may be confined by reference to the "duties and responsibilities" of those claiming the right. Nevertheless the starting point is the principle of free expression and it is for the person seeking to interfere with this to justify the interference.

Article 10 and whistleblowers

13–09   There is scant authority in the Strasbourg case law directly addressing the position of the whistleblower, in the sense of an employee who reports a matter of concern in relation to his current employer or employment. However guidance as to the likely approach of the courts can be gathered from the approach in related areas such as cases involving criticism of an ex-employer (*e.g. Jackubowski v. Germany*

[1994] E.H.R.R. 64)) or where the employer restricts the right of the employee to advocate a political view (*e.g. Glasenapp v. Germany* (1986) 9 E.H.R.R. 25) or to speak out in relation to matters unrelated to the employer (*X v. U.K.* (1979) 16 D & R 101).

Does the right to freedom of expression extend to the workplace?

13–10   Notwithstanding the scheme of Article 10, until recently the case law of the ECHR suggested that the right to free expression might have only a very limited application in the workplace. Both *Kosiek v. Germany* (1986) 9 E.H.R.R. 328 and *Glasenapp v. Germany* (above)involved the dismissal of teachers who held the status of probationary civil servant. Rolf Kosiek, a physics lecturer, was an active member of the extreme right wing German National Democratic Party (NPD). It was a condition for appointment and for continued employment in the civil service that he should abide by his obligation of loyalty and allegiance to the Constitution. He was dismissed because of the inconsistency between his political activities and writings and this duty of loyalty. The ECHR held that the dismissal did not constitute an interference with the right to freedom of expression. Instead it was held that Kosiek had been refused access to the civil service because he lacked one of the "personal qualifications" for the post in question, namely the ability to give the requisite oath of loyalty. That Kosiek had been refused tenure precisely due to the expression of his opinions was put to one side. By parity of reasoning, whilst to some extent different considerations might apply where a whistleblower seeks to reveal wrongdoing, an employer might argue that a whistleblower had been dismissed because in speaking out he had caused a breakdown of trust and confidence and thereby showed himself to be unfit for continued employment.

Such an approach conflicts with the caselaw of the ECHR which has recognised that sanctions imposed *after* publication can have a chilling effect and therefore interfere with freedom of expression.[8] More recently, however, in the important case of *Vogt v. Germany* [1996] 21 E.H.R.R. 205 the ECHR has sought to limit the application of the reasoning in *Kosiek* so that it would apply, at most, to conditions laid down for access to employment. Dorothea Vogt taught German and French at secondary school level. She was appointed as a permanent civil servant in February 1979 notwithstanding that the authorities were aware at that time that she was a member of the DKP (the German Communist Party). However disciplinary proceedings were commenced against her in July 1982 on the grounds that she had failed to comply with her duty of political loyalty as a result of her activities with the DKP since August 1980. She was dismissed in October 1987 on the grounds that by associating herself with the DKP she had betrayed the relationship of trust between herself and her employer. The majority of the ECHR held that this constituted interference with Ms Vogt's free speech rights as were protected by Article 10 of the Convention. The imposition of a disciplinary penalty in Ms Vogt's case was contrasted with the refusal to permit access to the civil service in *Kosiek* and *Glasenapp*. This distinction was not convincingly explained since in each case disciplinary action had resulted from the exercise of the right to free speech. It may be therefore that (as indeed was

---

[8] See *Thorgeirson v. Iceland* (1992) 14 E.H.R.R. 843 at para. 68 (conviction capable of discouraging discussion of police brutality—being a matter of public concern); *Barthold v. Germany* (1985) 7 E.H.R.R. 383, *Lingens v. Austria* (1986) 8 E.H.R.R. 407.

acknowledged by Judge Jambrek in *Vogt*) in truth the majority decision in *Vogt* was the product of a change in judicial policy.

In any event the gist of the decision in *Vogt* was a recognition that free speech rights are not given up when entering the workplace. A similar approach was taken by the Privy Council in *De Freitas v. Ministry of Agriculture* (1998) 4 BHRC 563. Relying on *Vogt* the Privy Council held that a provision in Bermuda and Antigua which prohibited civil servants from publishing information or expressions of opinion on matters of national or international controversy was unconstitutional due to the breach of free expression rights. The blanket restraint was held to be too wide, especially as it applied to all civil servants irrespective of how junior. The effect of this approach is that the whistleblower will at least be regarded as exercising a free speech right, albeit that it may then be necessary to address the matters raised within Article 10(2) of the Convention. Consideration of these issues cannot be evaded merely by referring to the need for the maintenance of trust and confidence as a qualification for continued employment.

Justification of interference

13–11   Once there has been shown to be an interference with freedom of expression the onus shifts to the State to justify the interference within Article 10(2). Essentially this involves consideration of three matters. Firstly the interference must be prescribed by law. Secondly it must be shown that the interference was in pursuance of a legitimate aim. If so it must still be established that the interference was "necessary in a democratic society".

Prescribed by law

13–12   Establishing that the restriction is prescribed by law has rarely been a difficulty. Even in cases where there may have been considerable doubt as to the proper construction of the law, the ECHR has generally been willing to accept that it is for the national authorities to interpret and apply domestic law.[9] Nor does a matter cease to be prescribed by law merely because a wide discretion is left to the judiciary provided that the scope of the discretion and the manner of its exercise are indicated with sufficient clarity.[10] In *Goodwin v. United Kingdom* [1996] 22 E.H.R.R. 123 (at 139–141) the ECHR applied this principle in finding that the possibility of a journalist being required to disclose his sources was sufficiently prescribed by law even though the Court had to carry out a balancing exercise between competing public interests and had to be satisfied that disclosure was "in the interests of justice".

Legitimate aim

13–13   Article 10(2) sets out the legitimate aims in pursuance of which Article 10(1) rights can be restricted. In practice this has not been a substantial hurdle of itself but, instead, has acted as an impetus to encourage states to identify the reasons for restrictions and as a reference point against which to consider whether the restriction is indeed necessary. There has in fact been no case where an infringement of Article 10 has been held to be unjustified merely because a legitimate aim was not pursued.

---

[9] See *e.g. Thorgeirson* at para. 58.
[10] *Goodwin v. United Kingdom* [1996] 22 E.H.R.R. 123 at 140, para. 31.

The most significant of the legitimate aims in the context of employees is the protection of the reputation and the rights of others and the prevention of the disclosure of information received in confidence. In most circumstances, other than the case where the employer acts in bad faith or imposes restrictions which have no rational relationship to the employment, a restriction of employee expression could be brought within one or both of these aims, albeit that it may not be possible for an employer to show the *necessity* for the restriction.

In many cases where the restriction on freedom of expression relates to whistleblowing it would appear likely that the restriction on expression could be said to be aimed at protecting the rights of employers. In *B v. United Kingdom* (1985) 45 D & R 41 a civil servant, who was also a local politician, participated in a television programme concerning safety at the atomic weapons research establishment at Aldermaston where he worked. The civil servant had been refused permission to speak on the programme and he received a severe reprimand which he challenged as being in breach of Article 10(1). The Commission found that there was an interference with free expression but that this was justified in order to protect the rights of the employers. Similar reasoning would apply in most whistleblowing cases since an employee would rarely have permission to criticise the employer, albeit that in the particular circumstances protection of the employer's rights may not justify the interference. Indeed interference need not even be for the purpose of protecting legally recognised rights. In *X v. U.K.* (1979) 16 D & R 101 the Commission was prepared to accept that protecting fellow members of teaching staff from being offended by a colleague's evangelical posters and stickers fell within the meaning of "protecting the rights of others". Thus the Commission was prepared to accept that there is a legitimate interest in protecting the rights of others not to be offended by speech.

Equally where the employee is involved in raising concerns about the employer, the imposition of a sanction might be regarded as being effected on the basis of protecting the employer's reputation. In *Morissens v. Belgium* (1988) 56 D & R 127 a Belgian teacher was dismissed after she had sought to highlight discrimination against homosexuals by complaining on Belgian television that she was not appointed as a head teacher because she was gay. The Commission held that the dismissal was in pursuance of the legitimate aim of the protection of the reputation of those whom she had implicitly suggested had refused to promote her on grounds of her homosexuality.

Even in cases which would not appear to fit neatly into any of the recognised categories of legitimate aim, such difficulties have been overcome by a flexible application of the legitimate aim test. In *Vogt*, for example, the insistence on political loyalty was imposed because, especially in the light of Germany's history, it was felt that there was a need for democracy to be able to defend itself and that the civil service was the guarantor of the constitution and democracy. On its face it is not apparent that defence of the constitution falls within any of the legitimate aims which can be pursued but the ECHR appears to have accepted the German Government's assertion that the restriction was aimed at protecting national security, preventing disorder and protecting the rights of others.

Necessary in a democratic society and the margin of appreciation

13–14 Since there will usually be a legitimate aim which can be said to be pursued by the interference with the whistleblower's freedom of expression, in almost every whistleblowing case the key issue for determination will be whether the legitimate aim in question (such as protecting the employers' right to fidelity or confidentiality or to protection of its reputation) justifies the interference with free expression. In each case this is to be resolved by enquiring as to whether the aim is "necessary" in a democratic society and the interpretation of this requirement and the evidential burden it imposes is therefore a matter of crucial importance to the whistleblower.

The ECHR has explained on several occasions (eg *Barthold v. Germany* at para. 55) that:

> "whilst the adjective 'necessary', within the meaning of Article 10(2) of the Convention, is not synonymous with 'indispensable', neither does it have the flexibility of such expressions as 'admissible', 'ordinary', 'useful', 'reasonable' or 'desirable'; rather, it implies a 'pressing social need'. The Contracting States enjoy a power of appreciation in this respect, but that power of appreciation goes hand in hand with a European supervision which is more or less extensive depending on the circumstances; it is for the Court to make the final determination as to whether the interference in issue corresponds to such a need, whether it is 'proportionate to the legitimate aim pursued' and whether the reasons given by the national authorities to justify it are 'relevant and sufficient'".

Thus it must be shown that the interference:

(a) corresponds to a "pressing social need";

(b) is proportionate to the aim pursued or, as it is sometimes put,[11] there is a reasonable relationship of proportionality between the legitimate aim pursued and the means deployed to achieve that aim; and

(c) is justified by reasons which are relevant and sufficient.

Further the ECHR has often emphasised that the exceptions contained in Article 10(2) are to be "narrowly interpreted" and must be "convincingly established".[12] Nevertheless while these general pronouncements require a particularly close scrutiny of any purported justification for interfering with free expression of the whistleblower, the case law of the Commission and Court is considerably less reassuring. In applying the test of necessity, especially as regards the scope of the margin of appreciation to be permitted, the ECHR and/or the Commission has had regard in particular to the following factors:

(a) whether the whistleblowing touches on matters of public concern;

(b) the duties and responsibilities of employment;

(c) the manner of expression;

(d) the extent to which the accusations made by the whistleblower are well-founded;

---

[11] *e.g.* Case 29183/95 *Fressoz and Roire v. France* (unreported, January 21, 1999), para. 56 (ECJ).

[12] See *Vogt v. Germany*; *Handyside v. The United Kingdom* (1976) 1 E.H.R.R. 737, para. 49; *Lingens v. Austria* (1986) 1 E.H.R.R. 407, para. 41; *Jersild v. Denmark* (1994) 19 E.H.R.R. 1, para. 31; *Goodwin v. United Kingdom* [1996] 22 E.H.R.R. 123, para. 40.

(e) the channel of communication used by the whistleblower;

(f) the nature of the employment;

(g) whether the sanction is imposed by the State.

It is pertinent therefore to consider in turn how the application of these factors has been applied and has influenced, or is likely to influence, the degree of protection afforded to the whistleblower.

(1) Does the whistleblower raise matters of public concern?

13–15 In seeking to rely upon Article 10 to broaden the protection of the Public Interest Disclosure Act, it will be in the interest of the whistleblower to emphasise that the matters raised are of public concern. In *Thorgeirson v. Iceland* (a non-employment case) the applicant made claims of police brutality. The Icelandic Government contended in response for a distinction between political discussion in which freedom of expression should have full rein and "discussion of other matters of public concern" in which expression could be restricted. This would potentially have provided a severe constraint on the freedom of the whistleblower. However the ECHR expressly rejected the proposition that the wide limits of acceptable criticism in political discussion do not apply equally to other matters of public concern. Equally the margin of appreciation for the State in interfering with free expression was correspondingly narrower in cases of political speech, and speech in relation to matters of public concern, than in other cases.

A similar approach was taken in *Barthold v. Germany* (1985) 7 E.H.R.R. 383 where the applicant was quoted in a newspaper interview as being critical of the absence of emergency veterinary services at night. Proceedings were brought on the basis that this infringed professional guidelines restricting advertising. Injunctions were issued under Germany's competition laws restraining the applicant from reporting to the press (except in professional journals) the difficulties in relation to the night service and the problems experienced by his own practice. The ECHR held that although this interference with expression was in pursuit of the legitimate aim of the protection of rights of other vets, it was not necessary in a democratic society. The newspaper article had sought to inform the public about the situation in Hamburg in respect of veterinary services at a time when new legislation was being considered. While the illustrations given by the applicant might have had the effect of publicising his own veterinary practise, the ECHR considered that this was secondary to the raising of a matter of public concern. The ECHR specifically expressed concern that if, as the German court had decided, an injunction could be imposed merely on the basis of an intention to act for a commercial motive, this could have a chilling effect in discouraging others from contributing to public debate.

Where a whistleblower seeks to raise issues of concern as to the management of his employer, there may well be a question as to whether in the circumstances this raises issues of public concern. Some assistance in relation to this might be derived from the recent decision of the ECJ in *Fressoz and Roire v. France*.[13] The weekly satirical newspaper *Le Canard Enchaine* published an article referring to salary increases awarded to Mr Jacques Calvet who was Peugeot's chairman and managing director.

---

[13] Case 29183/95, unreported, January 21, 1999.

The article was accompanied by extracts from Mr Calvet's tax assessments. The tax assessments could only have been obtained by virtue of disclosure in breach of confidence by a tax official, albeit that the identity of that tax official could not be identified. The journalist who reported the story and the editor of *Le Canard Enchaine* were convicted of handling the stolen photocopies. They then claimed that this was a breach of Article 10 of the Convention. In upholding this complaint, the ECHR noted that the article related to a matter of public concern in that it was published during a industrial dispute at Peugeot over pay and showed that the company chairman had received large pay increases whilst opposing the employees' pay claims. The ECHR rejected the argument advanced by the French Government that the disclosure of the remuneration of one person, even if he was the head of a major private company, did not contribute to debate on a matter of public interest and that the particular situation at Peugeot was too specific to be a matter of public interest.

The approach of the Court in *Fressoz* suggests that, at least in relation to employers that are substantial undertakings, a narrow argument to the effect that employment disputes raise matters of only private concern are unlikely to be successful. However the ECHR also emphasised that although the publication of tax assessments was prohibited, the information which they contained was not confidential and that it was particularly important to protect the entitlement of the press to impart information and ideas on matters of public interest. The Court was not called upon to consider the position of the unidentified tax official who had disclosed the tax assessments to the press.

(2) Duties and responsibilities

13–16 It may well be that a more restrictive approach would be taken where the disclosure is by an employee, especially if made otherwise than to the employer. Both the Commission and the ECHR have emphasised the duties and responsibilities involved in freedom of expression and it has been recognised that such duties and responsibilities require restrictions on the employee's freedom of expression. Thus in *Morissens v. Belgium* (1988) D & R 56, where a teacher made accusations of discrimination by her employers, the Commission noted that the applicant had accepted a responsible post in the provincial education service and that she had therefore accepted certain restrictions on the exercise of her freedom of expression as being inherent in her duties. Having regard to her professional responsibilities, the suspension of the applicant without pay was reasonably justified for the protection of the reputation of the teaching establishment where she worked and the reputation of her superiors.

Nevertheless reference to an employee's duties and responsibilities is unlikely to be decisive. Employees do assume duties of fidelity to the employer but the issue for the Court and Commission is how the tension between such duties and the norm of free speech is to be resolved. In *Morissens*, for example, the Commission also emphasised that the teacher had chosen to make her accusations on television without providing any proof for her claims. Nor was there any suggestion that she had previously raised these matters internally.

(3) Manner of the expression

13–17 One manifestation of the weight given to the duties and responsibilities of employment, perhaps unsurprisingly in the light of the need for a continuing

workable relationship between employer and employee, is in relation to the significance attached to the way in which the whistleblower criticises the employer.

In non-whistleblowing cases where matters of public concern have been raised, a
measure of intemperate speech has been accepted. In *Thorgeirson*, where a non-
employee made allegations of police brutality, the Government argued that even if
there was a factual basis for the allegations of police brutality the applicant had over-
stepped the reasonable limits of criticism by using malicious, insulting and vituper-
ative language in condemning the police and in calling them "beasts in uniform". In
rejecting this argument the ECHR conceded that the articles written by the applicant
were framed in particularly strong terms but denied that this could be regarded as
excessive in the light of the matters of public concern which they raised and the
impact which they were designed to have.

The approach in *Thorgeirson* may be contrasted with two whistleblowing cases,
one concerning a public health service employee and the other concerning a police
officer. In both these cases, although the applicant claimed to be raising matters of
serious public concern, the Commission was not prepared to investigate further into
this because of the intemperate way in which the applicants had criticised their
employers. In *Tucht v. FRG* 9336/81 (unreported) the applicant was dismissed from
his position as a specialist in mental and lung diseases in a regional public health
service in Germany. After being refused promotion he sent numerous letters to his
superiors heavily criticising their attitude and the organisation and working of the
regional public health service. These letters were copied to the regional parliament,
trade unions, professional associations, colleagues and political parties. After many
warnings he was dismissed from the civil service for various disciplinary offences.
These included insulting his employees, publicising abusive criticisms and communicating confidential information to third parties. He claimed that this interference was
unjustified on the basis that he was merely exercising his right freely to criticise the
"System". The Commission however accepted that the applicant was dismissed not
because of the fact that he was criticising his superiors but by reason of the abusive
and offensive form that this criticism had taken. Having regard to the duties and
responsibilities which his position carried, the interference with the applicant's
freedom of expression was held to be necessary for the protection of the rights of
others by preventing the disclosure of information received in confidence and by protecting the reputation of others. Indeed on this basis the Commission found the
application to be inadmissible without having regard to the detail of the criticisms
made by the applicant and, apparently, without considering whether the criticisms
were such as could provide a valuable contribution to the effective working of the
"System" (in the form of the regional public health service).

A similar approach was adopted by the Commission in *De Jong v. The Netherlands*
10280/83 (unpublished). In that case a police officer complained that he had been
transferred and then honourably discharged from the police on the grounds of the
opinions which he had expressed. The applicant, who was a former chief sergeant of
the Dutch national police, had strongly criticised persons, policies and situations
within both the police and the judiciary. He had done so both privately and publicly.
The Commission held that the applicant had been dismissed not because of the fact
that he was criticising his superiors but due to the abusive and offensive form the criticism had taken. As in *Tucht* it was held that having regard to the duties and
responsibilities which his position carried the interference with his freedom of expression rights was necessary for the protection of the reputation and rights of others and

for preventing disclosure of information received in confidence. Again the Commission appears to have found that the application was inadmissible without giving any weight to the value of such criticisms to public debate. Indeed the Commission was prepared to accept that the criticisms must have been confidential merely because the applicant was able to voice them only by virtue of the experience gained in his employment irrespective of whether the information disclosed was already in the public domain. Certainly the Commission's decision on admissibility does not disclose whether any attempt was made to identify what if any information was confidential.

This approach may be significant in construing the scope of the protection offered by the Public Interest Disclosure Act against victimisation of the whistleblower. The Act provides that a worker shall not be subjected to a detriment "on the ground that the worker has made a protected disclosure" (section 47B(1) of the ERA 1996). On its face this leaves open the possibility that an employer might argue that a worker has been disciplined not by reason of what the whistleblower said but by reason of the manner in which it was said. It is likely that, rather than allow the scope of the protection to be whittled away by such an argument, tribunals will adopt an approach similar to that applied in relation to victimisation of health and safety representatives or trade union officials. In that context the courts have refused to uphold the employer's claim that victimisation was due to the manner in which the safety representative or trade union official carried out their activities rather than the activities themselves, albeit that there might be some cases where the conduct was so extraneous, malicious or unreasonable as to fall outside the scope of the protection: *Goodwin v. Cabletel U.K. Limited* [1997] I.R.L.R. 665 (EAT) paras 39–40; *Bass Taverns Limited v. Burgess* [1995] I.R.L.R. 596 (CA). The decisions in *Tucht* and *De Jong* lend support to a narrower construction of the protection afforded against victimisation so that an employer could argue that the sanction was due to the language used by the worker in complaining. The Convention creates a floor of rights and, therefore it is suggested that it would not be appropriate to rely on *Tucht* or *De Jong* as a basis for narrowing the scope of protection set out in the Public Interest Disclosure Act.

(4) Whether the accusations are supported by evidence

13–18 The whistleblower who acts in good faith but without reasonable grounds in making disclosure other than to the employer may also look for assistance from the Convention in supplementing the Public Interest Disclosure Act. In *Thorgeirson* the ECHR emphasised that there is no general requirement in most cases where matters of public concern are raised to show that there is a sufficient evidential basis. However in *Morissens* the Commission took account of the absence of evidence in support of the allegations which the applicant made in relation to her employers. It appears to have been implicit that it was for the applicant at least to provide some proof that the allegations were well-founded. This would go beyond an obligation to act in good faith since there was apparently no suggestion that the applicant in *Morissens* had acted in bad faith. However it may be that this decision should be treated with some circumspection since it preceded the important case of *Thorgeirson* and the Commission does not appear to have considered the case law in relation to the need for a greater degree of protection in relation to speech upon matters of public concern.

(5) The audience

13–19   As with the emphasis in the Public Interest Disclosure Act on the person to whom disclosure should be made, so under the Convention a further factor which is often emphasised in considering the necessity of interference is the *means* used for the communication and the *audience* to be targeted. In non-employment cases one theme running through the case law has been an emphasis upon the role of the press as a watchdog and in imparting information and ideas.[14] By contrast, in cases where concern is expressed by employees about their employer, disclosure to the press or other media may be considered less deserving of protection (at least unless preceded by a genuine attempt to raise the matter with the employing organisation) than in a case where disclosure is to an appropriate regulatory body. Thus in *Morissens* the Commission took account of the fact that the applicant's comments had been made on television, and that she had therefore used a "means the impact of which is both wide and immediate".

This might be contrasted with *Grigoriades v. Greece* (1998) 4 BHRC 43. The applicant, a journalist, claimed to have discovered a series of abuses committed against conscripts in the course of his military service as a reserve officer on proba-tion. Criminal proceedings brought against him before the national court failed but a disciplinary penalty was imposed so that he had to spend additional time in the army. The language used by Mr Grigoriades in his articles about the army included a venomous attack on the army as "a criminal and terrorist mechanism which, by creating an atmosphere of intimidation and reducing to tatters the spiritual welfare of radical youth, clearly aims at transforming people to mere parts of a mechanism of domination". The Greek Government stressed the abusive contents of the letter and the need to protect the authority of the army and relied upon the wide margin of appreciation enjoyed by the national authorities. In finding that there had been a breach of Article 10, the ECHR emphasised that the letter was not sent to the press but to the commanding officer and one other officer. As such, together with the fact that the letter did not contain any insults directed against the recipients of the letter, it was held that any effect on military discipline must have been insignif-icant.

(6) Nature of the employing organisation

13–20   In a number of cases which do not involve whistleblowing, the Commission has paid attention to the nature of the employing organisation in assess-ing whether interference with free expression was justified. A breach of the obliga-tion of fidelity has been considered to be particularly serious and to justify a sanction where the views expressed inhibit the employee's ability to perform his duties. In *Van der Heijden v. The Netherlands* (1985) D & R 42, for example, the applicant's employment by an immigration foundation in Holland was terminated on the basis of his membership of a political party hostile to the presence of foreign workers in the Netherlands. The Commission held that the interference with the applicant's freedom of expression was justified because it was reasonable for the employer to have some discretion concerning the composition of its staff and because, having

---

[14] *Lingens v. Austria* (1986) 8 E.H.R.R. 407, para. 41; *Thorgeirson v. Iceland*, para. 63; *Goodwin v. The United Kingdom* (1996) 22 E.H.R.R. 123.

regard to the applicant's professional duties, the employer could reasonably take account of the adverse effects which his political activities might have on the employer's reputation, particularly in the eyes of the immigrants whose interests it sought to promote. Similarly in *X v. United Kingdom* (1979) 16 D & R 101, where a school teacher was dismissed for failing to obey an instruction that he was not to advertise his political, moral or religious beliefs by posters or stickers on school premises, the Commission found that the interference was justified and took into account the fact that the teacher was employed in a non-denominational school.

This approach again provides little comfort to the prospective whistleblower seeking to widen the protection offered by the Public Interest Disclosure Act. It may well be that the concerns which an employee raises inhibit his continuing per- formance of his duties by causing a breakdown of trust with the employer. It may also be that an employee seriously damages the employer's reputation by blowing the whistle on matters of concern at the workplace. The risk of this will be all the greater if an employee fails to meet the requirements of the Public Interest Disclosure Act, for example by disclosing his or concerns other than to the employer where this is not a protected disclosure.

(7) Is the sanction imposed by the State?—the scope of the positive obligation to protect the whistleblower

13–21 Although Article 10(1) proclaims that everyone has the right to freedom of expression, a complaint can only be made if the interference has been by a public authority. This requirement is likely to be satisfied where an employer relies upon the courts to provide a sanction against interference with free expression, such as by awarding an injunction or damages.[15] However where the interference is by way of a disciplinary measure imposed directly by the employer without the need for recourse to the court, there is then no scope for a claim unless it can be established that the State ought to have taken positive steps to protect freedom of expression.

In *Rommelfanger v. The Federal Republic of Germany* (1989) 62 DR 151 the Commission was required to consider the scope of the positive duty upon the state to protect free expression. The applicant was employed in a Catholic hospital and was dismissed because he had expressed in a newspaper an opinion which was not in conformity with the position of the Church. He signed, together with fifty others, a letter to the weekly magazine, *Stern*, criticising the attitude of leading personalities in medical organisations to abortion legislation which had been introduced some three years earlier. He was given notice of termination. He then appeared on televi- sion to defend his views. Herr Rommelfanger was initially successful in challenging the dismissal but the Federal Constitutional Court decided that the Labour Courts had not given sufficient weight to the principle of church autonomy.

The Commission held that the dismissal of the physician employee by a Roman Catholic foundation was an act of a private employer. The fact that in German law the Catholic Church could be regarded as a corporation of public law did not make the dismissal an act of the State. The Commission also held that the State would not be in breach of any positive obligation to protect the employee's free speech rights provided that it ensured that:

---

[15] See *e.g. Van der Heijden v. The Netherlands* (1985) D & R 42.

> "there is a reasonable relationship between the measures affecting freedom of expression and the nature of the employment as well as the importance of the issue for the employer."

Consistently with the approach endorsed in *Vogt*, the Commission did not accept the Government's view that Herr Rommelfanger had waived entirely his right to freedom of expression by entering into the employment contract but accepted that his right to freedom of expression was limited to some extent by the duty of loyalty to his employer. Having noted that the views expressed by Herr Rommelfanger upon abortion were contrary to the convictions and value judgments which the Church considered to be essential to the performance of its functions in society, the Commission concluded that the requisite reasonable relationship between the expression and the nature of employment and importance of the issue to the employer was satisfied here.

This approach would appear to leave the whistleblower who acts outside the regime of the Public Interest Disclosure Act in a precarious position. Often the matters raised by the whistleblower will be closely related to the employment and will touch on matters of great importance to the employer. Nevertheless in raising the prospect of positive obligations upon the State to protect free expression the Commission at least provided a basis for reliance upon Article 10 even where a sanction is imposed upon the whistleblower by a private employer. It may yet be that if the extent of such duties is considered in the context of an employer disclosing matters of public concern in relation to the employer, a more stringent requirement might be imposed upon the employer.

Conclusion

13–22   On many occasions the ECHR has emphasised the importance of the free speech rights provided by Article 10. Recent case law has emphasised that rights to free speech extend to the workplace (*Vogt*). Neither the ECHR nor the Commission has yet focused directly on the situation of the whistleblower. However the case law in analogous areas permit some tentative conclusions as to the likely treatment of the whistleblower.

Those wishing to argue in favour of extending the protection offered by the Public Interest Disclosure Act, whether by a generous construction of that statute or of other legislation (such as in relation to unfair dismissal) or by a direct remedy against a public authority, will emphasise the primacy of the norm of freedom of expression and the emphasis given to protection of speech in relation to matters of public concern (*Thorgeirson*; *Barthold*).

As against this, matters of public concern have so far been in non-employment context. Both the ECHR and Commission have recognised that employment involves duties and responsibilities. The nature of these duties will depend in part on the express terms of the contract (*Morissens*) and in part on terms to be implied from the employment relationship, such as duties of loyalty (*Rommelfanger*) and confidentiality (*Tucht*). Even where the whistleblower raises matters of public concern protection may be less extensive than in a non-employment context. Thus an employee who raises matters of public concern, in an intemperate way may, consistently with Article 10, be disciplined on the grounds of the way the issue has been raised (*Tucht*; *De*

Jong). Similarly discipline of a whistleblower is more likely if the matter is first raised with the mass media rather than being raised internally or with an appropriate regulatory body (*Grigoriades, Morissens*).

It may be that the decisions in *Thorgeirson* and *Vogt* will signal a more hospitable climate for the whistleblower. Nevertheless the Commission and Court have so far failed to give clear guidance as to when the whistleblower can be confident that the European Convention will offer protection. Even if the whistleblower uses temperate language and an appropriate channel of communication, it is as yet unclear what degree of proof s/he must also attain information to support the allegations (*Morissens*). Nor has consideration yet been given to the scope of a positive duty upon the State to ensure that private employers do not penalise the whistleblower, albeit it seems that there is a positive duty to protect free expression (*Rommelfanger*). Until such matters are directly addressed by the ECHR, the whistleblower would be well advised to keep within the scope of the protection offered by the Public Interest Disclosure Act.

CHAPTER 14

Litigation (Practice and Procedure)

14–01 We draw together in this Chapter the various applications which may be made by a worker and an employer in the context of whistleblowing. From the perspective of the worker we focus on the causes of action and remedies which are likely to be of most significance where the worker claims to have been victimised for blowing the whistle. As we have seen, however, the Public Interest Disclosure Act represents a balance between the need to protect the whistleblower who raises matters of public concern and the need to respect the employer's legitimate requirement for loyalty from the workforce. It is therefore also relevant to consider the employer's perspective and the remedies available to the employer where the worker does not make a protected disclosure. In particular, especially where there has been a leak to the media, the employer will have a legitimate concern in identifying a disloyal or untrustworthy employee and preventing future leaks or improper allegations.

CLAIMS ASSOCIATED WITH WHISTLEBLOWING BY THE WORKER

1. Unfair dismissal[1]

14–02 An application is made by an employee to an employment tribunal on a Form ET1 within three months of the effective date of dismissal (section 103A Employment Rights Act 1996). The time may be extended only if it was not reasonably practicable for the employee to claim within this period and the time which he claimed within is reasonable. This is the common formula applicable to most cases of unfair dismissal. There are three special features applicable to the whistleblower under the Public Interest Disclosure Act 1998. There is firstly a special remedy of interim relief available by which the employee may claim to be reinstated or that his pay and conditions continue before the tribunal hearing takes place but an application for such relief must be made within seven days of the effective date of termination. Secondly, there is no qualifying period which must be served before a claim can be made in respect of a dismissal by reason of the making of a protected disclosure. Compensation is unlimited (section 33 Employment Relations Act 1999).

It is noteworthy that the Council on Tribunals in its annual report for 1997/98 states that claims under the 1998 Act are likely to be complex and will be "vigorously contested". We would suggest however that this need not be so, especially in relation to first level disclosures where the conditions for protection are relatively straightforward and there is no need to enquire into whether the allegations made by

---

[1] See Chapters 6 and 11.

the whistleblower were well-founded. In any event, tribunals are now accustomed to dealing with complex litigation and, consistently with the modern approach to case management now adopted in the civil courts, can be expected to exercise a degree of control in managing complex cases, if necessary through considering the approach to the litigation with the parties at a directions hearing.

2. Right not to suffer detriment[2]

14–03   An application is made by a "worker" (the extended definition) to an employment tribunal on a Form ET1 within three months of the act or failure complained of (section 48(3) of the ERA). Where "the act or failure is part of a series of similar acts or failures" the relevant date is "the last of them". There is special provision for dating the action when there is a failure to act in that "in the absence of evidence establishing the contrary, an employer shall be taken to decide on a failure to act when he does an act inconsistent with doing the failed act or, if he has done no such inconsistent act, when the period expires within which he might reasonably have been expected to do the failed act if it was to be done" (section 48(4) of the ERA). It is for the employer to show the ground on which the act complained of was done (section 48(2) of the ERA).

3. Wrongful dismissal

14–04   At common law, where an employee is dismissed without notice there will be a claim for wrongful dismissal unless as a result of gross misconduct or express contractual provision the employer was entitled to dismiss without notice. The disclosure of confidential information or the failure to obey reasonable instructions, which will often be alleged in whistleblower cases, may however amount to gross misconduct entitling the employer to dismiss without notice. However as we have seen,[3] the employee may be able to establish a public interest defence to any alleged breach of confidence. In any event we would suggest that it is very unlikely that merely making a protected disclosure could amount to gross misconduct.

We consider below the remedies available to an employee who is, or is likely to be, wrongfully dismissed.

(1) Specific performance/injunctions

14–05   Insofar as a whistleblower who claims to have made a protected disclosure wishes to prevent a dismissal proceeding or to require an employer to take him back into employment, the appropriate course will be to seek interim relief in the employment tribunal. It is only where the disclosure was not a protected disclosure that it will be relevant to consider whether it is possible to apply in the High Court or county court for an injunction restraining the dismissal or specific performance requiring the employer to continue employing the employee. Usually the only common law remedy available to an employee for wrongful dismissal will be a claim for damages. The exceptional cases where such an order might be made fall, broadly, into two main categories:

---

[2] See Chapter 6.
[3] Chapter 7.

(a) Where the employee has retained the employer's trust and confidence, for example because the employer dismisses only reluctantly and/or has no doubt as to the employee's abilities.[4] In order to fall within this exception the employer must have retained complete confidence in the employee.[5] The court will not simply accept the employer's word that there has been a breakdown in trust and confidence. This will be judged by reference to all the circumstances of the case, including the nature of the work, the people with whom the work must be done and the likely effect upon employer's operations if the employer is required by injunction to suffer the employee's return to work. However where the disclosure is plainly not a protected disclosure we would expect the court readily to accept that as a result of the leak the employer has lost confidence in the employee and regards him as untrustworthy.

(b) Where the employee is dismissed in breach of a contractual disciplinary procedure or the rules of natural justice.[6] In such cases the duration of the injunction is usually relatively limited and the balance of convenience will tend more towards the granting of an injunction, particularly, where the employee would normally be suspended during the procedure.

The general principles applicable to the grant of interim injunctions are considered below. Essentially, the application should be made without delay, the applicant must show there is a serious issue to be tried and the court will then consider the wider balance of convenience. However where the dismissal has taken place and specific performance is sought it might be arguable that the more onerous conditions for a mandatory injunction would apply. In some cases, however, it may be possible to short circuit these tests on the basis that the court is able to determine the issue as a point of law, for example because on the construction of the contract it can be determined that the contractual disciplinary procedure has not been followed.[7]

(2) Declaration

14–06 In exceptional circumstances, an employee may be entitled to a declaration that a wrongful dismissal was invalid, although usually the employee will also seek an order restraining the termination of the employment. Declarations have most commonly been sought in cases involving statutory status and offices, especially where contractual safeguards have not been followed.[8]

(4) Damages

14–07 **(i) What damages are recoverable?** In most cases the employee's only common law remedy for wrongful dismissal will be a claim for damages or, in some

---

[4] *Hill v. C. A. Parsons & Co. Ltd* [1972] 1 Ch. 305 (CA); *Irani v. Southampton and South West Hampshire Health Authority* [1985] I.C.R. 590 (Warner J.).
[5] *Ali v. Southwark London Borough* [1988] I.C.R. 567; *Alexander v. Standard Telephones & Cables Plc* [1990] I.R.L.R. 55; *Alexander v. Standard Telephones & Cables Plc (No.2)* [1991] I.R.L.R. 286.
[6] *Robb v. London Borough of Hammersmith and Fulham* [1991] I.C.R. 514.
[7] *Jones v. Gwent County Council* [1992] I.R.L.R. 521.
[8] *Gunton v. London Borough of Richmond-Upon-Thames* [1980] I.C.R. 755 (CA); *Shook v. London Borough of Ealing [1986] I.R.L.R. 46 (EAT).

cases if there is an entitlement to payment in lieu of notice, in debt. The measure of loss is usually the salary/wages and benefits which the employee would have earned had he been given notice under his contract and this notice may be either as expressly provided in the contract or what the law would imply as reasonable notice, subject to the right of summary dismissal for gross misconduct or gross incompetence and subject to an entitlement to notice reflecting the minimum time it would have taken to carry out any contractual disciplinary procedure.[9]

In addition to claiming pay during the notice period, it may also be possible for an employee to recover "stigma damages", being financial loss resulting from damage to the prospects of future employment arising out of the employee's reputation being tarnished by the employer's conduct which is in breach of contract. This principle was established in *Malik v. BCCI* [1997] 3 W.L.R. 95 (HL). The right to *Malik*-style damages arises only when there is no reasonable and proper cause for the employer's conduct which breaks the implied duty of trust and confidence in the contract of employment (*per* Lord Nicholls at page 102A, Lord Steyn at page 116). The test is whether it was reasonably foreseeable that, as a result of the employer's action, there would be a serious possibility that the employees future employment prospects would thereby be handicapped. In that event, the employee may claim for the continuing *financial* losses. Lord Steyn explained (at p110G) that the employees in *Malik*:

> "may conceivably be able to prove that in the financial services industry they were regarded as potentially tarnished and therefore undesirable employees to recruit".

This may be of particular significance for the whistleblower who risks being branded a troublemaker as a result of speaking out, especially if the whistleblower "goes public" with the allegations.[10] If however there was no need to make a second level disclosure, perhaps because the matter was not raised internally, it may however be found that the employee is author of his own misfortune in failing to gain alternative work on the basis that the reason why the facts of his dismissal became known was that *he* chose to make wide disclosures in a way which would inevitably cause serious damage to the employer, and which might render other employers inevitably very cautious about employing him. If so, there would be a break in the chain of causation.

Subsequent authorities considering *Malik* have reiterated that nothing in that case was designed to detract from or overrule the general principle that damages in actions for breach of contract are designed to compensate for pecuniary losses only (as established in *Addis v. Gramophone Co Ltd* [1909] A.C. 488). Thus in *French v. Barclays Bank plc* [1998] I.R.L.R. 646 the Court of Appeal reaffirmed that damages for breach of contract made specifically could not be recovered for stress and annoyance unless there was, as the subject of the litigation, a contract with the object of providing peace of mind. Further, in *Johnson v. Unisys Ltd* [1999] I.R.L.R. 90 the Court of Appeal held that damages for wrongful dismissal could not include damages for the manner of the dismissal. As such even if the claimant had suffered a mental breakdown as a result of the manner of the dismissal, and as a result had suffered financial loss because as a result of the breakdown it was more difficult to find work, this

---

[9] *Janciuk v. Winerite Limited* [1998] I.R.L.R. 63.
[10] See Chapter 11 in relation to principles applying to compensation for unfair dismissal.

loss was not recoverable. On this basis a whistleblower who finds it difficult to find work because he is traumatised by the way in which he is victimised by the employer would be unable to recover the losses resulting from this by way of contractual damages, though such loss might be recoverable by way of compensation for unfair dismissal.[11]

Further, notwithstanding that damages for inability to find work due to stigma are in principle recoverable, the decision of Lightman J. in *Bank of Credit and Commerce International SA v. Ali* (No. 3) [1999] I.R.L.R. 508 suggests that it will be difficult to satisfy the evidential burden necessary to recover such damages. Lightman J. suggested that proceedings will rarely be justified before approaching a prospective employer for reasons as to the refusal to take on the worker. In the absence of evidence from prospective employers the claimants in *BCCI v. Ali* were not able to show that they had lost the chance of employment due to stigma. However, such an approach is unlikely to be a viable one for whistleblowers since prospective employers are most unlikely to admit that the whistleblowing activities were the reason for the refusal to take on a worker.

14–08   (ii) Impact of the 1998 Act.   The law as to wrongful dismissal is only directly altered by the 1998 Act insofar as it is not possible for the employer to enforce an agreement that the employee will not make a protected disclosure. There may also, however, be some indirect impact in that courts may draw by analogy upon the structure of the statute to determine what is a valid and invalid disclosure for the purposes of assessing what is and what is not gross misconduct on the part of the employee.

14–09   (iii) Where can the claim be brought?   At present, a contractual claim which is alive on termination of the employment may be made the subject of proceedings in the employment tribunal but only subject to a maximum of £25,000 (Employment Tribunals Extension of Jurisdiction (England and Wales) Order 1994 S.I. No. 1623). There has not yet been any decision as to whether an employee could claim up to the limit of £25,000 in the employment tribunal and then claim for the balance in the civil courts. It is at least arguable that the second action would be struck out as an abuse of process. If it were possible merely to claim the balance in the civil courts the £25,000 limit would merely serve to increase costs by requiring a further application in the civil courts—where it would be possible to rely on an issue estoppel arising from the tribunal's decision.

14–10   (iv) Overlap of contractual and unfair dismissal claims.   There may be circumstances in which the employee is entitled to recover for loss by way of damages or debt at common law *and* compensation under the statute. Usually the employee will claim both for contractual damages in relation to the notice period and for unfair dismissal. Where the contract provides that the employee has an entitlement either to notice or to pay in lieu of notice and the contract is summarily terminated but could have been terminated lawfully by making a payment in lieu, the employee can claim in debt rather than in damages (and in addition to claiming compensation for unfair dismissal). This has the advantage over both a contractual damages claim and

---

[11] See Chapter 11.

compensation for unfair dismissal that there will be no need to mitigate loss during the notice period and no need to give credit as against the sum claimed in debt for any earnings in fact made during the notice period.[12] However, whilst the first £30,000 of a damages claim would be tax free, a sum deemed as a payment in lieu would be taxable in full as an enulment from employment.[13]

The employee will not be able to recover twice for the same loss so that whichever forum adjudicates second will have to take into account by way of deduction what has been awarded by the first.

14–11   (v) Procedure for claiming in the High Court and County Court.   The claim for damages at common law for wrongful dismissal is brought on a Claim Form within six years of the relevant breach of contract. It may be allocated to the High Court or county court depending on the amount involved and the importance of the issues arising. Different rules apply to civil litigation depending on the track to which it is allocated. The matters relevant to the allocation of track are:

(1) the financial value of the claim;

(2) the nature of the remedy sought;

(3) the likely complexity of the facts, law or evidence;

(4) the number of parties of likely parties;

(5) the value of any counterclaim;

(6) the amount of oral evidence which may be required;

(7) the importance of the claim to persons who are not parties to the proceedings;

(8) the views expressed by the parties;

(9) the circumstances of the parties.

(Civil Procedure Rules 26.8(1)).

4. Judicial Review

14–12   Despite the wide definition of "worker" under the 1998 Act, protection is not provided to the police or members of the armed forces or to those involved in national security.[14] Equally, as in the case of police officers, workers in these categories may be holders of an office who are not in a contractual relationship with the "employer".[15] A whistleblower in this category may however still be able to challenge a decision which has the effect of victimising him for blowing the whistle by making an application for judicial review of the decision which is alleged to constitute victimisation.[16] The procedure to be followed is set out in RSC Ord. 53 in

---

[12] *Abrahams v. PRS* [1995] I.R.L.R. 486 (CA); *Gregory v. Wallace* [1998] I.R.L.R. 387 (CA); *Cerberus Software Limited v. Rowley* July 14, 1999, EAT.

[13] EMI Group Electronics Ltd v. Coldicoff (H.M. Inspector of Taxes) (Unreported, July 16, 1999, CA).

[14] See Chapter 6, para. 6.3.

[15] *Commissioner of Police for the Metropolis v. Lowrey-Nesbitt* [1999] I.C.R. 401 (EAT).

[16] *R. v. Secretary of State for the Home Office, ex p. Benwell* [1985] Q.B. 554; *R. v. Chief Constable of West Midlands Police, ex p. Carroll* (1994) 7 Admin. L.R. 45 (CA).

Schedule 1 to the Civil Procedure Rules. An application for judicial review can only be made with the permission of the court. The application for permission is made on Form No.86A supported by written evidence verifying the facts relied upon.[17] It must be made promptly and in any event within three months of the decision to be challenged unless the court considered that there is good reason for extending the time within which the application can be made.[18]

5. Application to the European Court of Human Rights

14–13   When the Human Rights Act 1998 is brought into force (on October 2, 2000) rights derived from the European Convention of Human Rights may be the subject of litigation in U.K. courts and tribunals. There may however be some cases in which an application to Strasbourg may be necessary. This will be so where the challenge is to primary legislation or the party has claimed certain rights under the Convention but the domestic courts have decided that the Convention does not have the effect contended for.

The relief sought in the Court of Human Rights is primarily a declaration that some action is unlawful but the Court also has a discretion under Article 41 of the Convention to award compensation or just satisfaction as it is known in "Eurospeak". Domestic legal aid is not available but conditional fees are permitted and some limited legal aid is offered by the Council of Europe which has responsibility for the European Court of Human Rights. Claims are initiated on a standard form and must be made within six months from the date on which the final decision (being the last in the chain of effective domestic remedies) was taken. The first stage is establishing whether the application is admissible and it may be held to be inadmissible on various grounds such as because the applicant has not exhausted all adequate and effective domestic remedies or does not have the correct *locus standi*, the time limit has expired or because the claim is manifestly ill-founded.

CLAIMS ASSOCIATED WITH WHISTLEBLOWING BY THE EMPLOYER AGAINST THE WORKER

1. Breach of confidence or copyright[19]

14–14   The employer may seek an injunction to restrain a worker from continuing to leak confidential information or using copyright documents. This will commonly be accompanied with an application made pursuant to section 4 of the Torts (Interference with Goods) Act 1977 for delivery up of documents removed by the employee. The principles and procedure relevant to injunctive relief are considered below.

In addition to seeking injunctive relief, the employer can claim damages and an account of profits (although ultimately at trial or earlier determination of the claim it will be necessary to elect which is claimed). This may be particularly important where the worker has been paid for making the disclosure. In such circumstances even if the employer cannot establish loss, he can be required to pay over profits made as a result of disclosing confidential or copyright material.

---

[17] R 53.3.
[18] R 53.4.
[19] See Chapters 7 and 9.

2. An informant injunction

14–15   In some cases it will be obvious to an employer when allegations appear in the media that there must have been a leak by an employee and the employer may be concerned to unmask the culprit. The circumstances in which such an application may succeed have been considered in Chapter 9.

3. Defamation[20]

14–16   The employer may seek to bring defamation proceedings as a result of the allegations made by the whistleblower. The defence most likely to be relied upon by the whistleblower will be qualified privilege. The action must be brought within one year of the defamation taking place. It is very rare that an injunction may be obtained if the defendant seeks (as it usually will) to justify the words used.[21]

INTERIM INJUNCTIONS

(i) Prohibitory injunctions

14–17   In deciding whether to grant an interim injunction, the court normally considers the principles set out by the House of Lords in *American Cyanamid Co. v. Ethicon Ltd* [1975] A.C. 396. Essentially this sets out three stages for consideration:

(1) The claimant must first establish that there is a serious question to be tried in the sense only that the claim is "not frivolous or vexatious".[22] This is a low threshold requirement.

(2) If the claimant overcomes the initial hurdle, the court must consider whether damages would provide an adequate remedy for the defendant or whether the claimant's undertaking in damages (if one is offered) would be an adequate remedy for the defendant. In a whistleblowing case damages will rarely be adequate since the employer may have an interest in unmasking a disloyal employee or preventing further leaks and the whistleblower will have an interest in making the disclosure.

(3) Where there is doubt as to whether the respective remedies in damages will be adequate, the court must consider the balance of convenience pending trial or, as it has subsequently been described, "the balance of the risk of doing an injustice".[23] Important considerations in this respect will include; the extent to which damages are likely to be an adequate remedy and the ability of the other party to pay, any clear view the court may reach as to the relative strength of the parties (although the court will not try to resolve conflicts of evidence on affidavit or in witness statements or difficult questions of law which call for detailed argument and mature consideration) and, where other factors appear equally balanced, the preservation of the status

---

[20] See Chapter 12.
[21] *e.g. Lion Laboratories Ltd v. Evans* [1985] 1 Q.B. 526; *Service Corp International v. Channel Four* [1999] E.M.L.R. 83.
[22] *per* Lord Diplock in *American Cyanamid* at 407G.
[23] May L.J. in *Cayne v. Global Natural Resources plc* [1984] 1 All E.R. 225 at 237H.

quo.[24] The *status quo* is the position that existed during the period immediately preceding the issue of the writ or if there is unreasonable delay between the issue of the writ and the application for the interim injunction the period immediately before the application. Delay in making the application may also be taken into account in relation to whether an injunction should be granted.

In many whistleblowing cases, however, it will not be appropriate to apply the first stage of the ordinary *American Cyanamid* test. Where the grant or refusal of the interim injunction application is likely substantially to dispose of the action, for example because the injunction will have substantially expired prior to trial or the information will have become stale, then the court can should first assess the relative strength of the parties' case.[25] This may be important in a whistleblowing case if the whistleblower is able to demonstrate that timely disclosure of a particular concern is essential since it may be too late to deal with the concern by the time a trial were to take place. Where it is uncertain where the merits lie it will be necessary to consider the balance of convenience. However in relation to this there is a developing line of authority to the effect that, at least in relation to press and broadcasters, disclosure of matters of public concern should not be prevented on the basis of a claim with limited or uncertain prospects of success.[26]

A good example of this line of authority is the decision of the Court of Appeal in *Secretary of State v. Central Broadcasting Limited* [1993] E.M.L.R. 253. The Home Office applied for an injunction to prevent the broadcast of an interview with Denis Nilsen, the convicted mass murderer. The interview had been conducted by a forensic psychologist employed by the Home Office. In support of the injunction it was argued that the Home Office was the equitable owner of the copyright in the film of the interview and, in the alternative, that the film was made pursuant to an agreement that it would not be shown without the agreement of the Home Office. In refusing the injunction, Hirst J. noted that the relative strength of the parties' case on the merits was not clear and that there were a number of conflicts of evidence that could only be resolved at trial. In those circumstances he held that, having regard to Article 10 of the European Convention of Human Rights, the Court should not interfere with the defendants freedom of speech including their freedom to publish the programme in full.

(ii) Mandatory injunctions

14–18 Different principles apply to an application for a mandatory injunction primarily because mandatory orders usually go further than the preservation of the status quo by requiring a party to take some new positive step or to undo what he has done in the past. It may thus carry a greater risk of injustice if the court should

---

[24] Laddie J. in *Series 5 Software Ltd v. Philip Clarke* [1996] F.S.R. 273 (Laddie J.); *American Cyanamid* at 407H, 408F.

[25] *Lansing Linde Limited v. Kerr* [1991] 1 All E.R. 418 (CA); *Cambridge Nutrition Limited v. BBC* [1990] 3 All E.R. 523 (CA); *Secretary of State for the Home Department v. Central Broadcasting Limited* [1993] E.M.L.R. 253 (CA), *per* Hirst L.J. at 274.

[26] *Cambridge Nutrition Limited v. BBC* [1990] 3 All E.R. 523 (CA); *Secretary of State for the Home Department v. Central Broadcasting Limited* [1993] E.M.L.R. 253 (CA), *per* Hirst L.J. at 274; *Beggars Banquet Records Ltd v. Carlton Television Ltd* [1993] E.M.L.R. 349; *Service Corporation International Plc v. Channel Four Television Corporation* [1999] E.M.L.R. 83 at 91–92.

turn out to be wrong at a later stage. In *Zockoll Group Ltd v. Mercury Communications Ltd* [1998] F.S.R. 354, the Court of Appeal approved the comments of Chadwick J. in *Nottingham Building Society v. Eurodynamics Systems* [1993] F.S.R. 468 at 474 that:

> "It is legitimate where a mandatory injunction is sought to consider whether the court does feel a high degree of assurance that the plaintiff will be able to establish this right at a trial. That is because the greater the degree of assurance the plaintiff will ultimately establish his right, the less will be the risk of injustice if the injunction is granted".

(iii) Procedure

14–19 The court may grant an interim remedy before a claim is made only if "the matter is urgent or it is otherwise desirable to do so in the interests of justice" (Civil Procedure Rules, P 25.2(2)(b)). The application notice and evidence in support of an interim injunction must be served "as soon as practicable after issue and in any event not less than 3 days before the court is due to hear the application" (*Practice Direction: interim injunctions*, para. 2.2). A draft of the order sought should be filed with the application notice and a disc containing the draft should be available to the court. Applications should be supported by evidence set out in a witness statement, a statement of case provided that it is verified by a statement of truth or the application provided that it is verified by a statement of truth (*Practice Direction: interim injunctions*, para. 3.2). This must include "all material facts of which the court should be made aware" (*Practice Direction: interim injunctions*, para. 3.3). "Any order for an injunction must set out clearly what the respondent must do or must not do" (*Practice Direction: interim injunctions*, para. 5.3).

CHAPTER 15

Whistleblowing procedures

WHY IS A WHISTLEBLOWING PROCEDURE NEEDED?

15–01   A key aspiration of those who supported the introduction of the Public Interest Disclosure Act 1998 was that it would encourage employers to develop appropriate procedures to encourage potential whistleblowers to raise their concerns within the employer organisation. To this effect, in the course of explaining why there would be no ceiling on compensation for dismissal for making a protected disclosure, the Secretary of State for Trade and Industry, Stephen Byers, stated:

> "I hope that businesses, including small business, will adopt best practice to ensure that the measures we are introducing today will never need to be used, because the climate has been created that precludes the occurrence of such wrongdoing."

There is good reason, both in terms of good practice and in terms of the employer's self-interest, for the employer organisation, whether large or small, to put in place adequate procedures to address concerns of staff. Encouraging staff to raise concerns first within the organisation produces benefits on several levels. First, it fosters a more healthy and accountable workplace where problems are more likely to be "nipped in the bud". Secondly, should a concern arise it is more likely that the member of staff would raise the matter internally using the procedure set out. This degree of control provides the employer organisation with every opportunity to address the concern and minimises the need for external involvement or the involvement of regulators. Finally, the internal system means that, should a worker make an external disclosure without first having made the disclosure internally or waiting for the matter to be addressed in accordance with the internal procedure, it is more likely that the disclosure will not be a protected disclosure. In some organisations there will be an added advantage in the impression made on those outside the employing organisation that good practice is being followed and that any concerns over malpractice are likely to be identified and addressed. This may be important in terms of fostering greater confidence amongst investors and in the market place, or on the part of an organisation with whom the employer organisation is tendering for work.

KEY FACTORS FOR ANY PROCEDURE

15–02   A whistleblowing procedure may therefore make the difference between the employer finding out about a concern from its staff rather than from a regulator or, in the worst case, in the media. To be successful, however, the procedure needs to be recognised by the potential users as being simple, possessing integrity, cheap, accessible, accountable and possessing the necessary teeth to investigate and sort out their concern. We summarise below key considerations when devising and implementing an appropriate procedure.

(a) In order to obtain the full benefit of a whistleblowing procedure it is important that it should be tailored to the specific needs and structure of the employer's organisation. Nevertheless, sample whistleblowing procedures provide a useful starting point and we set out some examples in Appendix 6.

(b) The process by which the procedure is introduced is itself important. It is not sufficient for an organisation merely to send staff a letter stating that there is a procedure. Although a whistleblowing procedure need not be agreed by the workforce and can simply be imposed, the better approach is for there to be a structured introduction involving consultation with all levels of staff and adequate publicity for the procedure and its essential elements. Proper consultation is more likely to result in a procedure in which the staff and managers have confidence. For example proper consultation is more likely to result in adequate consideration being given to the question of to whom concerns may be reported. If an unsuitable candidate is used, workers may be reluctant to use the procedure and may not only lose confidence in the person to whom the concerns should be reported, but also in the procedure and in management for appointing such an unsuitable person.

(c) Staff should receive training as to what concerns should be raised, when they should raise them and how to raise them. As we have seen, there is often a culture which discourages the raising of concerns. This will not just disappear upon the organisation adopting a procedure or through legislation. Workers need to be informed what the procedure is for and the fact that there will be no adverse repercussions for using it. At this stage workers can be sounded out as to whom they want to go to with concerns.

(d) Those who receive the information should also be trained as to what questions to ask and how to ensure that workers using the procedure are deterred from pursuing the procedure further due to the questions being asked. It would be advisable to create a form, preferably after consultation with worker representatives, that is completed by the person raising the concern. This would assist in ensuring that appropriate questions are asked. In addition if the form is distributed to staff this would assist in enabling those wishing to use the system to be properly prepared and to know what to expect. Typically the form might seek (1) details of the name, address and contact number of the worker, (2) details of the concern, such as whether it relates to health and safety, fraud or abuse, (3) details of the number of people at risk and (4) what evidence is available. It should be explained that the aim of such information is to enable the employer to investigate the concern with the goal of preventing the misconduct from continuing. An example of what not to do would be simply to set up an answering machine for users to record their concerns—this would not be good enough.

(e) If the organisation is large, then it may be sensible to consider different people being appointed for different areas of the organisation. For example, concerns over health and safety and over fraud may go to different people. It would be helpful, although not essential, for the recipient of the concern to have detailed knowledge of the area.

(f) The procedure could also have a tiered system so that if the concern is raised with the health and safety person and if the worker is not satisfied with the response, then the worker can go to another more senior person. It is desirable for the chief executive or managing director to be at the top of any such pyramid. It is they who are at the very top of the organisation and are likely to be most capable of readily addressing the concerns. Further, access to the most senior person in the organisation is likely to foster accountability.

(g) Ideally, although workers should be able to raise concerns on a confidential basis, it is preferable for the concerns not to be raised anonymously. If a concern is raised anonymously it may be difficult to pursue the issue due to being unable to gather further information that may be required. Further, anonymity should not be necessary if the procedure is working effectively since the introduction of the procedure ought to be accompanied with a recognition that the worker is in fact doing something that should be encouraged rather than hidden under a cloak of anonymity.

(h) If any procedure does receive anonymous information, however, it would be inadvisable to ignore the information received. The information might be true and it may be that the fact that the person making the disclosure wishes to remain anonymous is a reflection of a lack of confidence in the procedure. If the information is ignored in circumstances where, despite the disclosure being made anonymously, it could have been followed up, there will be an increased risk of a second level disclosure outside the employing organisation.

(i) The procedure should set out clearly to the person using it what will happen next and how long it will take for the investigator to respond and, should no response occur, what options are open to the user of the procedure.

(j) If there has been a protected disclosure then all effort should be made to ensure that no one victimises the user. If there is respect for the confidential basis on which concerns have been raised this should reduce the risk of such victimisation but will not necessarily eliminate the risk.

(k) The remit of the procedure may be widened to include those outside the employer organisation, such as contractors.

(l) The procedure should actively encourage concerns being reported to regulators.

(m) The procedure should be easily accessible. To this end it may be preferable to provide home and work phone number listings of those to whom concerns are reported. Workers should be encouraged to contact them at any time. An opportunity for meetings should be available.

(n) One means of publicising the procedure and fostering confidence in its use would be to keep staff informed as to its achievements, once the procedure is up and running, through the use of a newsletter.

APPENDIX 1

Public Interest Disclosure Act 1998 (Annotations by Public Concern at Work)

AN INTRODUCTION TO THE LEGISLATION WITH AUTHORITATIVE NOTES ON ITS PROVISIONS, SECTION BY SECTION.

These annotations were first published in October 1998 in Current Law Statutes. This edition is accurate at 1st September 1999.

Introduction

"All organisations face the risks of things going wrong or of unknowingly harbouring malpractice. Part of the duty of identifying such a situation and taking remedial action may lie with the regulatory or funding body. But the regulator is usually in the role of detective, determining responsibility after the crime has been discovered. Encouraging a culture of openness within an organisation will help: prevention is better than cure. Yet it is striking that in the few cases where things have gone badly wrong in local public spending bodies, it has frequently been the tip-off to the press or the local Member of Parliament – sometimes anonymous, sometimes not – which has prompted the regulators into action. Placing staff in a position where they feel driven to approach the media to ventilate concerns is unsatisfactory both for the staff member and the organisation."

Committee on Standards in Public Life
Second Report, Cm. 3270–1 p. 21 (1996)

While the Public Interest Disclosure Act (cap. 23) applies across the private, public and voluntary sectors, these words from the Nolan Committee were said to best summarise the purpose of the legislation (*Hansard*, H.L. col. 889, 1998)[1]. During the

---

[1] Parliamentary consideration of the Act can be found at
  a) *Parliamentary Debates*, H.C. Standing Committee D, March 11, 1998;
  b) *Hansard*, H.C. cols. 1124–1144, April 24, 1998;
  c) *Hansard*, H.L. cols. 888–904, May 11, 1998;
  d) *Hansard*, H.L. cols. 611–639, June 5, 1998; and
  e) *Hansard*, H.L. cols. 1798–1804, June 19, 1998.
  It should be noted that where the construction of this Act may be open to more than one interpretation, these annotations draw on the statements in Parliament not only of the Minister but of the joint promoters of the Bill (Richard Shepherd M.P. and Lord Borrie Q.C.). This is because along with Ministerial statements, those of the promoter are recognised as relevant authority for purposes of construction when permitted under the rule in *Pepper v. Hart* (1993) 1 All E.R. 42, per Lord Bridge at p. 49g and per Lord Browne-Wilkinson at p. 69e.

Bill's passage, Lord Nolan stated that his Committee had been persuaded of the urgent need for protection for public interest whistleblowers and he commended those behind the Bill "for so skilfully achieving the essential but delicate balance in this measure between the public interest and the interests of employers" (*Hansard*, H.L. col. 614, 1998).

To achieve such a balance, the Act sets out a framework for public interest whistleblowing. In doing this, it provides almost every individual in the workplace with full protection from victimisation where they raise genuine concerns about malpractice in accordance with the Act's provisions. Though the Act is part of employment legislation, no qualifying periods or age limits restrict the application of its protection.

Only a disclosure that relates to specified types of malpractice may qualify for protection under the Act. These include (s. 1, s. 43B) concerns about actual or apprehended breaches of civil, criminal, regulatory or administrative law; miscarriages of justice; dangers to health, safety and the environment; and the cover-up of any such malpractice. Cast so widely, and with its emphasis on the prevention of the malpractice, and with the guarantee of full compensation, the Act requires the attention of every employer in the UK. While the main issues for practitioners and their clients are set out at the end of this General Note, the key issue for employers will be to reduce any risk of creating grounds for protected public disclosures. Such steps will include (a) introducing a whistleblowing procedure; (b) ensuring that the workforce understands that victimisation for whistleblowing is not tolerated; and (c) making it clear that reporting malpractice to a prescribed regulator is acceptable.

The fullest—and most readily available—protection under the Act (s. 1, s. 43C) is where a worker, who is concerned about malpractice, raises the matter within the organisation or with the person responsible for the malpractice. The intended effect of this provision is to reassure workers that it is safe and acceptable for them to raise such concerns internally. Thereby, it is more likely that those in charge of the organisation (a) will be forewarned of potential malpractice, (b) will investigate it, and (c) will take such steps as are reasonable to remove any unwarranted danger. In this way, the Act aims to deter and facilitate the early detection of malpractice. Additionally, this approach furthers the principle of accountability. This is because – should the concern subsequently prove to be well founded – the law can more readily hold people to account for their actions where it can be shown they had actual (as opposed to constructive or implied) notice of the malpractice.

As the short title makes clear, the Act (s. 1. ss. 43E, 43F, 43G and 43H) also sets out the circumstances where the disclosure of the malpractice outside of the organisation is in the public interest and should be protected. In these provisions, the Act adopts and develops many of the signposts from the common law on whether particular information may, notwithstanding the fact it is confidential, lawfully be disclosed in the public interest. Before considering the relationship between these new statutory provisions and these established principles, it should be noted that the common law developed in cases about whether the confidential information might itself be published (usually by a newspaper) or disclosed (say, to a regulator), rather than whether the whistleblower should be protected.

In some respects, the Act imposes requirements additional to those in the law of confidence. To be protected, (a) the whistleblower must satisfy a good faith test in order to be protected; (b) as to all external disclosures, he needs to show a factual basis for his belief; and (c) as to wider public disclosures – unless there is some good reason why not – the concern should have been raised internally or with a prescribed regulator first. In other respects – such as factors to be weighed in deciding whether a public disclosure was reasonable under ss. 43G and 43H – the Act requires tribunals to have regard to issues, which will also be considered at common law. While relevant cases from the law of confidence may provide helpful guidance to tribunals, they are not binding. Indeed the Act only requires tribunals to consider duties of confidence where the disclosure was in breach of a duty of confidence which was owed to a third party by the employer: s. 43G(3)(d). For a comprehensive analysis of the case law in this area, the reader is referred to Dr Y. Cripps' monograph *The Legal Implications of Disclosure in the Public Interest*, (2nd ed., Sweet and Maxwell, London, 1994) and, more generally, to Toulson & Phipps, *Confidentiality* (Sweet & Maxwell, London, 1996).

Background

The Act was introduced as a Private Member's Bill into the Commons by the Conservative MP Mr Richard Shepherd and into the Lords by the Labour peer Lord Borrie Q.C. It received strong support from the Government. The new protection forms part of employment legislation and was put forward in the *Fairness at Work* White Paper Cm. 3968 (May 1998) as one of the key new rights for individuals. However, it was also recognised as a valuable tool to promote good governance and openness in organisations. This can be seen not only from the Parliamentary debates on the Bill but from the references to it in the White Papers on Freedom of information *Your Right to Know* Cm. 3818 (December 1997) and on *Modern Local Government* Cm. 4014 (July 1998) and also in ministerial guidance to the NHS (letter from Health Minister to NHS Trust Chairs, *Freedom of Speech in the NHS*, September 25, 1997). It was mostly on account of these wider implications for governance and their relevance across all sectors that the legislation received broad support from the Confederation of British Industry, the Institute of Directors and all key professional groups.

The legislation was closely linked to the work of the independent charity, Public Concern at Work[2]. This impartial organisation (a) provides educational and training services to organisations and (b) runs a free legal helpline from people who are concerned about serious malpractice in the workplace but are unsure whether or how to sound the alarm. The charity was launched in 1993 by the present commentator[3] with the assistance and under the guidance of, *inter alia*, Lord Borrie Q.C., the Rt. Hon Lord Oliver of Aylmerton, Ross Cranston M.P. (the Solicitor General), Maurice Frankel (director of the Campaign for Freedom of Information) and Marlene Winfield (senior policy officer at the National Consumer Council). The legal connection is maintained through Michael Brindle Q.C. as Chairman of the Trustees, the Rt. Hon Sir Ralph Gibson as Chairman of the Council and John Bowers Q.C. as Hon Legal Adviser.

The background to the Act and to the work of Public Concern at Work lies in the major disasters of the past decade. Almost every public inquiry found that workers had been aware of the danger but had either been too scared to sound the alarm or had raised the matter in the wrong way or with the wrong person. Examples of the

---

[2] Public Concern at Work, suite 306, 16 Baldwins Gardens, London EC1N 7RJ. Telephone 0171 4040 6609. Fax 0171 404 6576. Email *whistle@pcaw.demon.co.uk* Website www.pcaw.demon.co.uk
[3] These annotations were prepared by Guy Dehn, a practising barrister and founder director of Public Concern at Work.

former include the Clapham Rail crash (where the Hidden Inquiry heard that an inspector had seen the loose wiring but had said nothing because he did not want to rock the boat), the Piper Alpha disaster (where the Cullen Inquiry concluded that "workers did not want to put their continued employment in jeopardy through raising a safety issue which might embarrass management"), and the collapse of BCCI (where the Bingham Inquiry found an autocratic environment where nobody dared to speak up).

Examples of where the concern was raised but not heeded include the Zeebrugge Ferry tragedy (where the Sheen Inquiry found that staff had on five occasions raised concerns that ferries were sailing with their bow doors open), the collapse of Barings Bank (where the regulator found that a senior manager had failed to blow the whistle loudly or clearly) and the Arms to Iraq Inquiry (where the Scott Report found that an employee had written to the Foreign Office to tell them that munitions equipment was being produced for Iraq). Similar messages have come out of the inquiries into the abuse of children in care (over 30 reports of concern were ignored about the serial sex abuser Frank Beck) and investigations into malpractice in the health service (most recently the finding of the General Medical Council that a consultant anaesthetist who had warned about the high mortality rates at the paediatric unit at the Bristol Royal Infirmary had felt forced to give up his career in the NHS). The view of Public Concern at Work was that similar messages were likely to arise in a large proportion of those incidents and legal claims which did not justify a public inquiry.

Dr Tony Wright M.P. initiated the idea of a legislative framework for public interest whistleblowing in a ten minute rule bill in 1995. Broad support for such a measure led Don Touhig M.P. to introduce a private member's bill in 1996, which was drafted by Public Concern at Work and the Campaign for Freedom of Information. Although that Bill was unsuccessful, it had been supported by the Rt. Hon Tony Blair M.P. who – as leader of the Opposition – pledged that a future Government of his would introduce similar legislation. Don Touhig's 1996 Bill had been championed from the Labour front bench by Ian McCartney M.P., who after the election became the DTI minister who helped steer this Act onto the statute book.

Overview of the provisions

Malpractice

The Act applies to people at work raising genuine concerns about crimes, civil offences (including negligence, breach of contract, breach of administrative law), miscarriages of justice, dangers to health and safety or the environment and the cover up of any of these. It applies whether or not the information is confidential and whether the malpractice is occurring in the U.K. or overseas.

Individuals covered

In addition to employees, it covers workers, contractors, trainees, agency staff, homeworkers, and every professional in the NHS. The usual employment law restrictions on minimum qualifying period and age do not apply to this Act. It does not presently cover the genuinely self-employed (other than in the NHS), volunteers, the intelligence services, the army or police officers. (N.B. As to the police, see comment on s. 13).

Internal disclosures

A disclosure to the employer (which may include a manager or director) will be protected if the whistleblower has an honest and reasonable suspicion that the malpractice has occurred, is occurring or is likely to occur. Where a third party is responsible for the malpractice, this same test applies to disclosures made to him. It also applies where someone in a public body subject to ministerial appointment (*e.g.* the NHS and many "quangos") blows the whistle direct to the sponsoring Department.

Regulatory disclosures

The Act makes special provision for disclosures to prescribed persons. These are likely to be regulators such as the Health and Safety Executive, the Inland Revenue and the Financial Services Authority. Such disclosures will be protected where the whistleblower meets the tests for internal disclosures and, additionally, honestly and reasonably believes that the information and any allegation in it are substantially true.

Wider disclosures

Wider disclosures (*e.g.* to the police, the media, M.P.s, and non-prescribed regulators) are protected if, in addition to the tests for regulatory disclosures, they are reasonable in all the circumstances and they are not made for personal gain.

The whistleblower must, however, meet a precondition to win protection for a wider disclosure. This is either that (a) he reasonably believed he would be victimised if he had raised the matter internally or with a prescribed regulator; or (b) there was no prescribed regulator, and he reasonably believed the evidence was likely to be concealed or destroyed; or (c) the concern had already been raised with the employer or a prescribed regulator; or that (d) the concern is of an exceptionally serious nature.

If these provisions are met and the tribunal is satisfied that the disclosure was reasonable, the whistleblower will be protected. In deciding the reasonableness of the disclosure, the tribunal will consider all the circumstances, including the identity of the person to whom it was made, the seriousness of the concern, whether the risk or danger remains, and whether the disclosure breached a duty of confidence which the employer owed a third party. Where the concern had been raised with the employer or a prescribed regulator, the tribunal will also consider the reasonableness of their response. Finally, if the concern had been raised with the employer, the tribunal will consider whether any whistleblowing procedure in the organisation was or should have been used.

Full protection

Where a whistleblower is victimised in breach of the Act, he can bring a claim to an employment tribunal for compensation (s. 3). Where the victimisation falls short of dismissal, the Act provides that awards will be uncapped and based on what is "just and equitable" (s. 4). Dismissals in breach of the Act are automatically unfair (ERA, s. 103A as inserted by s. 5). Awards will be uncapped and based on the losses suffered. Where the whistleblower is an employee and he is sacked, he may, within seven days, seek interim relief so that his employment continues or is deemed to continue until the full hearing (s. 9). Where a tribunal makes a re-employment order at full hearing and the employer fails to comply with that order, the tribunal must make an additional award of not less than £5,720 and not more than £11,440.

Confidentiality clauses

Gagging clauses in employment contracts and severance agreements are void insofar as they conflict with the Act's protection.

Secrecy offences

Where the disclosure of the information is in breach of the Official Secrets Act or another secrecy offence, the whistleblower will lose the protection of the Public Interest Disclosure Act if he has been convicted of the offence or if an employment tribunal is satisfied, effectively beyond reasonable doubt, that he committed the offence.

Whistleblowing procedures

Though the Act does not require organisations to set up whistleblowing procedures, the existence of the Act will encourage the adoption of such procedures. Key aspects of such procedures[4], as endorsed by the Committee of Standards in Public Life (*supra*), are

- a clear statement that malpractice is taken seriously in the organisation;
- respect for the confidentiality of staff raising concerns, if they wish it;
- the opportunity to raise concerns outside the line management structure;
- access to independent advice;
- an indication of the proper way in which concerns may be raised outside the organisation if necessary; and
- penalties for making false allegations maliciously.

Commencement

The Government has announced that the legislation will be in force on or by the first anniversary of its enactment (which was July 2, 1998). The Act applies to England, Wales and Scotland. An Order in Council, which will provide the same protection to workers in Northern Ireland, is expected to be in force by the end of 1999.

Practical points

For those who advise employers, key issues to bear in mind are:

a) employers should make it clear that it is both safe and acceptable for workers to raise a concern they may have about misconduct or malpractice in the organisation;

---

[4] A comprehensive compliance toolkit, available from Public Concern at Work, gives detailed guidance and practical tools to help employers set up as an effective whistleblowing procedure and to comply with this Act.

b) where a worker raises a concern about a specified malpractice, every effort should be made to ensure that the employer responds [and can show it has responded: s. 1, s. 43G(3)(e)] to the message, rather than shoots the messenger;

c) the need that employers recognise it is in their own interests to introduce effective whistleblowing procedures. This will not only help both parties separate the message from the messenger but will also reduce the likelihood that a public disclosure will be protected under the Act: s. 1 s. 43G(3)(f);

d) where a protected disclosure has been made, employers should take all reasonable steps to try and ensure that no colleague, manager or other person under its control victimises the whistleblower: s. 2;

e) the implications of the Act on confidentiality clauses [s. 1, s. 43J] in severance agreements must be borne in mind by advisers and the use of such provisions in employment and related contracts should be reviewed;

f) employers should review the terms and conditions in their arrangements with contractors to ensure that those who work for key contractors also have access to the employer's whistleblowing policy insofar as the concern affects it;

g) disclosure to a prescribed regulator, though requiring a higher level of proof than internal whistleblowing, is protected [s. 1, s. 43F] whether or not the concern had first been raised internally. It is important to note that where the worker reasonably believes he will be victimised if he goes to a prescribed regulator, he will be entitled to protection if he makes a wider, public disclosure: s. 1, s. 43G(2)(a). Accordingly employers should make it clear that reporting concerns to a prescribed regulator is acceptable;

h) anything which might be construed as an attempt to suppress evidence of malpractice is now particularly inadvisable since (a) reasonable suspicion of a 'cover-up' would itself provide a basis for a protected disclosure: s. 43B(1)(f); (b) a disclosure to the media is more likely to be protected: s. 43G(2)(b); and (c) there is much reduced scope for containing any damage by a private settlement with a confidentiality clause: s. 43J;

i) if the employer is a public body subject to ministerial appointment, it should take account of the implications of the provisions which facilitate and protect whistleblowing direct to the sponsoring department: s. 1, s. 43E; and

j) depending on the employer's business, it may well be advisable that it – at a senior level – reviews its relationship with any regulator prescribed in its key areas of activity.

For those who advise individuals or potential claimants, essential issues to bear in mind are:

a) while the Act covers most of the workforce there are a few notable exceptions, (see overview above);

b) if the worker is seeking to engineer a claim or is seeking to misuse the Act to obtain or improve a settlement, it is unlikely he will satisfy the good faith test. If so, his disclosure will not be protected;

c) if the worker seeks advice about how to raise a concern, as the Act's strongest protection [s. 1, s. 43C] most readily applies where he raises the matter internally or with the responsible person, it is suggested that this should always be considered first as the initial and preferred step;

d) the worker is likely to face additional problems with causation [ss. 2, 5 and 6] if he blows the whistle anonymously as to win protection the tribunal must be satisfied that the employer believed he had made the disclosure and victimised him because of it;

e) if the worker is to disclose information externally because of fear of victimisation or fear of a cover-up or because of the seriousness of the matter, it is suggested that disclosures to Ministers [s. 1, s. 43E] and to prescribed regulators [s. 1, s. 43F] are fully considered first, even though a wider disclosure may also be protected [s. 1, ss. 43G(2) and 43H];

f) if the worker is to make a public disclosure of information [s. 1 s. 43G or s. 43H], two rules of thumb may be borne in mind: (a) a disclosure to a body whose duty is to investigate the malpractice is likely to be more readily protected; and (b) where the public interest will be equally protected by disclosures to two bodies, the disclosure which causes less damage to the employer is likely to be more readily protected than one which causes it much damage;

g) as to media disclosures [s. 1 ss. 43G and 43H], these are more likely to be protected (a) where the information was not confidential; (b) where, if it was confidential, there is or was a cover-up and there is no prescribed regulator; (c) where, if it was confidential, less public disclosures had failed to secure a reasonable response; or (d) where the matter was exceptionally serious and the client can show the media was a reasonable recipient of the disclosure;

h) if the worker suffers victimisation short of dismissal, he is also protected [s. 2]. Unless the detriment or damage is considerable, compensation awards under this head are likely to be small and, accordingly, it is suggested the main object should be to stop the victimisation; and

i) if the worker is an employee and is dismissed, he can and should within the first seven days apply for an interim order [s. 9] as this will strengthen his bargaining position.

Public Interest Disclosure Act 1998

CHAPTER 23

An Act to protect individuals who make certain disclosures of information in the public interest; to allow such individuals to bring action in respect of victimisation; and for connected purposes.

[2ND JULY 1998]

Section 1 PIDA

Protected disclosures

1.—After Part IV of the Employment Rights Act 1996 (in this Act referred to as "the 1996 Act") there is inserted—

PART IVA

PROTECTED DISCLOSURES

Section 43A ERA

Meaning of protected disclosure

43A—In this Act a "protected disclosure" means a qualifying disclosure (as defined by section 43B) which is made by a worker in accordance with any of sections 43C to 43H.

EXPLANATORY NOTE

The main effect of this provision is to insert into the Employment Rights Act 1996 the key provisions on the scope and detail of this Act. This contains eleven sections:

> 43A—defines a protected disclosure as a "qualifying disclosure" made in accordance with sections 43C–43H

> 43B—defines what information is capable of being protected ('a qualifying disclosure')

> *(43C—43H) set out the circumstances in which the following are protected)*

> 43C—raising the matter internally or with the person responsible

> 43D—disclosures in the course of obtaining legal advice

> 43E—disclosures concerning certain public bodies to a Minister of the Crown

> 43F—disclosures to persons (such as regulators) prescribed by Order

> 43G—other disclosures

> 43H—disclosures of exceptionally serious matters

> 43J—renders unenforceable contractual terms which preclude or restrict the making of a protected disclosure

> 43K—defines 'worker', giving it an extended meaning for the purposes of this Act

> 43L—is interpretative.

Section 43B ERA

Disclosures qualifying for protection

43B—(1) In this Part a "qualifying disclosure" means any disclosure of information which, in the reasonable belief of the worker making the disclosure, tends to show one or more of the following—

(a) that a criminal offence has been committed, is being committed or is likely to be committed,

(b) that a person has failed, is failing or is likely to fail to comply with any legal obligation to which he is subject,

(c) that a miscarriage of justice has occurred, is occurring or is likely to occur,

(d) that the health or safety of any individual has been, is being or is likely to be endangered,

(e) that the environment has been, is being or is likely to be damaged, or

(f) that information tending to show any matter falling within any one of the preceding paragraphs has been, is being or is likely to be deliberately concealed.

(2) For the purposes of subsection (1), it is immaterial whether the relevant failure occurred, occurs or would occur in the United Kingdom or elsewhere, and whether the law applying to it is that of the United Kingdom or of any other country or territory.

(3) A disclosure of information is not a qualifying disclosure if the person making the disclosure commits an offence by making it.

(4) A disclosure of information in respect of which a claim to legal professional privilege (or, in Scotland, to confidentiality as between client and professional legal adviser) could be maintained in legal proceedings is not a qualifying disclosure if it is made by a person to whom the information had been disclosed in the course of obtaining legal advice.

(5) In this Part "the relevant failure", in relation to a qualifying disclosure, means the matter falling within paragraphs (a) to (f) of subsection (1).

EXPLANATORY NOTE

Section 43B sets out the public interest information, which is capable of protection, provided that the particular disclosure meets the other conditions of the Act. It covers a wide class of information, applying to most malpractice. It is important to note that these provisions apply to all such information, whether or not it is confidential. It should also be noted that it does not matter whether the person to whom the disclosure is made is already aware of the information: s. 43L(3).

Subs. (1)

The requirement that the worker has a "reasonable belief" means that the belief need not be correct but only that the worker held the belief and it was reasonable for him to do so. Accordingly, it would still be a qualifying disclosure if the worker reasonably but mistakenly believed that a specified malpractice was occurring. Equally, if some malpractice were occurring which did not involve a breach of a legal obligation, the disclosure would still qualify if the worker reasonably believed it was such a breach. Unsubstantiated rumours will not be considered as qualifying disclosures as there must be, in addition to a reasonable belief, information that tends to show the specified malpractice. For the information to come within the definition of a qualifying disclosure, it matters not whether the malpractice was past, present or prospective or whether it related to particular conduct or to a state of affairs.

It will be noted that there is scope for considerable overlap between the six categories. As to the scope of several of the categories of information, the following points should be noted:

Failure to comply with a legal obligation includes a breach of any statutory requirement; contractual obligation, common law obligation (*e.g.* negligence, nuisance, defamation), or an administrative law requirement. As to government and public authorities, this subsection would include an official's reasonable belief that a decision of the authority could be overturned at judicial review (for example because of a procedural impropriety). It is submitted it would also cover the concern of a public servant that he had been asked to act in a way which breached a provision of the Civil Service Code or the Code for staff of non-departmental public bodies (NDPBs) (*e.g.* the requirement to act with "integrity, impartiality and honesty"). The Government confirmed by letter to Mr Shepherd that compliance with such codes is a contractual requirement binding on public servants.

Miscarriage of justice would include matters likely to lead to a wrongful conviction, such as reliance on unsound forensic techniques, failure to disclose evidence to the defence, or perjury (though this would come both under this heading and that covering crimes). As to cases at common law, reference may be made to the case of *Lion Laboratories v. Evans* [1985] QB 526 on suspect breathalyser equipment. However, the potential application of his Act to the famous miscarriages of justice (Birmingham Six, Guilford Four) is restricted while the Act's protection does not apply to police officers. It should be noted that the Government has given a firm commitment that the police officers will be provided equivalent protection—see Note to s. 13.

Health and safety risks apply whether they threaten a worker or any individual. As such, this provision includes risks to patients in a hospital, passengers on a train, children in care, consumers of electrical products or customers in a restaurant. It should be noted that the Act leaves in place the existing provisions in the ERA (ss. 44 and 100) on victimisation for health and safety matters.

'*Cover ups*' This category provides that qualifying disclosures include information not only about the substantive malpractice, but information which tends to show the deliberate concealment of information about the malpractice.

Subs. (2)

The Act applies regardless of the geographical location of the malpractice and subsection (1) applies regardless of whether the offence or breach of a legal obligation arises under UK law or the applicable law of another country. As explained in the Explanatory Note to s. 12, to be protected the worker must ordinarily work in Great Britain.

Subs. (3)

Where that disclosure of the information is itself a crime (*e.g.* it breaches the Official Secrets Act), it does not qualify. First it should be noted that raising such a concern formally within Whitehall or with the Civil Service Commissioner would not constitute a breach of (or disclosure under) a secrecy offence and so would qualify for protection in any event.

Where the disclosure was unauthorised and criminal proceedings were in progress or anticipated, it is expected that an employment tribunal would postpone any hearing under this Act. If the worker were acquitted at trial, he would be able to invoke its protection. Where no such proceedings were in prospect, the standard of proof the tribunal should apply is effectively a criminal one. This was the view of Lord Nolan (*Hansard*, H.L. June 5, 1998, col. 614) and Lord Borrie Q.C. (*ibid.*, cols 616/7), both of whom based their comments on the decision in *Re A Solicitor* [1992] 2 All E.R. 335. The Government spokesman, Lord Haskell, (*ibid.*, col. 616), while pointing out that the effects of such a finding would not be the same as in a criminal court, stated that a 'high standard of proof' would be required: reference may also be made to *Hornal v. Neuberger* (1957) 1QB 76.

Subs. (4)

This provision means that if a legal adviser cannot be compelled in court to give evidence about a matter, neither he nor the staff in his office can make a protected disclosure about it. Naturally, this does not affect the lawyer's ability to make disclosures on the instructions of a worker who is their client. This provision needs to be considered along with s. 43D, below.

DEFINITIONS

"disclosure": s. 43L(3)
"worker": s. 43K(1)

Section 43C ERA

Disclosure to employer or other responsible person

43C.—A qualifying disclosure is made in accordance with this section if the worker makes the disclosure in good faith—

(a) to his employer, or

(b) where the worker reasonably believes that the relevant failure relates solely or mainly to—

   (i) the conduct of a person other than his employer, or
   (ii) any other matter for which a person other than his employer has legal responsibility,

to that other person.

(2) A worker who, in accordance with a procedure whose use by him is authorised by his employer, makes a qualifying disclosure to a person other than his employer,

is to be treated for the purposes of this Part as making the qualifying disclosure to his employer.

EXPLANATORY NOTE

This section is, in the words of Lord Borrie Q.C., "absolutely at the heart" of the Act (*Hansard*, H.L., June 19, 1998 cols 1801/2) as it emphasises the vital role of those who are in law accountable for the conduct or practice in question. It does this by helping ensure that they are made aware of the concern, so they can investigate it. It sets out the wide circumstances in which a worker is protected if he raises the concern with his employer or the person responsible. No additional evidential test applies in this section beyond that in s. 43B, that the worker 'reasonably believes the information tends to show' the malpractice or misconduct.

Subs. (1)

Good faith—this requirement also appears in ss. 43E to 43H. A disclosure is made in good faith if it is made honestly, even though made negligently or without due care. Where the disclosure is demonstrably made for an ulterior and undesirable purpose (e.g. something approaching blackmail), it is submitted it would not be made in good faith. It should be pointed out that the issue of 'good faith' also arises in discrimination legislation and in the provisions in s. 104 ERA on the assertion of statutory rights.

Subs. (1)(a)

to his employer—this would, it is submitted, include a disclosure to any person senior to the worker, who has been expressly or implicitly authorised by the employer as having management responsibility over the worker. It would not cover a disclosure to a colleague. As to whistleblowing procedures, see the note on subs. (2) below.

Subs. (1)(b)

This subsection protects, for instance, a nurse employed by an agency who raises in the care home where she works a concern about malpractice. It would also protect a worker in an auditing firm who raises a concern with the client, and (it is submitted) it could also cover someone who works for a local authority highway contractor raising a concern with the local authority that the performance of the contract exposes the authority to negligence claims from injured pedestrians.

It is important to note that while such action is protected, (a) it does not amount to raising the matter with the employer for the purposes of a subsequent wider disclosure (under s. 43G); (b) this Act does not place any obligation on the person responsible to respond to the concern; and (c) if the worker is victimised for making a disclosure under this subsection, any claim he may have is against his employer and not against the person to whom he made this disclosure.

Subs. (2)

Where the organisation has a whistleblowing procedure which involves raising the concern with someone other than the employer (for example authorising a disclosure to a health and safety representative, a union official, its parent company, a retired non-executive director, its lawyers or external auditors, or to a commercial reporting hotline) a disclosure to that person will be treated as if it were a disclosure to the employer. As such, the reasonableness of the response to the concern is relevant in determining whether a subsequent wider disclosure may be protected: s. 43G(3)(e). While the Act does not require employers to set up whistleblowing procedures, a worker who makes a wide, public disclosure is more likely to be protected if there was no such procedure or it was not reasonable to expect him to use it: s. 43G(3)(f).

DEFINITIONS

"disclosure': s. 43L(3)
"employer": s. 43K(2)
"qualifying disclosure": s. 43B
"relevant failure": s. 43B(5)
"worker": s. 43K(1)

Section 43D ERA

Disclosure to legal adviser

43D. A qualifying disclosure is made in accordance with this section if it is made in the course of obtaining legal advice.

EXPLANATORY NOTE

This provision enables a worker to seek legal advice about a concern and to be protected in doing so. It should be noted that this is the only disclosure within the Act, which does not have to be made in good faith to be protected.

The lawyer, in turn, cannot of his own volition make a protected disclosure of the information—s. 43B(4). Of course, he can make such disclosure as the client instructs him to make on his behalf. As such, the disclosure will be judged as made by the client and it will only be protected if it is made in accordance with the other provisions of this Act. In terms of helping the client to raise the matter internally with the employer, the experience of Public Concern at Work is that this is best done by the client himself, rather than by the lawyer as this may unnecessarily suggest an adversarial stance. If the client does need some reassurance or backing, this may better be achieved by him mentioning that he has sought and is following legal advice.

While it is expected that, where a union is recognised in a workplace, disclosures to trade union officials will be protected under the whistleblowing procedures in s. 43C(2), the implications of this provision (and others) for general disclosures to union officials was considered at some length in the House of Lords at the Committee and subsequent stages. Lord Borrie Q.C. did make the point (*Hansard*, H.L. June 5, 1998, col. 624) that a disclosure by a union member for the purpose of obtaining legal advice from the union solicitor will, in any event, be protected under this section.

DEFINITIONS

"disclosure": s. 43L(3)
"qualifying disclosure": s. 43B

Section 43E ERA

Disclosure to Minister of the Crown

43E. A qualifying disclosure is made in accordance with this section if—

    (a) the worker's employer is—

        (i) an individual appointed under any enactment by a Minister of the Crown, or

        (ii) a body any of whose members are so appointed, and

    (b) the disclosure is made in good faith to a Minister of the Crown.

EXPLANATORY NOTE

Section 43E provides that workers in Government appointed bodies be protected if they report their concerns in good faith to the sponsoring Department rather than to their employer. The section refers to disclosure to a Minister, as legally this is what a disclosure to a Department is. This section provides a statutory framework for the recommendations that the *Committee on Standards in Public Life* made in its First Report, Cm. 2850–1 (1985) pp. 60 and 91–92 and Second Report (1996) p. 22.

This provision applies to bodies where the employer is an individual appointed under statute by a Minister (*e.g.* the utility regulators), or where one or more of the members of the body are appointed by a Minister (*e.g.* NHS Trusts, tribunals and non-departmental public bodies). While no requirement is placed on the Minister to respond to the concern, it does strengthen the accountability of Ministers for the conduct of bodies for which they are responsible and it is reasonable to expect that they will ensure the matter is investigated and any malpractice is corrected.

As under section 43C(1)(b), a disclosure under this section is not treated as one to the employer for the purposes of any subsequent, wider disclosure (s. 43G). It is also important to note that if the worker is victimised for making a disclosure under this subsection, any claim he may have is against his employer and not against the Minister to whom he made this disclosure.

Subs. 1(b)
"good faith": see note on s. 43C(1)

DEFINITIONS

"disclosure": s. 43L(3)
"employer": s. 43K(2)
"qualifying disclosure": s. 43B
"worker": s. 43K(1)

Section 43F ERA

Disclosure to prescribed person

43F—(1) A qualifying disclosure is made in accordance with this section if the worker—

(a) makes the disclosure in good faith to a person prescribed by an order made by the Secretary of State for the purposes of this section, and

(b) reasonably believes—

　(i) that the relevant failure falls within any description of matters in respect of which that person is so prescribed, and

　(ii) that the information disclosed, and any allegation contained in it, are substantially true.

(2) An order prescribing persons for the purposes of this section may specify persons or descriptions of persons, and shall specify the descriptions of matters in respect of which each person, or persons of each description, is or are prescribed.

EXPLANATORY NOTE

Section 43F protects a worker who makes a qualifying disclosure to a person prescribed by the Secretary of State for Trade and Industry by Order.

At September 1999, the following bodies have been prescribed. (The Public Interest Disclosure (Prescribed Persons) Order 1999 S.I. 1999 No. 1549) For further details, please visit our website at *www.pcaw.demon.co.uk*.

Health & Safety dangers: the relevant enforcing authority (HSE or local authority)

Environmental dangers: the Environment Agency, Scottish Environment Protection Agency

Utilities: OFTEL, OFFER, OFWAT, OFGAS

Financial Services & the City: Financial Services Authority (and pending its full operation, its predecessor bodies), H.M. Treasury (insurance)

Fraud & fiscal irregularities: Serious Fraud Office (Lord Advocate, Scotland), Inland Revenue, Customs & Excise

Public sector finance: Audit Commission, Accounts Commission for Scotland, National Audit Office, Auditor General for Wales

Company law: Department of Trade & Industry

Competition & consumer law: Office of Fair Trading or local authority

Others: Building Societies Commission, Certification Officer (Trade Unions), Charity Commission (and its Scottish sibling), Data Protection Registrar, Occupational Pensions Regulatory Authority, Rail Regulator.

However, an amendment was made to this section in Committee for the purposes (*Hansard* H.C. Standing Committee D, col. 8, 11 March 1998) of enabling classes of persons to be prescribed so as to ensure that health and safety representatives might be prescribed, should it transpire that employers were not including them within internal reporting procedures. Other classes of persons capable of being prescribed under this section could include certain trade union officials (*Hansard*, H.L. June 5, 1998, col. 623).

The preferential position this section will afford to disclosures made to prescribed regulators over other external disclosures reflects the position under the law of confidence. For example, in *Re. A Company* (1989) 3 W.L.R. 265, Sir Richard Scott, presently the Vice Chancellor, said:

"It may be the case that the information proposed to be given, the allegations to be made by the defendant to FIMBRA (*Commentator's note*: whose functions are performed by the Financial Services Authority now), and for that matter by the defendant to the Inland Revenue, are allegations made out of malice and based upon fiction or invention. But if that is so, then I ask myself what harm will be done. FIMBRA may decide that the allegations are not worth investigating. In that case no harm will have been done. Or FIMBRA may decide that an investigation is necessary. In that case, if the allegations turn out to be baseless, nothing will follow from the investigation. And if harm is caused by the investigation itself, it is harm implicit in the regulatory role of FIMBRA."

It should be noted, however, that not all regulators will be prescribed and that disclosures to such other regulators (and incidentally those to the police) will need to satisfy the provisions in ss. 43G or 43H if they are to be protected.

Where a regulator has been prescribed, it is important to note that there is no requirement (a) that the particular disclosure was reasonable; (b) that the malpractice was serious; nor (c) that the worker should have first raised the matter internally. However, the worker must meet a higher evidential burden than in s. 43C, which protects internal whistleblowing – see note on subs. (1)(b)(ii) below.

If it is not clear whether the matter should be raised internally or with a prescribed person, one practical approach to bear in mind will be for the worker or his adviser to contact the particular regulator informally first to check if it is prescribed and, without initially identifying the employer, to discuss the nature of the concern and to explore what action the regulator considers appropriate.

Subs. (1)(a)

As to good faith, see note on s. 43C(1), *supra*.

Subs. (1)(b)(i)

The worker must reasonably believe that the malpractice falls within the matters prescribed for that regulator.

Subs. (1)(b)(ii)

To be protected under this section, the worker must reasonably believe "that the information disclosed, and any allegation in it, are substantially true". While this is a higher evidential burden than that required for raising the concern under s. 43C, the worker will not lose protection if his belief was mistaken, provided the belief was reasonable. To be protected under this section, where a worker discloses the fact that another person has told him that a fraud has taken place, he would have to show he himself had a reasonable belief – and some factual basis for it – that the fraud has in fact taken place.

It should be noted that if the concern had been raised internally beforehand, the reasonableness of the worker's belief would have to take account of any response when the concern was raised internally.

DEFINITIONS

"disclosure": s. 43L(3)
"qualifying disclosure": s. 43B

"relevant failure": s. 43B(5)
"worker": s. 43K(1)

Section 43G ERA

Disclosure in other cases

43G—(1) A qualifying disclosure is made in accordance with this section if—

(a) the worker makes the disclosure in good faith,

(b) he reasonably believes that the information disclosed, and any allegation contained in it, are substantially true,

(c) he does not make the disclosure for purposes of personal gain,

(d) any of the conditions in subsection (2) is met, and

(e) in all the circumstances of the case, it is reasonable for him to make the disclosure.

(2) The conditions referred to in subsection (1)(d) are—

(a) that, at the time he makes the disclosure, the worker reasonably believes that he will be subjected to a detriment by his employer if he makes a disclosure to his employer or in accordance with section 43F,

(b) that, in a case where no person is prescribed for the purposes of section 43F in relation to the relevant failure, the worker reasonably believes that it is likely that evidence relating to the relevant failure will be concealed or destroyed if he makes a disclosure to his employer, or

(c) that the worker has previously made a disclosure of substantially the same information—(i) to his employer, or (ii) in accordance with section 43F.

(3) In determining for the purposes of subsection (1)(e) whether it is reasonable for the worker to make the disclosure, regard shall be had, in particular, to—

(a) the identity of the person to whom the disclosure is made,

(b) the seriousness of the relevant failure,

(c) whether the relevant failure is continuing or is likely to occur in the future,

(d) whether the disclosure is made in breach of a duty of confidentiality owed by the employer to any other person,

(e) in a case falling within subsection (2)(c)(i) or (ii), any action which the employer or the person to whom the previous disclosure in accordance with section 43F was made has taken or might reasonably be expected to have taken as a result of the previous disclosure, and

(f) in a case falling within subsection (2)(c)(i), whether in making the disclosure to the employer the worker complied with any procedure whose use by him was authorised by the employer.

(4) For the purposes of this section a subsequent disclosure may be regarded as a disclosure of substantially the same information as that disclosed by a previous disclosure as mentioned in subsection (2)(c) even though the subsequent disclosure extends to information about action taken or not taken by any person as a result of the previous disclosure.

EXPLANATORY NOTE

This section sets out the circumstances in which other disclosures, including those to the media, may be protected. Such disclosures must meet three tests to be protected. The first of these (s. 43G(1)(a)–(c)) deals with the evidence and motive of the whistleblower. The second (s. 43G(2)) sets out three preconditions, one of which must be met if the disclosure is to be capable of protection. Finally, to be protected the disclosure must be reasonable in all the circumstances (s. 43G(1)(e) and (3)).

Subs. (1)(a)
   good faith—See comment on subsection 43C(1), *supra*.

Subs. (1)(b)
   reasonable belief—See comment on s. 43F and 43F(1)(b)(ii), *supra*. If the concern had been raised internally beforehand or with a prescribed regulator, the reasonableness of the worker's belief will be assessed having regard to any response he had received from management or the prescribed regulator.

Subs. (1)(c)
   personal gain—This provision—that the whistleblower will not be protected if the purpose of the disclosure was personal gain—is aimed primarily at cheque book journalism. This provision does not catch any reward payable by or under any enactment (s. 43L(2)), such as a payment made by Customs and Excise. It covers not only payments of money, but benefits in kind. It would also catch a situation where the benefit did not go directly to the worker but to a member of his family, provided that its purpose was personal gain.

Subs. (1)(e)
   In all the circumstances of the case—In determining whether the disclosure was reasonable in all the circumstances, the tribunal should also have regard to the factors in s. 43G (3).

Subs. (2)
   The presumption is that, before any wider disclosure is protected, the concern will have been raised with the employer or with a prescribed regulator. This is reflected in three preconditions in this subsection, one of which must be met for a public disclosure under this section to be protected. These are that the worker reasonably believes he will be victimised; that he reasonably believes there is likely to be a cover-up; or that the matter had previously been raised internally or with a prescribed regulator.

Subs. (2)(a)
   The first precondition is that the worker reasonably believes he will be victimised were he to raise the matter internally or with a prescribed regulator. The belief must

exist at the time he makes the external disclosure, it must be objectively reasonable, and it must be that he *will be* victimised (note, by contrast, in subs. 2(b) that the test is reasonable belief that there is *likely to be* a cover-up).

To reduce the risk that this precondition is easily satisfied, it is suggested that organisations should (a) establish a whistleblowing procedure; (b) ensure that everyone knows victimisation is unacceptable and (c) make it clear that going to a prescribed regulator is acceptable. It is also suggested that organisations review how they handled any such matter beforehand, as a worker is more likely to be able to satisfy this precondition if in relation to a previous concern the employer's conduct could reasonably be interpreted as victimisation.

For those advising workers before any disclosure is made, it is important to note that – even though reasonable fear of victimisation may justify the protection of a wider disclosure – reporting to a prescribed regulator in such circumstances more readily secures protection for the client. However, where the worker has good reason to believe that, as a result of the unacceptably close relationship between the prescribed regulator and the employer, he will be victimised a wider disclosure will be protected provided it is reasonable in the circumstances

Subs. (2)(b)

This precondition deals with circumstances where the worker reasonably believes a cover-up of the malpractice is likely to occur.

It can only be satisfied where there is no regulator prescribed under s. 43F for that malpractice. Accordingly where there is a prescribed regulator, the Act suggests that a concern about a cover-up be raised with that regulator before any wider disclosure might be capable of protection (see subs. 2(c), below) unless the matter is exceptionally serious (s. 43H).

Subs. (2)(c)

This provides that wider disclosures may be protected where the matter has previously been raised internally or with a prescribed regulator. However, for such disclosures to be protected the tribunal must have particular regard to the reasonableness of the response of the employer or regulator (s. 43G(3)(e)). It should be noted that the disclosure does not have to be of exactly the same information, provided it is substantially the same.

Subs (2)(c)(i)

Where the concern was previously raised with the employer, in determining whether the particular disclosure should be protected, the tribunal must have particular regard (s. 43G(3)(f)) to whether the worker had complied with any whistleblowing procedure the organisation had.

Subs. (3)

In deciding whether the disclosure was reasonable in all the circumstances, the tribunal should have particular regard to the issues set out in this subsection. Where the disclosure was of non-confidential information, it is submitted that this reasonableness test should be more readily satisfied (reference may be made to the European Convention of Human Rights which, in the context of freedom of expression, distinguishes confidential from non-confidential information).

Where the information was confidential, it may be helpful to bear in mind the way the courts have weighed the same issue under the law of confidence. However, while the Act does not require that these are followed, it is submitted that tribunals should not apply this reasonableness test more restrictively than the courts permit disclosures of confidential information. This is because to be protected under this Act, the worker must meet certain criteria (good faith; some reliable evidence; and one of the preconditions in subs. (2) above) which do not apply to the decisions at common law. If the tribunal is satisfied that these criteria are met, the Act does no more than require the tribunal to consider whether the disclosure was reasonable in all the circumstances. The only explicit reference in the Act to any confidentiality in the information to the subject is where the rights of a third party have been breached: s. 43G(3)(d).

Subs. (3)(a)

The range of people to whom such a disclosure might be made is potentially vast. It could include the police, a professional body, a non-prescribed regulator, a union official, an MP, the relatives of a patient at risk, a contracting party whose rights were being flouted, shareholders or the media.

On the basis that the identity of the recipient of the disclosure may be in contention between the parties, we briefly summarise the decisions where this issue has been considered in the courts under the law of confidence. In 1984 the Court of Appeal, in *Francome v. Daily Mirror* [1984] 1 W.L.R. 892, held that the Daily Mirror could not publish confidential information which suggested that a jockey had been engaged in misconduct as the public interest would be just as well served by a disclosure to the police or the Jockey Club. This position was explained in *Spycatcher no. 2*, [1987] 3 W.L.R. p. 776, (*per* Lord Griffiths p. 794): "In certain circumstances the public interest may be better served by a limited form of publication perhaps to the police or some other authority who can follow up a suspicion that wrongdoing may lurk beneath the cloak of confidence. Those authorities will be under a duty not to abuse the confidential information and to use it only for the purpose of their inquiry."

As to cases where disclosures of confidential information to the media were justified, the following may be noted. In *Initial Services v. Putterill* [1968] 1 Q.B. 396 a disclosure to the Daily Mail about price-fixing was held to be lawful by the Court of Appeal because the public were being misled. Similarly in *Lion Laboratories v. Evans* [1984] 3 W.L.R. 539 a case about suspect roadside breathalysers, the Court of Appeal held the press was an appropriate recipient of the information as it was important that people had the information needed to challenge criminal charges and it seemed that the Home Office – which had approved the breathalyser—was an interested party. In *Cork v. McVicar The Times*, October 31, 1985, the High Court allowed the Daily Express to publish allegations of corruption in the Metropolitan Police.

Subs. (3)(b)

It is submitted that a lower level of seriousness would be expected where a disclosure of confidential information was made to the police or a non-prescribed regulator, than if the same information was disclosed to the media (see reference above to *Spycatcher no. 2*).

Subs. (3)(c)

This provision implies it is more likely to be reasonable if the disclosure is about an on-going or future threat. This picks up a theme from the jurisprudence on the law of confidence (*Weld–Blundell v. Stephens* [1919] 1 K.B. 520; *Malone v. Metropolitan Police Commissioner* [1979] 2 W.L.R. 700, p. 716; *Initial Services v. Putterill* [1968] 1 Q.B. 396, p. 405; *Schering Chemicals v. Falkman* [1981] 2 W.L.R. 848, p. 869). Where the threat is passed, there needs to be a clear public interest in any confidential information being disclosed. In *Spycatcher no. 2* [1987] 3 W.L.R. p. 776, Lord Griffiths (at p. 804) said such a public interest might be to bring those responsible to account.

Subs. (3)(d)

This provision was inserted at Committee in the Commons to ensure that tribunals took account of the interests of a third party about whom confidential information had been disclosed. In moving the amendment, the Minister explained (*Hansard*, H.C., Standing Committee D, cols. 8/9, 11 March 1998) that it was to deal with information subject to a banker-client or doctor-patient confidence. In such cases, tribunals would—it is submitted—do well to have close regard to the decision that would be reached if the third party sued the employer for breach of confidence. At report stage in the Commons, the Minister (*Hansard*, H.C., col. 1137, 24 April 1998) stated that "It is certainly not the intention that, where a bank has acted diligently, it should be liable for a breach of confidence by a client when a bank employee has made a public interest disclosure."

Its effect is not that the disclosure of such information should not be protected, rather that it is material in determining the reasonableness of the particular disclosure. A helpful example of this is in *W v. Egdell* [1990] 2 W.L.R. 471, where the Court of Appeal held that it was lawful for a consultant psychiatrist to disclose information about an in-patient to the medical director at the patient's hospital, where the consultant genuinely believed that a decision to release the patient was based on inadequate information and posed a real risk of danger to the public. However the court held that the sale of his story to the media would not have been justified, nor would an article in an academic journal unless it had concealed the patient's identity.

Where the disclosure did breach a duty of confidence owed by an employer to a third party, in determining the reasonableness of the disclosure it will be important to assess the effect of the breach on the rights of the third party and, in particular, any unjustifiable damage it caused him (Mr Shepherd, *Hansard*, H.C. Standing Committee D, col. 9, 11 March 1998).

Subs. (3)(e)

If the employer has investigated the concern and taken all reasonable action in respect of it but has left the whistleblower in ignorance of this, this may allow the worker to reasonably believe that no appropriate action was taken and to make a further disclosure. It is therefore highly desirable that the whistleblower is given feedback on, or is made aware of action taken as a result of, his concern and that this is provided within a reasonable period of time.

It is important to note that this section also applies where the concern has been raised with a prescribed regulator. As this has implications for employers, it is suggested that the organisation might sensibly request or instruct the prescribed regulator to communicate its findings to any whistleblower and to seek confirmation that this has been done.

Turning to the implications for prescribed regulators, this means that they too should be willing to provide the whistleblower with feedback. To this end it would be sensible that they advise the organisation that they propose to do this. Insofar as the secrecy offences which govern parts of the work of prescribed regulators may inhibit the provision of such feedback, it should be noted that (a) most such offences permit disclosures to be made with the consent of the person from whom the information has been obtained (and hence the employer can authorise the regulator to give feedback to the whistleblower); and (b) the Government is reviewing and revising the application of such offences in the forthcoming Freedom of Information legislation. Pending those changes, it is suggested that the prescribed regulator and the organisation should co-operate on how to ensure that reasonable feedback is made known to the whistleblower.

Subs. (3)(f)

As to the key elements of a whistleblowing procedure, see the reference in the section entitled Overview in the Explanatory Note to this Act and also the comment on s. 43C(2), *supra*. It should be noted that a grievance procedure is different from a whistleblowing procedure—a point made by Lord Borrie (*Hansard*, H.L., col. 627, 5 June 1998). Under a grievance procedure it is for the worker to prove his case. Under a whistleblowing procedure however, the worker raises the matter so that others may investigate it; it is not for the worker to prove the case or to dictate what the response should be from those in charge.

It is suggested it will not be enough to introduce such a procedure in a workplace if reasonable steps are not also taken to promote it to the workforce. Ideally once such a procedure is introduced, its use should be monitored and its role should be mentioned to the workforce (routinely depending on the size of the organisation), for example through team briefings, newsletters or posters.

Subs. (4)

This means that the worker will not lose protection if—in addition to disclosing the original concern—he comments on why he considers the initial response (be it of the employer or a prescribed regulator) was inadequate or unreasonable.

DEFINITIONS

"disclosure": s. 43L(3)
"employer": s. 43K(2)
"personal gain": s. 43L(2)
"qualifying disclosure": s. 43B
"relevant failure": s. 43B(5)
"worker": s. 43K(1)

Section 43H ERA

Disclosure of exceptionally serious failure

43H.—(1) A qualifying disclosure is made in accordance with this section if—

   (a) the worker makes the disclosure in good faith,

   (b) he reasonably believes that the information disclosed, and any allegation contained in it, are substantially true,

(c) he does not make the disclosure for purposes of personal gain,

(d) the relevant failure is of an exceptionally serious nature, and

(e) in all the circumstances of the case, it is reasonable for him to make the disclosure.

(2) In determining for the purposes of subsection (1)(e) whether it is reasonable for the worker to make the disclosure, regard shall be had, in particular, to the identity of the person to whom the disclosure is made.

EXPLANATORY NOTE

This section provides that other disclosures of exceptionally serious matters may be protected, even though they do not meet the conditions in the previous section.

Subs. (1)(a)
See comment on subsection 43C(1), *supra*.

Subs. (1)(b)
See Explanatory Note on s. 43F and comment on subsection 43F(1)(b)(ii), *supra*.

Subs. (1)(c)
See comment on 43G(1)(c), *supra*.

Subs. (1)(d)
This means that the concern should be of an exceptionally serious nature, were it to be well founded.

Subs. (1)(e) and Subs. (2)
These provisions were inserted by a Government amendment in Committee in the Commons (*Hansard*, H.C. Standing Committee D, 11 March 1998), following a concern of the Confederation of British Industry. The Minister said "The Government firmly believe that where exceptionally serious matters are at stake, workers should not be deterred from raising them. It is important that they should do so, and that they should not be put off by concerns that a tribunal might hold that they should have delayed their disclosure or made it in some other way. That does not mean that people should be protected when they act wholly unreasonably: for example, by going straight to the press when there could clearly have been some other less damaging way to resolve matters" (*ibid.*, col. 10).

Its submitted that a worker genuinely concerned that a child was being sexually abused would be protected under this section if he went to the police.

DEFINITIONS

"disclosure": s. 43L(3)
"personal gain": s. 43L(2)
"qualifying disclosure": s. 43B
"relevant failure": s. 43B(5)
"worker": s. 43K(1)

Section 43J ERA

Contractual duties of confidentiality

43J.—(1) Any provision in an agreement to which this section applies is void in so far as it purports to preclude the worker from making a protected disclosure.

(2) This section applies to any agreement between a worker and his employer (whether a worker's contract or not), including an agreement to refrain from instituting or continuing any proceedings under this Act or any proceedings for breach of contract.

EXPLANATORY NOTE

This provides that any clause or term in an agreement between a worker and his employer is void insofar as it purports to preclude the worker from making a protected disclosure. The agreement may be in an employment contract, in a contract of a worker who is not an employee or in any other agreement between a worker and employer. In particular it should be noted that it covers settlement agreements.

The section applies to 'gagging clauses' only insofar as they preclude a protected disclosure. In practical terms, their most significant effect will be in clauses in settlement agreements where the employer seeks to stop the worker from contacting a prescribed regulator under s. 43F. This provision would apply with equal strength and immediacy where a public body sought to stop workers contacting the sponsoring department under s. 43E.

Where important issues are at stake and the employer is seeking an injunction to restrain the disclosure of confidential information, it is suggested that the key issue for the court will be the identity of the recipient of the disclosure. This is because under the common law, courts are most unlikely to restrain a worker disclosing confidential information to a regulator or to the police, even where it is unclear the worker is acting in good faith or with reliable evidence (see Note on s. 43F, *supra*). Where the employer fears the worker will make a media disclosure, it will be open to the employer to seek an order or a declaration from the court that such a disclosure was not a protected one within this Act, even assuming the worker met the conditions in s. 43G(1) and (2).

Insofar as media disclosures go, this section will have no application where such a disclosure has already been held to be protected i.e. deemed to be in the public interest, as by that time the media will have covered the story.

It might apply however, where a worker was dismissed in a particularly unpleasant way because of making a protected disclosure to a prescribed regulator. In such an instance, his former employer might then settle a claim for unfair dismissal at an industrial tribunal and include within the settlement a clause preventing the whistleblower from disclosing the story of the malpractice and his dismissal to the media. However, the employer should recognise that even here such a clause may be unenforceable. If the whistleblower did tell the media, the issue would then arise whether this subsequent disclosure would have been protected. If it would not have been, then the employer might be able to claim that the money paid to the whistleblower be returned.

Such a risk would be greater where the employer's response to a concern which was raised internally was to dismiss the whistleblower and to cover-up the malpractice. If there was no prescribed regulator, then there is a good chance that any clause in the settlement of the whistleblower's claim which sought to prevent him or her telling the media would be unenforceable.

DEFINITIONS

"worker": s. 43K(1)

Section 43K ERA

Extension of meaning of "worker" etc. for Part IVA

43K.—(1) For the purposes of this Part "worker" includes an individual who is not a worker as defined by section 230(3) but who—

(a) works or worked for a person in circumstances in which—

  (i) he is or was introduced or supplied to do that work by a third person, and
  (ii) the terms on which he is or was engaged to do the work are or were in practice substantially determined not by him but by the person for whom he works or worked, by the third person or by both of them,

(b) contracts or contracted with a person, for the purposes of that person's business, for the execution of work to be done in a place not under the control or management of that person and would fall within section 230(3)(b) if for "personally" in that provision there were substituted "(whether personally or otherwise)",

(c) works or worked as a person providing general medical services, general dental services, general ophthalmic services or pharmaceutical services in accordance with arrangements made—

  (i) by a Health Authority under section 29, 35, 38 or 41 of the National Health Service Act 1977, or
  (ii) by a Health Board under section 19, 25, 26 or 27 of the National Health Service (Scotland) Act 1978, or

(d) is or was provided with work experience provided pursuant to a training course or programme or with training for employment (or with both) otherwise than—

  (i) under a contract of employment, or
  (ii) by an educational establishment on a course run by that establishment;

  and any reference to a worker's contract, to employment or to a worker being "employed" shall be construed accordingly.

(2) For the purposes of this Part "employer" includes—

(a) in relation to a worker falling within paragraph (a) of subsection (1), the person who substantially determines or determined the terms on which he is or was engaged,

(b) in relation to a worker falling within paragraph (c) of that subsection, the authority or board referred to in that paragraph, and

(c) in relation to a worker falling within paragraph (d) of that subsection, the person providing the work experience or training.

(3) In this section, "educational establishment" includes any university, college, school or other educational establishment.

EXPLANATORY NOTE

This provides an extended meaning to the definition of 'worker' and, as such, the scope of this Act goes beyond much of existing employment law. Under section 230(3) of the ERA, a worker includes an employee and an independent contractor who himself provides services other than in a professional – client or business – client relationship. In addition to these, this Act protects certain agency workers, home-workers, NHS doctors, dentists, opthalmologists and pharmacists, and trainees on vocational or work experience schemes.

Subs. (1)(a)

This covers agency workers, where the agency introduces them to or finds them the post and the terms of employment are substantially determined by the agency or the organisation where he performs the work. In this case, the 'employer' will be the person who substantially determined the terms of engagement (see subs. (2)(a)). It is anticipated that this will normally be the organisation where the person performs the work.

Subs. (1)(b)

This covers an independent contractor who provides services whether personally or otherwise from their home.

Subs. (1)(c)

This ensures that the Act applies across the NHS. Doctors, dentists, opthalmologists and pharmacists in the NHS are usually independently contracting profession-als and hence would not come under the definition of employee or worker in the ERA. Under this provision, for these professionals the Health Authority (or in Scotland, the Health Board) with which they contract is deemed to be their employer for the purpose of this Act (see subs. 2(b)).

Subs. (1)(d)

This provision ensures that trainees on work experience or vocational schemes will be protected against victimisation where they raise concerns within this Act. It does not cover trainees or students in education. For trainees covered by this section, the person providing the training is deemed to be the employer for the purposes of this Act (see subs. 2(c)).

DEFINITIONS

"contract of employment": ERA s. 230(2)
"employer": subs. 2 and ERA s. 230(4)
"worker": subs. 1 and ERA s. 230(3)

Section 43L ERA

Other interpretative provisions

43L.—(1) In this Part—

"qualifying disclosure" has the meaning given by section 43B;
"the relevant failure", in relation to a qualifying disclosure, has the meaning given by section 43B(5).

(2) In determining for the purposes of this Part whether a person makes a disclosure for purposes of personal gain, there shall be disregarded any reward payable by or under any enactment.

(3) Any reference in this Part to the disclosure of information shall have effect, in relation to any case where the person receiving the information is already aware of it, as a reference to bringing the information to his attention.

EXPLANATORY NOTE

These are interpretative provisions.

Subs. (2)

Disclosures for personal gain only arise under ss. 43G and 43H. The effect of this provision is where a regulator who is not prescribed under s. 43F makes a reward, it shall not be a bar to protection. Such rewards are occasionally made by statutory agencies in return for information supplied.

Subs. (3)

This makes clear that the worker does not unwittingly lose protection against victimisation where the recipient of the information was already aware of the situation. It avoids any argument that in such a case there could in law be no disclosure.

Section 2 PIDA

Right not to suffer detriment

2.—After section 47A of the 1996 Act there is inserted—
47B.—

Protected disclosures

(1) A worker has the right not to be subjected to any detriment by any act, or any deliberate failure to act, by his employer done on the ground that the worker has made a protected disclosure.

(2) Except where the worker is an employee who is dismissed in circumstances in which, by virtue of section 197, Part X does not apply to the dismissal, this section does not apply where—

(a) the worker is an employee, and

(b) the detriment in question amounts to dismissal (within the meaning of that Part).

(3) For the purposes of this section, and of sections 48 and 49 so far as relating to this section, "worker", "worker's contract", "employment" and "employer" have the extended meaning given by section 43K.

EXPLANATORY NOTE

This protects a worker who makes a protected disclosure under this Act from victimisation. It does this by inserting a new section into Part V of the ERA, which protects *inter alia* categories of workers who are performing statutory functions, such as health and safety representatives, trustees of occupational pension schemes and employee representatives from victimisation.

This section protects employees from action short of dismissal and protects other workers (who cannot be dismissed, as they are not technically employees) from any victimisation, including the termination of their contract. Protection for employees against dismissal and redundancy is provided in ss. 5 and 6, below. Note that no qualifying period or upper age limit applies to this protection.

The section does not confer a right of action against any third party who victimised the worker, such as clients of the employer (unless that third party comes within the extended definition of employer in s. 43K(2)). However, the failure of the employer to protect the worker against such action by others might itself be a detriment.

Subs. (1)

An employer subjects a worker to a detriment not only if he acts to the worker's detriment but if he causes him detriment by deliberately failing to act. Examples would include refusing promotion, not being given a pay rise; being disciplined; being singled out for relocation; or being denied facilities or training which would otherwise have been provided. Where the worker is not an employee, detriment includes termination of his contract.

Detriment, it is submitted, also includes the threat of a detriment. As the Government spokesman (*Hansard*, H.L., col. 634, 5 June 1998) said "An employee who has made a disclosure to his employer could be threatened with relocation to a remote branch of a company, for instance, where promotion prospects are poorer. That kind of threat is a detriment and even though the worker can be assured that the employer could not lawfully carry out the threat, the fear of the threat may well amount to detrimental action. Any threat which puts a worker at a disadvantage constitutes in itself detrimental action". See also *Mennell v. Newell & Wright* [1997] I.R.L.R. 519 where the Court of Appeal agreed with the EAT (while allowing an appeal on other grounds) that asserting a threatened infringement of a statutory right came within s. 104 ERA.

Subs. (2)

This provides that an employee who is dismissed cannot claim under this section but must claim under ss. 5 and 6 PIDA (ss. 103A and 105(6) ERA). However, the single exception to this is where an employee is on a fixed term contract of more than a year and he has agreed in accordance with s. 197 ERA to waive any claim for unfair dismissal if his contract is not renewed. In such a case, an employee can bring a claim that his employment contract was not renewed because he had made a protected disclosure.

DEFINITIONS

"employee': s. 230(1) ERA
"protected disclosure": s. 1 PIDA, s. 43A ERA
"worker": s. 1 PIDA, s. 43K(1) ERA

Section 3 PIDA

Complaints to employment tribunal

3.—In section 48 of the 1996 Act (complaints to employment tribunals), after subsection (1) there is inserted—

"(1A) A worker may present a complaint to an employment tribunal that he has been subjected to a detriment in contravention of section 47B."

EXPLANATORY NOTE

This enables a worker to make a complaint to an employment tribunal that he has been subjected to a detriment in breach of s. 2 PIDA, s. 47B ERA. Claims of an infringement of this right are not enforceable in any other forum.

Under this provision, it is for the employer to show the ground on which he subjected the worker to detriment: s. 48(2). Under s. 48(3) claims should be brought within three months of the act or the deliberate failure, or the last act or failure if the worker was subjected to a series of detriments. Where it was not reasonably practicable to claim within three months, the period may be extended to such extra time as is reasonable to bring the claim. However, tribunals are not known to grant such extensions freely.

Under s. 48(4) where the complaint relates to a deliberate failure to act, time runs from the date that the employer decided not to act. In the absence of evidence of this, it is the date the employer did an act inconsistent with the failed act or, in the absence of such evidence, the date by when the employer might reasonably have been expected to have acted.

DEFINITIONS

"worker": s. 1 PIDA, s. 43K(1) ERA

Section 4 PIDA

Limit on amount of compensation

4—(1) Section 49 of the 1996 Act (remedies) is amended as follows.
(2) At the beginning of subsection (2) there is inserted "Subject to subsection (6)".
(3) After subsection (5) there is inserted—

"(6) Where—

(a) the complaint is made under section 48(1A),

(b) the detriment to which the worker is subjected is the termination of his worker's contract, and

(c) that contract is not a contract of employment, any compensation must not exceed the compensation that would be payable under Chapter II of Part X if the worker had been an employee and had been dismissed for the reason specified in section 103A".

EXPLANATORY NOTE

This section deals with compensation for all forms of victimisation, other than the dismissal of an employee. For the reasons given below, the side-note is misleading as there is no limit to compensation under this section.

Where a tribunal has found that a worker was victimised in breach of s. 2 (s. 47B ERA), it must make a declaration to that effect and may make an award of compensation: s. 49(1) ERA. Compensation awards are assessed based on what is "just and equitable in all the circumstances", having regard to the infringement complained of and any loss suffered by the worker as a result of the detriment: s. 49(2). These losses specifically include expenses reasonably incurred by the complainant and the loss of any benefit he might otherwise have expected: s. 49(3). The worker is under a duty to mitigate his losses (s. 49(4)) – which if his contract is terminated includes obtaining or seriously seeking another job. Finally the tribunal has to reduce the award by such sum as it considers just and equitable where it finds the worker himself had contributed to or caused the detriment: s. 49(5).

Subs. (3)

This subsection has no effect as there will be no limit on compensatory awards where an employee is dismissed (see the Note to section 8 below). Had there been such a limit, this subsection would have ensured that a worker who was not an employee could not have received a larger award where his contract was terminated than if he had been an employee who had been dismissed in breach of this Act. However, *workers* whose contracts are terminated will still be less well protected in practice than *employees* who are dismissed. This is because *workers* cannot seek interim relief and they cannot seek re-employment orders.

DEFINITIONS

"contract of employment": s. 230(2) ERA
"employee": s. 230(1) ERA
"worker": s. 1 PIDA, s. 43K(1) ERA

Section 5 PIDA

Unfair dismissal

5.—After section 103 of the 1996 Act there is inserted—

"103A.

Protected disclosure

> An employee who is dismissed shall be regarded for the purposes of this Part as unfairly dismissed if the reason (or, if more than one, the principal reason) for the dismissal is that the employee made a protected disclosure."

EXPLANATORY NOTE

This provision makes the dismissal of an employee because or principally because he made a protected disclosure automatically unfair, because it is made a prohibited reason, within ss. 99–103 ERA. The effect is that the tribunal is not to consider whether or not the employer's actions were reasonable. If there were a number of reasons for the dismissal, it is still automatically unfair if the protected disclosure was the principal reason. Note that neither the normal qualifying period (two years at present) nor the upper age limit applies to this section (see s. 7, below).

Where the worker was not an employee (or if he was an employee on a fixed term contract and s. 197 ERA applies), and his contract was not renewed because he made a protected disclosure his protection is set out under ss. 3 and 4, *supra*.

DEFINITIONS

"employee": s. 230(1) ERA
"protected disclosure": s. 1 PIDA, s. 43A ERA

Section 6 PIDA

Redundancy

6.—After subsection (6) of section 105 of the 1996 Act (redundancy) there is inserted—

> "(6A) This subsection applies if the reason (or, if more than one, the principal reason) for which the employee was selected for dismissal was that specified in section 103A".

EXPLANATORY NOTE

This confers a new right on employees not to be selected for redundancy for making a protected disclosure. Note that no qualifying period or upper age limit applies to this section (see s. 7 below).

The effect is that the dismissal is unfair (s. 105(1) ERA) if (a) the principal reason for it was redundancy; (b) other employees in a similar position were not dismissed in the same circumstances; and (c) the reason or the principal reason the employee was selected was because he had made a protected disclosure

Where the worker was not an employee (or he was and he was on a fixed term contract and s 197 ERA applies), and his contract was not renewed because he made a protected disclosure his protection is set out under ss. 3 and 4, *supra*.

Section 7 PIDA

Exclusion of restrictions on right not to be unfairly dismissed

7.—(1) In subsection (3) of section 108 of the 1996 Act (cases where qualifying period of employment not required), after paragraph (f) there is inserted—

"(ff) section 103A applies"

(2) In subsection (2) of section 109 of the 1996 Act (disapplication of upper age limit), after paragraph (f) there is inserted—

"(ff) section 103A applies".

EXPLANATORY NOTE

This provides that neither the minimum qualifying period (presently two years, but being reduced to one) nor the upper age limit applies to claims under this Act for unfair dismissal or unfair selection for redundancy.

Subs. (1)

The effect is that rights in respect of dismissal for making a protected disclosure arise on the first day of employment. It should be noted that rights in respect of victimisation short of dismissal (see s. 2 *supra*) also arise on day one.

Subs. (2)

The effect is that the rights against unfair dismissal are not lost where the employee makes a protected disclosure after he has reached normal retirement age or, where there is none, the age of sixty-five.

Section 8 PIDA

Compensation for unfair dismissal

8.—(1) In section 112(4) of the 1996 Act (compensation for unfair dismissal) after "sections 118 to 127A" there is inserted "or in accordance with regulations under section 127B".

(2) In section 117 of that Act (enforcement of order for reinstatement or re-engagement)—

(a) in subsection (2) after "section 124" there is inserted "and to regulations under section 127B", and

(b) in subsection (3) after "and (2)" there is inserted "and to regulations under section 127B".

(3) In section 118 of that Act (general provisions as to unfair dismissal), at the beginning of subsection (1) there is inserted "Subject to regulations under section 127B".

(4) After section 127A of the 1996 Act there is inserted—

"127B.—

Dismissal as a result of protected disclosure

(1) This section applies where the reason (or, if more than one, the principal reason)—

    (a) in a redundancy case, for selecting the employee for dismissal, or

    (b) otherwise, for the dismissal, is that specified in section 103A.

(2) The Secretary of State may by regulations provide that where this section applies any award of compensation for unfair dismissal under section 112(4) or 117(1) or 117(3) shall, instead of being calculated in accordance with the provisions of sections 117 to 127A, consists of one or more awards calculated in such manner as may be prescribed by the regulations.

(3) Regulations under this section may, in particular, apply any of the provisions of sections 117 to 127A with such modifications as may be specified in the regulations."

EXPLANATORY NOTE

This section is being deleted by section 37 of the Employment Relations Act and will be of no effect. Pending this new section coming into force, regulations have been introduced under this section to provide that there is no limit on compensation awards under this Act (The Public Interest Disclosure Act 1998 (Compensation) Regulations 1999 S.I. 1999/1548). The regulations also provide for a higher additional award (currently not less than £5,720 and no more than £11,440) to be paid under section 117(3)–(6) ERA 1996, where a re-employment order has been made but not complied with. The same position will apply when section 37 is in force, namely no limit on awards for unfair dismissal and provision for a higher additional award.

It may be of assistance to explain the background to the regulation making power in this subsection. As the Government and Mr Shepherd were unable to agree on the correct approach to compensation for unfair dismissal at the time the Bill was introduced, a wide regulation making power was introduced in this section and Public Concern at Work was asked to consult key interests on the options. These were (a) applying the normal regime on unfair dismissal; (b) awarding compensation for losses, without any ceiling; or (c) extending the provisions for special awards (which hitherto applied to health and safety representatives, pensions fund trustees, union activities) to whistleblowers.

An unprecedented and overwhelming consensus among business, unions and professional interests favoured full compensation for whistleblowers. The Institute of Directors – which alone favoured normal awards – felt the precedent of special awards was "wholly inappropriate," while the Confederation of British Industry expressed reservations about the high minimum and the low maximum awards in it. It should be added that both bodies emphasised that they saw this Act primarily as a governance measure, rather than as a traditional employment matter. During the

Bill's passage (see *Hansard*, H.C. Standing Committee D, cols. 12–14, 11 March 1998; *Hansard*, H.C., cols. 1124–1139, 24 April 1998; *Hansard*, H.L., cols. 893, 895, 899, 900, 903, 11 May 1998), the Government came under pressure from all sides to endorse the view of the interested parties. Shortly before the Bill completed its passage, the Government published its White Paper *Fairness at Work (FaW)* (May 1998) Cm. 3968 and proposed to abolish the ceiling on unfair dismissal awards across employment law. While the Government has revised this proposal and decided that there will be a limit of £50,000 for general unfair dismissal awards, it has announced that no limit will apply under this Act.

Section 9 PIDA

Interim relief

9.—In sections 128(1)(b) and 129(1) of the 1996 Act (which relate to interim relief) for "or 103" there is substituted ", 103 or 103A".

EXPLANATORY NOTE

This provides that employees (but not other workers) who are dismissed because they made a protected disclosure are able to claim interim relief. This is a potentially significant provision because, if the tribunal finds that the employee is likely to win at the full hearing, it will order that, *pro tem.*, the employee is re-employed or that his employment is deemed to continue. If after the full hearing the tribunal finds for the employee, such an interim order is likely to increase the chances that the tribunal find it is practicable for the employer to comply with any re-employment order made at the full hearing. In these circumstances, if such a final order is not complied with, a higher additional award (currently between £5,720 and £11,440) must also be made.

Interim relief is available if the claim is made within 7 days of the dismissal (s. 128(2)); and the tribunal shall determine the application as soon as practicable thereafter (s. 128(3)); but giving the employer not less than 7 days notice of the hearing (s. 128(4)). The tribunal cannot postpone the hearing of an application for interim relief unless it is satisfied there are exceptional circumstances (s. 128(5)).

If at the interim relief hearing (s. 129(1)), the tribunal considers it likely that at a full hearing, it will find that the reason or the principal reason for the dismissal was because the employee made a protected disclosure, then a series of provisions apply. Briefly, these are that the tribunal first explains its powers (s. 129(2)) and asks the employer if he will reemploy the employee, pending the full hearing (s. 129(3)). If the employer is willing, then an order is made to that effect: s. 129(4)–(6). If the employee does not accept re-engagement (that is a different post, though on terms no less favourable: s. 129(3)(b)) then the tribunal decides whether that refusal is reasonable. If it is reasonable then the employee's contract is deemed to continue until the full hearing. If the refusal is not reasonable then no order is made pending full hearing: s. 129(8).

If the employer fails to attend the hearing for interim relief or says he is unwilling to reemploy the employee (s. 129(9)), then the tribunal makes an order under s. 130 that the employee's contract is deemed to continue until the full hearing. As pointed out above even if the whistleblower does not return to work, such an order will strengthen the employee's bargaining position in negotiations and may have some influence on the tribunal's decision whether to grant a reemployment order at full hearing and on whether it was practicable for the employer to comply with it.

Section 10

Crown employment

10.—In section 191 of the 1996 Act (Crown employment), in subsection (2) after paragraph (a) there is inserted—

"(aa) Part IVA,"

EXPLANATORY NOTE

The effect of this section is to apply this Act to people who are employees of, work for or are in the services of the Crown (s. 191 ERA). It does not, however, extend to those in the armed forces (s. 192 ERA) or to those involved in national security (s. 11, below).

Section 11

National security

11.—(1) Section 193 of the 1996 Act (national security) is amended as follows.
(2) In subsection (2) after paragraph (b) there is inserted—

"(bb) Part IVA"
"(bc) in Part V, section 47B."

(3) After subsection (3) of that section there is inserted—

"(4) Part IVA and sections 47B and 103A do not have effect in relation to employment for the purposes of the Security Service, the Secret Intelligence Service or the Government Communications Headquarters".

EXPLANATORY NOTE

This section restricts the application of this Act to those involved in national security and intelligence work.

Subs. (1)
This applies the general rule in s. 193 ERA that a Crown servant is protected under this Act, unless the worker is the subject of a ministerial certificate that his work safeguards national security.

Subs. (2)
This provides that this Act does not apply to people who work for the Security Service, SIS and GCHQ. Its effect is that a worker in one of these organisations will

not be protected from victimisation where he raises a concern internally that a manager has corruptly awarded a cleaning contract.

Section 12

Work outside Great Britain

12.—(1) Section 196 of the 1996 Act (employment outside Great Britain) is amended as follows.

(2) After subsection (3) there is inserted—

"**(3A)** Part IV A and section 47B do not apply to employment where under the worker's contract he ordinarily works outside Great Britain."

(3) In subsection (5), after "subsections (2)" there is inserted ", (3A)".

EXPLANATORY NOTE

This applies s. 196 of the ERA with the effect that this Act does not protect people who ordinarily work outside of Great Britain. It should be noted that under s. 196(5), someone who ordinarily works on a ship will, however, be protected under this Act unless (a) the ship is registered outside Great Britain; (b) the employment is wholly outside Great Britain; or (c) the worker is not ordinarily resident in Great Britain.

Section 13

Police officers

13.—In section 200 of the 1996 Act (police officers), in subsection (1) (which lists provisions of the Act which do not apply to employment under a contract of employment in police service, or to persons engaged in such employment)—

(a) after "Part III" there is inserted ", Part IV A", and

(b) after "47" there is inserted ", 47B".

EXPLANATORY NOTE

This section extends s. 200 ERA to this Act and thereby excludes police officers from this new legislative protection. It does not affect the rights of civilian staff in the police service to claim protection.

The proposed exclusion of police officers was criticised by both the Police Complaints Authority and the Association of Chief Police Officers and other consultees, particularly when miscarriages of justice are one of the specified malpractices expressly covered by the Act (see s. 43B(1)(c)). As a result of this criticism, the Government gave "an absolute commitment" that police officers will be given equivalent protection by regulation (*Hansard*, H.C., cols. 1143–44, 24 April 1998). The

Minister told the Standing Committee that the Home Office would immediately commence a review of the police regulations once the Bill was enacted and that if the police regulations could not provide 'equivalent' protection then other measures would be taken (*Hansard*, H.C. Standing Committee D, cols. 16–17, March 11, 1998).

Section 14

Remedy for infringement of rights

14.—In section 205 of the 1996 Act (remedy for infringement of certain rights) after subsection (1) there is inserted—

"(1A) In relation to the right conferred by section 47B, the reference in subsection (1) to an employee has effect as a reference to a worker."

EXPLANATORY NOTE

The effect of this is that complaints under this Act can only be brought to an industrial tribunal. In particular it provides that those covered by the extended meaning of "worker" in s. 43K(1) are able to bring claims to an industrial tribunal (which they would do under s. 2, s. 47B ERA *supra*).

Section 15

Interpretative provisions of 1996 Act

15.—At the end of section 230 of the 1996 Act (employees, workers etc) there is inserted—

"(6) This section has effect subject to sections 43K and 47B(3); and for the purposes of Part XIII so far as relating to Part IVA or section 47B, "worker", "worker's contract" and, in relation to a worker, "employer", "employment" and "employed" have the extended meaning given by section 43K".

(2) In section 235 of the 1996 Act (other definitions) after the definition of "position" there is inserted—

"protected disclosure" has the meaning given by section 43A,"

EXPLANATORY NOTE

This provision amends the interpretative provisions in the ERA to provide that the definition of 'workers' in s. 230 is given the extended meaning in s. 43K (*supra*) for the purposes of this Act. It also provides that the term 'protected disclosure' which is inserted (by ss. 2 and 5 *supra*) into other parts of the ERA has the meaning given by s. 1 PIDA, s. 43A ERA.

Section 16

Dismissal of those taking part in unofficial industrial action.

16.—(1) In section 237 of the Trade Union and Labour Relations (Consolidation) Act 1992 (dismissal of those taking part in unofficial industrial action), in subsection (1A) (which provides that the exclusion of the right to complain of unfair dismissal does not apply in certain cases)—

(a) for "or 103" there is substituted ", 103 or 103A", and

(b) for "and employee representative cases)" there is substituted "employee representative and protected disclosure cases)".

EXPLANATORY NOTE

While s. 237(1A) TULRA 1992 provides that generally an employee who is taking part in unofficial industrial action at the time of his dismissal cannot bring a claim for unfair dismissal, this amending provision means that this bar will not apply where the employee was dismissed or made redundant because he had made a protected disclosure.

Section 17

Corresponding provision for Northern Ireland.

17.—An Order in Council under paragraph 1(1)(b) of Schedule 1 to the Northern Ireland Act 1974 (legislation for Northern Ireland in the interim period) which states that it is made only for purposes corresponding to those of this Act—

(a) shall not be subject to paragraph 1(4) and (5) of that Schedule (affirmative resolution of both Houses of Parliament), but

(b) shall be subject to annulment in pursuance of a resolution of either House of Parliament

EXPLANATORY NOTE

The Act applies only to England, Scotland and Wales. This section enables its provisions to be extended to Northern Ireland by Order in Council, and this was done by statutory instrument 1998 No.1763 (NI. 17).

Section 18

Short title, interpretation, commencement and extent.

18.—(1) This Act may be cited as the Public Interest Disclosure Act 1998.

(2) In this Act "the 1996 Act" means the Employment Rights Act 1996.

(3) Subject to subsection (4), this Act shall come into force on such day or days as the Secretary of State may by order made by statutory instrument appoint, and different days may be appointed for different purposes.

(4) The following provisions shall come into force on the passing of this Act—

    (a) section 1 so far as relating to the power to make an order under section 43F of the 1996 Act,

    (b) section 8 so far as relating to the power to make regulations under section 127B of the 1996 Act,

    (c) section 17, and

    (d) this section.

(5) This Act, except section 17, does not extend to Northern Ireland.

EXPLANATORY NOTE

The substantive provisions of the Act were brought into force on July 2, 1999 by the Public Interest Disclosure Act 1998 (Commencement) Order S.I. 1999 No. 1547. As to Northern Ireland, the Order (see section 17, *supra*) is expected to be in force by the end of 1999.

Relevant extracts from the Employment Rights Act 1996

(as amended by the Public Interest Disclosure Act 1998 and the Employment Relations Act 1999)

Meaning of "protected disclosure"

43A. In this Act a "protected disclosure" means a qualifying disclosure (as defined by section 43B) which is made by a worker in accordance with any of sections 43C to 43H.

Disclosures qualifying for protection

43B.—(1) In this Part a "qualifying disclosure" means any disclosure of information which, in the reasonable belief of the worker making the disclosure, tends to show one or more of the following—

(a) that a criminal offence has been committed, is being committed or is likely to be committed,

(b) that a person has failed, is failing or is likely to fail to comply with any legal obligation to which he is subject,

(c) that a miscarriage of justice has occurred, is occurring or is likely to occur,

(d) that the health or safety of any individual has been, is being or is likely to be endangered,

(e) that the environment has been, is being or is likely to be damaged, or

(f) that information tending to show any matter falling within any one of the preceding paragraphs has been, is being or is likely to be deliberately concealed.

(2) For the purposes of subsection (1), it is immaterial whether the relevant failure occurred, occurs or would occur in the United Kingdom or elsewhere, and whether the law applying to it is that of the United Kingdom or of any other country or territory.

(3) A disclosure of information is not a qualifying disclosure if the person making the disclosure commits an offence by making it.

(4) A disclosure of information in respect of which a claim to legal professional privilege (or, in Scotland, to confidentiality as between client and professional legal adviser) could be maintained in legal proceedings is not a qualifying disclosure if it is made by a person to whom the information had been disclosed in the course of obtaining legal advice.

(5) In this Part "the relevant failure", in relation to a qualifying disclosure, means the matter falling within paragraphs (a) to (f) of subsection (1).

Disclosure to employer or other responsible person

43C.—(1) A qualifying disclosure is made in accordance with this section if the worker makes the disclosure in good faith—

(a) to his employer, or

(b) where the worker reasonably believes that the relevant failure relates solely or mainly to—

(i) the conduct of a person other than his employer, or
(ii) any other matter for which a person other than his employer has legal responsibility,

to that other person.

(2) A worker who, in accordance with a procedure whose use by him is authorised by his employer, makes a qualifying disclosure to a person other than his employer, is to be treated for the purposes of this Part as making the qualifying disclosure to his employer.

Disclosure to legal adviser

43D. A qualifying disclosure is made in accordance with this section if it is made in the course of obtaining legal advice.

Disclosure to Minister of the Crown

43E. A qualifying disclosure is made in accordance with this section if—

(a) the worker's employer is—

(i) an individual appointed under any enactment by a Minister of the Crown, or
(ii) a body any of whose members are so appointed, and

(b) the disclosure is made in good faith to a Minister of the Crown.

Disclosure to prescribed person

43F.—(1) A qualifying disclosure is made in accordance with this section if the worker—

(a) makes the disclosure in good faith to a person prescribed by an order made by the Secretary of State for the purposes of this section, and

(b) reasonably believes—

(i) that the relevant failure falls within any description of matters in respect of which that person is so prescribed, and
(ii) that the information disclosed, and any allegation contained in it, are substantially true.

(2) An order prescribing persons for the purposes of this section may specify persons or descriptions of persons, and shall specify the descriptions of matters in respect of which each person, or persons of each description, is or are prescribed.

Disclosure in other cases

43G.—(1) A qualifying disclosure is made in accordance with this section if—

(a) the worker makes the disclosure in good faith,

(b) he reasonably believes that the information disclosed, and any allegation contained in it, are substantially true,

(c) he does not make the disclosure for purposes of personal gain,

(d) any of the conditions in subsection (2) is met, and

(e) in all the circumstances of the case, it is reasonable for him to make the disclosure.

(2) The conditions referred to in subsection (1)(d) are—

(a) that, at the time he makes the disclosure, the worker reasonably believes that he will be subjected to a detriment by his employer if he makes a disclosure to his employer or in accordance with section 43F,

(b) that, in a case where no person is prescribed for the purposes of section 43F in relation to the relevant failure, the worker reasonably believes that it is likely that evidence relating to the relevant failure will be concealed or destroyed if he makes a disclosure to his employer, or

(c) that the worker has previously made a disclosure of substantially the same information—

(i) to his employer, or
(ii) in accordance with section 43F.

(3) In determining for the purposes of subsection (1)(e) whether it is reasonable for the worker to make the disclosure, regard shall be had, in particular, to—

(a) the identity of the person to whom the disclosure is made,

(b) the seriousness of the relevant failure,

(c) whether the relevant failure is continuing or is likely to occur in the future,

(d) whether the disclosure is made in breach of a duty of confidentiality owed by the employer to any other person,

(e) in a case falling within subsection (2)(c) (i) or (ii), any action which the employer or the person to whom the previous disclosure in accordance with section 43F was made has taken or might reasonably be expected to have taken as a result of the previous disclosure, and

(f) in a case falling within subsection (2)(c) (i), whether in making the disclosure to the employer the worker complied with any procedure whose use by him was authorised by the employer.

(4) For the purposes of this section a subsequent disclosure may be regarded as a disclosure of substantially the same information as that disclosed by a previous disclosure as mentioned in subsection (2)(c) even though the subsequent disclosure extends to information about action taken or not taken by any person as a result of the previous disclosure.

Disclosure of exceptionally serious failure

43H.—(1) A qualifying disclosure is made in accordance with this section if—

(a) the worker makes the disclosure in good faith,

(b) he reasonably believes that the information disclosed, and any allegation contained in it, are substantially true,

(c) he does not make the disclosure for purposes of personal gain,

(d) the relevant failure is of an exceptionally serious nature, and

(e) in all the circumstances of the case, it is reasonable for him to make the disclosure.

(2) In determining for the purposes of subsection (1)(e) whether it is reasonable for the worker to make the disclosure, regard shall be had, in particular, to the identity of the person to whom the disclosure is made.

Contractual duties of confidentiality

43J.—(1) Any provision in an agreement to which this section applies is void in so far as it purports to preclude the worker from making a protected disclosure.

(2) This section applies to any agreement between a worker and his employer (whether a worker's contract or not), including an agreement to refrain from instituting or continuing any proceedings under this Act or any proceedings for breach of contract.

Extension of meaning of "worker" etc. for Part IV A

43K.—(1) For the purposes of this Part "worker" includes an individual who is not a worker as defined by section 230(3) but who—

(a) works or worked for a person in circumstances in which—

(i) he is or was introduced or supplied to do that work by a third person, and
(ii) the terms on which he is or was engaged to do the work are or were in practice substantially determined not by him but by the person for whom he works or worked, by the third person or by both of them,

(b) contracts or contracted with a person, for the purposes of that person's business, for the execution of work to be done in a place not under the control or management of that person and would fall within section 230(3)(b) if for "personally" in that provision there were substituted "(whether personally or otherwise)",

(c) works or worked as a person providing general medical services, general dental services, general ophthalmic services or pharmaceutical services in accordance with arrangements made—

(i) by a Health Authority under section 29, 35, 38 or 41 of the National Health Service Act 1977, or
(ii) by a Health Board under section 19, 25, 26 or 27 of the National Health Service (Scotland) Act 1978, or

(d) is or was provided with work experience provided pursuant to a training course or programme or with training for employment (or with both) otherwise than—

(i) under a contract of employment, or
(ii) by an educational establishment on a course run by that establishment;

and any reference to a worker's contract, to employment or to a worker being "employed" shall be construed accordingly.

(2) For the purposes of this Part "employer" includes—

(a) in relation to a worker falling within paragraph (a) of subsection (1), the person who substantially determines or determined the terms on which he is or was engaged,

(b) in relation to a worker falling within paragraph (c) of that subsection, the authority or board referred to in that paragraph, and

(c) in relation to a worker falling within paragraph (d) of that subsection, the person providing the work experience or training.

(3) In this section "educational establishment" includes any university, college, school or other educational establishment.

Other interpretative provisions

43L.—(1) In this Part—

"qualifying disclosure" has the meaning given by section 43B;
"the relevant failure", in relation to a qualifying disclosure, has the meaning given by section 43B(5).

(2) In determining for the purposes of this Part whether a person makes a disclosure for purposes of personal gain, there shall be disregarded any reward payable by or under any enactment.

(3) Any reference in this Part to the disclosure of information shall have effect, in relation to any case where the person receiving the information is already aware of it, as a reference to bringing the information to his attention.

PART V

PROTECTION FROM SUFFERING DETRIMENT IN EMPLOYMENT

Rights not to suffer detriment

Protected disclosures

47B.—(1) A worker has the right not to be subjected to any detriment by any act, or any deliberate failure to act, by his employer done on the ground that the worker has made a protected disclosure.

(2) . . . [*Repealed*] This section does not apply where—

  (a) the worker is an employee, and

  (b) the detriment in question amounts to dismissal (within the meaning of that Part).

(3) For the purposes of this section, and of sections 48 and 49 so far as relating to this section, "worker", "worker's contract", "employment" and "employer" have the extended meaning given by section 43K."

Enforcement

Complaints to industrial tribunals

48.—(1) An employee may present a complaint to an employment tribunal that he has been subjected to a detriment in contravention of section 44, 45, [46, 47 or 47A].

[(1A) A worker may present a complaint to an employment tribunal that he has been subjected to a detriment in contravention of section 45A.]

(2) On such a complaint it is for the employer to show the ground on which any act, or deliberate failure to act, was done.

(3) An employment tribunal shall not consider a complaint under this section unless it is presented—

  (a) before the end of the period of three months beginning with the date of the act or failure to act to which the complaint relates or, where that act or failure is part of a series of similar acts or failures, the last of them, or

(b) within such further period as the tribunal considers reasonable in a case where it is satisfied that it was not reasonably practicable for the complaint to be presented before the end of that period of three months.

(4) For the purposes of subsection (3)—

(a) where an act extends over a period, the 'date of the act' means the last day of that period, and

(b) a deliberate failure to act shall be treated as done when it was decided on;

and, in the absence of evidence establishing the contrary, an employer shall be taken to decide on a failure to act when he does an act inconsistent with doing the failed act or, if he has done no such inconsistent act, when the period expires within which he might reasonably have been expected to do the failed act if it was to be done.

(5) In this section and section 49 any reference to the employer includes, where a person complains that he has been subjected to a detriment in contravention of section 47A, the principal (within the meaning of section 63A(3)).

Remedies

49.—(1) Where an employment tribunal finds a complaint under section 48 well-founded, the tribunal—

(a) shall make a declaration to that effect, and

(b) may make an award of compensation to be paid by the employer to the complainant in respect of the act or failure to act to which the complaint relates.

(2) [Subject to subsections (5A) and (6)] the amount of the compensation awarded shall be such as the tribunal considers just and equitable in all the circumstances having regard to—

(a) the infringement to which the complaint relates, and

(b) any loss which is attributable to the act, or failure to act, which infringed the complainant's right.

(3) The loss shall be taken to include—

(a) any expenses reasonably incurred by the complainant in consequence of the act, or failure to act, to which the complaint relates, and

(b) loss of any benefit which he might reasonably be expected to have had but for that act or failure to act.

(4) In ascertaining the loss the tribunal shall apply the same rule concerning the duty of a person to mitigate his loss as applies to damages recoverable under the common law of England and Wales or (as the case may be) Scotland.

(5) Where the tribunal finds that the act, or failure to act, to which the complaint relates was to any extent caused or contributed to by action of the complainant, it shall reduce the amount of the compensation by such proportion as it considers just and equitable having regard to that finding.

(5A) Where—

(a) the complaint is made under section 48(1ZA),

(b) the detriment to which the worker is subjected is the termination of his worker's contract, and

(c) that contract is not a contract of employment,

any compensation must not exceed the compensation that would be payable under Chapter II of Part X if the worker had been an employee and had been dismissed for the reason specified in section 101A.

"(6) Where—

    (a) the complaint is made under section 48(1A),

    (b) the detriment to which the worker is subjected is the termination of his worker's contract, and

    (c) that contract is not a contract of employment,

any compensation must not exceed the compensation that would be payable under Chapter II of Part X if the worker had been an employee and had been dismissed for the reason specified in section 103A."

PART X

Unfair Dismissal

Chapter I

Right not to be Unfairly Dismissed

The right

The right

94.—(1) An employee has the right not to be unfairly dismissed by his employer.

(2) Subsection (1) has effect subject to the following provisions of this Part (in particular sections 108 to 110) and to the provisions of the Trade Union and Labour Relations (Consolidation) Act 1992 (in particular sections 237 to 239).

Circumstances in which an employee is dismissed

95.—(1) For the purposes of this Part an employee is dismissed by his employer if (and, subject to subsection (2) and section 96, only if)—

    (a) the contract under which he is employed is terminated by the employer (whether with or without notice),

    (b) he is employed under a contract for a fixed term and that term expires without being renewed under the same contract, or

    (c) the employee terminates the contract under which he is employed (with or without notice) in circumstances in which he is entitled to terminate it without notice by reason of the employer's conduct.

(2) An employee shall be taken to be dismissed by his employer for the purposes of this Part if—

    (a) the employer gives notice to the employee to terminate his contract of employment, and

(b) at a time within the period of that notice the employee gives notice to the employer to terminate the contract of employment on a date earlier than the date on which the employer's notice is due to expire;

and the reason for the dismissal is to be taken to be the reason for which the employer's notice is given.

Effective date of termination

97.—(1) Subject to the following provisions of this section, in this Part 'the effective date of termination'—

(a) in relation to an employee whose contract of employment is terminated by notice, whether given by his employer or by the employee, means the date on which the notice expires,

(b) in relation to an employee whose contract of employment is terminated without notice, means the date on which the termination takes effect, and

(c) in relation to an employee who is employed under a contract for a fixed term which expires without being renewed under the same contract, means the date on which the term expires.

(2) Where—

(a) the contract of employment is terminated by the employer, and

(b) the notice required by section 86 to be given by an employer would, if duly given on the material date, expire on a date later than the effective date of termination (as defined by subsection (1)),

for the purposes of sections 108(1), 119(1) and 227(3) the later date is the effective date of termination.

(3) In subsection (2)(*b*) 'the material date' means—

(a) the date when notice of termination was given by the employer, or

(b) where no notice was given, the date when the contract of employment was terminated by the employer.

(4) Where—

(a) the contract of employment is terminated by the employee,

(b) the material date does not fall during a period of notice given by the employer to terminate that contract, and

(c) had the contract been terminated not by the employee but by notice given on the material date by the employer, that notice would have been required by section 86 to expire on a date later than the effective date of termination (as defined by subsection (1)),

for the purposes of sections 108(1), 119(1) and 227(3) the later date is the effective date of termination.

(5) In subsection (4) 'the material date' means—

(a) the date when notice of termination was given by the employee, or

(b) where no notice was given, the date when the contract of employment was terminated by the employee.

(6) . . . [*Repealed*]

Fairness

General

98.—(1) In determining for the purposes of this Part whether the dismissal of an employee is fair or unfair, it is for the employer to show—

    (a) the reason (or, if more than one, the principal reason) for the dismissal, and

    (b) that it is either a reason falling within subsection (2) or some other substantial reason of a kind such as to justify the dismissal of an employee holding the position which the employee held.

(2) A reason falls within this subsection if it—

    (a) relates to the capability or qualifications of the employee for performing work of the kind which he was employed by the employer to do,

    (b) relates to the conduct of the employee,

    (c) is that the employee was redundant, or

    (d) is that the employee could not continue to work in the position which he held without contravention (either on his part or on that of his employer) of a duty or restriction imposed by or under an enactment.

(3) In subsection (2)(a)—

    (a) 'capability', in relation to an employee, means his capability assessed by reference to skill, aptitude, health or any other physical or mental quality, and

    (b) 'qualifications', in relation to an employee, means any degree, diploma or other academic, technical or professional qualification relevant to the position which he held.

(4) Where the employer has fulfilled the requirements of subsection (1), the determination of the question whether the dismissal is fair or unfair (having regard to the reason shown by the employer)—

    (a) depends on whether in the circumstances (including the size and administrative resources of the employer's undertaking) the employer acted reasonably or unreasonably in treating it as a sufficient reason for dismissing the employee, and

    (b) shall be determined in accordance with equity and the substantial merits of the case.

(5) . . . [*Repealed*]

Protected disclosure

103A. An employee who is dismissed shall be regarded for the purposes of this Part as unfairly dismissed if the reason (or, if more than one, the principal reason) for the dismissal is that the employee made a protected disclosure.

Assertion of statutory right

104.—(1) An employee who is dismissed shall be regarded for the purposes of this Part as unfairly dismissed if the reason (or, if more than one, the principal reason) for the dismissal is that the employee—

    (a) brought proceedings against the employer to enforce a right of his which is a relevant statutory right, or

(b) alleged that the employer had infringed a right of his which is a relevant statutory right.

(2) It is immaterial for the purposes of subsection (1)—

(a) whether or not the employee has the right, or

(b) whether or not the right has been infringed;

but, for that subsection to apply, the claim to the right and that it has been infringed must be made in good faith.

(3) It is sufficient for subsection (1) to apply that the employee, without specifying the right, made it reasonably clear to the employer what the right claimed to have been infringed was.

(4) The following are relevant statutory rights for the purposes of this section—

(a) any right conferred by this Act for which the remedy for its infringement is by way of a complaint or reference to an employment tribunal,

(b) the right conferred by section 86 of this Act,

(c) the rights conferred by sections 68, 86, 146, 168, 169 and 170 of the Trade Union and Labour Relations (Consolidation) Act 1992 (deductions from pay, union activities and time off) [and

(d) the rights conferred by the Working Time Regulations 1998.]

(5) In this section any reference to an employer includes, where the right in question is conferred by section 63A, the principal (within the meaning of section 63A(3)).

Redundancy

105.—(1) An employee who is dismissed shall be regarded for the purposes of this Part as unfairly dismissed if—

(a) the reason (or, if more than one, the principal reason) for the dismissal is that the employee was redundant,

(b) it is shown that the circumstances constituting the redundancy applied equally to one or more other employees in the same undertaking who held positions similar to that held by the employee and who have not been dismissed by the employer, and

(c) it is shown that any of subsections (2) and to (7A) applies.

(2) . . . [Repealed]

(3) This subsection applies if the reason (or, if more than one, the principal reason) for which the employee was selected for dismissal was one of those specified in subsection (1) of section 100 (read with subsections (2) and (3) of that section).

(4) This subsection applies if either—

(a) the employee was a protected shop worker or an opted-out shop worker, or a protected betting worker or an opted-out betting worker, and the reason (or, if more than one, the principal reason) for which the employee was selected for dismissal was that specified in subsection (1) of section 101 (read with subsection (2) of that section), or

(b) the empoyee was a shop worker or a betting worker and the reason (or, if more than one, the principal reason) for which the employee was selected for dismissal was that specified in subsection (3) of that section.

[(4A) This subsection applies if the reason (or, if more than one, the principal reason) for which the employee was selected for dismissal was one of those specified in section 101A.]

(5) This subsection applies if the reason (or, if more than one, the principal reason) for which the employee was selected for dismissal was that specified in section 102(1).

(6) This subsection applies if the reason (or, if more than one, the principal reason) for which the employee was selected for dismissal was one that specified in section 103.

(6A) This subsection applies if the reason (or, if more than one, the principal reason) for which the employee was selected for dismissal was that specified in section 103A.

(7) This subsection applies if the reason (or, if more than one, the principal reason) for which the employee was selected for dismissal was one of those specified in subsection (1) of section 104 (read with subsections (2) and (3) of that section).

[(7A) This subsection applies if the reason (or, if more than one, the principal reason) for which the employee was selected for dismissal was one of those specified in subsection (1) of section 104 (read with subsection (2) that section).]

(8) For the purposes of section 36(2)(b) or 41(1)(b), the appropriate date in relation to this section is the effective date of termination.

(9) In this Part 'redundancy case' means a case where paragraphs (a) and (b) of subsection (1) of this section are satisfied.

Exclusion of right

Qualifying period of employment

108.—(1) Section 94 does not apply to the dismissal of an employee unless he has been continuously employed for a period of not less than two years ending with the effective date of termination.

(2) If an employee is dismissed by reason of any such requirement or recommendation as is referred to in section 64(2), subsection (1) has effect in relation to that dismissal as if for the words 'two years' there were substituted the words 'one month'.

(3) Subsection (1) does not apply if—

(a) ... [*Repealed*]

(b) subsection (1) of section 99 (read with subsection (2) of that section) or subsection (3) of that section applies,

(c) subsection (1) of section 100 (read with subsections (2) and (3) of that section) applies,

(d) subsection (1) of section 101 (read with subsection (2) of that section) or subsection (3) of that section applies,

[(dd) section 101A applies,]

(e) section 102 applies,

(f) section 103 applies,

(ff) section 103A applies,

(g) subsection (1) of section 104 (read with subsections (2) and (3) of that section) applies, ...

(gg) subsection (1) of section 104A (read with subsection (2) of that section) applies, or

(h) section 105 applies.

Upper age limit

109.—(1) Section 94 does not apply to the dismissal of an employee if on or before the effective date of termination he has attained—

(a) in a case where—

(i) in the undertaking in which the employee was employed there was a normal retiring age for an employee holding the position held by the employee, and

(ii) the age was the same whether the employee holding that position was a man or a woman,

that normal retiring age, and

(b) in any other case, the age of sixty-five.

(2) Subsection (1) does not apply if—

(a) . . . [*Repealed*]

(b) subsection (1) of section 99 (read with subsection (2) of that section) or subsection (3) of that section applies,

(c) subsection (1) of section 100 (read with subsections (2) and (3) of that section) applies,

(d) subsection (1) of section 101 (read with subsection (2) of that section) or subsection (3) of that section applies,

(dd) Section 101A applies

(e) section 102 applies,

(f) section 103 applies,

(ff) section 103A applies,

(g) subsection (1) of section 104 (read with subsections (2) and (3) of that section) applies, . . .

(gg) subsection (1) of section 104A (read with subsection (2) of that section) applies, or

(h) section 105 applies.

CHAPTER II

REMEDIES FOR UNFAIR DISMISSAL

Introductory

Complaints to employment tribunal

111.—(1) A complaint may be presented to an employment tribunal against an employer by any person that he was unfairly dismissed by the employer.

(2) Subject to subsection (3), an employment tribunal shall not consider a complaint under this section unless it is presented to the tribunal—

(a) before the end of the period of three months beginning with the effective date of termination, or

(b) within such further period as the tribunal considers reasonable in a case where it is satisfied that it was not reasonably practicable for the complaint to be presented before the end of that period of three months.

(3) Where a dismissal is with notice, an employment tribunal shall consider a complaint under this section if it is presented after the notice is given but before the effective date of termination.

(4) In relation to a complaint which is presented as mentioned in subsection (3), the provisions of this Act, so far as they relate to unfair dismissal, have effect as if—

(a) references to a complaint by a person that he was unfairly dismissed by his employer included references to a complaint by a person that his employer has given him notice in such circumstances that he will be unfairly dismissed when the notice expires,

(b) references to reinstatement included references to the withdrawal of the notice by the employer,

(c) references to the effective date of termination included references to the date which would be the effective date of termination on the expiry of the notice, and

(d) references to an employee ceasing to be employed included references to an employee having been given notice of dismissal.

The remedies: orders and compensation

112.—(1) This section applies where, on a complaint under section 111, a tribunal finds that the grounds of the complaint are well-founded.
(2) The tribunal shall—

(a) explain to the complainant what orders may be made under section 113 and in what circumstances they may be made, and

(b) ask him whether he wishes the tribunal to make such an order.

(3) If the complainant expresses such a wish, the tribunal may make an order under section 113.
(4) If no order is made under section 113, the tribunal shall make an award of compensation for unfair dismissal (calculated in accordance with sections 118 to 127A . . . [*repealed*]

Orders for reinstatement or re-engagement

The orders

113.—An order under this section may be—

(a) an order for reinstatement (in accordance with section 114), or

(b) an order for re-engagement (in accordance with section 115),

as the tribunal may decide.

Order for reinstatement

114.—(1) An order for reinstatement is an order that the employer shall treat the complainant in all respects as if he had not been dismissed.
(2) On making an order for reinstatement the tribunal shall specify—

(a) any amount payable by the employer in respect of any benefit which the complainant might reasonably be expected to have had but for the dismissal (including arrears of pay) for the period between the date of termination of employment and the date of reinstatement,

(b) any rights and privileges (including seniority and pension rights) which must be restored to the employee, and

(c) the date by which the order must be complied with.

(3) If the complainant would have benefited from an improvement in his terms and conditions of employment had he not been dismissed, an order for reinstatement shall require him

to be treated as if he had benefited from that improvement from the date on which he would have done so but for being dismissed.

(4) In calculating for the purposes of subsection (2)(a) any amount payable by the employer, the tribunal shall take into account, so as to reduce the employer's liability, any sums received by the complainant in respect of the period between the date of termination of employment and the date of reinstatement by way of—

    (a) wages in lieu of notice or ex gratia payments paid by the employer, or

    (b) remuneration paid in respect of employment with another employer,

and such other benefits as the tribunal thinks appropriate in the circumstances.

(5) . . . [Repealed]

Order for re-engagement

115.—(1) An order for re-engagement is an order, on such terms as the tribunal may decide, that the complainant be engaged by the employer, or by a successor of the employer or by an associated employer, in employment comparable to that from which he was dismissed or other suitable employment.

(2) On making an order for re-engagement the tribunal shall specify the terms on which re-engagement is to take place, including—

    (a) the identity of the employer,

    (b) the nature of the employment,

    (c) the remuneration for the employment,

    (d) any amount payable by the employer in respect of any benefit which the complainant might reasonably be expected to have had but for the dismissal (including arrears of pay) for the period between the date of termination of employment and the date of re-engagement,

    (e) any rights and privileges (including seniority and pension rights) which must be restored to the employee, and

    (f) the date by which the order must be complied with.

(3) In calculating for the purposes of subsection (2)(d) any amount payable by the employer, the tribunal shall take into account, so as to reduce the employer's liability, any sums received by the complainant in respect of the period between the date of termination of employment and the date of re-engagement by way of—

    (a) wages in lieu of notice or ex gratia payments paid by the employer, or

    (b) remuneration paid in respect of employment with another employer,

and such other benefits as the tribunal thinks appropriate in the circumstances.

(4) . . . [Repealed]

Choice of order and its terms

116.—(1) In exercising its discretion under section 113 the tribunal shall first consider whether to make an order for reinstatement and in so doing shall take into account—

    (a) whether the complainant wishes to be reinstated,

    (b) whether it is practicable for the employer to comply with an order for reinstatement, and

    (c) where the complainant caused or contributed to some extent to the dismissal, whether it would be just to order his reinstatement.

(2) If the tribunal decides not to make an order for reinstatement it shall then consider whether to make an order for re-engagement and, if so, on what terms.

(3) In so doing the tribunal shall take into account—

(a) any wish expressed by the complainant as to the nature of the order to be made,

(b) whether it is practicable for the employer (or a successor or an associated employer) to comply with an order for re-engagement, and

(c) where the complainant caused or contributed to some extent to the dismissal, whether it would be just to order his re-engagement and (if so) on what terms.

(4) Except in a case where the tribunal takes into account contributory fault under subsection (3)(c) it shall, if it orders re-engagement, do so on terms which are, so far as is reasonably practicable, as favourable as an order for reinstatement.

(5) Where in any case an employer has engaged a permanent replacement for a dismissed employee, the tribunal shall not take that fact into account in determining, for the purposes of subsection (1)(b) or (3)(b), whether it is practicable to comply with an order for reinstatement or re-engagement.

(6) Subsection (5) does not apply where the employer shows—

(a) that it was not practicable for him to arrange for the dismissed employee's work to be done without engaging a permanent replacement, or

(b) that—

    (i) he engaged the replacement after the lapse of a reasonable period, without having heard from the dismissed employee that he wished to be reinstated or re-engaged, and

    (ii) when the employer engaged the replacement it was no longer reasonable for him to arrange for the dismissed employee's work to be done except by a permanent replacement.

Enforcement of order and compensation

117.—(1) An industrial tribunal shall make an award of compensation, to be paid by the employer to the employee, if

(a) an order under section 113 is made and the complainant is reinstated or re-engaged, but

(b) the terms of the order are not fully complied with.

(2) Subject to section 124, [and to regulations under section 127B, and] the amount of the compensation shall be such as the tribunal thinks fit having regard to the loss sustained by the complainant in consequence of the failure to comply fully with the terms of the order.

(3) Subject to subsections (1) and (2) [and to regulations under section 127B], if an order under section 113 is made but the complainant is not reinstated or re-engaged in accordance with the order, the tribunal shall make—

(a) an award of compensation for unfair dismissal (calculated in accordance with sections 118 to [127A]), and

(b) except where this paragraph does not apply, an additional award of compensation of the appropriate amount,

to be paid by the employer to the employee.

(4) Subsection (3)(b) does not apply where—

(a) the employer satisfies the tribunal that it was not practicable to comply with the order ... [repealed]

(7) Where in any case an employer has engaged a permanent replacement for a dismissed employee, the tribunal shall not take that fact into account in determining for the purposes of subsection (4)(a) whether it was practicable to comply with the order for reinstatement or re-engagement unless the employer shows that it was not practicable for him to arrange for the dismissed employee's work to be done without engaging a permanent replacement.

(8) Where in any case an employment tribunal finds that the complainant has unreasonably prevented an order under section 113 from being complied with, in making an award of compensation for unfair dismissal . . . it shall take that conduct into account as a failure on the part of the complainant to mitigate his loss.

General

118.—(1) . . . [*Repealed.*] Where a tribunal makes an award of compensation for unfair dismissal under section 112(4) or 117(3)(a) the award shall consist of—

(a) a basic award (calculated in accordance with sections 119 to 122 and 126), and

(b) a compensatory award (calculated in accordance with sections 123, 124, 126 [and 127A(1), (3), and (4)]).

(2), (3) . . . [*Repealed*]
(4) Where section 127A(2) applies, the award shall also include a supplementary award.

Basic award

119.—(1) Subject to the provisions of this section, sections 120 to 122 and section 126, the amount of the basic award shall be calculated by—

(a) determining the period, ending with the effective date of termination, during which the employee has been continuously employed,

(b) reckoning backwards from the end of that period the number of years of employment falling within that period, and

(c) allowing the appropriate amount for each of those years of employment.

(2) In subsection (1)(c) 'the appropriate amount' means—

(a) one and a half weeks' pay for a year of employment in which the employee was not below the age of forty-one,

(b) one week's pay for a year of employment (not within paragraph (a)) in which he was not below the age of twenty-two, and

(c) half a week's pay for a year of employment not within paragraph (a) or (b).

(3) Where twenty years of employment have been reckoned under subsection (1), no account shall be taken under that subsection of any year of employment earlier than those twenty years.
(4) Where the effective date of termination is after the sixty-fourth anniversary of the day of the employee's birth, the amount arrived at under subsections (1) to (3) shall be reduced by the appropriate fraction.
(5) In subsection (4) 'the appropriate fraction' means the fraction of which—

(a) the numerator is the number of whole months reckoned from the sixty-fourth anniversary of the day of the employee's birth in the period beginning with that anniversary and ending with the effective date of termination, and

(b) the denominator is twelve.

(6) . . . [*Repealed*]

Basic award: minimum in certain cases

120.—(1) The amount of the basic award (before any reduction under section 122) shall not be less than [£2,900] where the reason (or, if more than one, the principal reason)—

(a) in a redundancy case, for selecting the employee for dismissal, or

(b) otherwise, for the dismissal

is one of those specified in section 100(1)(a) and (b), [101A(d),] 102(1) or 103.

(2) . . . [*Repealed*]

Basic award of two weeks' pay in certain cases

121.—The amount of the basic award shall be two weeks' pay where the tribunal finds that the reason (or, where there is more than one, the principal reason) for the dismissal of the employee is that he was redundant and the employee—

(a) by virtue of section 138 is not regarded as dismissed for the purposes of Part XI, or

(b) by virtue of section 141 is not, or (if he were otherwise entitled) would not be, entitled to a redundancy payment.

Basic award: reductions

122.—(1) Where the tribunal finds that the complainant has unreasonably refused an offer by the employer which (if accepted) would have the effect of reinstating the complainant in his employment in all respects as if he had not been dismissed, the tribunal shall reduce or further reduce the amount of the basic award to such extent as it considers just and equitable having regard to that finding.

(2) Where the tribunal considers that any conduct of the complainant before the dismissal (or, where the dismissal was with notice, before the notice was given) was such that it would be just and equitable to reduce or further reduce the amount of the basic award to any extent, the tribunal shall reduce or further reduce that amount accordingly.

(3) Subsection (2) does not apply in a redundancy case unless the reason for selecting the employee for dismissal was one of those specified in section 100(1)(a) and (b), [101A(d),] 102(1) or 103; and in such a case subsection (2) applies only to so much of the basic award as is payable because of section 120.

[(3A) Where the complainant has been awarded any amount in respect of the dismissal under a designated dismissal procedures agreement, the tribunal shall reduce or further reduce the amount of the basic award to such extent as it considers just and equitable having regard to that award.]

(4) The amount of the basic award shall be reduced or further reduced by the amount of—

(a) any redundancy payment awarded by the tribunal under Part XI in respect of the same dismissal, or

(b) any payment made by the employer to the employee on the ground that the dismissal was by reason of redundancy (whether in pursuance of Part XI or otherwise).

Compensatory award
[amended by the Employment Relations Act 1999]

123.—(1) Subject to the provisions of this section and sections 124 [, 126, 127 and 127A(1), (3) and (4)] the amount of the compensatory award shall be such amount as the tribunal considers just and equitable in all the circumstances having regard to the loss sustained by the complainant in consequence of the dismissal in so far as that loss is attributable to action taken by the employer.

(2) The loss referred to in subsection (1) shall be taken to include—

(a) any expenses reasonably incurred by the complainant in consequence of the dismissal, and

(b) subject to subsection (3), loss of any benefit which he might reasonably be expected to have had but for the dismissal.

(3) The loss referred to in subsection (1) shall be taken to include in respect of any loss of—

(a) any entitlement or potential entitlement to a payment on account of dismissal by reason of redundancy (whether in pursuance of Part XI or otherwise), or

(b) any expectation of such a payment,

only the loss referable to the amount (if any) by which the amount of that payment would have exceeded the amount of a basic award (apart from any reduction under section 122) in respect of the same dismissal.

(4) In ascertaining the loss referred to in subsection (1) the tribunal shall apply the same rule concerning the duty of a person to mitigate his loss as applies to damages recoverable under the common law of England and Wales or (as the case may be) Scotland.

(5) In determining, for the purposes of subsection (1), how far any loss sustained by the complainant was attributable to action taken by the employer, no account shall be taken of any pressure which by—

(a) calling, organising, procuring or financing a strike or other industrial action, or

(b) threatening to do so,

was exercised on the employer to dismiss the employee; and that question shall be determined as if no such pressure had been exercised.

(6) Where the tribunal finds that the dismissal was to any extent caused or contributed to by any action of the complainant, it shall reduce the amount of the compensatory award by such proportion as it considers just and equitable having regard to that finding.

(7) If the amount of any payment made by the employer to the employee on the ground that the dismissal was by reason of redundancy (whether in pursuance of Part XI or otherwise) exceeds the amount of the basic award which would be payable but for section 122(4), that excess goes to reduce the amount of the compensatory award.

Limit of compensatory award etc

124.—(1) The amount of—

(a) any compensation awarded to a person under section 117(1) and (2), or

(b) a compensatory award to a person calculated in accordance with section 123,

shall not exceed [£12,000].

(2) . . . [Repealed]

(3) In the case of compensation awarded to a person under section 117(1) and (2), the limit imposed by this section may be exceeded to the extent necessary to enable the award fully to reflect the amount specified as payable under section 114(2)(a) or section 115(2)(d).

(4) Where—

(a) a compensatory award is an award under paragraph (a) of subsection (3) of section 117, and

(b) an additional award falls to be made under paragraph (b) of that subsection,

the limit imposed by this section on the compensatory award may be exceeded to the extent necessary to enable the aggregate of the compensatory and additional awards fully to reflect the amount specified as payable under section 114(2)(a) or section 115(2)(d).

(5) The limit imposed by this section applies to the amount which the employment tribunal

would, apart from this section, award in respect of the subject matter of the complainant after taking into account—

(a) any payment made by the respondent to the complainant in respect of that matter, and

(b) any reduction in the amount of the award required by any enactment or rule of law.

Special award

125.—. . . [*Repealed*]

Internal appeal procedures

[**127A.**—(1) Where in a case in which an award of compensation for unfair dismissal falls to be made under section 112(4) or 117(3)(a) the tribunal finds that—

(a) the employer provided a procedure for appealing against dismissal, and

(b) the complainant was, at the time of the dismissal or within a reasonable period afterwards, given written notice stating that the employer provided the procedure and including details of it, but

(c) the complainant did not appeal against the dismissal under the procedure (otherwise than because the employer prevented him from doing so),

the tribunal shall reduce the compensatory award included in the award of compensation for unfair dismissal by such amount (if any) as it considers just and equitable.

(2) Where in a case in which an award of compensation for unfair dismissal falls to be made under section 112(4) or 117(3)(a) the tribunal finds that—

(a) the employer provided a procedure for appealing against dismissal, but

(b) the employer prevented the complainant from appealing against the dismissal under the procedure,

the award of compensation for unfair dismissal shall include a supplementary award of such amount (if any) as the tribunal considers just and equitable.

(3) In determining the amount of a reduction under subsection (1) or a supplementary award under subsection (2) the tribunal shall have regard to all the circumstances of the case, including in particular the chances that an appeal under the procedure provided by the employer would have been successful.

(4) The amount of such a reduction or supplementary award shall not exceed the amount of two weeks' pay.]

Dismissal as a result of protected disclosure

127B.—. . . [*Repealed*]

Interim relief

Interim relief pending determination of complaint

128.—(1) An employee who presents a complaint to an employment tribunal—

(a) that he has been unfairly dismissed by his employer, and

(b) that the reason (or, if more than one, the principal reason) for the dismissal is one of those specified in section 100(1)(a) and (b), [101A(d),] 102(1)[103 or 103A.],

may apply to the tribunal for interim relief.

(2) The tribunal shall not entertain an application for interim relief unless it is presented to the tribunal before the end of the period of seven days immediately following the effective date of termination (whether before, on or after that date).

(3) The tribunal shall determine the application for interim relief as soon as practicable after receiving the application.

(4) The tribunal shall give to the employer not later than seven days before the date of the hearing a copy of the application together with notice of the date, time and place of the hearing.

(5) The tribunal shall not exercise any power it has of postponing the hearing of an application for interim relief except where it is satisfied that special circumstances exist which justify it in doing so.

Procedure on hearing of application and making of order

129.—(1) This section applies where, on hearing an employee's application for interim relief, it appears to the tribunal that it is likely that on determining the complaint to which the application relates the tribunal will find that the reason (or, if more than one, the principal reason) for his dismissal is one of those specified in section 100(1)(a) and (b), [101A(d),] 102(1). [103 or 103A.]

(2) The tribunal shall announce its findings and explain to both parties (if present)—

(a) what powers the tribunal may exercise on the application, and

(b) in what circumstances it will exercise them.

(3) The tribunal shall ask the employer (if present) whether he is willing, pending the determination or settlement of the complaint—

(a) to reinstate the employee (that is, to treat him in all respects as if he had not been dismissed), or

(b) if not, to re-engage him in another job on terms and conditions not less favourable than those which would have been applicable to him if he had not been dismissed.

(4) For the purposes of subsection (3)(b) 'terms and conditions not less favourable than those which would have been applicable to him if he had not been dismissed' means, as regards seniority, pension rights and other similar rights, that the period prior to the dismissal should be regarded as continuous with his employment following the dismissal.

(5) If the employer states that he is willing to reinstate the employee, the tribunal shall make an order to that effect.

(6) If the employer—

(a) states that he is willing to re-engage the employee in another job, and

(b) specifies the terms and conditions on which he is willing to do so,

the tribunal shall ask the employee whether he is willing to accept the job on those terms and conditions.

(7) If the employee is willing to accept the job on those terms and conditions, the tribunal shall make an order to that effect.

(8) If the employee is not willing to accept the job on those terms and conditions—

(a) where the tribunal is of the opinion that the refusal is reasonable, the tribunal shall make an order for the continuation of his contract of employment, and

(b) otherwise, the tribunal shall make no order.

(9) If on the hearing of an application for interim relief the employer—

(a) fails to attend before the tribunal, or

(b) states that he is unwilling either to reinstate or re-engage the employee as mentioned in subsection (3), the tribunal shall make an order for the continuation of the employee's contract of employment.

Order for continuation of contract of employment

130.—(1) An order under section 129 for the continuation of a contract of employment is an order that the contract of employment continue in force—

(a) for the purposes of pay or any other benefit derived from the employment, seniority, pension rights and other similar matters, and

(b) for the purposes of determining for any purpose the period for which the employee has been continuously employed,

from the date of its termination (whether before or after the making of the order) until the determination or settlement of the complaint.

(2) Where the tribunal makes such an order it shall specify in the order the amount which is to be paid by the employer to the employee by way of pay in respect of each normal pay period, or part of any such period, falling between the date of dismissal and the determination or settlement of the complaint.

(3) Subject to the following provisions, the amount so specified shall be that which the employee could reasonably have been expected to earn during that period, or part, and shall be paid—

(a) in the case of a payment for any such period falling wholly or partly after the making of the order, on the normal pay day for that period, and

(b) in the case of a payment for any past period, within such time as may be specified in the order.

(4) If an amount is payable in respect only of part of a normal pay period, the amount shall be calculated by reference to the whole period and reduced proportionately.

(5) Any payment made to an employee by an employer under his contract of employment, or by way of damages for breach of that contract, in respect of a normal pay period, or part of any such period, goes towards discharging the employer's liability in respect of that period under subsection (2); and, conversely, any payment under that subsection in respect of a period goes towards discharging any liability of the employer under, or in respect of breach of, the contract of employment in respect of that period.

(6) In an employee, on or after being dismissed by his employer, receives a lump sum which, or part of which, is in lieu of wages but is not referable to any normal pay period, the tribunal shall take the payment into account in determining the amount of pay to be payable in pursuance of any such order.

(7) For the purposes of this section, the amount which an employee could reasonably have been expected to earn, his normal pay period and the normal pay day for each period shall be determined as if he had not been dismissed.

Application for variation or revocation of order

131.—(1) At any time between—

(a) the making of an order under section 129, and

(b) the determination or settlement of the complaint,

the employer or the employee may apply to an industrial tribunal for the revocation or variation of the order on the ground of a relevant change of circumstances since the making of the order.

(2) Sections 128 and 129 apply in relation to such an application as in relation to an original application for interim relief except that, in the case of an application by the employer,

section 128(4) has effect with the substitution of a reference to the employee for the reference to the employer.

Consequence of failure to comply with order

132.—(1) If, on the application of an employee, an industrial tribunal is satisfied that the employer has not complied with the terms of an order for the reinstatement or re-engagement of the employee under section 129(5) or (7), the tribunal shall—

(a) make an order for the continuation of the employee's contract of employment, and

(b) order the employer to pay compensation to the employee.

(2) Compensation under subsection (1)(b) shall be of such amount as the tribunal considers just and equitable in all the circumstances having regard—

(a) to the infringement of the employee's right to be reinstated or re-engaged in pursuance of the order, and

(b) to any loss suffered by the employee in consequence of the non-compliance.

(3) Section 130 applies to an order under subsection (1)(a) as in relation to an order under section 129.

(4) If on the application of an employee an employment tribunal is satisfied that the employer has not complied with the terms of an order for the continuation of a contract of employment subsection (5) or (6) applies.

(5) Where the non-compliance consists of a failure to pay an amount by way of pay specified in the order—

(a) the tribunal shall determine the amount owed by the employer on the date of the determination, and

(b) if on that date the tribunal also determines the employee's complaint that he has been unfairly dismissed, it shall specify that amount separately from any other sum awarded to the employee.

(6) In any other case, the tribunal shall order the employer to pay the employee such compensation as the tribunal considers just and equitable in all the circumstances having regard to any loss suffered by the employee in consequence of the non-compliance.

PART XIII

MISCELLANEOUS

CHAPTER I

PARTICULAR TYPES OF EMPLOYMENT

Crown employment etc

Crown employment

191.—(1) Subject to sections 192 and 193, the provisions of this Act to which this section applies have effect in relation to Crown employment and persons in Crown employment as they have effect in relation to other employment and other employees or workers.

(2) This section applies to—

    (a) Parts I to III,

"(aa) Part IV A"

    (b) Part V, apart from section 45,

    (c) Parts VI to VIII,

    (d) in Part IX, sections 92 and 93,

    (e) Part X, apart from section 101, and

    (f) this Part and Parts XIV and XV.

(3) In this Act 'Crown employment' means employment under or for the purposes of a government department or any officer or body exercising on behalf of the Crown functions conferred by a statutory provision.

(4) For the purposes of the application of provisions of this Act in relation to Crown employment in accordance with subsection (1)—

    (a) references to an employee or a worker shall be construed as references to a person in Crown employment,

    (b) references to a contract of employment, or a worker's contract, shall be construed as references to the terms of employment of a person in Crown employment,

    (c) references to dismissal, or to the termination of a worker's contract, shall be construed as references to the termination of Crown employment,

    (d) references to redundancy shall be construed as references to the existence of such circumstances as are treated, in accordance with any arrangements falling within section 177(3) for the time being in force, as equivalent to redundancy in relation to Crown employment, and

    (e) references to an undertaking shall be construed—

        (i) in relation to a Minister of the Crown, as references to his functions or (as the context may require) to the department of which he is in charge, and
       (ii) in relation to a government department, officer or body, as references to the functions of the department, officer or body or (as the context may require) to the department, officer or body.

(5) Where the terms of employment of a person in Crown employment restrict his right to take part in—

    (a) certain political activities, or

    (b) activities which may conflict with his official functions,

nothing in section 50 requires him to be allowed time off work for public duties connected with any such activities.

(6) Sections 159 and 160 are without prejudice to any exemption or immunity of the Crown.

National security

193.—(1) The provisions of this Act to which this section applies do not have effect in relation to any Crown employment in respect of which there is in force a certificate issued by or on behalf of a Minister of the Crown certifying that employment of a description specified in the certificate, or the employment of a particular person so specified, is (or, at a time specified in the certificate, was) required to be expected from those provisions for the purpose of safeguarding national security.

(2) This section applies to—

    (a) Part I, so far as it relates to itemised pay statements,

    (b) Part III,

  (bb) Part IV A,

  (bc) in Part V, section 47B.

    (c) in Part VI, sections 50 to 54,

    (d) in Part VII, sections 64 and 65, and sections 69 and 70 so far as relating to those sections,

    (e) in Part IX, sections 92 and 93, except where they apply by virtue of section 92(4),

    (f) Part X, except so far as relating to a dismissal which is treated as unfair—

        (i) by section 99(1) to (3), 100 or 103, or
       (ii) by subsection (1) of section 105 by reason of the application of subsection (2, (3) or (6) of that section, and

    (g) this Part and Parts XIV and XV (so far as relating to any of the provisions specified in paragraphs (a) to (f)).

(3) Any document purporting to be a certificate issued as mentioned in subsection (1)—

    (a) shall be received in evidence, and

    (b) unless the contrary is proved, shall be deemed to be such a certificate.

[Part IVA and sections 47B and 103A do not have effect in relation to employment for the purposes of the Security Service, the Secret Intelligence Service or the Government Communications Headquarters.]

Employment outside Great Britain

196.—. . . [*Repealed*]

Police officers

200.—(1) Sections 8 to 10, Part III, Part IV A, and sections . . . 45, [45A,] 47, ", 47B" 50 to 57 and 61 to 63, Parts VII and VIII, sections 92 and 93, Part X [[(except sections 100 and 134A and the other provisions of that Part so far as relating to the right not to be unfairly dismissed in a case where the dismissal is unfair by virtue of section 100)]] and section 137 do not apply to employment under a contract of employment in police service or to persons engaged in such employment.

(2) In subsection (1) 'police service' means—

    (a) service as a member of a constabulary maintained by virtue of an enactment, or

    (b) subject to section 126 of the Criminal Justice and Public Order Act 1994 (prison staff not to be regarded as in police service), service in any other capacity by virtue of which a person has the powers or privileges of a constable.

Law governing employment

204.—(1) For the purposes of this Act it is immaterial whether the law which (apart from this Act) governs any person's employment is the law of the United Kingdom, or of a part of the United Kingdom, or not.

(2) . . . [*Repealed*]

Remedy for infringement of certain rights

205.—(1) The remedy of an employee for infringement of any of the rights conferred by section 8, Part III, Parts V to VIII, section 92, Part X and Part XII is, where provision is made for a complaint or the reference of a question to an industrial tribunal, by way of such a complaint or reference and not otherwise.

[(1A) In relation to the right conferred by section 47B, the reference in subsection (1) to an employee has effect as a reference to a worker.]

(1ZA) In relation to the right conferred by section 45A, the reference in subsection (1) to an employee has effect as a reference to a worker.

(2) The remedy of a worker in respect of any contravention of section 13, 15, 18(1) or 21(1) is by way of a complaint under section 23 and not otherwise.

CHAPTER III

OTHER INTERPRETATION PROVISIONS

Employees, workers etc

230.—(1) In this Act 'employee' means an individual who has entered into or works under (or, where the employment has ceased, worked under) a contract of employment.

(2) In this Act 'contract of employment' means a contract of service or apprenticeship, whether express or implied, and (if it is express) whether oral or in writing.

(3) In this Act 'worker' (except in the phrases 'shop worker' and 'betting worker') means an individual who has entered into or works under (or, where the employment has ceased, worked under)—

   (a) a contract of employment, or

   (b) any other contract, whether express or implied and (if it is express) whether oral or in writing, whereby the individual undertakes to do or perform personally any work or services for another party to the contract whose status is not by virtue of the contract that of a client or customer of any profession or business undertaking carried on by the individual;

and any reference to a worker's contract shall be construed accordingly.

(4) In this Act 'employer', in relation to an employee or a worker, means the person by whom the employee or worker is (or, where the employment has ceased, was) employed.

(5) In this Act 'employment'—

   (a) in relation to an employee, means (except for the purposes of section 171) employment under a contract of employment, and

   (b) in relation to a worker, means employment under his contract;

and 'employed' shall be construed accordingly.

[(6) This section has effect subject to sections 43K and 47B(3); and for the purposes of Part XIII so far as relating to Part IV A or section 47B, "worker", "worker's contract" and, in relation to a worker, "employer", "employment" and "employed" have the extended meaning given by section 43K.]

Other definitions

235.—(1) In this Act, except in so far as the context otherwise requires—

'act' and 'action' each includes omission and references to doing an act or taking action shall be construed accordingly, 'basic award of compensation for unfair dismissal' shall be construed in accordance with section 118,

'business' includes a trade or profession and includes any activity carried on by a body of persons (whether corporate or unincorporated),

'childbirth' means the birth of a living child or the birth of a child whether living or dead after twenty-four weeks of pregnancy,

'collective agreement' has the meaning given by section 178(1) and (2) of the Trade Union and Labour Relations (Consolidation) Act 1992,

'conciliation officer' means an officer designated by the Advisory, Conciliation and Arbitration Service under section 211 of that Act,

'dismissal procedures agreement' means an agreement in writing with respect to procedures relating to dismissal made by or on behalf of one or more independent trade unions and one or more employers or employers' associations,

'employers' association' has the same meaning as in the Trade Union and Labour Relations (Consolidation) Act 1992,

'expected week of childbirth' means the week, beginning with midnight between Saturday and Sunday, in which it is expected that childbirth will occur,

'guarantee payment' has the meaning given by section 28,

'independent trade union' means a trade union which—

(a) is not under the domination or control of an employer or a group of employers or of one or more employers' associations, and

(b) is not liable to interference by an employer or any such group or association (arising out of the provision of financial or material support or by any other means whatever) tending towards such control,

'job', in relation to an employee, means the nature of the work which he is employed to do in accordance with his contract and the capacity and place in which he is so employed,

'maternity leave period' shall be construed in accordance with sections 72 and 73,

'notified day of return' shall be construed in accordance with section 83,

'position', in relation to an employee, means the following matters taken as a whole—

(a) his status as an employee,

(b) the nature of his work, and

(c) his terms and conditions of employment,

"'protected disclosure' has the meaning given by section 43A,"

'redundancy payment' has the meaning given by Part XI,

'relevant date' has the meaning given by sections 145 and 153,

'renewal' includes extension, and any reference to renewing a contract or a fixed term shall be construed accordingly.

'statutory provision' means a provision, whether of a general or a special nature, contained in, or in any document made or issued under, any Act, whether of a general or special nature,

'successor', in relation to the employer of an employee, means (subject to subsection (2)) a person who in consequence of a change occurring (whether by virtue of a sale or other disposition or by operation of law) in the ownership of the undertaking, or of the part of the undertaking, for the purposes of which the employee was employed, has become the owner of the undertaking or part,

'trade union' has the meaning given by section 1 of the Trade Union and Labour Relations (Consolidation) Act 1992,

'week'—

(a) in Chapter I of this Part means a week ending with Saturday, and

(b) otherwise, except in section 86, means, in relation to an employee whose remuneration is calculated weekly by a week ending with a day other than Saturday, a week ending with that other day and, in relation to any other employee, a week ending with Saturday.

(2) The definition of 'successor' in subsection (1) has effect (subject to the necessary modifications) in relation to a case where—

(a) the person by whom an undertaking or part of an undertaking is owned immediately before a change is one of the persons by whom (whether as partners, trustees or otherwise) it is owned immediately after the change, or

(b) the persons by whom an undertaking or part of an undertaking is owned immediately before a change (whether as partners, trustees or otherwise) include the persons by whom, or include one or more of the persons by whom, it is owned immediately after the change,

as it has effect where the previous owner and the new owner are wholly different persons.

(3) References in this Act to redundancy, dismissal by reason of redundancy and similar expressions shall be construed in accordance with section 139.

(4) In section 136(2), 154 and 216(3) and paragraph 14 of Schedule 2 'lock-out' means—

(a) the closing of a place of employment,

(b) the suspension of work, or

(c) the refusal by an employer to continue to employ any number of persons employed by him in consequences of a dispute,

done with a view to compelling persons employed by the employer, or to aid another employer in compelling persons employed by him, to accept terms or conditions of or affecting employment.

(5) In sections 91(2), 140(2) and (3), 143(1), 144(2) and (3), 154 and 216(1) and (2) and paragraph 14 of Schedule 2 'strike' means—

(a) the cessation of work by a body of employed persons acting in combination, or

(b) a concerted refusal, or a refusal under a common understanding, of any number of employed persons to continue to work for an employer in consequence of a dispute,

done as a means of compelling their employer or any employed person or body of employed persons, or to aid other employees in compelling their employer or any employed person or body of employed persons, to accept or not to accept terms or conditions of or affecting employment.

Relevant Statutory Instruments

The Public Interest Disclosure (Compensation) Regulations 1999

The Secretary of State, in exercise of the powers conferred on him by section 127B of the Employment Rights Act 1996(a), hereby makes the following Regulations—

Citation and commencement

1. These Regulations may be cited as the Public Interest Disclosure (Compensation) Regulations 1999 and shall come into force on 2nd July 1999.

Interpretation

2. In these Regulations—
"the 1996 Act" means the Employment Rights Act 1996.

Compensation

3. Sections 117 to 127A(b) of the 1996 Act shall apply to compensation awarded, or a compensatory award made, to a person in a case where he is regarded as unfairly dismissed by virtue of section 103A(c) or 105(6A)(d) of the 1996 Act, with the following modifications—

(a) as if, after section 124(1), there was inserted the following subsection—

"(1A) Subsection (1) shall not apply to compensation awarded, or a compensatory award made, to a person in a case where he is regarded as unfairly dismissed by virtue of section 103A or 105(6A)."; and

(b) as if, in section 117(6)(a)—

(i) after paragraph (b), the word "and" was omitted; and
(ii) after paragraph (c), there was inserted "and

(d) a dismissal where the reason (or, if more than one, the principal reason)—

(i) in a redundancy case, for selecting the employee for dismissal, or
(ii) otherwise, for the dismissal.

is that specified in section 103A."

The Public Interest Disclosure (Prescribed Persons) Order 1999

The Secretary of State, in exercise of the powers conferred on him by section 43F of the Employment Rights Act 1996(a), hereby makes the following Order:—

Citation and commencement

1. This Order may be cited as the Public Interest Disclosure (Prescribed Persons) Order 1999 and shall come into force on 2nd July 1999.

Prescribed Persons

2.—(1) The persons and descriptions of persons prescribed for the purposes of section 43F of the Employment Rights Act 1996 are the persons and descriptions of persons specified in the first column of the Schedule.

(2) The descriptions of matters in respect of which each person, or persons of each description, specified in the first column of the Schedule is or are prescribed are the descriptions of matters respectively specified opposite them in the second column of the Schedule.

SCHEDULE Article 2

FIRST COLUMN *Persons and descriptions of persons*	SECOND COLUMN *Descriptions of matters*
Accounts Commission for Scotland and auditors appointed by the Commission to audit the accounts of local government, and health service, bodies.	The proper conduct of public business, value for money, fraud and corruption in local government, and health service, bodies.
Audit Commission for England and Wales and auditors appointed by the Commission to audit the accounts of local government, and health service, bodies.	The proper conduct of public business, value for money, fraud and corruption in local government, and health service, bodies.
Building Societies Commission.	The operation of building societies.
Certification Officer.	Fraud and other irregularities, relating to the financial affairs of trade unions and employers' associations.
Charity Commissioners for England and Wales.	The proper administration of charities and of funds given or held for charitable purposes.
Lord Advocate. Scotland.	The proper administration of charities and of funds given or held for charitable purposes. Serious or complex fraud.
Chief Executive of the Criminal Cases Review Commission.	Actual or potential miscarriages of justice.
Chief Executive of the Scottish Criminal Cases Review Commission.	Actual or potential miscarriages of justice.
Chief Registrar of Friendly Societies.	The operation of credit unions, clubs, housing associations, co-operatives and other industrial and provident societies, benevolent societies, working men's clubs and specially authorised societies.

FIRST COLUMN *Persons and descriptions of persons*	SECOND COLUMN *Descriptions of matters*
Assistant Registrar of Friendly Societies for Scotland.	The operation of clubs, housing associations, co-operatives and other industrial and provident societies, benevolent societies, working men's clubs and specially authorised societies.
Civil Aviation Authority.	Compliance with the requirements of civil aviation legislation, including aviation safety.
The competent authority under Part IV of the Financial Services Act 1986(a).	The listing of securities on a stock exchange; prospectuses on offers of transferable securities to the public.
Commissioners of Customs and Excise.	Value added tax, insurance premium tax, excise duties and landfill tax. The import and export of prohibited or restricted goods.
Commissioners of the Inland Revenue.	Income tax, corporation tax, capital gains tax, pretroleum revenue tax, inheritance tax, stamp duties, national insurance contributions, statutory maternity pay and statutory sick pay.
Comptroller and Auditor General of the National Audit Office.	The proper conduct of public business, value for money, fraud and corruption in relation to the provision of centrally-funded public services.
Auditor General for Wales.	The proper conduct of public business, value for money, fraud and corruption in relation to the provision of public services.
Data Protection Registrar.	Compliance with the requirements of legislation relating to data protection.
Director General of Electricity Supply.	The generation, transmission, distribution and supply of electricity, and activities ancillary to these matters.
Direct General of Fair Trading	Matters concerning the sale of goods or the supply of services which adversely affect the interests of consumers. Matters relating to consumer credit and hire, estate agency, unfair terms in consumer contracts and misleading advertising. The abuse of a dominant position in a market and the prevention, restriction or distortion of competition.
Direct General of Gas Supply.	The transportation, shipping and supply of gas through pipes, and activities ancillary to these matters.
Direct General of Telecommunications	The provision and use of telecommunication systems, services and apparatus.
Director General of Water Services.	The supply of water and the provision of sewerage services.
Director of the Serious Fraud Office.	Serious or complex fraud.

FIRST COLUMN *Persons and descriptions of persons*	SECOND COLUMN *Descriptions of matters*
Environment Agency.	Acts or omissions which have an actual or potential effect on the environment or the management or regulation of the environment, including those relating to pollution, abstraction of water, flooding, the flow in rivers, inland fisheries and migratory salmon or trout.
Scottish Environment Protection Agency.	Acts or omissions which have an actual or potential effect on the environment or the management or regulations of the environment, including those relating to flood warning systems and pollution.
Financial Services Authority.	The carrying on of investment business or of insurance business; the operation of banks, deposit-taking businesses and wholesale money market regimes: the functioning of financial markets, investment exchanges and clearing houses; the functioning of other financial regulators: money laundering, financial crime, and other serious financial misconduct, in connection with activities regulated by the Financial Services Authority.
Friendly Societies Commission.	The operation of friendly societies and industrial assurance companies.
Health and Safety Executive.	Matters which may affect the health or safety of any individual at work; matters which may affect the health or safety of any member of the public, arising out of or in connection with the activities of persons at work.
Local authorities which are responsible for the enforcement of health and safety legislation.	Matters which may affect the health or safety of any individual at work; matters, which may affect the health or safety of any member of the public, arising out of or in connection with the activities of persons at work.
Investment Management Regulatory Organisation.	The activities of persons regulated by the Investment Management Regulatory Organisation.
Occupational Pensions Regulatory Authority.	Matters relating to occupational pension schemes and other private pension arrangements.
Personal Investment Authority.	The activities of persons regulated by the Personal Investment Authority.
Rail Regulator.	The provision and supply of railway services.
Securities and Futures Authority.	The activities of persons regulated by the Securities and Futures Authority.
Treasury.	The carrying on of insurance business.

FIRST COLUMN *Persons and descriptions of persons*	*SECOND COLUMN* *Descriptions of matters*
Secretary of State for Trade and Industry.	Fraud, and other misconduct, in relation to companies, investment business, insurance business, or multi-level marketing schemes (and similar trading schemes); insider dealing. Consumer safety.
Local authorities which are responsible for the enforcement of consumer protection legislation.	Compliance with the requirements of consumer protection legislation.
A person ("person A") carrying out functions, by virtue of legislation, relating to relevant failures falling within one or more matters within a description of matters in respect of which another person ("person B") is prescribed by this Order, where person B was previously responsible for carrying out the same or substantially similar functions and has ceased to be so responsible.	Matters falling within the description of matters in respect of which person B is prescribed by this Order, to the extent that those matters relate to functions currently carried out by person A.

The Public Interest Disclosure Act 1998 (Commencement) Order 1999

The Secretary of State, in exercise of the powers conferred on him by section 18(3) of the Public Interest Disclosure Act 1998(a), hereby makes the following Order:—

Citation

1. This Order may be cited as the Public Interest Disclosure Act 1998 (Commencement) Order 1999

Commencement

2. The Public Interest Disclosure Act 1998, so far as not already in force, shall come into force on 2nd July 1999.

Illustrative Flow Chart

WORKER
Are they:
1. Employee
2. Contractor
3. Trainee
4. Agency staff
5. Homeworker
6. Any professional in the NHS whether or not they are a volunteer, or self employed

THEN THE PIDA APPLIES

WORKER
Are they:
1. Genuine Self employed person
2. A volunteer
3. Working in the Intelligence services
4. in the Army
5. in the Police Force

THEN THE PIDA DOES NOT APPLY

WHAT IS THE MALPRACTICE
1. CRIME.
2. BREACH OF LEGAL OBLIGATION (inc. Negligence, Breach of Contract, Breach of Administrative Law)
3. MISCARRIAGE OF JUSTICE
4. DANGER TO HEALTH & SAFETY
5. DANGER TO THE ENVIRONMENT
6. ANY ATTEMPT TO COVER ANY OF THE ABOVE.

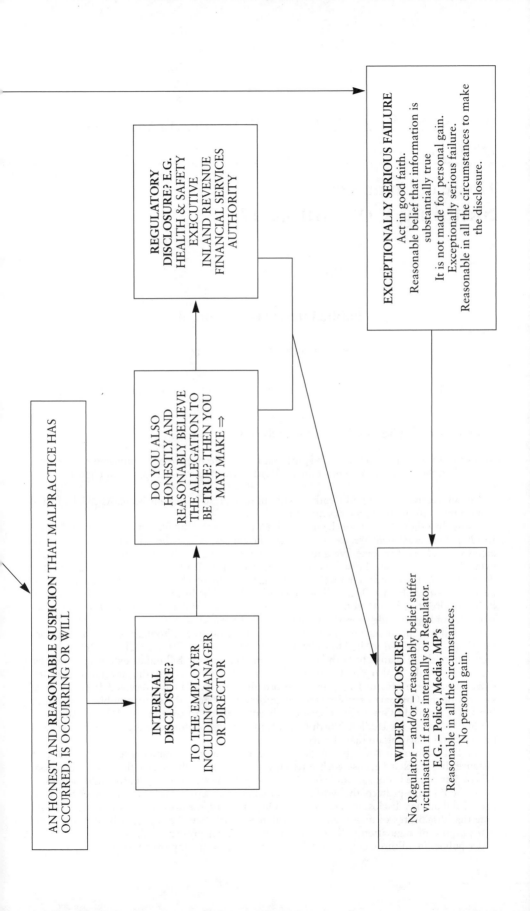

AN HONEST AND **REASONABLE SUSPICION** THAT MALPRACTICE HAS OCCURRED, IS OCCURRING OR WILL

INTERNAL DISCLOSURE?

TO THE EMPLOYER INCLUDING MANAGER OR DIRECTOR

DO YOU ALSO HONESTLY AND REASONABLY BELIEVE THE ALLEGATION TO BE **TRUE**? THEN YOU MAY MAKE ⇒

REGULATORY DISCLOSURE? E.G. HEALTH & SAFETY EXECUTIVE INLAND REVENUE FINANCIAL SERVICES AUTHORITY

EXCEPTIONALLY SERIOUS FAILURE
Act in good faith.
Reasonable belief that information is substantially true
It is not made for personal gain.
Exceptionally serious failure.
Reasonable in all the circumstances to make the disclosure.

WIDER DISCLOSURES
No Regulator – and/or – reasonably belief suffer victimisation if raise internally or Regulator.
E.G. – Police, Media, MP's
Reasonable in all the circumstances.
No personal gain.

APPENDIX 5: EXTRACTS FROM PARLIAMENTARY DEBATES

House of Commons
Standing Committee D

Public Interest Disclosure Bill

MR ROGER GALE IN THE CHAIR

WEDNESDAY MARCH 11, 1998

Mr. Richard Shepherd (Aldridge-Brownhills): I beg to move.

> That if proceedings on the Public Interest Disclosure Bill are not completed at this day's sitting, the Committee do meet on Wednesday 18 March at half-past Ten o'clock.

The Bill received its Second Reading without debate, so with your leave, Mr. Gale, I shall make a few introductory remarks about it.

Normally, I should be one of the first to think it remiss if a Bill were not debated on Second Reading. However, there are, extenuating circumstances, in that the subject was fully considered by the House for some five hours on 1 March 1996. The hon. Member for Makerfield (Mr. McCartney), now Minister of State, Department of Trade and Industry, said that that debate had been won more comprehensively than any other he had heard in the nine years that he has been in the House. That Bill—also entitled the Public Interest Disclosure Bill—received its Second Reading by 118 votes to nil. Regrettably, it did not reach the statute book last year, notwithstanding its wide support in the House and outside.

That Bill was introduced by the hon. Member for Islwyn (Mr. Touhig) following an initiative that was launched in the House by the hon. Member for Cannock Chase (Dr. Wright), I record my debt of thanks to both hon. Members, because the Bill builds extensively on their earlier proposals. I also thank the Minister and his officials for the assistance that the Government have afforded me, and I record the help that I have received from Maurice Frankel of the Campaign for Freedom of Information, from the charity Public Concern at Work and from Mr. Guy Dehn. I have also been fortunate to have received the assistance of the hon. Member for Dudley, North (Mr. Cranston) who, before coming to the House, was instrumental in setting up that charity.

The Bill's approach is to encourage the worker to raise the matter internally in the first instance. It does that because such internal reports most easily attract the Bill's protection. Where that course is not safe and sound, or where the matter is not properly addressed internally, the Bill also protects the worker who makes an external disclosure in a specified way, provided that such disclosure is reasonable. On that point, members of the Committee should note that disclosures of malpractice to regulators which have been expressly authorised for that purpose by regulation will be more likely to attract protection than disclosures to the wider public. In all those cases, the Bill will protect only an employee who is acting in good faith. I am grateful to the Government, who have agreed in the light of Minister's oversight for public bodies to make special provisions for those who work in quangos and in the national health service.

The clearest illustration of the need for the Bill is to be found in the major disasters and scandals of the last decade. Almost all official inquiries report that workers had seen the dangers, but either had been too scared to sound the alarm, or had raised the matter with the wrong person or in the wrong way. Examples include the rail inspector who, for fear of rocking the boat, did not report loose wiring before the Clapham rail disaster in which 35 people died. There were five warnings that ferries were sailing with their bow doors open before the tragedy at Zeebrugge took 193 lives. At Barlow Clowes and the Bank of Credit and Commerce International and in Maxwell's empire a culture of fear and silence deterred workers from blowing the whistle, costing investors and pensioners billions of pounds. Finally, a Matrix Churchill employee wrote a letter to the Foreign Secretary about munitions equipment for Iraq but it was ignored by civil servants.

Those examples show how devastating the effects of a culture of silence can be when things are going wrong on a grand scale. However, hon. Members will know from their constituency work that employees who feel cowed—whether or not with good reason—may not wish to express concern about the types of malpractice specified in this Bill for fear of losing their jobs or careers.

A telling example of the need for the Bill was contained in a letter from Mrs. Bonnie Tall, who had been forced out of her post as secretary to the vice-chancellor at the university of Portsmouth after she had refused to turn a blind eye to his sophisticated and proven fiddling of public money. Mrs. Tall won a claim for unfair dismissal and received £10,000. She has been out of work since. By contrast, the vice-chancellor left with a golden handshake, while the university spent £200,000 on an inquiry by a Queen's counsel. As Mrs. Tall wrote, her experience was hardly likely to encourage others in her situation to act properly when they see public money being flagrantly misused for personal benefit.

I hope that the Bill will signal a shift in culture so that it is safe and accepted for employees such as those I have mentioned to sound the alarm when they come across malpractice that threatens the safety of the public, the health of a patient, public funds or the savings of investors. I hope that it will mean that good and decent people in business and public bodies throughout the country can more easily ensure that where malpractice is reported in an organisation, the response deals with the message, not the messenger.

The Bill is, as its name implies, a public interest measure. Were it merely an employee—rights measure, I doubt that I would be able to inform the committee that its objectives are supported by the Institute of Directors, the Confederation of British Industry and the Committee on Standards in Public Life as well as the Trades Union Congress.

In all but one area—compensation, the detail of which is yet to be settled—the Bill adopts or improves on the approach of last year's Bill. As just one example, the public interest test is set out more clearly in this Bill—neither employee nor employer will have to second guess the likely decision of the courts in an action for breach of confidence. Credit for those improvements largely belongs to the Minister and those who advise him, and I am grateful for the careful and positive consideration that they have given to the general points that were made by me and on my behalf.

In the light of extensive agreement between myself and the Minister of State, Department of Trade and Industry and the overwhelming support that the Bill has received from consultees, there is a good chance that we may complete our considerations of it this morning. If we need more time. I hope that the Committee may sit next on 18 March.

Mr. Shepherd: As originally drafted, the Bill did not require tribunals to give weight to whether the information was confidential and, if so, what damage the disclosure may have caused to the third party whose confidence had been breached.

In consultations, the Minister and I agreed that any cross-reference to the law of confidence in the Bill was inappropriate for a number of reasons. First, we were keen to make the public interest in all disclosure of wrong-doing the pre-eminent factor. Secondly, we feared that it would not be sufficiently clear to employers and employees how this area of case law might apply, if there were some umblicical link. Thirdly, we recognised that workers who reported a serious wrong-doing should not forfeit protection because it later transpired that that information was not in law confidential. When the courts have granted or refused an injunction to stop the disclosure of that same confidential information, the view of the Minister, with which

I acquiesced, was that those decisions should be relevant, but not binding on the tribunal. As such, no reference was made to the law of confidence in the Bill.

During consultation, the point was made that there are some particularly important obligations of confidence—for example, those owed by a doctor to his patient or a bank to its customer. A fear was expressed that the Bill as drafted might unwittingly permit or encourage a secretary in a doctor's surgery or a clerk in a bank to disclose a concern about malpractice or misconduct without regard to the fact that that information was subject to an important obligation of confidence owed by the employer to a third party. The amendment has been tabled simply to allay those fears. Its purpose is not to thwart protection simply because the information was subject to a routine claim of confidentiality. It covers those exceptional cases in which there is a particularly important duty of confidence, as between doctors and patients, when a worker's disclosure breaches that duty and harms the third party. In such cases, it is right that the tribunal should consider the breach and the degree of any harm that it causes in deciding whether the disclosure was reasonable.

HOUSE OF LORDS

Lord Borrie: My Lords, I beg to move that this Bill be now read a second time.

It is a pleasure and an honour to introduce this Bill into your Lordships' House. It passed through another place with strong support from both the Government and the Opposition. I pay tribute to both Mr. Richard Shepherd MP and to the Minister of State at the DTI, Mr. Ian McCartney, for the careful consideration that they and their advisers gave to this matter. The results of that careful consideration can be seen not only in the detail of the Bill but also in the support that the Bill has received from the CBI, the Institute of Directors, the TUC, consumer groups, various professions such as the medical, legal and accountancy professions, and numerous other bodies.

I myself have particular reasons to be proud of this measure as it is, to a large extent, based on the work of a charity, Public Concern at Work, which I helped to found some six years ago. It was not an easy initiative to launch, but its importance was recognised at the outset by, among others, the noble and learned Lord, Lord Oliver of Aylmerton, the noble Lord, Lord Gladwin of Clee, the noble Baroness, Lady Dean of Thornton-le-Fylde, the noble Lord, Lord Alexander of Weedon and the noble Baroness, Lady Wilcox. They all kindly offered support and advice to help the charity to find its feet. It also had the advantage of securing the services of Mr. Guy Dehn as director. He has been indefatigable in assisting with this Bill and, indeed, with the work of the charity generally.

There is one other noble and learned Lord I must particularly thank. I refer to the noble and learned Lord, Lord Nolan. Under his chairmanship, the Committee on Standards in Public Life championed the work of the charity and the issue which lies behind this Bill. Indeed, the noble and learned Lord and his committee took up the issue with such eloquence that I can best summarise the purposes of this Bill by quoting from his committee's second report:

> "All organisations face the risks of things going wrong or of unknowingly harbouring malpractice. Part of the duty of identifying such a situation and taking remedial action may lie with the regulatory or funding body. But the regulator is usually in the role of detective, determining responsibility after the crime has been discovered. Encouraging a culture of openness within an organisation will help: prevention is better than cure. Yet it is striking that in the few cases where things have gone badly wrong in local public spending bodies, it has frequently been the tip-off to the press or the local Member of Parliament—sometimes anonymous, sometimes not—which has prompted the regulators into action.

Placing staff in a position where they feel driven to approach the media to ventilate concerns is unsatisfactory both for the staff member and the organisation".

While the committee's words referred explicitly to public bodies, the issue it addresses does sadly apply to the private and voluntary sectors as well.

The official reports in recent years into the Zeebrugge ferry disaster, the rail crash at Clapham Junction, the explosion on Piper Alpha and the scandals at BCCI, Maxwell. Barlow

Clowes and Barings have all revealed that staff were well aware of the risk of serious physical or financial harm but that they were either to scared to raise their concern or that they did so in the wrong way or with the wrong person. This culture, which encourages decent ordinary citizens to turn a blind eye when they suspect serious malpractice in their workplace, has not only cost lives and ruined livelihoods, but it has also damaged public confidence in some of the very organisations on which we all depend.

The purpose of this Bill is to give a clear signal to people in places of work up and down the country that if they suspect wrongdoing, the law will stand by them provided they raise the matter in a responsible and reasonable way. Where a worker is aware of fraud, a price-fixing cartel, the sexual abuse of a child in a home or a danger to health, safety, or the environment, or some other malpractice, this Bill provides welcome and much needed guidance.

If today a worker feels unable to raise the matter with his immediate manager for whatever reason, he may well feel that the only options are to stay silent or to blow the whistle in some underhand way, perhaps by leaking information anonymously to the media. Once this Bill is enacted and taken to heart by the British people, which I am sure it will be, there will be a much improved chance that concerns about dangers to the public interest will be raised and addressed within the organisation itself. Where there are good reasons why such concerns cannot be raised and resolved internally, the Bill sets out a tight structure whereby the concern can be raised outside the organisation, thereby protecting the public interest. Where the worker follows the Bill's framework and satisfies its requirements, he will be protected from victimisation and can bring a claim before an industrial tribunal if he is victimised.

As to that protection, the Bill provides that where a worker is disciplined or demoted for raising such a concern, he can apply for relief to an industrial tribunal and be awarded such compensation as it just and equitable. Where, however, he is dismissed, his remedies are not set out on the face of the Bill but are to be determined by regulation. That is because the Government rightly recognise that the matter warrants careful and further consideration. There has been much support for the view that, like discrimination legislation, awards under the Bill should compensate for the victim's loss where he loses his job. There is alternatively the option, favoured by the Government, that the awards should follow the best available under employment law, such as those provided for health and safety representatives. These not only substantially exceed the normal awards in employment cases, but also include specific incentives to encourage the employer to take back a worker who has acted in the public interest. Bearing in mind the wider implications any departure from existing employment provisions will have, I hope the House accepts the Government's case that they should consider the matter further, not least in the light of the forthcoming proposals on fairness at work.

Your Lordships will have gathered that this Bill is to be part of wider employment legislation. However, recognising the importance of the issue, it covers individuals such as trainees, homeworkers and professionals in the NHS who are not normally protected by employment law. While its scope is wide, the House should note that it does not cover the genuinely self-employed, the intelligence services, the armed forces and the police. As to the last category, however, I am pleased to report that the Government undertook in another place to ensure that police officers are to be provided with comparable protection to that provided in the Bill.

I turn to how the Bill will work in practice. Clause 1 incorporates new provisions into Section 43 of the Employment Rights Act 1996. As a starting point, it clearly directs the worker towards raising the matter internally first. What will be Sector 43C will afford protection where a worker raises within his own organisation an honest and reasonable belief about one of the specified malpractices. New Section 43E will provide like protection to staff within public bodies who raise such concerns with the sponsoring department.

The Bill then addresses the particular circumstances where an external disclosure of the concern is protected. First and most importantly, new Section 43F will provide something of a halfway house in that it recognises the particular role of regulatory authorities which are charged to oversee and investigate malpractice within organisations. Where a regulator—it might be the Financial Services Authority or the Health and Safety Executive—has been prescribed for the purposes of the Bill, a worker who contacts them will be protected if, in addition to the tests I have referred to for internal disclosures, he also reasonably believes the information and any allegation within it is substantially true.

Where a wider disclosure is made the worker must not only pass the tests that apply to disclosure to prescribed regulators, but also the additional hurdles set out in what will be new

Sections 43G and 43H. New Section 43G will address the circumstances in which a disclosure is made to the police, a professional association, a regulator which has not been prescribed by Ministers, and the media may also be capable of protection. As to such disclosures, your Lordships will be pleased to note that these will not be protected where their purpose was the personal gain of the worker.

Apart from deciding whether the particular recipient of that disclosure was appropriate, the tribunal must be satisfied that that disclosure was reasonable, having regard, among other things, to the seriousness of the threat to the public interest, whether the danger is continuing or likely to occur again, whether the disclosure was in breach of an obligation of confidentiality owed to a third party and, where appropriate, whether use was made of any whistle-blowing procedure which the organisation had in place. Most importantly, the Bill indicates that such wider disclosures—wider than one's own employer or specified regulator—should be protected only where the concern had been raised internally or with a prescribed regulator first, in which the reasonableness of his response will also be the key issue.

This requirement within the Bill's structure that the concern should have been raised first does not apply where the worker can demonstrate a reasonable belief that he will be victimised or that evidence of the malpractice will be destroyed or covered up. Equally, no such conditions presently exist where the matter is exceptionally serious, such as the sexual abuse of a minor, an issue addressed in Section 43H.

As I hope I have made clear, this measure will encourage people to recognise and identify with the wider public interest and not just their own private position. It will reassure them that if they act reasonably to protect the legitimate interests of others who are being threatened or abused, the law will not stand idly by should they be vilified or victimised.

It is not my view, in the light of my experience with the charity Public Concern at Work, that serious malpractice is endemic or widespread in organisations throughout the country. However, I am satisfied that when it occurs, the law needs to be strengthened so that those decent people who too often stay silent for fear of losing their own job are protected. I mention as one example the case of Judy Jones who was the deputy matron in a nursing home in Yorkshire. She suspected that the manager of the home was sexually abusing women in his care suffering from senile dementia. She could not raise the issue with the manager or the owner who was the manager's wife. Her fear was that if she went to the authorities it would be the manager's word against hers and her career might be destroyed. Fortunately, with the assistance of the charity, she collected incontrovertible evidence before she contacted the police. It subsequently transpired that the manager had been sexually assaulting people in his care for some nine years; and last February he was gaoled for four years. As one victim's family said, "If it hadn't been for Mrs. Jones, it could still be going on and no one would ever have known".

I hope your Lordships will agree that the situation in which Mrs Jones found herself is an invidious one and one which we should not allow to flourish unchecked.

This Bill addresses that dilemma in a sound and practical way while protecting the interests of responsible employers. As such, I commend it to your Lordships' House, I beg to move.

Moved. That the Bill be now read a second time.—(*Lord Borrie.*)

Baroness Turner of Camden: My Lords, I welcome the Bill. It provides long needed protection for employees who whistle-blow on unsafe, fraudulent and other undesirable practices by employers. I am glad to note that it is welcomed by both the CBI and the TUC, and although substantially about employment rights it is regarded as a public interest measure.

I am particularly glad that it has been introduced. I recall with, I may say, some pride that when I had been a Member of your Lordships' House for several years I was successful in introducing a Private Member's Bill designed to give employment protection to employees engaged in North Sea oil ventures who blew the whistle on unsafe practices. My noble friends Lord Wedderburn and Lord McCarthy and I worked together to introduce the Bill following the appalling "Piper Alpha" disaster. Many of the employees were engaged on short-term contracts and although some were apprehensive about the level of safety precautions they were unwilling to risk continued employment by exposing the problems involved. I was briefed by my union, MSF. We managed to get the Bill through this House and it was later approved in another place. It was then absorbed into a more comprehensive Health and Safety at Work Act.

The present Bill goes much further than that of course. It deals not only with health and safety issues, but fraud and other malpractices. I note from the Bill that a qualifying disclosure within the terms of the Bill occurs when this is made to a "prescribed person". It seems to me that for some workers an appropriate person might often be his or her union representative. The union might be expected to have the appropriate knowledge of the way to proceed and whether the failure concerned was of a sufficiently serious nature to qualify under the terms of the legislation. That raises a further point in my mind. It might well be said that a recognised union holding a collective bargaining agreement with the employer is clearly an appropriate person within the meaning of the new Bill. However, as the "Piper Alpha" disaster disclosed, unsafe practices often occur in situations where the employer is anti-union and refuses union recognition, making it as difficult as possible for the union to recruit.

In such circumstances, the individual employee who has detected something unsafe, or a serious failure within the meaning of the legislation, is in even more need of protection if he reports the circumstances to his union official. I would welcome the Minister's comment on that.

Other issues also occur to me. I note that enforcement of employees' rights is, as one would expect, ultimately to be a matter for employment tribunals and, I assume, for the EAT. I am concerned, as many are, about the level of work that might be imposed upon the system. It is true that a recent Bill, now the Job Dispute Resolution Act, has introduced another means of dealing with straightforward unfair dismissal cases via arbitration. That should lighten the workload somewhat.

However, colleagues who are more involved with ETs and EATs than I am are concerned about whether sufficient resources will be made available to deal with these new tasks. I therefore welcome the Minister's comment on that when he replies to the debate.

Finally, I wish to raise a point that has already been discussed in Committee in another place—the cap on levels of compensation. I think that the issue could be important. I note that the Government wish to stay within the limits imposed within employment law. However, as my noble friend Lord Borrie said, the Bill is intended to deal with fraud and malpractices of all kinds. The *Maxwell* and *BICC* cases come immediately to mind, but there have been other less publicised cases.

People capable of bringing malpractice to the attention of the appropriate authorities in such cases are likely to be specialist and managerial personnel. It is clear from what is now known about the Maxwell affair that people who might have been able to throw some light on what was going on were too intimidated to come forward. They would have risked not only the jobs they then had; they might not have been able to find anything else in the same specialism. In other words, a whole career could have been put at risk. In such circumstances, a cap does not seem a good idea.

There is an even more pressing need to look at the cap. The employer is ordered by an employment tribunal to reinstate an employee. Let us suppose that that employer stubbornly refuses to do so. That is likely to occur in only a small minority of cases. But in such instances, when the case is finally settled, a cap on compensation offered does not seem appropriate. When I was a union official, I remember a case where reinstatement was ordered by the tribunal. It took four years before the case was settled. In such circumstances, it does not seem reasonable that a cap should be applied to the compensation eventually paid.

I am pleased that it is accepted that there has to be some protection against false allegations. That is clear from the Bill and from what my noble friend Lord Borrie said. Presumably that is the reason for saying that qualifying disclosure will not apply if the individual makes disclosure for personal gain. I welcome that.

In these days when the media are so totally irresponsible, and interested so much in sensation, that is important. I note that in another place my honourable friend made it clear that simply going off to the press rather than attempting to raise the issue in the first place internally would not be acceptable. The disclosure should be to a "prescribed person" able to deal with it in an informed and responsible way.

I commend the Bill. I have raised a few points that I think are of some interest. However, I have no doubt that overall it is greatly to be welcomed. I congratulate my noble friend on introducing it.

Baroness Dean of Thornton-le-Fylde: My Lords, I welcome the Bill and support it. I congratulate my noble friend Lord Borrie on introducing it to the House. I have to declare an interest, although my noble friend has declared it for me. I, too, am a member of the charity Public Concern at Work. I supported that organisation when it was founded because of my practical experience as a trade union officer. Over a number of years I have seen the often traumatic situation in which employees found themselves.

As a result of those experiences, I quickly formed the view not only that this kind of measure was necessary, but that it would be brought about only if there was wide consensus across the whole range of employment activity, not merely among trade unions but among businesses and various institutions. It is to the credit of the charity and it has been able to bring together a large group of support. One would expect support from the TUC; but it has come also from the CBI, the Institute of Directors and large public companies, and not least from both Government and Opposition Benches in the other place.

This is a practical Bill. It is short—it has 18 clauses—but, my goodness, I wish it had been around some years ago! I would certainly have made the lives of employees in Britain in certain selected cases far easier, and made it easier for them to rest in their employment. Such matters can be traumatic. Even if an employee is represented by his or her union, the issue that he or she may feel they need to raise may not necessarily affect them individually; it may affect a third party. It may be a health and safety issue in relation to the production process which does not affect the employees, but affects the user of the goods in question.

Having a piece of legislation on the statute book is a great thing. If you are a member of a trade union, the union will make sure that you know about it. But if you are not in a trade union, it is important that you know that the Act is there. I can think of many isolated situations in which an individual employee knows that something is wrong, wants to speak out and yet does not know where to turn. In those circumstances, it is not unusual for an employee possibly to visit a citizens advice bureau, where he may receive help. But how can he or she share what may be private information without being protected?

My noble friend Lady Turner of Camden raised the issue of capping on compensation. I am concerned about that matter too. It may be argued that if reinstatement is required and the employer does not do it, capping is not an issue. I do not accept that. I see this as a weakness that needs to be addressed.

Those are my two key concerns. However, they do not in any way prevent me from giving the Bill my wholehearted support. It is a step forward. I know that many employees will feel a confidence that they may not have felt before when they believe that matters are going wrong—and not necessarily for them as individuals: in the example I have given. Harry Templeton was concerned about his fellow workers; and when he spoke out, he lost his job. This Bill will help prevent such a situation. It will build on employment guidelines to which employers will have to refer when they would like to respond aggressively—as they do from time to time—and in a way that is damaging to the employee. I support the Bill despite those two reservations. Perhaps the Minister will comment on those points when he replies.

Lord McCarthy: My Lords, this is an excellent and overdue Bill. Those of us on this side of the House only want to probe as to the detail of the Bill because it has not received a Second Reading before coming before the House.

All I wish to do is explore a point made by several previous speakers. It relates to the role of the employer. As the noble Lord, Lord Borrie, said, the assumption behind the Bill is that in the first—the primary—instance, the worker who has a problem will go first to his or her employer. The explanatory memorandum states that in general it is envisaged that the matter has been raised with the employer, or with the prescribed regulatory body.

I suggest that we examine the type of matters for which this Bill will be used. We may take, for instance, the example of Mrs. Jones, cited by the noble Lord, Lord Borrie. That relates to the type of matter than an employee might very well feel he or she cannot take to the employer. In cases such as a criminal offence, a miscarriage of justice, some danger in the machinery, some situation where an employee believes the employer has concealed information, to whom does he or she go? On the employer's side, one can go to an immediate superior with these matters; or possibly the level above that; or perhaps the managing director? To whom do you go? I suggest that in the majority of cases employees may very well not feel confident in such a case in going to anybody on the management side. Yet the Bill envisages that in general the matter has been raised with the employer. I question how far that is likely to be the case, and ask the Government to comment.

It will be said, as it was by the noble Lord, Lord Borrie, that there are exceptions. If I am correct, the Bill envisages six situations in which a person does not go to his or her employer. The first is when the matter does not involve the employer but is related to the misconduct of some other person. In that case a person is covered if he or she does not go to the employer first. A second exception, introduced in new Section 43D, is when an employee goes to a lawyer. In relation to the comment made by the previous speaker, why does that not apply if he or she goes to the union representative? Why should the union representative not be protected in the same way? That is the second case: the employee may go to some adviser , possibly a lawyer. If a lawyer is consulted, the employee does not have to go first to the employer. As I understand it, if the issue has no element of confidentiality, a person might be able to avoid the employer. If a person is likely to be victimised or penalised in some way, that may be possible. If there is some residuary body, such as the Health and Safety Commission, it may be possible to refer the problem to that body rather than go to the employer. And the most difficult circumstance for the average worker, introduced in new Section 43H, is if the employee takes the view that it is an exceptionally serious matter.

How on earth does the average worker know that it is an exceptionally serious matter, not just a serious matter or not just an exceptional matter? It must be "exceptionally serious". How does the employee know that? The noble Lord, Lord Borrie, gave us an example, but it was not a list. That is the part of the Bill that I find unsatisfactory in its present state.

I believe that in many cases—I cannot say the majority—workers will feel that they do not wish to go to the employer; they wish to go elsewhere. Unless the Government tell us that there will be specified residuary bodies established across the whole area covered by the Bill—and maybe they will tell us that tonight—so that everyone will have someone to go to, it will remain a problem. Unless one receives guidance on what is an "exceptionally serious" matter, one is in difficulty.

I would like the Government to comment on those matters. Shall we have better definitions in the regulations? Will the regulations make clear how the various exceptions relate to each other? Surely, after the Bill is passed there must be something like a code of practice or an explanatory memorandum. The noble Baroness said that the citizens' advice bureaux could help. Yes, of course, but we cannot expect them to advise in a vacuum as to what is an exceptionally serious case. We must have guidance; there must be documentation if we are to give people some idea so that they know when they are protected and when they are not. Nevertheless, it is an excellent Bill and we look forward to hearing what the Minister says.

APPENDIX 6

Extracts from Nolan Committee on Standards in Public Life

First Report of the Committee on Standards in Public Life

CHAIRMAN LORD NOLAN

VOLUME 1: REPORT

[MAY 1995]

We Recommend that departments and agencies should nominate one or more officials entrusted with the duty of investigating staff concerns raised confidentially.

54.   We recognise that this represents something of a novelty, although the use of confidential appeal systems and hotlines is not uncommon in the private sector. Structured in the way we suggest, however, such a system could be introduced within the framework of the constitutional conventions governing the work of civil servants and their relations with Ministers. We accept the Government's view that most issues can safely be resolved by the normal mechanisms within departments and agencies. We think, however that the prevention of corruption and maladministration is hampered if an individual civil servant has to identify him or herself as a complainant before superiors who may have direct influence over his or her career. That has been found to be a powerful disincentive to 'whistleblowers' in other organisations. The independent charity, Public Concern at Work, has set out Good Practice Guidelines which recommend that employees are offered confidential routes to raise concerns[*]. Indeed, the result of failing to provide a confidential system for matters of conscience is, ironically, to encourage leaks, which are damaging to the cohesiveness of civil service bodies and weaken the relationship between Ministers and civil servants.

"Whistleblowing"

112.   One of the conditions which can lead to an environment in which fraud and malpractice can occur, according to the Metropolitan Police, is the absence of a mechanism by which concerns can be brought to light without jeopardising the informant[†]. The Audit Commission figures (see Table 3) show that information from staff is a major contribution to the detection of fraud and corruption in the NHS. Concerned staff were instrumental in uncovering serious irregularities at two colleges of further education[‡]. As Public Concern at Work, a leading

---

[*]   Public Concern at Work, First Annual Report (1994), page 12.
[†]   Metropolitan Police, Fraud Squad, Public Sector Corruption Unit, written evidence.
[‡]   As described to us by the Chairman and Chief Executive of the Further Education Funding Council.

charity in this field, told us in their submission, "if there is a breach of the standards appropriate in a public body it is likely that the first people to suspect it will be the staff who work there"

Table 3: Method of detection of proven fraud and corruption in the NHS, over 3 years to 1994.

Information from staff	22%
Information from patients	9%
Accidental	8%
Internal controls	22%
Internal audit	18%
External audit	10%
Other	11%

Source: Audit Commission, in 'Protecting the Public Purse 2: Ensuring in the NHS', 1994

113.   However, it seems that staff concerns come to light despite rather than because of the system. We are not aware of any central guidance for executive NDPBs, and whilst the NHS have issued comprehensive central guidance[§], the Audit Commission's 1994 report found that none of the 17 NHS bodies they visited had a well-publicised system which informed staff whom they should contact if they suspect fraud and corruption.

114.   There is public concern about "gagging clauses" in public employees' contracts of employment, which prevent them from speaking out to raise concerns about standards of propriety. Where a loyal employee has concerns about impropriety, making public allegations in the media is unlikely to be their first recourse. However, without some way of voicing their concern, and without some confidence that it will be taken seriously and dealt with if necessary, they may feel they have no other option. We agree with the sentiment expressed by Robert Sheldon MP, Chairman of the Public Accounts Committee that "public money must never be allowed to have silence clauses". On the other hand, we would not wish to encourage vexatious or irresponsible complaints which undermine public confidence in institutions without due cause. We believe the best way to achieve this balance is to develop sound internal procedures backed by an external review.

115.   Non-executives often see themselves as a safeguard against such problems but staff may be suspicious or reluctant to approach them. The Audit Commission found a third of the NHS staff they interviewed would take no action in the face of impropriety because of fears of losing their jobs if they 'rock the boat'. Alan Langlands, the Chief Executive of the NHS, recognised that, "a sustained effort is required to ensure that these guidelines are properly carried through, both in spirit and in detail at local level". As Public Concern at Work point out, "although the employee is well placed to sound the alarm, he or she has most to lose by raising the matter".

116.   In Chapter 3, we propose that each government department and agency nominate an officer to provide a clear route for staff concerns about improper conduct. This will be supported by a further route of appeal to the Civil Service Commissioners. The NHS guidance suggests that NHS bodies might wish to designate such an officer.

We recommend that each executive NDPB and NHS body that has not already done so should nominate an official or board member entrusted with the duty of investigating staff concerns

---

Guidance for staff on relations with the public and the media, issued by the NHS Management Executive, June 1993.

about propriety raised confidentially. Staff should be able to make complaints without going through the normal management structure, and should be guaranteed anonymity. If they remain unsatisfied, staff should also have a clear route for raising concerns about issues of propriety with the sponsor department.

Local Public Spending Bodies

Further and Higher Education Bodies (including universities)
Grant-maintained schools
Training and Enterprise Councils and local Enterprise Companies
Registered Housing Associations

Second Report of the Committee on Standards in Public Life

CHAIRMAN LORD NOLAN

VOLUME 1: REPORT

Blowing the Whistle

41. All organisations face the risks of things going wrong or of unknowingly harbouring malpractice. Part of the duty of identifying such a situation and taking remedial action may lie with the regulatory or funding body. But the regulator is usually in the role of detective, determining responsibility after the crime has been discovered. Encouraging a culture of openness within an organisation will help: prevention is better than cure. Yet it is striking that in the few cases where things have gone badly wrong in local public spending bodies, it has frequently been the tip-off to the press or the local Member of Parliament—sometimes anonymous, sometimes not—which has prompted the regulators into action.

42. Placing staff in a position where they feel driven to approach the media to ventilate concerns is unsatisfactory for both the staff member and the organisation. We observed in our first report that it was far better for systems to be put in place which encouraged staff to raise worries within the organisation, yet allowed recourse to the parent department where necessary. In the course of the present study, we received evidence from the independent charity, Public Concern at Work, which specialises in this area. They proposed that an effective internal system for the raising of concerns should include:

- a clear statement that malpractice is taken seriously in the organisation and an indication of the sorts of matters regarded as malpractice

- respect for the confidentiality of staff raising concerns if they wish, and the opportunity to raise concerns outside the line management structure

- penalties for making false and malicious allegations

- an indication of the proper way in which concerns may be raised outside the organisation if necessary.

43. We agree. This approach builds on some aspects of existing practice, for example the duty of accounting officers in education bodies to notify the funding councils of the misuse of public funds. It goes further by inviting *all* staff to act responsibly to uphold the reputation of their organisation and maintain public confidence. It might help to avoid the cases when the first reaction of management faced with unwelcome information has been to shoot the messenger.

R2. Local public spending bodies should institute codes of practice on whistleblowing, appropriate to their circumstances, which would enable concerns to be raised confidentially inside and, if necessary, outside the organisation.

44. In the next three chapters we examine the main issues sector by sector, before drawing some general conclusions in chapter 6.

96.   In practice, it seems that universities and funding councils have struck a practical bargain between the benefits of autonomy and the need for accountability. We agree with the maxim that 'the exact counter-balance to autonomy is accountability'. As HEFCE argued, that meant that universities could be required to act reasonably, not to misuse public funds, not to withhold information from HEFCE, and not to ignore probity, value for money, or good governance—all requirements that can be imposed without infringing academic freedom.

97.   That view does not lead us to underestimate the true importance of academic freedom if properly defined. The right of individuals to pursue lines of research and publication which may be unpopular or controversial seems to us to be fundamental to the success of universities, reflected in the debates of senates and the like, as an academic institution. By extension, it has created a tradition of freedom of speech within a university which is an important check on impropriety. Comparisons with the requirements of confidentiality normal in a commercial business are misleading and misguided, as Sir Michael Davies observed in his visitorial report on University College, Swansea: 'the point is that neither the University of Wales nor the University College Swansea is a 'company' in the profit-making or any other sense. They are academic institutions.' He added that, when drawing the line between the exercise of proper academic freedom and unacceptable dissent, 'the fact that it is a line to be drawn in an adult academic world and not in a commercial jungle is of profound importance'.

R7.   Institutions of higher and further education should make it clear that the institution permits staff to speak freely and without being subject to disciplinary sanctions or victimisation about academic standards and related matters, providing that they do so lawfully, without malice, and in the public interest.

Confidentiality clauses

98.   In Chapter 1 we discussed the importance for organisations of setting up a proper system of whistleblowing within the organisation. Yet cases of misconduct and maladministration involving a risk to public funds will occur from time to time. In some cases, the embarrassment to the institution has been such that disincentives to whistleblowing, in the form of confidentiality clauses, have been used.

99.   In their report *Severance Payments to Senior Staff in the Publicly Funded Education Sector*, the Public Accounts Committee observed that 'We are strongly opposed to the 'gagging' clause such as that which was included in the original severance agreement [at the University of Huddersfield]. Such a restriction should not be employed to prevent disclosure of the use of public funds'. We have come across instances in higher and further education of clauses in service and severance contracts which place extremely wide restrictions on the ability of staff to discuss with outsiders events within the body in which they work. There may of course be a place for restrictions of some sort in these contracts: genuinely confidential material may need to be protected and severance agreements may contain personal details which the individual would want to keep private. Yet it is against the public interest for confidentiality clauses to inhibit the disclosure of maladministration or the misuse of public funds.

100.   The charity Public Concern at Work provided us with an extract from the standard contract for staff in new universities and colleges of further education. In part it reads:

'*15.3   Confidential information must be determined in relation to individual employees according to their status, responsibilities or the nature of their duties. However, it shall include all information which has been specifically designated as confidential by [the institution] and any information which relates to the commercial and financial activities of [the institution], the unauthorised disclosure of which would embarrass harm or prejudice [the institution].*'

101.   We consider that this clause is unacceptably wide and will tend to inhibit staff from raising concerns in the public interest, even with the proper authorities. If clauses of this type are necessary, for example, to protect commercially sensitive details of a forthcoming purchase, they should contain a statement of a public interest exception, permitting staff to raise

matters with the funding councils or some other outside person or body, such as the Visitor. Protecting institutions from embarrassment cannot be weighed in the balance with ensuring the proper conduct of public business.

R8.   Where it is absolutely necessary to include confidentiality clauses in service and severance contracts, they should expressly remind staff that legitimate concerns about malpractice may be raised with the appropriate authority (the funding council, National Audit Office, Visitor, or independent review body, as applicable) if this is done in the public interest.

Third Report of the Committee on Standards in Public Life

CHAIRMAN LORD NOLAN

VOLUME 1: REPORT

Whistleblowing

193. The Local Government (Access to Information) Act 1985 imposed demanding standards of openness on local government, which compare favourably with other parts of the public sector. We received some evidence, notably from the local media, that these standards were not always observed, which, if true, would be reprehensible. The statutory arrangements, however, seem to us to be very much in line with the best practice we have recommended for other public bodies. High standards of openness should be coupled with a positive approach to whistleblowing. This is a matter on which we have, in our previous reports, adopted a consistent and firm approach which has been fully accepted by government. In our first report we recommended that:

> *. . . each . . . [public] body should nominate an official or board member entrusted with the duty of investigating staff concerns about propriety raised confidentially. Staff should be able to make complaints without going through the normal management structure, and should be guaranteed anonymity'.*

194. We made similar recommendations in our second report. The essence of a whistle-blowing system is that staff should be able to by-pass the direct management line, because that may well be the area about which their concerns arise, and that they should be able to go outside the organisation if they feel the overall management is engaged in an improper course.

195. We consider that local government should be expected to adopt this approach, and we note that the LGMB has produced recommendations on these lines. In some ways there is less need for local government employees to go to external sources, because there will usually be opposition councillors only too ready to pick up on matters of concern. That may not be a desirable way to ventilate an issue, however, and it would be sensible for councils to adopt the following approach:

- creating a route for confidential whistleblowing within the management structure, perhaps as part of the duties of the monitoring officer:

- permitting staff to raise matters in confidence with the local government ombudsman or district auditor:

- allowing access to some other external body, such as an independent charity.

196. In all cases the usual test would apply that the concerns are raised in good faith and without malice, in order for the whistleblower to be immune from disciplinary sanctions for breach of confidence.

R26 Every local authority should institute a procedure for whistleblowing, which would enable concerns to be raised confidentially inside and, if necessary, outside the organisation. The Standards Committee might well provide an internal destination for such complaints.

> 'We are not adversarial at all. We are inquisitorial and we set out to have a common aim with complainants and local authorities which is (a) to get at the truth and (b) to co-operate to try to put things right not just for the complainant but also for other people so that they do not suffer the same consequences. Our concern is that enforcement might change that, that it might become adversarial, that it might become much more like the courts and we think that might not be in the interests of complainants' **Edward Osmotherley, Chairman, Commission for Local Government in England**
>
> 'Overall, and to our disappointment as a strong supporter of the Ombudsman in principle, our experience is of a service which is not living up to its potential. Inevitably the Ombudsman deals with contentious cases and frustrated individuals who use the service as a last resort. This can colour perceptions of its effectiveness. Nevertheless, we have encountered genuine problems with both the scope of the Ombudsman's powers and the complaint procedures for individuals. On too many occasions the public are left dissatisfied with the service provided by local authority and by the sanctions available to them when seeking redress. In many cases this dissatisfaction is not related to the question of whether a local authority has handled an issue fairly or not.' **Tony Burton, Head of Planning and Natural Resources, Council for the Protection of Rural England**

a contractor has a complaints system of its own should not prevent the local authority's complaints system being able to handle a problem where the complainant was dissatisfied with the response from the contractor.

R31   Local authorities should ensure that people who receive services through a contractor to the local authority have access to a properly publicised complaints system.

258.   We commented in chapter 4 about the importance of whistleblowing systems in local government. We have considered whether it would be realistic to recommend that organisations tendering for local authority services should be required, by a contract term, to have their own confidential mechanisms for reporting malpractice. The existence of such a mechanism is now considered best practice within the private sector and we would not wish to discourage organisations tendering for local authority contracts from putting their own systems in place. We recognise, however, that in the short term the existence of such procedures will be the exception rather than the rule. We therefore believe it is important that local authorities should seek to provide, through their contracts, access to their own internal whistleblowing procedures for the staff of contracting organisations. This could involve requiring the contracting organisation to declare, as part of the contract, that any confidentiality clauses relating to its staff should not apply in relation to a formal reference by that member of the staff to the council's internal whistleblowing procedures.

R32   Staff of contracting organisations should have access to the local authority's whistleblowing procedures.

> 'A combination of mid-career changes and early retirement has launched a skilled and potentially predatory class of knowledgeable senior local authority managers into the market place. Their skills and knowledge, gained in a local authority setting, are not only potentially of advantage to any new employer organisation offering them a job, but also potentially to the disadvantage of their former local authority.' **David Winchurch, Chief Executive, Walsall Metropolitan Borough Council**
>
> 'We believe that there are many examples of officers who have been responsible or very closely involved in the award of contracts to private sector organisations or in the award of grants to voluntary organisations who, shortly after the decision of the authority concerned, have then taken up employment with those organisations. Most members of the
>
> *[Continued on next page]*

[Continued from previous page]

public would clearly regard that as an abuse. We believe it is one that should be prevented and we believe that it is capable of prevention and capable of being policed at the local level.' Steven Bundred, Member, Society of London Treasurers, and Chief Executive, Camden Borough Council

'I think it is an illustration of the potential conflict situation, inasmuch as it may tempt certain officers, or members also for that matter, to promote the contracting out of services with a view to their taking positions in it. That is the danger. How real a danger it is, I do not know, but it is around sufficiently for a mechanism to be required to test it.' Sir Jeremy Beecham, Chairman, Association of Metropolitan Authorities (now Chair, Local Government Association)

Review of Standards of Conduct in Executive NDPBs, NHS Trusts and Local Public Spending Bodies

Fourth Report of the Committee on Standards in Public Life

Chairman Lord Nolan

Common Themes

14.   There is a number of issues which apply to all the bodies covered in this review which have force in more than one area of the report.

Whistleblowing

66.   Responses on whistleblowing were patchy. Most executive NDPBs had formal procedures for staff to raise concerns over malpractice which were outlined in staff handbooks or codes of conduct. These allowed individuals to raise concerns confidentially with line management in the first instance. The individual then had the option to take the matter further with a nominated officer within the executive NDPB, and then to a nominated individual within the sponsor department. However some executive NDPBs had no such procedures or statement of confidentiality. Nor was there any indication that such procedures were being considered within those organisations.

67.   The response we received from Public Concern at Work (the leading organisation in this field) noted that of the fourteen public bodies who commissioned them to help introduce a whistleblowing policy, one quarter had some difficulty distinguishing between a whistleblowing policy from a grievance procedure. In these organisations, Public Concern at Work were not convinced that staff would have sensed a genuine commitment that management wanted concerns to be raised.

68.   The responses to our questionnaire noted that the whistleblowing arrangements had been put to the test in only four cases. The first two instances were (in general terms) allegations of dishonesty and/or conduct incompatible with high standards of regularity and propriety; and allegations of financial misconduct. A third case did not specify the occasions on which the arrangements had been used; and the fourth case related to personnel issues and not the use for which the mechanism was devised.

69.   All organisations face the risks of things going wrong or of unknowingly harbouring malpractice. In these days of greater openness of government, those organisations who do not have arrangements to give staff the opportunity to act responsibly to uphold the reputation of the organisation and maintain public confidence, will be looked upon as failing in their duty adequately to protect the public purse.

70.   It is clear that executive NDPBs and their sponsor departments are making efforts to provide avenues which enable staff to raise concerns about misconduct and malpractice, while offering safeguards about confidentiality. However, much still needs to be done to encourage a culture of openness within some organisations. **It is important that all Departments, executive NDPBs and NHS bodies should institute codes of practice on whistleblowing, appropriate to their circumstances, so as to enable concerns about malpractice to be raised confidentially inside and, if necessary, outside the organisation.** It is important that these arrangements are well publicised within organisations so that staff are left in no doubt about the avenues open to them. The proposal by Richard Shepherd MP to introduce a 'Public Interest Disclosure Bill' in the current Parliamentary session is likely to receive support from the Government, and will require a whole-hearted response from public sector bodies.

Standard Chartered Policy

Group Instruction

[1 DECEMBER 1997]

SPEAKING UP-POLICY

Introduction

Trust and integrity are vital to the Group. We must be able to trust each other to behave honestly. Our customers must be able to trust in the Bank absolutely.

Misconduct and malpractice breach trust and endanger the Bank's reputation and, in some cases, licences. The best way of protecting trust is for staff who have genuine suspicions about wrongdoings to speak up. Usually, staff will raise concerns with their line management but there will be times when this might not be possible.

This policy tells you what to do in such a case. Any report which you make will be listened to, investigated and treated in confidence. Victimisation of anyone who comes forward will not be tolerated. Remember "Speaking Up" is an essential principle of our compliance policy.

What should I speak up about?

Any actual or planned wrongdoing or bad practice which:

—is against the law

—is against banking regulations

—does not comply with Group rules or the Code of Conduct.

What if I have a grievance?

The system is *not* intended to deal with staff grievances, for which separate procedures exist.

What if I'm not sure of my facts?

You don't have to be 100% sure. If you have a genuine suspicion then come forward and explain your concerns. It may just be a mistake in the system or process, rather than deliberate wrongdoing.

In any event, don't leave it until it is too late.

Won't I be thought malicious?

If you genuinely act in the best interests of the Bank and its employees, then your actions will be viewed as courageous, not malicious.

Wouldn't it be disloyal?

No—quite the opposite! Your action will help protect the interests of our Bank. Staff involved in wrongful behaviour are the ones who are being disloyal. They are putting at risk not only the achievements of their business, but possibly those of the Group as a whole.

Who should I speak to?

If you can, then you should speak to your line manager. However, the Bank accepts that there will be certain circumstances when staff could feel uncomfortable doing this. **Compliance Officers** will therefore act as alternative first points of contact—his or her number is in your directory.

Can I come forward anonymously?

Yes. But it is much harder to investigate suspicions which are reported anonymously—and often it is impossible. It is best to declare your identity if you can.

Can I bring a colleague along?

Yes—if you wish.

What will happen next?

Your Compliance Officer will discuss with you whether anyone else needs to be put in the picture in order for your suspicions to be investigated and, if so, who. They will not mention your involvement to your line manager or anyone else implicated without your consent.

Will it be in confidence?

Every effort will be made to protect your confidence. The principle will always be to involve as few people as possible. Although you may be asked if you can provide further information, you will not be directly involved in the investigation.

What will be the consequences for *me*?

You will *not* be blamed for speaking up or for any failure to speak up earlier. Staff may have taken time to form their suspicions, or to build up the courage to act on them. However, those who have been actively involved in wrongdoing will not have automatic immunity from disciplinary or criminal proceedings.

How will I know whether action has been taken?

Your Compliance Officer will give you feedback on the outcome. Any investigation may take some time, but you will be told in due course whether your suspicions were well-founded and (where possible) what action is being taken about them.

Martin Hayman
Group Secretary

Leonard Cheshire

NOVEMBER 1998

Reasons for policy

Leonard Cheshire recognises that there are, from time to time, situations where employees/volunteers become aware of bad practice which can affect the well being of users of services, and the long-term reputation of the organisation. Suspecting or even knowing of such bad practice may cause contradictory feelings; for example employees or volunteers may be worried about raising such issues or want to keep their concerns to themselves. They may feel that raising the matter would be disloyal to colleagues, managers or to Leonard Cheshire. They may have decided to say something but find that they have spoken to the wrong person or raised the issue in an inappropriate way and feel they still want to pursue it.

This policy and procedure has been introduced to enable employees and volunteers to raise their concerns at an early stage. Leonard Cheshire wants matters raised when they are a concern rather than wait for proof.

Policy statement

1. Leonard Cheshire acknowledges its duty to encourage and empower employees and volunteers to speak out when they encounter bad practice.

2. All staff employed by Leonard Cheshire have a duty to care and assist people who use Leonard Cheshire Services. This duty extends to having an obligation not to overlook bad practice, but to speak out and seek to correct it.

3. No one who raises a genuine concern about bad practice will be at risk of losing their job or suffering any form of retribution as a result of doing so.

4. Trustees expect all people in management positions to recognise their responsibilities in this matter and to adopt and implement this policy and to adhere to its procedures with regard to whistleblowing by any employee or volunteer.

This Policy has accompanying Procedures which must be followed.

This Policy statement has been agreed by the Trustees of Leonard Cheshire and is mandatory on all its Departments and Services.

Whistleblowing

These Procedures should be used in conjunction with the relevant policy document.

Procedures

Introduction

- Bad practices may occur from time to time in the operation of Leonard Cheshire's Services

- Leonard Cheshire is committed to the principle that disclosing bad practice is good practice.

- These procedures are designed to enable and encourage employees and volunteers to raise concerns about bad practices without fear of reprisals, and to reassure employees and volunteers that such matters will be dealt with seriously and effectively by the organisation.

- The procedures apply to ALL employees and volunteers unless expressly stated otherwise.

- Managers of services, local committees and central and regional staff are required to implement these procedures and to ensure that all employees and volunteers are aware that they are available.

- The type of malpractice covered by the Whistleblowing Policy and Procedures includes:
    * failure to uphold professional standards of practice and/or behaviour; (e.g. abuse in all its forms, breaches of confidentiality)
    * danger to health and safety (e.g. ignoring manual handling regulations)
    * criminal activity including fraudulent and corrupt behaviour; (e.g. theft, fraud)
    * breach of legal duties; (e.g. staffing arrangements)
    * cover-up of the above

There are existing procedures in place to enable employees to lodge a grievance relating to their own employment. The Whistleblowing Policy is intended to cover concerns that fall outside the scope of those procedures and is not a substitute for Leonard Cheshire's Grievance Procedures. There is a separate Complaints Procedure for service users.

How to raise a concern

If employees or volunteers suspect malpractice they should act promptly and follow the procedure detailed below. The earlier they raise their concern the easier it is to take action. They will need to explain to the person they contact the reasons for their concerns and give as much information as they possibly can. It will help if they keep notes of the dates, times and details of their concerns but, even if they don't have all this information, it is important that they raise their concerns anyway.

- Employees/volunteers should raise their concerns about bad practices with one of the following people (list 1):
    1. their supervisor, line manager, volunteer co-ordinator; or
    2. the local health and safety representative; or

    3. the manager of the Service/Section/Department; or
    4. the local committee chairman.

- If they are not reassured by the response they receive from the person they have contacted in list 1, or they do not feel able to contact any of the above, they should raise their concerns with one of the following people (list 2):

    1. the Regional Complaints Co-ordinator; or
    2. the Regional Health & Safety Co-ordinator; or
    3. the Regional Director (or any other Director); or
    4. the Manager Internal Audit (Finance) c/o Wales & West Regional Office; or
    5. any Trustee; or
    6. the Head of Standards at Leonard Cheshire's Central Office, Millbank.

    It will help considerably at this stage if they are able to put their concerns in writing. This will assist the person carrying out any investigation into their concerns.

- All people listed above will be trained to deal with concerns raised through these procedures.

- The intention in these procedures is that wherever possible any employee's or volunteer's concerns should be raised within Leonard Cheshire, in the ways outlined above. If, however, they feel unable to raise the matter in this way they may contact the Registration and Inspection Department of the relevant Local Authority, or in matters relating to fraud or corruption, the external Auditor Pricewaterhouse-Coopers.

Independent Advice

If at any stage in the procedures employees or volunteers are unsure about what to do and would like independent advice they may like to discuss their concerns with someone at Public Concern at Work (PCaW). PCaW is an independent charity staffed by lawyers which offers confidential free legal and practical advice on how people can raise concerns about malpractice at work. They can also give advice on who else employees or volunteers may contact and about what legal protection may be available. The most enquiries that PCaW receive are from people working in the health and care fields. PCaW's legal helpline can be contacted on 0171 404 6609.

Professional associations and trade unions can also offer advice to members considering raising concerns.

Safeguards

- Harassment or victimisation of whistleblowers will not be tolerated. Information about available support for the whistleblower will be offered to any employee or volunteer who whistleblows by the person they contact within Leonard Cheshire (Lists 1 & 2).

- Every effort will be made to ensure that the employee's or volunteer's identity is kept confidential if they so wish. However, it must be appreciated that an investigation process may reveal the source of the information. Leonard Cheshire may need them to give evidence at disciplinary or criminal proceedings. If it becomes necessary to reveal the employee's or volunteer's identity in order to pursue the investigation, this will be discussed with them at the earliest stage. In such circumstances it may affect Leonard Cheshire's ability to continue the investigation if they do not agree to be identified.

- If an allegation is made in good faith but it is not confirmed by any investigation, no action will be taken against them. If, however, they maliciously make false allegations, disciplinary action will be taken against them.

- Leonard Cheshire hopes that all employees and volunteers will feel able to put their name to the allegation, as concerns expressed anonymously are more difficult to investigate. If employees or volunteers raise a concern anonymously their identity may be deduced. If, contrary to this policy, they then suffer reprisals, it may be difficult to show that this was the result of raising a concern.

How Leonard Cheshire will respond

- All concerns raised under these procedures must be followed up and documented.

- The action taken will depend on the nature of the concern. The matters raised may be:
    * investigated internally
    * referred to the police
    * referred to the external Auditor
    * form the subject of an independent inquiry

- Initial enquiries will be made to determine whether an investigation is appropriate, and, if so, what form it should take. Concerns or allegations which fall within the scope of specific procedures (for example the Grievance Procedure) will normally be referred for consideration under those procedures.

- If requested, within 5 working days of a concern being received, the person raising the concern will be written to by the person in Leonard Cheshire who received it. The letter will acknowledge the concern has been received and provide information on who is dealing with the matter and who to contact if they have any questions.

- So that the person who raised the concern can be sure that the matter has been properly addressed, they will be given feedback on how their concern has been handled and the outcome of any investigation. However, Leonard Cheshire may not be able to disclose full details due to confidentiality in relation to other people involved or due to legal constraints, in which case this will be explained.

November 1998

APPENDIX 8

Other Jurisdictions

Whistleblowing protection only exists in a handful of countries around the world. Whilst these jurisdictions may afford some employment protection for employees raising concerns, such protection is not specifically related to whistleblowing and will not provide the degree of certainty that statutory whistleblowing affords. This appendix provides a brief glance at the protection provided by the United States of America, Australia, Europe. Whilst this book is published South Africa is presenting a Whistleblowing Bill through its Parliament. The distinction from protection provided elsewhere in the world is that the Public Interest Disclosure Act is the only Act to provide protection to private sector. In this regard the United Kingdom's legislation albeit younger is more advanced and drew from what was seen as the inadequacies within other systems.

The United States of America

Employment Law

Generally in the United Kingdom most employees enjoy statutory protection against arbitrary dismissal from the Employment Rights Act 1996. In the U.S.A. there is no such statutory protection at a federal level or within individual states. Generally speaking such protection can not be found within the U.S.A.'s common law. As such, employees in the U.S. may be arbitrarily dismissed at the whim of their employer. Whilst the U.S. cites strong economic based arguments for creating such a fluid but insecure workforce, without this fundamental right there exists no foundation upon which general protection for whistleblowers may be built. Nevertheless that is not to say that there is no protection for certain whistleblowers within specified sectors or where certain concerns are to be raised.

There are pressure groups within the U.S.A. who regularly comment and criticise the protection afforded to whistleblowers attempting to widening its availability. One such body is the Government Accountability Project run by Tom Devine. This organisation disseminating information from their website have produced numerous publications one of which is *The Whistleblower's Survival Guide*.[1] Whilst the U.S. may be considered as one of the most litigious countries in the world, its whistleblowing protection has been introduced piecemeal and as such remains specific to areas of malpractice or work.

Common Law

Protection against dismissal—generally

Protection was thought to have been available in the Constitutional right to free speech but the courts have not yet been persuaded that this right should provide an employee with pro-

---

[1] Tom Devine, *The Whistleblower's Survival Guide* (Government Accountability Project, July 1997), Ch. 5, pp. 116–151.

tection against dismissal. The First and Fourteenth Amendments to the Constitution do provide Federal employees with some protection in that they protect federal workers from discrimination where they raise matters of public concerns. Federal employees include federal employees and local and state government workers. Within the U.K. and a major factor in the British Legal System is that anyone may consult with their lawyers without fear of breaching any implied or written duty of confidentiality. Within the U.S. no such protection is provided to disclosure to their attorney and is not accepted by the U.S. Justice Department.

The first case cited[2] as the case establishing general whistleblowing protection in certain states was the Appellate Court's decision in state of California in the case *Petermann v. International Brotherhood of Teamsters, Chauffeurs, Warehousemen and Helpers of America* (1959) 396,344 P.2d 25. This case founded implied protection against arbitrary dismissal where such a dismissal was founded on a breach of public policy. In this case the breach of public policy was that an employee had refused to perjure himself for the purposes of an investigation and was dismissed as a direct result. The Appellate Court holding that such a dismissal was wrong created an actionable tort whereby the employee would be entitled to compensation if the employee successfully proved that their dismissal was as a result of the employers breach of public policy.

PROTECTION AGAINST DISMISSAL—WHISTLEBLOWERS

Since this 1959 case, courts in other States have followed its precedent but the definition of what is and what is not an employer's breach of "public policy" has provided scope for this protection to be widened and narrowed. One case showing how narrowly "public policy" has been defined is the case of *Schudolski v. Michigan Consolidated Gas Co.* (1982) 316 NW 2d 710 where an employee who raised concerns over internal accounting procedures relied upon his code of ethics provided by his Institute of Internal Auditors. The court did not accept that this code was public policy.

Forty two states provide some level of protection for whistleblowers by accepting the precedent of *Petermann* preventing arbitrary dismissal where the reason is a breach of public policy. Of these only eighteen states possess some form of protection for "private whistleblowers" and two states provide some protection for "independent contractors".

STATUTORY PROTECTION

STATE PROTECTION

One of the earliest states to have created their own legislation[3] was the Michigan Whistleblower Protection Act 1981. This Act provides both compensation and reinstatement to whistleblowers. Further this protection is enjoyed by those close to reporting their concern or where they have been dismissed for reporting a concern. This protection is only where the concern relates to an infringement of the law or a regulations and that they report it to a public body.

More recently new State statutes such as the Clean Air Act, the Safe Drinking Water Act and the Toxic Substances Control Act have begun to protect employees who raise concerns in areas such as Health and Safety and within the Environment. These Acts provide protection only if the disclosure is made to a public body and that the whistleblower has been dismissed or suffered discrimination as a result of their disclosure. By requiring the disclosure to be to a public body prior to protection being provided such legislation does not incite or encourage internal reporting. This important distinction with the U.K.'s legislation has an important impact on employers.

---

[2] *ibid.*
[3] *ibid.*

FEDERAL STATUTORY PROTECTION

The first piece of general protection was found within the False Claims Act of 1863 although this Act will is discussed later under "Profits from Whistleblowing". The Civil Service Reform Act 1978 provided protection only to federal employees who reported any "waste, abuse or fraud" from within their departments. The federal workers could only report matters which had occurred. This Act created three agencies, namely The Office of Personal Management, the Merit Systems Protection Board and the Office of Special Counsel. The Office of Personnel Management was put in place to administer the civil service. The Merit System Protection Board was charged with the adjudication of appeals of personnel of any matter—which included the prohibited practices. Finally the Office of Special Counsel was to be a "watchdog" in the defence and to assist whistleblowers in raising their concern and in pursuit of redress together with the Merit Systems Protection Board (M.S.P.B.). The Government Accountability Project cite[4] that between 1979 and 1988 the Office of Special Counsel turned down 99 per cent of cases referred to it and undertook no litigation attempting to reinstate a whistleblower. In fact a Congressional Research Service Report for Congress published in 1990 stated that "no measurable progress had been made in overcoming federal employee resistance to reporting instances of fraud, waste and abuse".[5] In the face of such criticism and apparent inaction the Whistleblower Protection Act 1989 addressed the position of the Federal Whistleblower.

WHISTLEBLOWER PROTECTION ACT 1989 (AMENDED 1994)

Under Section 1213 of the 1989 Act federal employees were permitted to disclose evidence where they have a reasonable belief that there is evidence of "(1)(A) violation of any law, rule, or regulation or; (B) gross mismanagement, a gross waste of funds, an abuse of authority or a substantial and specific danger to public health or safety . . ." Gross mismanagement "is defined as 'patterns or significant single instances of arbitrary activity that interferes with efficient accomplishment of the agency mission'".

Where a present or former federal employee reported such concerns and suffered prohibited personal practices their first avenue was to report the matter to the Merit Systems Protection Board alleging the prohibited practices against the employee. A further avenue was to seek the Office of Special Counsel to initiate action. Finally as an alternative an individual could embark upon their own action negotiating with the relevant parties.

The position of the Merit System Protection Board was changed only to adjudicate on the employees allegation whereas the Office of Special Counsel became an independent agency away from the Merit System Protection Board (1994 amendment) with its role squarely defined so as to protect federal workers from prohibitive practices although it may still initiate inquiries and investigate allegations. The Office of Special Counsel also had to consult more and keep informed those they represented. This move placed the emphasis more on the whistleblower's interests becoming the paramount concern of the agency and attempted to change the image that the O.S.C. had cultivated prior to this Act.

The W.P. Act ensured that federal agencies encouraged whistleblowing through the enforcement of the *Government Code of Ethics*. Further it opened the avenue to obtain interim relief removing a financial lacuna providing the employers with the duty to permit those raising concerns either to return to their job or at least to remain on the pay roll whilst awaiting the determination of their concern. Should the concern be substantiated then whistleblowers were provided with the right to request a move to another position within their federal employer where they were to be permitted to make a fresh start.

Further, the National Performance Review which examined the position of federal employees after the Whistleblowing Protection Act and the Merit Systems Protection Board and the Office of Special Counsel and concluded that some 5000,000 federal workers annually witnessed serious misconduct. The Act protected present and former federal employees.

---

[4] *ibid.*, p. 119.
[5] L. Paige Whitaker, *Whistleblower Protections for Federal Employees*, January, 10, 1990, p. 2.

ONUS OF PROOF

When considering the level of protection afforded to an employee it is important to focus on the level of proof that the employee must achieve for their claim to succeed. In the U.K. the onus of proof can be reversed so that the onus is placed on the employer to prove that they were not victimised or dismissed or suffering from any detriment due to raising their concern. Under the previous Civil Service Reform Act 1978, the whistleblower first had to permit the illegal act to occur before they could report the malpractice. Within the Whistleblowing Protection Act 1989 this was changed to make mere threat to act sufficient for a concern to be raised. Nevertheless for a claim to succeed the federal employee **must** establish that a *significant* factor causing the "reprisal" was the disclosure by the federal employee. "Reprisal" was interpreted widely so as to include dismissal and other discrimination such as the employee being passed over for promotion, or the reduction in responsibility or wages. Within the 1979 Act the federal employee had to show the "action" or "inaction" of the employer to receive protection. This proved in practise to be a difficult hurdle for the federal employee to clear. As such in the 1994 Act the burden was not reversed but lowered so that now the employee had to show that behind the retaliation by their employer a contributing factor was their involvement in the disclosure. This change from the "significant factor" to that of a "contributing factor" was welcomed by most commentators. Contributing was defined as "any factor, which alone or in connection with other factors, tends to affect in any way the outcome of the decision". Finally the whistleblower must possess a "reasonable belief" that there is evidence of those acts set out within Section 1213 of the W.P. Act.

PROFITS FROM WHISTLEBLOWING

The False Claims Act 1863 which was revised in 1986 is commonly referred to as the "Lincoln Law", and is based on the Common Law principal of *qui tam pro domino rege sequitur quam pro se ipso* or *He who sues on behalf of the King also sues as well as for himself*. This Common Law principal was turned into statutory form in the False Claims Act which was introduced to protect the Union Arms against fraudulent suppliers during the American Civil War. The Act established that anyone who sued in the name of the U.S. Government in relation to charges of fraud also sues for themselves. The Act as amended in 1986 permitted those who exposed financial malpractice against a Federal Agency such as a contracting body with the Federal Agency, may receive compensation based on a 15–25 per cent share of the savings recouped by the Federal Government Agency. If the Federal Government is informed of the concern but they fail to litigate when a claim is filed this may increase to 25–30 per cent.

An example of this "Lincoln Law" principle is case of an English worker, Frederick Copeland who worked for Western Geared System, a subsidiary of Lucas Industries. Mr Copeland received $18 million after claiming successfully that his employers had falsely certified work on the gearboxes of American fighter aircraft.

Australia

This common law country comprises six states and two territories each possessing local government powers encompassing the power to create statute. Of these eight units only the state of Victoria fails to have Whistleblowing protection whereas the only territory to possess protection is the Australian Capital Territory which possesses its own Public Interest Disclosure Act 1994.

COMMON LAW

It will be of no surprise that being a Commonwealth country the position for the whistleblower in Australia at Common Law mirrors that of the U.K. As such there exists an implied duty of confidentiality together with the defence to a breach of confidence be it the implied or express obligation in that there can be no confidence in iniquity.

STATUTORY PROTECTION

The statutory language and the practical approach used in Australia is similar to that of the U.K. Act. The position in Australia however is the same as the U.S.A. in that protection in Australia also does not extend to private organisations. The protection in the States of Western Australia, South Australia, New South Wales and Queensland will be discussed briefly.

WESTERN AUSTRALIA

In 1988 this state established the Official Corruption Commission, to assist public sector employees. It provides protection only to those raising concerns about criminal activity. For a concern to be raised it must be presented to the Commission in the form of an allegation, whether of actions or omissions. In making a disclosure to the Commission the whistleblower is protected in respect of any retaliatory action or any legal proceedings being issued for breach of confidence. If any reprisals are taken against the whistleblower that act is in itself an offence although there is no redress for the whistleblower for the reprisals and there is no scope for any civil action.

SOUTH AUSTRALIA

The Whistleblowing Protection Act 1993 provides protection within this state but again only in regard to the public sector. This permits concerns to be disclosed where there are allegations of maladminstration and or waste. Maladministration has been defined in South Australia in a manner similar to that of the U.S.A.: "illegal activity; irregular or unauthorised use of public money; substantial mismanagement of public resources; conduct that is a substantial risk to public health and safety or to the environment". The onus is that the whistleblower must show that the evidence "tends to show" that there has been a breach of the Act. This is a low level evidential burden for the whistleblower to achieve for protection to follow. To be protected, unlike Western Australia, there is not a prescribed body. Within South Australia the whistleblower is under a duty to assist with any investigation, although their identity may not be revealed. There is also created a statutory act of victimisation which entitles the victim to recover compensation on a tort basis.

This is also a Public Interest Disclosure Act 1994. This Act applies to any person so it is not restricted to public sector employees although it only relates to concerns of a public nature. Disclosure must be made to a proper authority and government agencies are prescribed as recipients of such concerns. This Act ensured that every Government Agency undertook to establish proper procedures to facilitate concerns being raised.

NEW SOUTH WALES

In a similar manner to Western Australia, the first legislation created the Independent Commission Against Corruption 1988. All concerns had to be raised through the Commission. Although the Act permitted concerns to be raised by anyone, the concern had to relate to public corruption. Corruption was defined as criminal or disciplinary offences. The whistleblower did not need to have a reasonable belief in the allegation and the Commissioner had no discretion as to which concerns they investigated as they had to investigate all allegations.

The Public Disclosures Act 1994 widened the matters which could be reported to the

Commission to include "maladministration and serious and substantial waste". The Act ensured that the public sector set up procedures for concerns to be raised and that these procedures were to protect the whistleblower from reprisals. Protection is afforded if the concern is raised to the head of the organisation or within its whistleblowing procedure. Alternatively they are protected if the matter is raised with the Commission, the relevant Ombudsman and the Auditor-General. These three bodies now possess discretion not to investigate matters which appear to be frivolous or vexatious. The whistleblower must within 6 months receive a report from who they raised the concern. Similar to the U.K. Act the whistleblower must believe that the allegation is "substantially true". There is no protection if the disclosure is made frivolously or to avoid disciplinary action. Where the disclosure is made falsely or to mislead then unusually they will be guilty of an offence.

This Act does not permit concerns to be raised with journalists and Members of Parliament although in such circumstances the whistleblower must not only believe that the allegation is "substantially true" but they must also have made "substantially the same disclosure" to either one of the investigatory bodies or within the internal procedure. If it has been raised with the investigatory body or internally it must be shown by the whistleblower that the concern was not investigated or that the investigation was not completed within the six months provided or that they raised it and there has been no response. The protection provides that should any reprisals occur for making a protected disclosure then that person commits an offence.

The Criminal Justice Commission investigates official misconduct in public administration. The Whistleblowing Protection Act 1994 built upon the existing Criminal Justice Act 1989. Within Queensland again it is only concerns relating to the Public sector which are protected. The whistleblower must "honestly believe" that there are "reasonable grounds" that there has been negligent, unlawful or improper conduct, or a danger to the environment. If the disclosure is malicious or intentionally misleanding then that person commits an offence. By protecting the genuine discloser from any detriment from reprisals they are defined in statute and it includes the attempt to reprisal. Such action is both criminal and tortious, providing a compensatory element for the victim. Internal procedures are also a requirement under this Act.

The Commission in Queensland provides a "Whistleblower Support Program" that encompasses advice, counselling and psychologist.

Europe

There are a range of duties placed on professionals or specific employees to report crimes or threats against the state. A few shall be discussed below.

EUROPEAN COMMUNITY

The European Community ["E.C."] does not provide protection for whistleblowers. The closest example of protection is where the E.C. has placed a prositive duty or obligation on certain workers with the 1991 Money Laundering Directive. Under this Directive organisations which provide financial services and or relevant professionals, such as accountants, must report any suspicious financial transactions connected with money laundering.

The duty imposed rests on the relevant person possessing a mere suspicion. As soon as the individual has such a suspicion then have a duty to report the transaction. The Directive avoids any issue of confidentiality through Article 9 which releases the employee or individual from any duty of confidence. It is Article 10 that requires the institution to report the suspicions to the authorities. Further, a step which must be considered as constructive, Article 11 requires that the institution actually creates an internal procedure to train the employees with regard to the requirements of the Directive.

FRANCE

There is no specific statutory legislation to protect whistleblowers. This must be however understood against a background that under the French legal system an individual has a legal duty to report a serious crime. This duty is enforced with a penalty of up to Ff. 300,000 or up to 3 years imprisonment which may be imposed for a failure to report that a crime is about to take place. Where the crime is more serious or the threat is one against the state then the punishment can be greater.

ITALY

Under Article 33(1) of the Italian Code of Criminal Procedure, Public officials who become aware of illegal acts (which include frauds to the E.U. budget) have a positive duty to report the fact in writing. This duty even exists where the perpetrator's identity is unknown.

In Italy there exists statutory mechanism to prevent the disclosue of business secrets. Should an individual disclose a business secret under Article 622 of the Code of Criminal Procedure they may be punishable by a sentence of up to one years imprisonment and or a fine. Such a system could undermine any public spirited employee were it not for the equivalent of a "just cause" defence.

THE NETHERLANDS

The Dutch system has no protection for whistleblowers. In 1996 a government advisory body called the Socio-Economic Council discussed the desirability of "*klokkeluiden*" [bell-ringing] their equivalent to whistleblowing. Through a majority of the Council it was decided such legislation was unnecessary because it was felt that under Article 611 of the Book VII of Dutch Criminal Code employers have a duty to be a good employer. As such it sets down the principles of "reasonableness" and "fairness" of an employer. Employees dismissed for reporting malpractice may receive protection. However whether the protection is sufficient to encourage whistleblowing remains uncertain.

The *Working Conditions Act* places a duty on employees to report concerns about health and safety risks to their employer. If having reported the risk the employer fails to take sufficient steps to alleviate the risk then the employee may report the failure to the relevant Government official.

Canada

There is no federal protection for whistleblowers. At provincial level there exists some protection.

New Zealand

In June 1994 a Whistleblowers Protection Bill was introduced as a private member's bill in the New Zealand House of Representatives. This bill provided for the disclosure of "public interest information" which is defined as any "conduct or activity in the public or private sector that concerns unlawful, corrupt or unauthorised use of public funds or resources; is otherwise unlawful; or constitutes a significant risk or danger, or is injurious to public health or safety, the environment or the maintenance of the law and justice".

Such information must be disclosed to a Whistleblowers Protection Authority and can be made by any person who "believes on reasonable grounds" that the information is "true or if not in a position to do so, believes that the information may be true and is of sufficient significance to justify its disclosure so that the truth may be investigated".

Any person who makes such a disclosure is protected and the bill provides remedies for discrimination or harassment.

Worked Examples

The following case studies are fictional cases. There is first a description of a particular scenario. Then each case study is followed by a short analysis showing how the concern may be disclosed and the different options available to both the member of staff and the company at each stage.

The cases cover diverse organisations from different sectors with a range of staff. The practical approach as to whom the "whistleblower" may disclose such critical information is different when one considers the sector or the business structure.

Case 1

PUBLIC SECTOR—MIDDLE MANAGEMENT EMPLOYEE—FRAUD

1. James is 36 years old and started working for **Big Heap Local Authority** six months ago as an assistant auditor. Recently he was promoted to Manager of the Payments Section.

2. Within the Finance section of the Housing Benefit Department there exists a computer system to enable payments to be made directly to landlords.

3. As the Manager James is responsible for overseeing all payments to ensure that they are sent out on a specified date. Most of the payments are made direct to the landlords' bank/building society accounts, although there are a large number where cheques are sent through the post to the landlords.

4. Whilst cross tabulating the payments being sent to landlords James came across the name of the Director of Housing. It is an unusual name and James recognised it immediately. James then examined how many payments the Director was receiving. After this cursory investigation James discovered that the Director has, according to the payments, eight tenants living in two properties. In total she received £640 per week for the properties. He noted however when investigating a little further that both properties are listed on the computer as properties within the ownership of a company called "LETTINGS ARE US".

5. James becomes more curious later that evening. He remains at work under the pretext that he is doing some overtime. He endeavours to find the file on the property which would contain all the necessary documents substantiating the claims—but the file is missing. Files can only be removed by being signed out. James checks the appropriate book and finds no record of the file being taken.

The Position of James

James appears to have come across some suspicious payments but they may not be fraudulent. The first question is whether Big Heap has its own internal whistleblowing procedure. If it does then this procedure would be best followed.

[Continued on next page]

[Continuned from previous page)

It may be that the evidence before James is sufficient to possess a *"reasonable belief that it tends to show"* one of the six items of malpractice or misconduct [sections 43C, E, F, G]. Of the six items these possibilities arise:

a. There may be a crime committed if the properties do not exist—although there is no evidence at present that this is correct.

b. It may be that the Director has a legal obligation to declare such interests and this may not have been done, although this would probably not be a crime.

c. It may be that there has been an attempt, with the removal of the file and another name being used, to cover up (a) and (b) above.

There is no issue as to James acting in bad faith.
There is no fear of "victimisation" or that there would be a "cover-up".

At this stage there is no evidence to suggest that the allegation is true and an internal disclosure appears appropriate. If following an internal disclosure Big Heap fail to ensure that James is fully aware as to the outcome of any investigation into his concern, it may be that James can consider a disclosure to the Audit Commission as a Government prescribed person, but for this he would have to satisfy the requirements under section 43F.

The Position of the Big Heap Local Authority

The internal procedure may designate a person within the Audit section to whom financial concerns may be raised. Should this person or the Chief Executive be contacted by James it is important that James is made aware that an investigation will occur and provide James with an approximate date for a conclusion. No one else in his department should be informed as to his concern. Should they fail to investigate then this may provide James with the ammunition to raise the concern externally. Big Heap does not need to inform James as to what disciplinary action has been taken as this may be confidential information between the Director and Big Heap.

Case 2

SMALL PRIVATE SECTOR—PART-TIME EMPLOYEE—ABUSE

1. Joanne is 26 years old and started a part-time job working for SPRING retirement home four years ago. The home is owned by Mr and Mrs B who lived close to the retirement home. The home employs 20 staff, although only three staff are required for the night shifts. The home has a capacity for 40 residents although at present only 28 beds are in use.

2. Joanne works two nights a week starting at 8.00 p.m. finishing at 8.00 a.m. The home is a large Edwardian property with an extension to the rear. The other two members of staff in the home during Joanne's shifts are Billy and Stephanie.

3. Joanne, Stephanie and Billy have a number of responsibilities that must be performed. Whilst responding to calls from the residents and the hourly *"walk round"* the home, they are required to use the washing and drying machines, dishwashers with some ironing and carry out the occasional stocktake. Providing these duties are performed there is no rule preventing staff from sleeping.

4. Bob, the nephew of Mr B was a new member of staff who worked day shifts. Whilst Billy was on holiday Bob had been asked to cover for him. One night Stephanie had called in sick and the shift was to be undertaken by Stephanie and Bob alone.

5. The residents were all in bed and Bob suggested that Joanne start to do the washing and drying whilst Bob attended to each room to ensure that the televisions were all switched off and plugs removed from the walls. Joanne happily agreed.

6. After Joanne had finished she went to look for Bob. Joanne was concerned that Bob should have returned. She decided to walk round the home and check that everything was all right.

7. On approaching the door to Mrs A's room Joanne noticed a lamp on. The policy at the Home is that should a female resident need attending to then a female member of staff must assist or perform any necessary tasks.

8. Mrs A was unfortunately both blind, deaf and suffering from Alzheimer's disease. Joanne noticed the door was ajar and she thought through the darkness that she saw Bob moving around Mrs A whilst she was in her night gown. Bob appeared startled when Joanne walked into the room and appeared to be adjusting his trousers whilst at the same time moving around the bed.

The Position of Joanne

Joanne may have caught Bob abusing a resident. The first question is whether the Home has its own internal whistleblowing procedure. If they do then this procedure should be followed.

It may be that what Joanne saw was merely a case of Bob attending to Mrs A but not following the in-house procedures. As there appears to be no independent corroborative evidence to support Joanne it is likely that she possesses more than a *"reasonable belief that it tends to show"* one of the six items of malpractice or misconduct [sections 43C, E, F, G]], that is Crime—sexual and/or abuse.

There is no issue as to Joanne acting in bad faith.
There is no fear of "victimisation" although because of the relationship of the accused and proprietor it may be that Joanne fears there would be a "cover-up".

With allegations of this nature there is not normally any corroborative evidence to support what Joanne suspects she saw. As there is a possibility that there was merely a failure to follow internal procedures with regard to the presence of a female member of staff an internal disclosure is appropriate. If following an internal disclosure SPRING fail to reassure Joanne that they have properly investigated her allegation, she may consider contacting the social services department of her local authority.

The Position of the SPRING

In small organisations an internal procedure usually designates one person to whom all concerns should be reported. Should the designated person or one of the owners be contacted by Joanne it is important that Joanne is made aware that the allegation will be taken seriously whether or not the allegation is against a relative.

Bill should be suspended until the investigation is concluded. Should SPRING fail to investigate adequately then this may provide Joanne with the opportunity to raise her concern with the local authority.

SPRING should consider the involvement of the police during their investigation.

Case 3

1. Jim is 29 and works in a factory making cars, where he has been working for ten years and he is a member of the union. Jim was recently elected by the fitters as their representative within B-Cars plc. Through this position he gained responsibility for health and safety.

2. Jim's responsibilities are to oversee the assembly of the car doors, boots and bonnets and other external parts. In his new position he is the first tier for whistleblowing should a member of staff have a concern.

3. A new car model was now in production and there was extreme work pressure on the staff. Some teething problems had occurred with its production and the manager had recently addressed all the staff requesting an efficient and speedy job as there were deadlines which had to be met in order to ensure the availability of the car in August.

4. Trevor approached Jim at the start of the week. Trevor was concerned with a new solvent which was being used to adhere leather to a panel to be fitted to the car doors. Trevor stated that this adhesive was making him feel unwell and he stated that other colleagues were also complaining about nausea.

5. Jim said to Trevor that he would approach his manager—Jim's line manager. He said he would contact his union to see whether they had any records of the solvent or could provide some general assistance.

6. Jim approached his line manager and described the problem to him reiterating the staff concerns and that he was considering approaching his union.

The Position of Jim

Jim should approach his line manager before contacting his union. The concern at this stage is not one for which it would be considered necessary to invoke a whistleblowing procedure. If, however, his line manager does not respond adequately then it could be used.

Jim at present is not likely to possess a *"reasonable belief that it tends to show"* one of the six items of malpractice or misconduct [sections 43C, E, F, G]. If B-Cars plc fail to act then it could be that there exists a health and safety concern and the staff should be provided with breathing masks, or only be permitted to work with the solvent for limited periods.

There is no issue as to Jim acting in bad faith. There is no fear of "victimisation" or that there would be a "cover-up".

Jim may consider seeking legal advice from his union or he could contact the Health and Safety Executive, a Government prescribed person, requesting some assistance from them as to the side effects of the adhesive and in doing so he need not provide his name or address or his place of work. Should Jim discover that the adhesive is dangerous then he should inform B-Cars of the danger.

If B-Cars fail to act or reassure Jim then he may consider approaching the H.S.E. as they are a prescribed person.

The Position of the B-Cars plc

B-Cars should investigate the side effects of the adhesive as soon as possible. It may be best for them to contact the manufacturers. Should any breathing equipment be required then this should be obtained as soon as possible and in the interim whilst waiting for such equipment they should limit the time spent by each worker using the adhesive.

If Jim was to use the internal whistleblowing procedure the matter should be addressed as a concern over health and safety. The staff should be informed as to what the company is proposing to do (a) to investigate the possibility that the adhesive is causing the sickness—such as contacting the manufacturer and in the interim (b) they should put in place some system to reduce the workers' exposure to the fumes.

Case 4

VOLUNTARY SECTOR—EMPLOYEE—MISCARRIAGE OF JUSTICE

1. Jill was very interested in charitable work.

2. Jill applied and obtained a temporary position with B-Help for two months as a volunteer. She was to use her secretarial skills in order to assist a director in the day to day running of the charity. Jill was proficient on the word processor and had particularly good shorthand skills and previous experience of office work.

3. When she joined she immediately put her skills to good use. The Director was extremely pleased with her work and Jill felt that they had a good working relationship.

4. At the start of the second month the Director explained that there was an impending visit with regard to a court case. He explained that it was necessary to tidy the office in preparation for the visit where the lawyers were to have access to a particular filing cabinet. The Director explained that the aim of the exercise was to remove other confidential information which was not relevant to the case. The Director asked Jill whether she could work the next evening to assist the Director. Jill accepted the offer.

5. The next evening Jill was asked to type pre-dated letters which were passed to the Director to sign. He would then place these letters in the filing cabinet. Jill thought this an unusual practice but the amount of work she was doing meant that she did not really consider what she was doing. Whilst this was taking place the Director was sifting through the filing cabinet and shredding documents.

6. That evening when Jill returned home late she discussed her interesting day with her flat mate who stated that her actions could implicate Jill in an attempted miscarriage of justice.

The Position of Jill

Jill is a volunteer and has come across suspicious behaviour. As a volunteer under section 43K she is not a protected class of worker. Nevertheless should she wish to raise the concern in a small charity it is doubtful that they have their own internal whistleblowing procedure, but it may be that she should approach a trustee of the Charity or some other designated person. If they do then Jill should follow this procedure and contact this person.

[Continued on next page]

[Continued fromprevious page]

If Jill was not a volunteer and was instead a protected worker, she would possess suffi-cient to possess a "reasonable belief that it tends to show" one of the six items of mal-practice or misconduct [sections 43C, E, F, G]. Of the six items it would most likely be that:

There appears to be a crime such as perjury being committed or an attempt to bring about a miscarriage of justice. The evidence though may already have been disposed of.

There may be an issue as to whether or not Jill is acting in good faith in that she was to some extent involved herself, although the information suggests that she was asked to perform the task without realising the consequences. There is no fear of "victimisation" or that there would be a "cover-up".

It may be that Jill would consider contacting the Police if the case is of a criminal nature or the other party if the matter is a civil one. The Charity Commission would most prob-ably not be able to deal with this matter, although they are a prescribed person, but she may still contact them if she reasonably believes they are the appropriate body.

The Position of the charity B-Help

As a volunteer Jill is not a protected worker. Should any internal procedure be used it may be that they or a trustee is approached by Jill.

Should a trustee or the Chairman of the charity be contacted by Jill it is important that she is made aware that the information has been received in confidence.
If they fail to investigate Jill may raise her concern with the Charity Commission or with the lawyers who came to examine the documents.

Case 5

PUBLIC SECTOR—EMPLOYEE—FAILED TO COMPLY WITH THE LEGAL OBLIGATIONS

1. John is an executive director for a large NHS Trust. Although not medically quali-fied he has been involved in the management of hospitals for over 25 years.

2. John's responsibilities included the non-medical staffing of the hospital and facility management. His responsibilities include all the orderlies, the catering, the cleaning, the maintenance and health and safety at the hospital.

3. John was preparing for the fitting and renovation of three wards within the east wing of the hospital where the new elderly patients unit was to be placed.

4. John was approached by a senior manager who wanted to know how he was to deal with large deposits of brown asbestos which had been found within the previ-ous ceiling of these wings. The Senior Manager had been told that the budget had not taken into account the cost of its removal and that they needed to obtain the funds to remove it from the Chief Executive involving a specialist firm in its removal.

5. John referred the matter to the Chief Executive. The Chief Executive assumed imme-diate control of the project.

6. Over the following three months John took no part in the project. In May, John was presented with the breakdown of costs for the renovation. Despite the transfer of responsibility it appeared that this document had been inadvertently sent through to him. John examined the cost sheets and could not find within the breakdown any costs attributable to the removal of the asbestos—it alarmed John however that there had been included a payment of £10,000 to the Managing Director of the renovating contractors under the heading "Bonus for Early Completion".

The Position of John

John appears to have come across the possible leaving of brown asbestos in the ceiling of a hospital ward. The first question is whether the NHS Trust has its own internal whistle-blowing procedure. If they do then this procedure would be best followed. However as the matter involves the Chief Executive this may make an internal disclosure difficult.

The evidence before John is sufficient for him to possess a "reasonable belief that it tends to show" one of the six items of malpractice or misconduct [sections 43C, E, F, G]. Of the six items it could be:

a. Danger to health and safety.
b. That there has been an attempt to cover up (a) above.

There is no issue as to John acting in bad faith. There is no fear of "victimisation" although there may be a fear of a "cover-up".

John should consider contacting the Health and Safety Executive (H.S.E.), a Government prescribed person, with regard to an inspection. Such a referral may be made anonymously although it would then be difficult to invoke protection. There are many people who are aware of the asbestos who could contact the HSE. In such circumstances it may be that the Chief Executive would not suspect John. As to the payment for early completion it may be that this comes out when the asbestos is investigated.

The Position of the NHS Trust

It is doubtful that any disclosure would be made internally. Should the HSE find asbestos at a time when contractors have been working on the same area of a building it would be sensible to investigate why it was not reported or why it was not discovered.

Should John raise his concern over the payment John must be reassured that the matter will be investigated in confidence and they should ask John for the breakdown of costs.

Case 6

MARKETING MANAGER—PUBLIC LIMITED INTERNATIONAL COMPANY—

1. Philip is a marketing manager of the Big Plc a multinational company. Philip has been employed for six and a half years.

2. Last year the Director of Marketing had discussed with Philip the various options open to him within the company. Recently he had been put forward by the Director for a position abroad and he was placed in the Kuala Lumpur office in Malaysia for a year.

3. Whilst in Malaysia Philip reported to the East Asian Director, Brian, who was responsible for the marketing over East Asia. Brian visited Philip every two months.

4. Big Plc manufacture computer chips for mobile phones and the factories in Malaysia were spearheading the company's research and development with regard to technology.

5. The latest piece of technological equipment on which Big Plc were working was the XXX1. This was a computer chip which it was hoped would revolutionise the mobile phone industry. On Friday September 28 Brian, the Director, came to Kuala Lumpur on his fourth regular visit.

6. Philip and Brian went out for a meal and as the evening wore on Brian was becoming more and more relaxed. Brian started claiming that he was soon to become *very* rich. Towards the end of the evening Brian let it slip that on the Wednesday there was to be an announcement which would make all those who had shares in Big Plc very rich indeed provided that they were sold within two days.

7. All the senior staff received share options and Philip made a mental note of the forecast as Big Plc shares were traded on the London Stock Exchange.

8. On Tuesday night, Philip was aghast to see on an international news channel a bulletin about Big Plc. The announcement was that a new computer chip was to be launched which would revolutionise the mobile phone market.

9. Philip remembered that only a few days earlier the Research & Development Director had expressed grave concerns over the capability of the XXX1 chip. Philip was shocked by the bulletin and quickly thought about the reasons behind this development. It was not unusual for the company to instigate high profile news items on their achievements, but Philip would be briefed.

10. The news bulletin then moved on to an interview with Brian who explained that it was the Malaysian team who had produced the chip. Philip's first reaction was anger that he had not been told of this breakthrough.

11. Philip reassured himself that he could speak to Brian on the Wednesday. When he tried Brian was unavailable. It was only on the Friday that Philip's concern crystallised. He was still in his office when he received an e-mail from the Managing Director of Marketing in London. It read that the press release over the XXX1 by Big Plc had been premature and a flaw in the chip had been discovered and that its launch was to be delayed.

12. Philip was not a conspiracy theorist but the conversation with Brian had sinister implications to him. Philip logged onto the internet and he was able to look at the share price of Big Plc over the last five days.

13. To his surprise, the shares which usually had traded at £6.50 each had increased by £6 to £12.50 a share on the Wednesday and peaked with an increase of £7.50 on the Thursday. By close of business on the Friday however following the latest release they were down to £6 each.

14. Philip knew that the directors such as Brian each had major share holdings. It was only now that Philip considered there to be orchestration.

Philip's Position

Philip is acting in good faith. He would have to first consider whether Big Plc had an internal procedure to follow.

He possesses enough information to "reasonably believe that the information tends to show" that one or more of the catalogue of six items exists, namely—crime; in that it is possible that individuals within the company are obtaining of a pecuniary advantage by deception [sections 43C, E, F, G].

[Continued on next page]

[Continued from previous page]

The fact that Philip works abroad is relevant under section 12 of the Public Interest Disclosure Act 1998. To be protected Philip must not "ordinarily work outside the United Kingdom". It would be an arguable point as to whether Philip is or is not ordinarily a worker outside the United Kingdom, although because he is on a short term contract he is probably covered.

On the facts Philip is unlikely to have much faith in raising his concern within the organisation. It is unclear whether he is in the position to make any other form of disclosure. He is able to make a disclosure to a Government appointed body. For disclosure to a person appointed by the Secretary of State, Philip will need to ensure that the matter is within the regulator's remit. In this case it may be that the ramifications of the share price rigging has such important consequences that Philip should consider whether he believes the allegation is "substantially true" to enable a wider disclosure to be appropriate [section 43H]. On the facts it would appear that he does possess the belief that the allegation is "substantially true" and he may then make a wider disclosure providing that he has a fear of "victimisation" or that there would be a "cover-up".

Big Plc's position

If Philip raises this concern internally Big Plc should investigate fully. They must also reassure Philip that they are treating the allegation seriously and provide him with some indication as to how long an investigation will take.

If Philip has made an external disclosure it is imperative that no action is taken against Philip for raising this concern without considering the options. Should any action be taken he may suffer a detriment and be entitled to compensation.

Case 7

CONTRACT—"GAGGING CLAUSE"

1. Peter was a self-employed computer systems analyst.

2. ABCD contracted Peter to set up a new mainframe computer system. Peter signed the contract and started to work on what was a six-month contract.

3. Peter was in his second week when he started to check the file allocation presently used. It was for this process that Peter had access to all the files on all the computers. Whilst reorganising the file management, Peter came across many "J.PEG" files. These were common on many computers but it was the names of the files that made Peter suspicious. A large number of files were held on the Commercial Director's computer.

4. Peter opened these files and found that the pictures stored were all pornographic and appeared to be of young children. There was little doubt in Peter's mind that these pictures were illegal.

5. Unsure about what he should do, Peter contacted an old friend who was a lawyer to get some advice. Terry spoke to him on the phone and stated that whilst he was not an employment lawyer he perceived that the best starting point would be to examine his contract.

6. Peter got out the contract. Whilst there was no clause specifically dealing with this scenario, Peter was very concerned over a clause which stated:

The contractor herein undertakes not to disclose any information obtained or discovered whilst the contractor is working for the contractee such information being either confidential, a trade secret, private or any other information. Should the contractor consider that it may be appropriate to disclose any information the contractor must only disclose such information to their appointed line manager or to the Managing Director. Under no circumstances may any information be disclosed outside ABCD. Such a disclosure by a contractor will result in termination of the contract and if necessary legal action

---

The Position of Peter

Should ABCD have an internal whistleblowing procedure for contractors as highlighted within the clause, then Peter should raise the matter internally.

Peter possesses a "reasonable belief that it tends to show" one of the six items of malpractice or misconduct [sections 43C, E, F, G], that is there may be a crime committed.

There is no issue as to Peter acting in bad faith. There appears to be no fear of "victimisation" or that there would be a "cover-up".

An internal disclosure is appropriate to enable ABCD to address Peter's concern. Should Peter feel that having raised the concern internally that it has not been addressed he may wish to consider a disclosure to the Police. Although they are not listed as a prescribed person by the Government they are the appropriate body to investigate such crimes. In these circumstances the clause which appears to be a "gagging clause" conflicts with the options open to workers to enable them to raise their concern prescribed within the Act and as such under section 43 J it is void.

The Position of ABCD

The internal procedure designated a line manager or the Managing Director of ABCD. Should they be contacted by Peter it is important that Peter is made aware that an investigation will occur and provide Peter with an approximate date for a conclusion to the investigation. No-one else in his department should be informed as to his concern. Should they fail to investigate then Peter may raise the concern externally.

Case 8

PUBLIC FINANCE—SUPPRESSION OF CONCERN

1. Tommy worked for Dumpsville Local Authority as a refuse collector. He worked six days a week on the trucks that drive around the borough collecting domestic rubbish.

2. The driver of the refuse truck is the shift leader. The driver is responsible for the team and must ensure that the correct route is taken and that all the refuse is collected.

3. Tommy had worked with the Local Authority for over seven years.

4. Tommy had recently been ill with the flu and had been off work for a couple of weeks. When he returned to work he was scheduled to work with another shift, and Tommy had never worked this shift area before.

5. Grant was the driver on this shift. Tommy had no reason to dislike Grant—but Tommy was aware that he was "trouble". Grant was big and he was best friends with the Supervisor of the Refuse department. Tommy understood that it was best to keep in Grant's "good books" to avoid trouble.

6. The truck stopped at the High Street. Grant stopped the truck and he got out of the cab the collectors loaded what was clearly business waste into the truck. Tommy knew very well that it was a Local Authority policy not to take commercial waste on these trucks. Grant spoke to the owners of a couple of premises, one a kebab shop and the other a grocer's. Tommy helped the collectors place the refuse in the truck. It was whilst he was doing this that he was sure that Grant was handed paper envelopes by the shop assistants.

7. At the end of the shift when the team were all in the cabin Grant pulled out some money and gave £10 to each collector including Tommy.

8. Tommy knew that this was against the Local Authority's policy. Businesses had a separate system for them to pay for the disposal of their waste. Tommy was concerned as to his personal safety and his future should he raise this breach of policy.

9. When Tommy was next in the main office he made the point of looking at the shift rota. Tommy quickly realised that Grant was responsible for all routes which covered or passed close to commercial areas.

10. Tommy spoke with his wife and together they decided that something had to be done. A week later Tommy had a day off and he went to the Director of the Refuse Department. Tommy made a point of visiting him whilst he knew the other teams were out so that no one would see him.

11. Tommy outlined the situation and the Director listened and made notes. The Director did not appear as surprised as Tommy had thought he would be—but Tommy put this down to the fact that this sort of behaviour had probably occurred before. Tommy was reassured that the discussion had been in complete confidence and that the Director would look into the "serious issues raised".

12. The next week Tommy went to work as usual. As he opened his locker to change into his uniform, he found that his locker had been filled to the top with grass.

The Position of Tommy

Tommy has been victimised following raising a legitimate concern internally.

Tommy possesses a "reasonable belief that it tends to show" one of the six items of malpractice or misconduct [sections 43C, E, F, G], that there may be a crime committed if the properties do not exist—although there is no evidence at present that this is correct.

There is a possible issue as to Tommy acting in bad faith in that he received money from Grant.

Tommy has a fear of "victimisation" should he raise the concern further. Tommy is protected from suffering victimisation short of dismissal under section 2 of the Act. Compensation is likely to be small but will prevent the victimisation continuing. It would also raise the issue of Grant and the Director.

It may be that Tommy can raise the issue with another department head within the Local Authority.

The Position of the Big Heap Local Authority

The internal procedure has been used and has failed.

The Local Authority are liable for compensation to Tommy. Should any other person or the Chief Executive be contacted by Tommy it is important that Tommy is made aware that an investigation will occur and provide Tommy with an approximate date for a conclusion.

Further it is essential that the victimisation stops once the company are aware that it is occuring. Failure to do so may increase any award that Tommy will be entitled to.

Case 9

CIVIL SERVANT—DISCLOSURE TO M.P.

1. Theo had been working for the Planning Inspectorate for three years. He was a junior civil servant but enjoyed the mix of policy and project work.

2. Theo started to work for the most senior inspector, Mr C, earlier in the year. Unfortunately the Inspector had recently had a number of appeals upheld against his decisions. Theo and he were working on tightening up his decision letters to ensure that lawyers were less able to find grounds of appeal within them.

3. For this reason Theo decided to collect all decisions of the Inspector and to examine them. Theo did not consult the Inspector on his idea. Theo thought that this may make it easier to contrast those decisions which had been successfully appealed with those which had not.

4. Theo put together the 200 cases creating a table of the decisions. It was in the formulation of these tables that Theo came across a certain phenomenon. On the table Theo had made a note of the name of each party, the names of the planning consultants or law firm advising each party and the essential facts of each case. Theo became concerned when he discovered that over the last ten years the Inspector had never determined a planning inquiry against a particular firm of planning consultants.

5. Theo at first put this down to sheer coincidence. However upon a cursory examination of the letters he saw that whilst a couple had been successfully appealed, the decision letters appeared to be less comprehensive than he was used to preparing. Theo decided to investigate his suspicions a little further.

6. Theo arranged for this year's annual report from the planning consultants to be sent to his home. It was upon examining this that a more serious coincidence occurred. The senior planning consultant at the firm was a Dr A Wormals. This was an unusual name and Theo distinctly remembered Mrs Wormals describing herself as the Inspector's sister.

7. Theo was troubled as to whom he could approach with this concern. Whilst the Inspector did not know Theo had drawn up this table, it did appear to him that these decisions were irregular and would not normally be noticed as they had taken place over a ten-year period.

8. Theo was concerned as to his future and did not wish to raise the alarm bells himself. He decided that he would write to the Secretary of State for the Environment.

The Position of Theo

Theo appears to have discovered the fraudulent granting of planning permissions. The first question is whether the Planning Inspectorate have an internal whistleblowing procedure. If they do then this procedure would be best followed before Theo contacts the Secretary of State.

Theo possess a "reasonable belief that it tends to show" one of the six items of malpractice or misconduct [sections 43C, E, F, G]. It may be:

    a.   A crime.

    b.   A breach of a legal obligation under administrative law.

    c.   A miscarriage of justice.

There is no issue as to Theo acting in bad faith. There is on the facts no fear of "victimisation" or that there would be a "cover-up".

At this stage there is no evidence to suggest that the allegation is true and as such an internal disclosure appears appropriate. If Theo raises the concern directly with the Secretary of State this would be protected under section 43E of the Act as the Inspector is an individual appointed under an enactment by the Minister of the Crown.

The Position of the Planning Inspectorate

The internal procedure may designate a person within the Inspectorate to whom concerns may be raised.

Should this person be contacted by Theo, it is important that Theo is made aware that an investigation will occur and provide Theo with an approximate date for a conclusion. It may be that Theo's name need not be used in any investigation as the facts alone are sufficient for an investigation.

Should they fail to investigate, Theo may go to the Secretary of State and this disclosure will be protected.

Case 10

AGENCY MEMBER OF STAFF—VICTIMISATION

1. Chris had been a chef for over 12 years. Chris had recently married and with his wife they decided that he should move to contract and event catering. The aim was for Chris to have more time at home without having to work nights.

2. The move was essentially quite smooth. Chris was placed in a large company catering for all their staff and directors. Basically the large company paid the contract catering company a flat rate in addition to the cost of providing all the food and other incidental costs.

3. Chris had been working for a couple of months when he became concerned that the catering company insisted that supplies were always purchased from particular com-

panies. He contacted head office and was informed that this was company policy and to get on with it. Chris pointed out that he knew of certain suppliers who as a matter of fact could supply the produce much cheaper.

4. Chris asked the manager at the unit why all produce was purchased in this way. He soon learnt that the reason for this system was that the contract catering company had negotiated a printed rate for the supplies sold to the companies and that later the suppliers would send back a percentage of the money paid. Effectively this was a system where there was one price for the catering company and another inflated price for the customer.

5. Chris raised his concern with the financial director of the catering company and he was dismissive of Chris's concerns.

6. A week later Chris received a phone call from the Human Resources Department informing him that he was to move to another unit. The new unit was over two hours' drive from his home. It was a smaller unit with only two other staff.

The Position of Chris

Chris appears to have come across some suspicious charging of clients. An agency member of staff is protected under section 43K. Chris has raised the concern internally.

The evidence before Chris is sufficient to possess a "reasonable belief that it tends to show" one of the six items of malpractice or misconduct [sections 43C, E, F, G] that:

a. There may be a crime committed, *i.e.* fraud.

b. Possibly a breach of a legal obligation—breach of contract.

There is no issue as to Chris acting in bad faith.

Chris has suffered "victimisation" short of dismissal. Compensation is available to him. It may be that Chris can raise the concern within the large company as an agency worker and he would be protected and he may have access to their whistleblowing procedure.

The Position of the Catering Company

Compensation may be claimed for victimisation. Compensation is likely to be small but attempts to prevent the victimisation continuing. Any compensation would be (at present) uncapped under section 3 and based on his losses under section 4.

The catering company would be best to investigate the issue and if necessary raise it with the large company as an issue themselves rather than leaving Chris to raise it with them.

Chris may raise the concern externally as he believes the allegation to be substantially true. There is no issue as to personal gain. As to addressing his concern should be raise it again internally Chris must be reassured that the matter will be investigated and if there has been any under or over payment that such money will be returned.

APPENDIX 10

Precedents

Form 1

CONFIDENTIALITY/INFORMANT/DELIVERY UP INJUNCTION

IN THE HIGH COURT OF JUSTICE   *Claim No.*
QUEEN'S BENCH DIVISION
THE HONOURABLE MR. JUSTICE
BETWEEN:

BIG BUCKS PLC   *Applicant*

—and—

THE DAILY RAG   *Respondent*

MINUTE OF ORDER

IMPORTANT

NOTICE TO THE DEFENDANT

You should read the terms of this Order and the Guidance Notes very carefully. You are advised to consult a Solicitor as soon as possible.

This Order prohibits you, the Respondent, from doing and obliges you to do the acts set out in this Order. You have a right to ask the Court to vary or discharge this Order.

If you disobey this Order you may be found guilty of Contempt of Court and you may be sent to prison or fined. In the case of a Corporate respondent, it may be fined, its directors may be sent to prison or fined or its assets may be seized.

THE ORDER

An Application was made on   by Counsel for the Applicant, [and attended by Counsel for the Respondent] to Mr. Justice [   ] who heard the application. The Judge read the affidavits listed in Schedule A and accepted the undertakings set out in Schedule B at the end of this Order. As a result of the application **IT IS ORDERED** that:

1. Until [   ] or further Order of the Court, the Respondent shall be restrained, whether by its directors, officers, employees or agents or any of them, or otherwise howsoever:

    (1) from making any use (to include the passing to any third party) of the draft pre-liminary financial statement ("the Draft Statement"), referred to in the 29th May

2000 of the publication "All the News that's fit to print", or any of its content; and

(2) from defacing, deleting any part of, or otherwise altering or tampering with the format or appearance of any and all documents and records which are the property of the Applicant.

2. The Respondent shall forthwith deliver up to the Applicant all property belonging to the Applicant in its possession, including:

(1) the Draft Statement or any extracts from it and all documents containing information derived from the Draft Statement.

(2) all documents and records (in hard copy, digital or electronic form) which are the property of the Claimant.

3. The Respondent shall swear an affidavit within two days of the date of this Order:

(1) confirming compliance with paragraph 2 of this Order.

(2) to the extent that any copy of the Draft Statement or any other documentation belonging to the Applicant was, but is no longer, in the possession of the Respondent, and has not been returned to the Applicant, stating what has become of it.

(3) stating when, how and to whom the Draft Statement or any of its contents has been disclosed by the Respondent.

(4) identifying the person or people who disclosed the Draft Statement to the Respondent and what other information relating to the Applicant, or property belonging to the Applicant, was disclosed by that person or people to the Respondent and stating when and how the disclosure was made.

4. The costs of the Applicant's application shall be the Applicant's costs in case.

GUIDANCE NOTES

Effect of this Order

1) A respondent who is an individual who is ordered not to do something must not do it himself or in any other way. He must not do it through others acting on his behalf or on his instructions or with his encouragement.

2) A respondent which is a corporation and which is ordered not to do something must not do it itself or by its directors, officers, employees or agents or in any other way.

Variation or discharge of this Order

The Respondent (or anyone notified of this Order) may apply to the Court at any time to vary or discharge this Order (or so much of it as affects that person) but anyone wishing to do so he must first inform the Applicant's legal representatives at least 48 hours beforehand.

Interpretation of this Order

1) In this Order the words "he" "him" or "his" include "she" or "her" and "it" or "its".

2) Where there are two or more respondents then (unless the contrary appears):

(a) References to "the Respondent" means both or all of them;

(b) A requirement to serve on "the Respondent" means on each of them. However, the order is effective against each Respondent on whom it is served.

(c) An Order requiring "the Respondent" to do or not to do anything applies to all Respondents.

Communications with the Court

All communications to the Court about this Order should be sent, where the Order is made in the Chancery Division, to Room TM 510, Royal Courts of Justice, Strand, London WC2A

2LL quoting the case number. The telephone number is 0171 936 6927; and where the order is made in the Queen's Bench Division, to Room W11 (0171 936 6009). The offices are open between 10 a.m. and 4.30 p.m. Monday to Friday.

SCHEDULE A

Witness Statements

The Judge read the following witness statements before making this Order:
[*name*] [*number of witness statements*] [*date sworn*] [*filed on behalf of*]

(1)

(2)

SCHEDULE B

Undertakings given to the Court by the Applicant

(1) If the Court later finds that this Order has caused loss to the Respondent and decides that the Respondent should be compensated for that loss, the Applicant will comply with any order the Court may make.

(2) As soon as practicable the Applicant will issue and serve on the Respondent a Claim Form in the form of the draft produced to the Court claiming the appropriate relief, together with this Order.

(3) Anyone notified of this Order will be given a copy of it by the Applicant's legal representatives.

Name and address of the applicant's legal representatives

The Applicant's Solicitors are:—
[*Name, address, reference, fax and telephone numbers both in and out of office hours.*]

Form 2

CONFIDENTIALITY/INFORMANT/DELIVERY UP/COPYRIGHT

PARTICULARS OF CLAIM

IN THE HIGH COURT OF JUSTICE   *Claim No.*
QUEEN'S BENCH DIVISION
BETWEEN:

BIG BUCKS PLC   Claimant
—and—
THE WEEKLY RAG   Defendant

PARTICULARS OF CLAIM

The Parties

1. At all times material to this action:

    (1) the Claimant has been authorised to run a game of chance; and

    (2) the Defendant was the proprietor and publisher of a weekly magazine bearing the title "All The News That's Fit To Print" ("the Magazine").

The Draft Statement

2.The Claimant's financial and accounting year ends on 31st March. In preparation for publication on 1st June 2000 of a preliminary financial statement, the Claimant prepared a draft preliminary financial statement ("the Draft Statement").

3. The Draft Statement and its contents:

    (1) constituted confidential information the property of the Claimant which was only to have been disseminated to third parties with the authority of the Claimant; and

    (2) had been passed in confidence to the Claimant's auditors ("the Auditors") for the sole purposes of enabling them:

    (a) to audit the Claimant's draft accounts;
    (b) otherwise and generally to advise, as appropriate, on the contents of such document.

Copyright

4. Further, the Draft Statement is an original literary work which was prepared by employees of the Claimant in the course of their employment with the Claimant and accordingly the Claimant is the first owner of the copyright in the Draft Statement.

Unauthorised disclosure of the Draft Statement

5. On a date of which the Claimant is unaware, but which fell prior to 28th May 2000, an individual or individuals ("the Informant(s)") whose identity is unknown to the Claimant, acting without the authority or knowledge of the Claimant, wrongfully caused and/or permitted a copy of the Draft Statement to be passed to a journalist employed by the Defendant ("the Journalist").

Equitable duty of confidence owed by the Defendant

6. The Journalist received the copy of the Draft Statement in circumstances where it was obvious that the Draft Statement had been disclosed in breach of an equitable duty of confidence owed to the Claimant.

7. Accordingly upon receipt of the Draft Statement the Defendant was under a duty not to use any part of the Draft Statement or divulge any part of its content without the Claimant's consent.

Receipt and publication of the Draft Statement by the Defendant

8. Following the receipt by the Defendant of the Draft Statement, in the issue of the Magazine dated 29th May 2000 (published and/or distributed on 28th May 2000) the Defendant published an article written by the Journalist under the heading "Big Bucks' chiefs' pay soars as lottery pay outs fall" ("the Article"). The Article made express references to (parts of) the Draft Statement as having been the source for the conclusions drawn by the Journalist and included extracts from the Draft Statement.

Breach of confidence

9. Accordingly the Defendant has acted in breach of its equitable duty of confidence owed to the Claimant.

Infringement of copyright

10. Further:
    (1) by making unauthorised use of the Draft Statement, including printing extracts from the Draft Statement, the Defendant has infringed the Claimant's copyright in the Draft Statement.
    (2) the Defendant has in its possession custody or control in the course of its business, infringing copies of the Claimant's copyright work, The Draft Statement.

Wrongful Interference with Property

11. Further, the Defendant has failed or refused to return the copy or copies of the Draft Statement supplied to it without authority, notwithstanding demand made for the return of such copies in a facsimile message dated 28th May 2000. Accordingly the Defendant has wrongfully interfered with the Claimant's property.

Duty of disclosure

12. Further and in any event, the Defendant has become mixed up in, and has facilitated, the wrongdoing of the Informant(s). Accordingly the Defendant is under a duty to assist the Claimant by providing full information of matters within its knowledge relating to such wrongdoing, including information as to the identity of the Informant(s). The Claimant contends that such disclosure is in the interests of justice within the meaning of that phrase in section 10 of the Contempt of Court Act 1981. In particular:

    (1) it is likely that the Informant(s) is or are employed by either the Claimant or the Auditors and, as such, the Claimant and the Auditors have a legitimate interest in identifying a disloyal employee who will have access to confidential information of the Claimant and the Auditors.
    (2) it is in any event necessary to identify the Informant(s) so as to prevent further disclosures of confidential information.

Threat of further use of Draft Statement

13. Unless restrained by this Honourable Court, the Defendant threatens and intend to make further use of the Draft Statement and/or part(s) of it in breach of its equitable

duty of confidence to the Claimant and by way of infringement of the Claimant's copyright interest in the Draft Statement.

Loss and damage/Account of Profits

14. By reason of the matters set out above the Claimant has suffered loss and damage. Alternatively, and at the election of the Claimant, the Defendant is liable to account to the Claimant for the profits earned by reason of its breach of the equitable duty of confidence and infringement of copyright.

15. Further the Claimant claims interest pursuant to the equitable jurisdiction of the Court, alternatively pursuant to section 35A of the Supreme Court Act 1981, on such sums as are found to be due to Plaintiff at such rate and for such period as the Court shall think fit.

AND the Claimant claims:

(1) An injunction restraining the Defendant, whether by its directors, officers, employees or agents or any of them, or otherwise howsoever:

    (a) from making any use (to include the passing to any third party) of the Draft Statement or any of its content; and

    (b) from infringing the Claimant's copyright interest in the literary work constituted by the Draft Statement; and

    (c) from defacing, deleting any part of, or otherwise altering or tampering with the format or appearance of any and all documents and records which are the property of the Claimant.

(2) An Order for delivery up to the Claimant of all property belonging to the Claimant in its possession including:

    (a) the Draft Statement and any extracts from it and all documents containing information derived from the Draft Statement, alternatively destruction upon oath of all such documents.

    (b) all documents and records (in hard copy, digital or electronic form) which are the property of the Claimant.

(3) An Order for disclosure by the Defendant of the identity of the Informant(s) and of the precise circumstances in which each and every piece of confidential information, or other property of the Claimant, received by the Defendant from the Informant(s) came to its attention and into its possession.

(4) Damages consequential upon the Defendant's wrongful interference with the Claimant's property.

(5) An Inquiry into the damages which have been, and may be, suffered by the Claimant by reason of the Defendant's wrongful use of confidential information the property of the Claimant and infringement of copyright.

(6) Alternatively, and at the election of the Claimant, an Account of profits made by the Defendant with the assistance of confidential information the property of the Claimant and/or by reason of the Defendant's infringement of copyright.

(7) Payment of the amount certified in answer to such Inquiry or Account as set out above.

(8) Interest pursuant to section 35A of the Supreme Court Act 1981 as above.

(9) Such further or other relief as the Court shall consider appropriate.

STATEMENT OF TRUTH
STATEMENT OF VALUE

APPENDIX 11

Useful Addresses

Action on Elder Abuse

1268 London Road
London SW16
0181 679 2648

Audit Commission

1 Vincent Square
London SW1P 2PN
0171 828 1212

Health & Safety Executive

Broad Lane
Sheffield S3 7HQ
0114 289 2345

Insurance Ombudsman Bureau

135 Park Street
London SE1 9EA
0171 928 7600
0171 938 4488

Law Centres Federation

Duchess House
Warren Street
London W1P 5DA
0171 387 8570

Local Government Ombudsman
(E Anglia, SW, W, S, Central)

The Oaks
Westwood Way
Westwood Business Park
Coventry CV4 8JB
01203 695 999

Local Government Ombudsman
(E Midlands & N)

Beverly House
17 Shipton Road
York YO3 6FZ
01904 663 200

Local Government Ombudsman
(London, Kent, Surrey,
E & W Sussex)

21 Queen Anne's Gate
London SW1H 9BU
0171 915 3210

Ministry of Agriculture,
Fisheries & Food

W Block
Whitehall Place
London SW1A 2HH
0171 270 3000
01645 335577

National Association of Citizens' Advice Bureax	115 Pentonville Road London N1 9LZ **0171 833 2181**
Occupational Pensions Advisory Service	11 Belgrave Road London SW1V 1RB **0171 233 8080**
Office of Fair Trading	15–25 Breams Buildings London EC4A 1PR **0171 211 8000**
Office of Health Service Commissioner	Church House Great Smith Street London SW1P 3BL **0171 276 3000**
Office for the Supervision of Solicitors	Victoria Court 8 Dormer Place Leamington Spa Warks CV32 5AE **01926 820 082**
Pollution Inspectorate	43 Marsham Street London SW1P 3PY **0171 276 8061** **01342 312 016**
Public Concern at Work	Suite 306 16 Baldwin's Gardens London EC1N 7RJ
Railway Inspectorate	4th Floor SW Rose Court 2 Southwark Bridge London SE1 9HS **0171 717 6533**
Securities and Investments Board	Gavrelle House 2–14 Bunhill Row London EC1Y 8RA **0171 638 1240**
Society for the Prevention of Asbestos & Industrial Diseases	38 Drapers Road Enfield Middlesex EN2 8LU **0181 360 6413**

Index

All references are to to paragraph number.